D0712402

# WILD SPORTS

## OF THE WEST

# WILD SPORTS

## OF THE WEST..

INTERSPERSED

WITH LEGENDARY TALES, AND LOCAL SKETCHES.

BY

## WILLIAM HAMILTON MAXWELL

AUTHOR OF "STORIES OF WATERLOO."

" And sure it is yet a most beautifull and sweete countrey as any is
under heaven, being stored throughout with many goodly rivers, replenished
with all sorts of fish mo̊st abundantly, sprinkled with many very sweet
islands and goodly lakes, like little inland seas, that will even carry shippes
upon their waters."—*Spenser's State of Ireland*, 1596.

Republished
EP Publishing Limited
1973

Copyright © in reprint EP Publishing Limited
East Ardsley, Wakefield
Yorkshire, England

First published in 1832. This is a
reprint of the 1850 edition
published by Richard Bentley, London.

ISBN 0 85409 973 5

Please address all enquiries to EP Publishing Limited
(address as above)

*Printed in Great Britain by*
The Scolar Press Limited, Ilkley, Yorkshire

# PREFACE

## TO THE FIRST EDITION.

SOME explanation may be necessary for obtruding upon the public the private details of a sportsman's life, and particularly when the scene of his exploits is laid within "the four seas of Britain." In the customary course of field adventure, few besides the individual concerned are much interested in the successes and disappointments he experiences; and rural sports are, in all their general incidents, so essentially alike, as to render their minute description almost invariably a dull and unprofitable record.

Circumstances, however, may occasionally create an interest which in ordinary cases would be wanting. From local connexions, a field almost untrodden by any but himself, was opened to the writer of these Sketches. He was thrown into an unfrequented district, with a primitive people to consort with. With some advantages to profit from the accident, a remote and semi-civilized region was offered to his observation; and although within a limited distance of his Majesty's mail-coach, a country was thus disclosed, as little known to the multitude as the interior of Australasia; and where, excepting some adventurous grouse-shooter, none had viewed its highlands or mingled with its inhabitants,

That the scenic and personal sketches are faithful, the reader is assured; some were written on the spot, and others traced from vivid recollection. Those with whom the author shot these wild moors, or fished these waters, will best estimate the fidelity of the descriptions; and *one* valued friend, though now beneath another sun, will probably recall the days he spent by "fell and flood," and bring to memory those light and joyous hours when he caroused in a mountain bivouac, and rested in a moorland hut.

Of the actors in the following scenes, some are still living, while others are no more. The Colonel, that best and honestest of boon companions, sleeps with his fathers; and old John and the Otter-killer have gone the way of all flesh. The priest, "mine honoured friend," I rejoice to say, is still healthy and vigorous; in his wild but happy retirement he holds "the noiseless tenour of his way," exercises hospitality most liberally to the stranger, and throws forty feet of silk and hair better than any artist in the empire. Last of the "dramatis personæ," Hennessey is in full force, and "*mutato nomine,*" may still be found in Ballycroy.

With regard to the tales and legends narrated in the succeeding pages, the former were told just as they are introduced. "The Blind Seal" is known to be substantially true—I have heard it from many, and never knew its veracity impugned. My lamented friend was himself the principal actor in "the Night Attack;" and he, poor fellow, was exactly the man who, in an affray or a carouse, might be depended on. The heroes of the " Gold Snuff-box" are alive and merry, and long may they continue so ! for truer friends and " better company" never listened to the " chimes at midnight." " Mr. Dawkins" is, I believe, engaged in seeking, through Doctors' Commons, to be relieved " *è vinculo matrimonii*,"—and " Mr. Burke" duly announced among the last arrivals in the Sydney Gazette.

Respecting the legendary stories, I have no pledge to offer for their authenticity,—old Antony believed them to the letter—I have given them nearly in his own words, and I may say with Sir Walter Scott,

> " I cannot tell how the truth may be,
> I say the tale as 'twas said to me."

" The Legend of Knock-a-thample" remains as the Otter-killer related it ; but with " Rose Roche" I confess to have taken liberties, in suppressing a portion of her flirtation with the " black-eyed page," which, although, upon the lady's part, I feel convinced, was perfectly platonic, yet by uncharitable constructions might be tortured into something like indiscretion.

If I have undervalued those rural recreations in which many a worthy citizen sometimes dissipates, I hope my contempt for his avocations will be ascribed to the true cause, namely, that local advantages have spoiled my taste and rendered me fastidious. He who can shoot grouse upon the moor, will spend little time in killing pigeons from the trap ; the angler who in a morning hooks some half-score salmon, would reckon it but sorry amusement to dabble in a pond. To a Galway rider, the Epping hunt would be a bore, and he would probably treat it with the same contumely that one of this redoubted body did hare-hunting, by riding to the hounds in morocco slippers, and carrying an open umbrella to protect him from the sun.

As I have casually named " an honoured name," I lament that it was not his fortune to have visited those interesting scenes, where I have been so long a useless wanderer. The wild features and wilder associations of that romantic and untouched country, would have offered him a fresh field whereon to exercise his magic pencil— and many a tale and legend still orally handed down, but which in a few years must of necessity be forgotten, would have gained immortality from the touch of " the mighty master." But alas! the creations of his splendid imagination will no more delight an enchanted world. The wand is broken, the spell is over, the lamp of life is nearly exhausted—and even now, Scotland may be mourning for the mightiest of her gifted sons.

As a votive offering, these Volumes are inscribed to that matchless genius, by an humble, but enthusiastic admirer of SIR WALTER SCOTT.

SYDENHAM,
SEPTEMBER 12, 1832.

# CONTENTS.

## CHAPTER I.

## CHAPTER II.

## CHAPTER III.

## CHAPTER IV.

## CHAPTER V.

## CHAPTER VI.

## CHAPTER XIV.

## CHAPTER XV.

## CHAPTER XVI.

## CHAPTER XVII.

## CHAPTER XVIII.

## CHAPTER XXXVIII.

## CHAPTER XXXIX.

## CHAPTER XL.

## CHAPTER XLI

## CHAPTER XLII.

## CHAPTER XLIII.

## CHAPTER XLIV.

# WILD SPORTS OF THE WEST.

## CHAPTER I.

London, July 1st, 1829.

NOTWITHSTANDING its dust and desertion, I am still lurking in the metropolis. The heat has become intolerable—yesterday, I imagined myself in Calcutta—for never but in the land of curries and red pepper did I experience anything so oppressive.

I breakfasted this morning at the Club-house. My air and attitude, as I caught a glimpse of them in a concave mirror, looked exquisitely disconsolate. Never was mortal more *ennuyé* than I. Town has become a desert—the world has abandoned it by general consent—the streets feel as if they had been recently fanned by a sirocco; and of divers unhappy beings whom I encountered in my walk from Grafton-street to St. James's, none seemed at ease but a bilious gentleman from Bombay, and the French fellow who exhibits in the oven. The thermometer, in a shaded corner of the room, is stationary at 82°. To remain longer here would be suicidal; but, where to go—whither to fly—alas! I know not.

Would that you were near me, then should I be certain of sympathy and counsel—for at this moment, there is not a more persecuted gentleman in the King's dominions. But I will make a clean breast—and to render my confessions explanatory, I must favour you with some particulars of my private history.

As autobiographers enjoy a prescriptive privilege of exhibiting their ancestors, I shall take the liberty of introducing my

B

papa. In his twenty-second year, Mr. Hector O'Brien was a bold Lieutenant of Grenadiers in his Majesty's 50th Foot, then distinguished by the flattering title of " The Dirty Half Hundred."* My father was a strapping fellow as ever wore a wing, kept a showy horse, and was decidedly the best dancer in the regiment. Being quartered in the vicinity of Bath, he attended the assemblies, and " in double quick" managed to effect a conquest. The lady had a fortune, and my father required one. Unluckily, she had a brother's consent to gain ; and on being consulted, he was unmoved by importunity, and deaf to " every plea of love." The case was hopeless. Mr. Wamsley disliked Ireland, detested military men, and above all things, abominated " The Dirty Half Hundred."

To account for the gentleman's antipathy to this celebrated corps, it will be necessary to remark, that the regiment was then afflicted with a mad Major. His, the Major's delight, ley in drinking port wine and slaying pheasants. Mr. Wamsley, on the contrary, preferred water and preserved game. The Major beat up preserves without remorse, and deforced keepers who, though good men and true, prudently declined joining issue with mad Majors and double-barrelled guns. Now Mr. Wamsley resisting an invasion of his rights, applied to the Justice for redress, whereas Major O'Farrell considered that a reference to the pistol would be much more gentlemanly —a deadly feud was the consequence, and Mr. Wamsley was closely blockaded within his park walls by the military delinquent. Fortunately for all concerned, the regiment got the route ; Mr. Wamsley recovered his liberty, and his detestation of the gallant 50th only ended with his life.

But his sister held a very different opinion respecting the merits of the brave " Half Hundred." She was devoted to the Lieutenant of Grenadiers, and the route hurried matters to a crisis. The result may be anticipated. Despising park walls and surly keepers, Mr. O'Brien overcame every difficulty, and with the assistance of a garden-ladder, the mad Major, and his double-barrelled gun, he carried off the lady, and at Gretna they became " one flesh."

Mr. Wamsley was irritated beyond the possibility of being appeased. Ten thousand pounds, which his wife possessed without the control of her brother, enabled my father to leave

---

* From their black facings, the 50th received this *sobriquet.*

the army, and settle on his hereditary estate in Roscommon ; and there he hunted, shot, fished, and farmed, and lived just as Irish gentlemen lived some thirty years ago.

I was the only issue of the marriage. All communication had ceased between my parents and Mr. Wamsley, and eighteen years passed away, and no appearance of abated displeasure had ever been evinced by this implacable relative. I left a public school for the Dublin University, was destined for the church, and had nearly completed my college course, when an unforeseen event changed my prospects and profession. It was the death of both my parents within the brief space of a month.

My father's affairs were in great disorder—his estate was heavily embarrassed, and if his debts were paid, it was ascertained that I should be left nearly destitute. The intelligence reached Mr. Wamsley, and to the astonishment of all acquainted with his unrelenting animosity to my deceased parents, a letter was received from him, inviting me to visit him at his magnificent place, Lalworth Castle.

The invitation was of course accepted. I arrived, and found him a stern, disagreeable old man. My first appearance was against me—for the resemblance I bore to my father was most striking, and it seemed to recall my uncle's long-cherished prejudices. He abruptly asked me on the succeeding morning, " What course of life I had selected ?" I replied, " That the army appeared best adapted to my taste and broken fortunes." His only observation was, " Be it so ;" and here this laconic conversation ended.

That evening, Mr. Wamsley wrote to his neighbour, Lord Ulverston. The peer was his debtor to a·large amount, and generally trafficked with him for his borough of ——bury. My uncle's request was promptly attended to. Lord Ulverston stood well at the Horse Guards ; and in a few weeks, to my unfeigned satisfaction and surprise, I was gazetted to a Cornetcy in the Blues.

But my joy at this event was but of short duration. The miserly disposition of my uncle took alarm at the large outlay attendant on entering an expensive corps. Each hundred was doled out with painful reluctance, and the knowledge that a certain annual allowance would be requisite for my support, made him still more wretched. I joined the regiment; my subsidies—generally drafts for a paltry fifty—were " few and far between." To hold a certain place in society, with an income incompetent to its expenses, is a state of inexpressible misery. Gradually I became embarrassed, and in two years found it necessary to exchange from the Blues to a Light Cavalry regiment, then stationed in the East Indies. My uncle made no objection; he was tired of what he termed supplying my boundless extravagance, bade me a cold farewell, and his parting words, as I stepped into the carriage, were a request that I would "write but seldom, as postage from the East, his lawyer told him, was enormous."

I obeyed him to the letter, I only wrote once, and that was conveying an entreaty that he would purchase a majority likely to become vacant; I got a coarse refusal, and thus our correspondence terminated. For four years I never heard from him, and had nearly forgotten that I had left a relation behind me.

I was surprised, however, at this distant period with a letter, worded in his stiff and peculiar style. It briefly stated that his health was indifferent, and that he would recommend me to return to Europe with as little delay as possible.

This recommendation was anything but gratifying. I liked India well enough—the climate agreed with me—my health was unimpaired—the mess was good—the regiment gentlemanly—and better still, I could live most comfortably upon my pay. I felt, however, that my uncle's invitation should not be neglected; applied for leave; succeeded, and made immediate preparations for a return to Europe. My brother officers congratulated me on my good fortune in so speedily revisiting my native country; but to me it was a subject of regret. I was leaving pleasant quarters, cheerful society, and comparative independence, to become a slave to the caprice and ill-humour of a morose and splenetic invalid.

It was late in December when I landed at Portsmouth. The voyage had been remarkably quick, and without delay I started for my uncle's residence, and in the gloom of a wet wintry evening re-entered the gates of Lalworth Park. I looked down the long vista of splendid elms, but in the twilight the house was not visible; not a candle glanced from a window, and no indication of its being inhabited appeared about this melancholy mansion. The postboy stopped—I alighted, ran up the steps and rang gently—no one answered

—I rang again—louder yet—and a step came hastily over the oaken floor. The old porter at last approached, cautiously affixed the chain, opened a few inches of the door, and raised his candle suspiciously to examine the late visiter. Instantly recollecting me, he uttered a suppressive exclamation of astonishment, removed the fastenings, and muttered, "Thank God, it is himself!" and, as he admitted me, whispered that my uncle was not expected to survive till midnight.

In silence I was conducted to a back drawing-room, where, on a large, old-fashioned sofa the dying man was laid. The porter advanced before, and in a low voice notified my arrival. The news appeared to gratify the invalid; he turned his dim eyes to the spot where I stood waiting for permission to advance. "Are you there, Frank!" he said in a feeble voice —"Ha, ha, ha! it was *touch and go* with you!" and he uttered a weak and sarcastic laugh.—"Call Doctor Dodwell and the lawyer—desire them to bring the *other will*—and tell Moore and Hubert to attend to witness it." While he gave these orders, I gazed on the wasted features of the dying miser, and there was a strange expression of stern satisfaction visible on his countenance, as his cold glance rested fixedly on me. Immediately the doctor, solicitor, and witnesses entered the room.—"Raise me up," he said to the ancient domestic, his personal attendant. It was done, and he motioned to the solicitor to unfold the parchment. Carefully he passed his eye over the surface to assure himself that the document was the one he required, and having ascertained the fact, he pointed to a pen. With difficulty he placed it in his trembling fingers, and with a painful exertion, affixed his signature to the deed—then looking at the witnesses as they annexed their names—"This is my last will and testament," he said with a feeble emphasis, "and thus do I revoke all others!" —then turning to me, while a ghastly smile overspread his face, "Half an hour later would have served hospitals and almshouses, Francis:" he leaned himself back and expired without a struggle.

For a few moments we were not aware that he was dead; the strength with which his last remark was uttered led us at first to believe that he had reclined in consequence of the exertion. In a few minutes the physician took his hand and sought for a pulse, but in vain; he raised the eyelid and applied a candle to the fixed and deadly stare, and then announced that the patient had departed.

A scene, a disgusting scene ensued; the attorney, when certified of his client's death, seized my hand and coarsely congratulated me on my good fortune. The doctor abandoned the corpse to join the solicitor in his compliments—and between them the truth transpired. I had, indeed, been luckily expeditious in my journey, and the old man's phrase of *touch and go*, was fully explained. The preceding day he had signed a testament conveying his entire property to a variety of charitable institutions; and the will which had been originally made in my favour, and been kept over by this singular relative, would have remained imperfect, had I not so providentially arrived the evening of his death.

We left the room while the body was being laid out preparatory to interment. What a turn one hour had given to my fortunes! I entered Lalworth Park at four o'clock, a poor miserable dependant; at five, I was master of all around me, possessed of twelve thousand pounds a year, owner of a borough, with fifty thousand in the funds and twenty at my banker's. Such a mingled yarn is the web of human life.

The obsequies of my uncle were duly performed, and for many days I was engaged in examining papers, and taking possession of the plate and valuables of Lalworth Park. The house was sadly out of repair, and the grounds and gardens utterly neglected. The old man had limited the fuel for the mansion to such fallen wood as could be collected throughout the domain; and the few domestics he employed were scarcely sufficient to ventilate, without attempting to keep in order the numerous and once splendid apartments. For some time I was busily occupied; I hired additional servants, engaged an architect, fiated my agent's accounts, and started then for London so soon as a decent respect towards the deceased would permit my appearing in the metropolis. Of the rest, my dear Baronet, you know sufficient particulars; a presentable man, *olim* in the Blues, and recently succeeding to a large and unencumbered property, would soon "find room in any place." I was speedily admitted to those chosen circles which are impassable to those who want birth, impudence, or money. I ran the full round of dissi—— but, on this head, *you*, my constant companion, require but little information.

In human life, George, every thing has its limits. I am

probably too rich to be permanently happy. I tired of
Brookes's and Willis's and Crockford's : I had little taste
for the play, and betted moderately, and with even success :
if I lost I was not depressed : if I won I was not exhilarated.
The season was drawing to its close, and I began to discover
that I was not fated to escape from sublunary annoyances.
I was bored by the dull dinners of stupid placemen who
calculated on my borough; I was persecuted by ancient
gentlewomen who wished to rid themselves of daughters that
years ago were *passées ;* a young and titled widow almost
wooed me to desperation ; and the Dowager of —— shocked
me by an assurance that Lord Leatherby expected, from my
marked attention at the Horticultural fête, that I would *forthwith* propose for that sandy-haired fright his daughter. God
help me ! little did I suppose that an act of common humanity, in sheltering her red ringlets with a broken umbrella,
would have been thus tortured by that leaden-headed Lord
her sire !

I forgot in its proper place to notify an important occurrence ; it was the death of Mr. James Jones. This personage
was owner of a property in Surinam, and one of the representatives for the borough of ——bury. A year before his
death my late uncle had pocketed three thousand pounds, and
returned as inoffensive a gentleman as ever snored upon the
benches of St. Stephen's. I took his place, next the oaths,
and had sufficient grace to sit quiet and listen to other de-
claimers, who possessed more talent or more impudence than
myself. For some time I was rather undecided in my politics ;
but the Ministerial were the quieter benches,—there I established myself, and for half a session none slept through a
debate with a quieter conscience—but curse upon blighted
beauty, I was not permitted to remain in happy and unam-
bitious celibacy.

From my first appearance I had been exposed to distant
attacks, but as the weather warmed and the town thinned, my
persecutors became more daring in their approaches. Did I
venture to a Refugee concert, there I was waylaid by the
widow. Did I endeavour to steal a ride in Rotten-row, I was
directly hunted off by the *dame rouge* and that infernal Peer
her father ; and all that was penniless or *passé* marked me as
an object of unrelenting importunity. Eventually, I was
driven from every place approachable by woman, and having

no other refuge, turned to the turf, and engaged myself deeply in the Derby.

That event is over, and I shall write the man " mine enemy" who ever recalls it to my recollection—but as this is a confession to thee, George, I must make a clean breast. I was as well acquainted with the mysteries of a betting-book, as I was with the financial department of Timbuctoo ; when luckily "a d——d good-natured friend" came to my aid, and with his experience, why should I not get on cleverly ? A horse was going for nothing, my friend was on the alert, made the discovery, and I bought him for five hundred. He was a dead bargain, quite *a dark one,* and in proof of the same, the odds against him were thirty-five to one ; but, as I was informed, *there* lay the beauty of the thing.

As the races drew near, I discovered that my book was what the *legs* call a *queer concern.* I had picked up the halt and blind as first favourites and betted accordingly. My *dark one* proved a *roarer,* and my faithful friend recommended me to hedge immediately, and I did so, as the result will tell.

Off went the horses ; Phenomenon, my courser, in the chance medley got a splendid start, but from his pace the spectators alleged that he was hamstrung. In three hundred yards he was passed by the slowest of the *bad ones,* and before the leading horses reached the distance, every thing I was interested in was beaten fairly off. All I had left for consolation under this accumulation of disappointment was the smart hedge that I had so prudently effected before starting.

The settling-day came ; I was at Tattersall's and so were my winners to a man ; I disbursed five thousand to divers legs with and without titles, and furthermore disposed of the celebrated horse Phenomenon for fifty pounds. But where was the worthy gentleman with whom I had hedged half my losses ? Till four o'clock I waited in painful expectation, and at that hour, he being still invisible, I ventured to hazard an inquiry, and was favoured with the comfortable tidings, that my absent friend was a broken wine-merchant, and that he had levanted the evening of the race.

This wind up of the season, united to sultry weather and a tender persecution, determined me to fly " east, west, or north, I care not whither." This, however, was more easily decided on than effected, for to retreat is the difficulty, as I find myself hemmed in by my enemies on every side. The widow cuts me off from Cheltenham; the Honourable Juliana Thistleton would haunt me in Hastings; the Dowager of —— and her *protégée* abide in the pleasant town of Brighton; and my Lord Leatherby has taken out a sort of roving commission, to infest every retirement of fashionable repute; and from his cunning inquiries as to the particular point, seaside or suburban, to which I purpose to remove, I perceive I am as deliberately doomed to matrimony by this relentless nobleman, as ever a country bonnet-maker was devoted to destruction by an immoral captain of horse.

And shall I fall without a struggle to avert my fate? forbid it honour! Yes, my determination is fixed—I will counteract this conspiracy against my freedom, and call my Connaught cousin "to the rescue." He is a determined duellist, and has been regularly jilted—consequently he abominates the sex (I hope) and will protect me from the widow; while his truculent propensities for the pistol will keep the Peer at a distance. Adieu! I'll write anon—thine always.

------

## CHAPTER II.

Letters—An Escape—Connaught—Topographical and Moral Description
—Ballinasloe—A Virtuous and Flourishing Town—A Bible Meeting
and Radical Reform.

I APPRIZED you in my last letter, that in this my hour of need, I would seek succour from my Irish kinsman. I wrote to him accordingly, implored him to abandon his mountain den and join me at Lalworth Park. To my invitation I received a decisive, and I would almost say, insulting refusal; "He hated puppies, avoided flirts, was neither a fool or a fortune, and therefore had no business with such society as I should expose him to." The man appears to be a misanthrope; I gave him in return a tart rejoinder, and he seems disinclined to remain my d btor. Hear what he says:

"Francis, I pity thee! Like the Moor, your 'occupation's gone,' and your letter seals your condemnation.

"You talk of exercise: pshaw! what is it? You knock some party-coloured balls over the smooth surface of a green table ; you hazard suffocation for an hour in Rotten-row, and should you survive the dust, endure eternal dread of empalement by a carriage-pole; you shoot a score of rascally pigeons within the enclosures of Battersea, or make a grand excursion to slaughter pheasants in a preserve; last and proudest feat comes the *battu*, when, with noble and honourable confederates, you exterminate a multitude of semi-civilized fowls, manfully overcoming the fatigue of traversing an ornamented park, and crossing a few acres of turnips. And is this ignoble course befitting one of 'lith and limb' like thine? *You*, the best of your day in Trinity ;—you, whose prowess is still recorded in the annals of the watchhouse, and whose hurling is yet chronicled in the Park ;—you, whom no six-feet wall could turn, whom no mountain-herd could tire in the dog-days ;—you, who could swim with Byron, and walk with Barclay,—what are you become? an elegant and fashionable idler—lolling life away, the morning in a club-house window, the evening in the Park, and the night *gallopading* some scion of nobility, who has discovered that you possess twelve thousand pounds a year, and that her own funds are insufficient to satisfy the corset-maker in Regent-street.

"Would that I could reform your taste and habits! Could I but induce you to pass one autumn here, your conversion would be a certainty. Come to me, Frank; ay, come to the wilds of Connaught: avoid an atmosphere surcharged with villanous impurities, and brace your relaxed nerves in the waves of the Atlantic; seek life and energy in the mountain-breeze; abandon the gymnasium to scriveners and shopmen; and leave Crockford's to ruined dupes and titled swindlers.

"You have hitherto been a silent Member of the Honourable Commons, and St. Stephen's has never heard from you 'the popular harangue, the tart reply.' Hast thou any aspirations after fame? any 'longing after immortality?' Listen; the means are simple. Indict the Red-house as a nuisance, and propose a bill, making the being aiding or accessory to a *battu*, death without benefit of clergy. Thy name will live when Joe Hume, that ready-reckoner, shall be forgotten; and Dick Martin's senatorial renown will fade before the perennial glory of the present member for ——bury !"

Need I say how opportunely came this invitation? "I embraced his offer ;" and here I am fairly over the border, and

safely deposited in the kingdom of Connaught, without injury
or interruption worth recording.

On the subject of my travels I intend to be laconic, inas-
much as, with a temporary intervention of steam, I have resided
in the royal mail since I left the lamps of London. I believe
I am not exactly cut out for a traveller : I am incurious as
to names of guards and coachmen—never inquire after their
wives, or take the population of their families ; I generally
sleep from the start to the close of the stage. I did observe
that the colour of corn was nearly alike in both countries ; and
remarked further, that English drivers seemed partial to ale
and overalls, and Irish ones preferred frieze coats and naked
whiskey.

And now, George, you shall have the particulars of my
escape; and, since the times of the Anabasis, or the more
recent exploits of Lavalette and Ikey Solomons, never was
retreat effected in more masterly style. Candour obliges
me to admit, that mine was unaccompanied by sound of
trumpet, or other "pomp and circumstance of war;" and
rather resembled the hasty retirement of a detected thief
from a tabernacle, than a bold operation in noonday, and in
the face of the enemy. But let that pass. I embarked a
miscellaneous cargo of guns, dogs, and fishing-tackle, under
the *surveillance* of a trusty servant, on board a Dublin
steamer, and the following evening started quietly for "the
Head;" leaving directions with mine host in Grafton-street
to acquaint Lord Leatherby, and all suspicious-looking in-
quirers, that I had departed for Constantinople, and that any
commands for me must be forwarded, under cover, to the
Sublime Porte.

I have no talent for statistics, but if my memory serve,
the interesting portion of the British empire from which I
write, is thus laid down by a modern tourist :—"It lieth,"
says this intelligent traveller, " under a dark gray cloud, which
is evermore discharging itself on the earth, but, like the
widow's curse, is never exhausted. It is bounded on the south
and east by Christendom and part of Tipperary, on the north
by Donegal, and on the west by the *salt say*. It abounds in
bogs, lakes, and other natural curiosities ; its soil consists of
equal quantities of earth and stone ; and its surface is so
admirably disencumbered of trees, shrubs, hedges, and ditches,
that an intelligent backwoodsman from Louisiana was heard to

declare with rapture, that it was the most perfectly-cultivated territory in Europe.

" Further," saith the tourist, " its gentry are a polished and religious race, remarkable for their punctuality in pecuniary transactions, and their freedom from a litigious or quarrelsome disposition. The prevailing mode of belief among the upper classes is *anythingarianism*—that of the people, pure Popery."

This premonitory sketch will save you and me, George, an infinity of trouble. You have here the country graphically placed before you, as well as the distinguishing traits of character, for which the pleasant and virtuous community who abide in this interesting department of the Emerald Isle are so eminently distinguished.

The town of Ballinasloe is seated on a river, the name of which I neglected to inquire. It is much frequented by saints and cattle dealers, carries on a smart trade in sheep and proselytes, and Bibles and bullocks are " thick as leaves in Vallombrosa." The cabins, moreover, are whitewashed; pigs and popery are prohibited; and travellers wayfaring on the seventh day denounced, and, under perilous amercements, enjoined to take their ease in their respective inns.

While the horses were being brought out, I strolled into the street, and, in a show-room of the Farming Society, discovered a collection of biblicals in full activity. From a short gentleman with soiled linen and an impeded delivery, I learned the gratifying fact, that the spread of the Gospel was progressive in California; and, further, that a second-cousin of the King of Siam had been baptized by a Moravian Missionary. This latter annunciation elicited a thunder of applause; and a young lady with a lisp pinched my elbow playfully, and requested me to propose that a piece of plate be transmitted to the convertee. Now, pinching one's elbow on a five minutes' acquaintance is alarming; I accordingly levanted, leaving *Lispy* to propose the plate in person. I observed in my retreat a mob assembled round the chapel, and, pushing through a crowd of ragged urchins, established myself in the doorway. Within there was a meeting of Radical Reformers, and a tall man was pouring forth a philippic from the altar, in which he made an awful example of the king's English, and, in his syllabic arrangements, differed totally from modern orthoepists. The gist of his oration went to prove, that Catholic Emancipation was a humbug—concession a farce—and luck or grace would never visit this unhappy island, until Mr. Cornelius Cassidy, of Killcooney House, was sent to represent us in the Imperial Parliament.

The horses are being put to, and I must say farewell. I shall, however, note my adventures, and in due time favour you with another epistle.

Adieu, always yours.

## CHAPTER III.

Journey continued—Inn of Glantane—Tuam—A Bad Night—Out of the Frying-pan into the Fire—A Country Ball, and the Finish.

As my journey hither has been singularly propitious, I shall only trouble you with the leading incidents.

My carriage broke down close to the inn of Glantane, a solitary house, as the song goes, " delightfully placed in a bog." As some delay must necessarily occur before the repairs of the vehicle could be effected, after the example of that accomplished cavalier, Major Dalgetty, I determined to seize on this opportunity to provision the garrison. To this prudent proceeding on my part I found there was an insurmountable obstacle: the landlady assured me that the " *matériel*" was in the house—there was bacon in the chimney, and chickens in the yard, but there was no turf within, till *the boys—the devil bother them for staying!*—came home from the blacksmith's funeral. Now, that the hotel of Glantane should be deficient in this point was marvellous. The surface of the circumjacent country, in its proportion of tillage-ground to turbary, bears an acreable ratio of one to five hundred; and yet, though in the bosom of a bog, there could not be a sufficiency of fire obtained to boil a potato-pot! But human ingenuity is surprising: after a delay of three mortal hours I reascended my chaise, and, without further accident, was deposited in the town of Tuam.

On the merits of the Mitre Inn I shall be silent; it produced in good time a respectable quarter of cold lamb, and a dish of exquisite potatoes. By the way, we cannot cook this latter esculent in England. Had my fare been worse, I would have submitted without a murmur; for the waiter assured my servant that I had got the best bedroom in the house. Now, in the course of my narrative, I omitted to mention, that on the preceding night I had scarcely closed an eye. On retiring to my dormitory, I remarked that the grate was heaped with black turfs, apparently in the same state in which they had been removed from their parent moor; but, anxious to court the drowsy god, I extinguished the candle, sprang into bed, and too late discovered that I was overloaded with a mass of ponderous blanketing, while a faint spark twinkled in the bottom of the grate, and, like the cry of wisdom in the streets, was disregarded. I fell into a temporary doze, and awoke an hour afterwards in a burning fever; for the grate, in place of cold turfs, exhibited a roaring fire. In vain I opened door and window; in vain I tumbled blanket after blanket on the floor: hours elapsed before the fever-warmth of the apartment could be abated. At last, exhausted by heat and exertion, I threw myself upon the outside of the bed-coverings, and made myself up for repose. Just then a brace of obstinate curs determined to " bay the moon :" one established himself beneath my window, and the other took up a position at the opposite side of the street, and for three long hours they barked incessantly, relieving themselves occasionally by indulging in a mournful and nerve-torturing howl. Human forbearance could not support the martyrdom I suffered: I was driven to desperation, and, collecting every missile article in the chamber, with repeated discharges routed my persecutors, and once more endeavoured to procure some rest.

I sank into a delicious slumber; but suddenly the door was flung open, and in rushed the waiter with portentous speed. " The house must be on fire !" I ejaculated as I somerseted into the centre of the floor. My fears were fortunately groundless : Dennis merely awoke me to inquire if I would drive three miles out of town to see two scoundrels fight, who had quarrelled the preceding night about a game of cribbage. Judge then, dear George, after all these visitations, whether the annunciation of a quiet bed at Tuam was not to me " a sound ecstatic !"

I swallowed a pint of rascally sherry without a murmur, fortified it with a dose of diluted alcohol, yawned my way to my room, found clean linen—no fire, and, in five minutes, was buried in sleep " fast as a watchman."

Presently arose a hum of many voices; dreams and phantasies disturbed my uneasy slumbers; a noise like distant music at times was faintly audible;—at last a crash of instruments awoke me, and the first quadrille was in full execution within four feet of my distracted head!

Heaven granted me patience, although I was on the very brink of a country ball-room, and separated from " the gay throng" only by the intervention of a slip of deal-board, while through the chinks you might have passed the poker, or interchanged a parasol.

I raised myself up on my elbow, and what a group was there! A short man, in a claret-coloured coat, was paired with a stout gentlewoman in bright scarlet: she must have been descended from " the giant;" I would as soon grapple with her in a waltz, as commit myself to the embraces of a boa-constrictor. *Vis-à-vis* was a police-officer, in state uniform, with a pale beauty in cerulean blue; and a personage of immense calf, in black *tights*, confronted a skeleton in nankeen *unmentionables*. The ladies were gloriously adorned with silver ribbon, gilt wreaths, and every flower that blows, from a pink to a peony; the lords of the creation sported stiffened cravats and a plurality of waistcoats; and the ball-room emitted " an ancient and fish-like smell"—a miasm of musk, assisted by every abomination in perfumery.

I was in an intermediate state between frenzy and fever, and turned over in my mind the expediency of setting fire to the bed-curtains, and sending myself, the quadrille, and the whole company to the skies, by igniting ten pounds of Harvey's *treble strong*, which was stowed away somewhere in my luggage. Did tired Nature quiesce for a moment, I was fearfully roused with a tornado of torturous sounds. " Places, gentlemen!"—" Ladies-chain!"—" Now, don't dance, Patsey; you know you're drunk!"—" Arrah! Charley, are you stupid?"—" *Dos-à-dos*, Miss Rourke!"—" Up with the Lancers!"—" Aisy, Mr. Bodkin! remember there are ladies here!"—" Waiter! there's porter wanted at the card-table!" Somnus! deity of my adoration! never expose me to such misery as I endured in the archiepiscopal town of Tuam!

Morning came, and the company retired to supper below stairs. Anticipating the consequences, I fortified my chamber-door with all the moveables I could collect. It was a prudent precaution; for, blessed be God! a row ensued, that finished both delph and dancing. I suffered nothing in person, but my less-fortunate valet got a black eye from a Connemara gentleman, who, unluckily for poor Travers, mistook him for the master of the ceremonies, with whom he of Connemara was at feud.

For the present, farewell.

## CHAPTER IV.

Loss of a Waiter—Precocious Talent—The Mad Major and the Mendicants of Mullingar—Cursing an Adjutant—Death of Denis O'Farrell.

It was noon when I arose, and the inmates of the Mitre were still in exquisite confusion. Breakfast, after much delay, was provided by the agency of the housemaid. She apologized for the non-attendance of the waiter, at present a patient in the Infirmary; he having, in the course of the entertainment, been ejected from the window by a pleasant gentleman of Loughrea.

Anxious to be off as soon as possible, I ordered the horses to; but an unforeseen difficulty occurred in removing my luggage to the carriage, as the door was blocked up four deep by a gang of beggars. With relation to the sizes of the respective places, the lazaroni of Naples are far out-numbered by the mendicants of Tuam. A trace broke at starting, and thus enabled me to form a pretty correct idea of this multitude. I reckoned to fifty-seven, and then became confused. Although beset on every side, I was proof against importunity, and refused parting with a sixpence. Cursing was next tried; and to the curious in that accomplishment, I would suggest a week's residence at the Mitre. One boy, a cripple in a dish, excelled the united talent of the remainder. English and Irish epithets were with him " common as household words;" he used both languages with surpassing fluency, and there was an originality of conception in his style of execration, which was what the Cockneys call most refreshing. This precocious prodigy could not be much above fifteen; and, if he lives, will in this peculiar department of national eloquence be without a parallel. I have " erst while" passed through Billingsgate, when the fair

inhabitants betrayed symptoms of irritation ; I have heard
hackney-coachmen cursing at a crowded opera over a fractured
panel or broken pole ; I have listened to a score of watermen
squabbling for a fare at Westminster Bridge ; I have been on
board a transport in a gale of wind, with an irreligious commander ; but Tuam for ever! there cursing is perfection.

Mine, George, is but a rambling narrative, and my details,
however interesting, lay no claim to the *lucidus ordo* ; therefore I reserve full liberty from the very start to bolt into digres-
sions when and as I please.

Of the many anecdotes that I have heard my father narrate
of his friend, the Mad Major, one was particularly characteristic.

When the gallant 50th were removed to Mullingar, it was
supposed that this town produced a greater number of beggars
than any in the king's dominions : a swarm of paupers rendered
the streets almost impassable, and ingress or egress to or from
a shop was occasionally impracticable.  Now, beggars were
to the Mad Major an abomination ; and for two days he ensconced himself in his lodgings, rather than encounter the mendicants of Mullingar.  Confinement will increase bile, and bile
may induce gout ; and at last, wearied of captivity, he sallied
forth, and to every application for relief, he specified an early
day, requesting the numerous supplicants to be punctual to the
appointed time.  His wish was faithfully attended to ; and on
the expected morning, the street where he resided was literally blocked up.  The Major, under a volley of blessings,
appeared at the hall-door.  " Are you all here?" he inquired,
in accents of the tenderest compassion.  " All, your honour—
all, young and owld!" responded a big beggarman.  " We're
all here, colonel, *avorneen !*" exclaimed a red virago, " but my
own poor man, *Brieney Bokkogh* ;* and he, the crater ! fell into
the fire a Sunday night, and him hearty, and sorrow stir he
can make good nor bad."—" Ah, then," said the humane
commander, " why should poor Brien be left out ?  Arrah !
run yourself, and bring the cripple to us."  In a twinkling
off went the red virago, and, after a short absence, issued
from a neighbouring lane, with Brieney on her shoulders.
" Are you all here now?" inquired the tender-hearted chief-
tain.  " Every single sowl of us," said an old woman in reply.

* Bryan the Cripple.

" Ogh! that the light of heaven may shine on his honour's dying hour; but it's he that's tender to the poor!"—" Amen, sweet Jasus!" responded a hundred voices. " Silence!" said the Mad Major, as he produced a small book neatly bound in red morocco. " Whisht, your sowls!" cried the big beggarman. " Are ye listening?"—" Sha, sha! yes, yes!" was responded in English and Irish. " Then, by the contents of this blessed book—and it's the Bible—a rap I won't give one of ye, you infernal vagabonds, if I remained a twelvemonth in Mullingar!" A yell of execrations followed; but the Major bore the cursing like a philosopher, and kept his promise like a monk. To the surprise of all, the beggars left the way when he walked out, and absconded from the shop he entered. They crossed themselves devoutly if they encountered him unexpectedly at a corner, adjuring the Lord to " stand between them, the Mad Major, and the devil!"

*Apropos* to cursing; the late Sir Charles Asgill told a story of this eccentric personage. During the time the 50th remained in Ireland, the Colonel was mostly absent from ill health, and the command of course devolved upon the Major. By one of the military abuses at that time too common, a little Scotch Doctor, who had somehow been appointed Adjutant to a Fencible regiment, was transferred from it to the 50th. Incompetent from professional inability, he was further afflicted by a constitutional nervousness, that made him badly calculated to come in contact with such a personage as the Mad Major.

Shortly after the little Scotchman joined, the half yearly inspection took place. Major O'Farrell, in the course of his evolutions, found it requisite to deploy into line, and called to his field-assistant " to take an object." " Have you got one?" cried the commander, in a voice of thunder. " Yes, Sir," replied the alarmed Adjutant, in a feeble squeak. The word was given, and the right wing kept moving, until the face of the regiment assumed the form of a semicircle. " Hallo!—where or what is your object?" roared the Major. " A crow, Sir," replied the unhappy Scotsman. " And where is the crow?" roared the Commander. " Flown off," was the melancholy response. " May the devil fly away with you, body and bones! Halt — dress! Stop, Sir Charles; do stop. Just allow me two minutes to curse that rascally Adjutant." To so reasonable a request, Sir Charles,

who was a most obliging officer, readily assented. The
General mentioned often, that the damning of a stupid Adjutant was no novelty; but that he never saw a man cursed to
his perfect satisfaction, until he heard the Scotch Doctor
anathematized in the Phœnix Park.

The death of poor Denis was in such perfect keeping with
his life, that I am tempted to give it to you.

The regiment was in garrison, and at a race-ball a trifling
misunderstanding occurred between a young Ensign and a
country-gentleman. It was, however, instantly adjusted.
A few days afterwards, some intemperate expressions which
had fallen from the gentleman at the ball, were reported to
the Mad Major. These he considered as reflecting upon
the character of his corps, and he despatched the senior
Captain for an explanation. The answer to this demand
was unsatisfactory, and the Captain was directed to deliver
a hostile message. The officers of the " Half Hundred"
were a brave body—they vainly endeavoured to make it a
regimental affair, and insisted that the person to resent
the insult should be indifferently selected (by lot) from the
corps.

" Gentlemen, I thank you;" said the Mad Major, as he
struck his broad hand upon the mess-table. " Your motives
are personally kind—but as I am at the head of this regiment,
I hòld myself to be the conservator of its honour."

That evening the Major had a violent attack of gout, to
which for years he had been a martyr—but he concealed it
carefully, and when his friend called him on the morning,
he was found dressed and powdered, but unable to move
without assistance. Captain M—— pressed upon him the
necessity of postponing the meeting, or permitting another
officer to be his substitute; but Denis was immovable in his
resolve. He proceeded to the ground, and supported by a
crutch, after a discharge of pistols, received a satisfactory
apology. Poor fellow! this was his last feat. Exposure to
the cold of a damp spring morning brought on a renewed
attack of gout—that night the disorder settled in his stomach
—and the morning after he was a corpse.

The body was carried to its last resting-place, accompanied
by all the pomp of a military funeral. His own beloved company, the grenadiers, who had often followed their lion-
hearted leader into action, now formed his guard of honour

to the grave; and when his remains were committed to the
earth there was not a dry eye among the " Dirty Half
Hundred."

Two months afterwards, when an Irish soldier was questioned on the merits of his successor—" The man is well
enough," said Pat, with a heavy sigh, " but where will we
find the equal of the Mad Major ?  By Jasus, it was a comfort to be cursed by him !"

## CHAPTER V.

Castlebar—Newport—Departure from Christendom—Progress into Terra
Incognita—Roads and scenery—Mulranny—Passage down the Inlet—
Incidents—Lodge in the Wilds of Erris—Description of the establish-
ment.

WITHOUT any adventure worthy of a place in this itinerary,
I reached in safety the capital of Mayo.  From other provincial cities, this town is distinguished in having a new drop
and an old gaol; a swamp in the centre of the town surrounded by an iron chain, judiciously placed there, I imagine,
to prevent cattle and children being lost in the morass which
it environs; a court-house, with a piazza and façade, of an
original order of architecture, only known to Irish professors
of the art of building; trade and manufactures are limited to
felt-hats and poteen whisky; and the only machinery I could
discover was the drop, aforesaid.  I was informed that the
chapel and petty-sessions are generally crowded, as is the
market, upon a hanging-day.

I was called next morning at five o'clock by the waiter, to
proceed by the Sligo mail, although on the preceding night I
had taken considerable pains to persuade him that my course
lay westward.  One hour afterwards, the chamber-maid roused
me to inquire if I had any intention of proceeding to Holly-
mount by a hackney car.  To save these worthy people further
trouble, I arose and dressed, and, wishing to avoid a vestry to
be that day holden in the town, and where, in the course of argument, it was believed that divers lives would be lost, I took
an early breakfast, and departed.

I stopped at Newport; it was the last cluster of houses arrogating to itself the title of a town, that I should now meet with, for I had reached the *ultima Thule* of civilized Europe— and when I had given directions to the post-master touching the transmission of my letters in my cousin's bag, I looked around me, and took a silent but mournful farewell of Christendom.

I found at the public-house that my kinsman had provided for my farther progress into *terra incognita*. A couple of rudely-constructed vehicles were waiting to receive myself and personal property, and a wild bare-legged mountaineer, with a leathern bag strapped across his shoulders, announced himself as guide. "Had he no horse?"—"*Devil a harse!* but he would warrant he would keep up with me,"—and away we went under a salute of our dogs, and the furtive glances of sundry ladies with their hair in papers.

Some distance from the town, we crossed an ancient bridge of many arches, through which an extensive lake communicates with the sea, and farther on passed the old tower of Carrigahowla. Our route was contiguous to the sea—on the left were the numerous islands of Clew Bay; on the right an extensive chain of savage hills and barren moorland. The road now became hardly passable; constructed without the least regard to levelness,—*here* it dipped into a ravine, and *there* breasted some sudden hill, inaccessible to any carriage but the light machines we travelled with. Its surface was rough, and interrupted by a multitude of loose stones; while some of the bridges were partially dilapidated, and others had never been completed. In these, the ragged line of granite which formed the key-stones of the arches stood nakedly up, and presented a barrier that no common carriage could overtop without endangering its springs and harness. Yet this forlorn road is the only communication with a highly improvable country, covering at least fifty square miles, with numerous and profitable islands attached, and an immense line of sea-coast, possessing rich fisheries, and abounding in kelp-weed and manure! And why was this neglect? Were the proprietors of this deserted district so cold to that true spring of human action, self-aggrandizement, as to omit providing an outlet for the sources of their opulence? Were there no public monies allocated to these abandoned corners of the earth, and so much lavishly expended on many a useless undertaking elsewhere? Yes : large sums have been presented and *re-presented* by the Grand Juries for the last twenty years, but they have been regularly pocketed by those to whose good faith they were entrusted. Would it be believed in England, George, that this atrocious system of peculation has been carried to such an extent, that roads have been passed, *as completed*, when their lines have been but roughly marked out—and bridges been actually paid for, the necessary accounting affidavits having been sworn to in open court, when not a stone was ever laid, and to this day the stream runs without a solitary arch to span its flood from the source to the debouchement? Ay—these delinquencies have been often and notoriously perpetrated, and none have had the courage to drag the criminals to justice.

At the *clachan* of Mulranny we struck into a pass in the mountains, and turned our backs upon Clew Bay. A branch from the waters of Black Sod runs some ten miles inland, and meets this opening in the hills, affording a communication by boats with Erris. There my kinsman's galley was waiting for me, and in it I embarked my person and establishment. Taking advantage of a south-westerly wind, the boatmen hoisted their close-reefed lug, and away we shot rapidly towards the entrance of the inlet. From the high lands which rose on every side, the squalls fell more heavily and frequent than I found agreeable ; but in an hour we cleared this confined and dangerous channel, and, running between Currane Point and the island of Innis Biggle, entered Black Sod Bay.

The passage down the inlet, was marked with several incidents which were in perfect keeping with the wild and savage scenery around. A seal would suddenly raise his round head above the surface, gaze for a moment at the boat, and, when he had apparently satisfied his curiosity, sink quietly from our view. In rounding the numerous headlands through which this inlet irregularly winds, we often started flocks of curlews,*

* The bill is long, equally incurvated, and terminated in a blunt point ; nostrils linear, and longitudinal near the base ; tongue short and sharp-pointed ; and the toes are connected as far as the first joint of the membrane.

With the curlew, Linnæus begins a numerous tribe of birds under the genuine name of Scalopax, which, in his arrangement, includes all the snipes and godwits, amounting, according to Latham, to forty-two species

which, rising in an alarm at our unexpected appearance, made
the rocks ring with their loud and piercing whistle. Skirting
the shore of Innis Biggle, we disturbed an osprey or sea-eagle,*
in the act of feeding on a bird. He rose leisurely, and, lighting on a rock, waited till we passed, and then returned to his

prey. We ran sufficiently close to the shore to observe the

and eight varieties, spread over various parts of the world, but nowhere
very numerous.

Buffon describes fifteen species and varieties of the curlew, and Latham
ten, only two or three of which are British birds. They feed upon
worms, which they pick up on the surface, or with their bills dig from the
soft earth : on these they depend for their principal support; but they
also devour the various kinds of insects which swarm in the mud and
in the wet boggy grounds, where these birds chiefly take up their
abode.

* " Eagles are well knowne to breed here, but neither so bigge, nor
so many, as books tell. Cambrensis reporteth of his own knowledge,
and I heare it averred by credible persons, that barnacles, thousands
at once, are noted along the shoares to hang by the beakes about the

size and colour of the bird, and concluded that a grouse had been the eagle's victim.

When we had cleared the islands, the breeze blew fresh and steadily; the boatmen shook out the reefs, which had hitherto confined their canvass; the galley, with increased velocity, rushed through the rippling water, till, doubling a neck of land surmounted by a ruined castle, and running up a sheltered creek, I found myself at the termination of my voyage, and warmly welcomed by my Irish kinsman, from whom for fifteen years I had been separated.

---

I have oeen here three days, and am as much domesticated in the mansion as my cousin's Newfoundland dog. I know the names and "*sobriquet*" of the establishment; can discriminate between "*Hamish-a-neilan*" (James of the island) and *Andy-bawn* (Fair Andy); I hold converse with the cook, and am hand-and-glove with the housemaid. Really I am delighted with the place, for every thing is wild, new, and out-of-the-way; but I must describe the *locale* of my kinsman's domicile.

At the bottom of a narrow creek, you must imagine "a low snug dwelling, and in good repair." The foam of the Atlantic breaks sometimes against the windows, while a huge cliff, seaward, defends it from the storm, and, on the land side, a sudden hill shelters it from the north wind. Here, when the tempest roars abroad, your friend Laura might venture forth and not endanger a *papillotte*. The bent* roof is impervious to the rain; the rooms are neat, well arranged, and comfortable. In the parlour, if the evening be chilly, a turf fire sparkles on the hearth; and when dried bog-deal is added to the embers, it emits a fragrant and delightful glow, superseding the necessity of candles. The long and measured swell of the Atlantic would almost lull a troubled conscience to repose; and that rural hum, which attends upon the farm-yard, rouses the refreshed sleeper in the morning. In the calm of evening I hear the shrill cry of the sand-lark; and in

---

edges of puttified timber, shippes, oars, anchor-holders, and such like, which in processe, taking lively heate of the sunne, become water-fowles, and, at their time of ripenesse, either fall into the sea, or fly abroad into the ayre."—*Campion's Historie.*

* The customary thatch in parts of Erris.

the early dawn, the crowing of the cock-grouse. I see the
salmon fling themselves over the smooth tide, as they hurry
from the sea to reascend their native river. And while I
drink claret that never paid the revenue a farthing, or indulge
over that proscribed beverage—the produce and the scourge
of this wild district—I trace from the window the outline of
a range of hills, where the original red-deer of Ireland are
still existing—none of your park-fed venison, that tame,
spiritless diminutive, which a boy may assassinate with his
" birding-piece," but the remnant of that noble stock, which
hunters of other days, *O'Connor the Cus Dhu*,* and *Cormac
Bawn Mac Tavish* once delighted in pursuing.

The offices of this wild dwelling are well adapted to the
edifice. In winter, the ponies have their stable; and kine
and sheep a comfortable shed. Nor are the dogs forgotten;
for them a warm and sheltered kennel is fitted up with
benches, and well provided with straw. Many a sporting-
lodge in England, on which thousands have been expended,
lacks the comforts of my kinsman's unpretending cottage.
Where are the coach-houses ? Those, indeed, would be
useless appendages; for the nearest road on which a wheel
could turn, is ten miles distant from the lodge.

---

## CHAPTER VI.

Periodicals—Cockney sports and sportsmen—Mountain angler and his
attendant—Fishing-tackle—Antony the otter-killer—Visit the river—
Flies—Hooking my first salmon—Return to the lodge—Sporting
authors — Sir Humphry Davy—Colonel Hawker—Salmonia—Criti-
cisms.

THE last post-bag brought a large supply of newspapers
and monthly literature. "Gad-o'-mercy!" what notions the
fishermen of Cockaign must have of the " gentle art!" It is
amusing to read the piscatory articles so seriously put forth
in the sporting periodicals. No persons on earth suffer more
personal inconvenience than the Cockney artist, or submit so
patiently to pecuniary imposition — and like virtue, their

* Blackfoot.

trouble is its own reward. Punt-fishing and perch-fishing, baiting-holes, and baiting-hooks, appear to the mountain fisherman so utterly worthless, that I do not wonder at the sovereign contempt with which he regards the unprofitable pursuits of the city angler.*

What a contrast to the Cockney bustle of a Londoner does my cousin's simple preparation for a morning's sport exhibit! If the wind and clouds are favourable, the rod, ready jointed and spliced, is lifted from beneath the cottage eave, where it "lay like a warrior taking his rest," on a continuation of level pegs. The gaff and pannier are produced by a loose-looking mountaineer, whose light-formed but sinewy limbs are untrammelled by shoe or stocking. Fond of the sport himself, he evinces an ardent interest in your success; on the moor and by the river he is a good-humoured and obliging assistant; traverses the mountains for a day, and lies out on the hill-side through the long autumnal night, to watch the passage of the red deer as they steal down from the mountain-top to browse on the lower grounds by moonlight.

How different from this wild and cheerful follower are the sporting attendants of the unhappy Cockney! he must consort with "bacon-fed knaves," be the companion of your brawny jolter-headed porter-swollen waterman, who in sulky silence paddles his employer into some phlegmatic pool, where the disciple of Walton is secure of the lumbago, but by no means certain of a sprat.

In truth, dear George, I am half ashamed of myself: I came here loaded with rods, flies, and baskets, with the "thousand and one" nameless *et cetera* furnished from a city tackle-shop, in their uses and appearance various as the cargo of the ark. When I displayed yesterday this accumulation of "engines and cunning devices," my cousin burst into a roar of laughter, and inquired if I intended to annihilate the fishery?" Then, turning, leaf by leaf, three immense fly-books over, he praised the pretty feathers, commended the brightness of the tinsel, and good-naturedly assured me

* " To induce fish to come to any particular spot, boiled wheat, grains of malt graves (from the tallow-chandler's) cut small, should be thrown in *plentifully* two or three times. A composition of *ground malt, blood, and clay* is the best for salmon and trout: to which some add ivy-gum."—*Daniel.*

that this rich assemblage did not possess· a fly of the value
of one farthing. I fear his verdict was a true one; I have
tried two days consecutively and never hooked a fish. But
no, the water was too low, the wind too high, or something
was amiss, for I have the best flies procurable in the best shop
in London.

The storm terminated as summer gales do, in a heavy fall
of rain. Although the wears are raised to intercept the
passage of the fish from the sea, the late *freshes*, joined to a
spring tide, have enabled both trout and salmon to overleap
the barrier and fill the pools above it. Want of success had
damped my ardour for piscation; and besides, I had involved
myself in a most amusing article in Blackwood, and felt an
unwillingness to lay aside the book. At this moment of
indecision, old Antony the otter-killer, one of that numerous
and nondescript personages who *locate* themselves in the
houses of the Irish gentry, passed the window with a fine
salmon and a brace of trout sixteen inches long. How fresh
and sparkling is the phosphoric shading of the scales, as the
old man turns them round for my inspection! What a beautiful fish! it barely measures thirty inches, and is fully
ten pounds weight! That short and deep-shouldered
*briddawn*\* is worth all the lubberly roach, dace, perch, and
gudgeons, that the Thames contains from its source to its
debouchement.

I looked after the ancient otter-hunter with envy. How
lowly would he be estimated in the eyes of a Cheapside
fisherman; one, who wears a modest-coloured jacket,† lest
a showy garment might annoy the plethoric animals he is
dabbling for, — whose white basket is constructed of the
finest wicker work — with rods and reels, floats and flies,
pastes and patties, lines and liqueurs sufficient to load a
donkey, — how contemptuously would he look down upon
honest Antony! Figure to yourself a little feeble man, dressed

\* A salmon.
† " Our forefathers were wont to pursue even their amusements with
great formality: an angler, a century and a half back, must have his
fishing-coat, which, if not black, must at least be of a very dark colour, a
*black velvet cap*, like those which jockeys now wear, and a rod with a
stock like a halberd; thus equipped, he stalked forth, followed by the
eyes of a whole neighbourhood."—*Daniel.*

in a jerkin of coarse blue cloth, with an otter (a fancy of my cousin's) blazoned on his arm : in one hand he holds a fish-spear, which assists him when he meets with rugged ground, in the other, a very unpretending angle, jointed rudely with a penknife, and secured by waxen threads ; a *cast* of flies are wound about his hat, and his remaining stock, not exceeding half-a-dozen, are contained between the leaves of a tattered song-book : in the same depository he has some silk, dyed mohair, a hare's ear, and a few feathers from the cock, brown turkey, and mallard ; and these simple materials furnish him with most efficient flies, but he requires a bright day to fabricate them, as his sight is in-different.

It required much persuasion and a positive assurance of success, before I ventured with my kinsman to the river. Ten minutes' easy walking brought us to a noble pool above the Wear, where my friend never fails to kill a salmon, if the wind be westerly and the water not too low. The water was in beautiful order, and my cousin insisted that, under his direction, I should once more try my fortune with the fishing-rod. Discarding my gaudy flies with a malediction upon the knave who tied them, he affixed two of his upon the casting-line ; and nothing could be of a simpler character than those selected from his book. The tail-fly was a plain black and orange mohair body, with a long and pointed turkey-feather wing ; the dropper was formed of blue and scarlet wool, ribbed with silver, a pheasant sprit for legs, and mixed wings of the turkey and mallard.

I made several unsuccessful casts : " A bad look-out, friend Julius. Heaven forfend that the cook has placed any dependence on the angle !" Again I tried the pool, and, like all disappointed fishermen, began to prognosticate a change of weather. " I had remarked mares' tails in the sky yesterday evening, and there was rain over head, for a hundred !" My cousin smiled ; when, suddenly, my nebulous speculations were interrupted by a deep, sluggish roll at the dropper. " *Monamondiaoul !*"* exclaimed *Mortien Beg*,† as he caught a momentary glance of the broad and fan-like tail. " He is fifteen pound weight !" Obedient to the directions of my Mentor, I left the spot the salmon leaped in, and commenced

* An Irish imprecation.　　　　† Little Martin.

casting a dozen yards below it. Gradually I came over him again. "A light cast, Frank, and you have him!" I tried, and succeeded gallantly. I sent the fly across the water with the lightness of the thistle's down, as at the same moment the breeze eddied up the stream, and curled the surface deliciously. A long dull ruffle succeeded — whish! span the wheel; whish-h-h-h-h, whish-h-h-, whish! I have him!

Nothing, my dear George, can be more beautiful than the play of a vigorous salmon. The lubberly struggles of a pond-fish are execrable to him who has felt the exquisite pleasure that attends the conquest of "the monarch of the stream." His bold rushes—his sudden and rapid attempts to liberate himself from the fisher's thrall—the energy with which he throws his silver body three or four feet above the surface of the water—and the unwearied and incessant opposition he makes, until his strength is exhausted by the angler's science; all this must be experienced to be adequately conceived. In ten minutes I mastered my beautiful victim; and Mortien Beg gaffed and landed a splendid summer fish, which, if the cook's scales be correct, weighed *thirteen pounds and seven ounces.*

Overjoyed with my success, I proceeded up the river. My cousin brought me to several delightful pools ; and, with his assistance, I raised and hooked several capital fish, but only landed one of them, a nice and active salmon of about eight pounds weight. From half a dozen white trout fresh from the sea, I received excellent amusement; and at six o'clock returned to dinner, gratified with my sport, pleased with myself, and at peace with all mankind, excepting that confounded cozener, the tackle-merchant in —— Street.

Over our wine, the conversation naturally turned upon the "gentle art." My kinsman is both a practical and a scientific angler. "Holding, with few exceptions, all published sporting productions in disrepute, one that I remarked on your book-stand, Julius, strikes me as being at the same time clever and useful: I mean Sir Humphry Davy's."

"It is both, Frank: his account of the habits and natural history of the salmon species is just, ingenious, and amusing; and there is a calm and philosophic spirit that pervades the whole, rendering it a work of more than common interest. But, practically, it is as useless as all *Guides* and *Manuals,*

since the days of Walton. Of the uninitiated it will make
fishermen, where *Colonel Hawker's* directions enable a man to
shoot, who has never been five miles from Holborn-bars. I
doubt not but Sir Humphry was an ardent and *scientific*
fisherman, but in many practical points I differ with him.
He angled well, but he fished like a philosopher. If he
haunted this river for a season, unless he altered his system
materially, he would not kill a dozen salmon. Flies, such as
he describes, would never, in any seasons or weathers, be
successful here. He fairly says, that ' different rivers require
different flies ;' but nothing like those he recommends would
answer this one ;—and, although many of the theories and
speculative opinions are very ingenious, I question much their
validity.

" Admiring Sir Humphry as I do, I would pardon his
philosophy and fine flies, his ' golden pheasant, silken-bodied,
orange, red, and pale-blue, silver-twisted, and king's-fisher
mixtures,' even to his ' small bright humming-bird' itself;
but, with all my Christian charity and personal affection, there
is one fatal passage, for which, like Lady Macbeth's soiled
hand, there is no remedy. Would that I could ' pluck from
the memory' that luckless page ! But, alas ! whenever I see
*Salmonia*, it rushes to my recollection. Think, Frank, of a
man who limited a party of sporting tourists to *half a pint of
claret !* and threatened an honest gentleman, who called for
another bottle, with ' an overflow of blood,' ' a suffusion of the
hæmorrhoidal veins,' and, worse than all, ' a determined
palsy,'* if he persevered ! I could have forgiven the philosopher any thing—every thing—even to the comparison of
that rascally fish, the perch, with the rich and luxurious
mullet; but to *fob off* four stout gentlemen with a solitary

---

* Doctors will disagree—*vide* Daniel's Account of Joe Man, game-
keeper to Lord Torrington. " He was in constant strong morning exercise;
he went to bed always betimes, *but never till his skin was filled with ale.*
This," he said, " would do no harm to an early riser, and to a man who
pursued field-sports. At seventy-eight years of age he began to decline,
and then lingered for three years ;—his gun was ever upon his arm,
and he still crept about, not destitute of the hope of fresh diversion."—
Vol. ii. p. 172.

" Inhabitants (especially new comers) are subject to distillations,
rhumes, and fluxes; for remedy whereof they use an ordinary drink
of aqua-vitæ, so qualified in the making, that it dryeth more, and in-
flameth lesse, than other hote confections."—*Campion's Historie*, 1571.

bottle of the *vin ordinaire* ycleped claret, that one meets with in a country inn ! For God's sake, ring the bell ! Here, John, some wine ! Nothing but a fresh bottle can allay my indignation, and restore my tranquillity."

" Well, we must admit that Sir Humphry would not be exactly the man to fill the chair at an Irish ' symposium ;'. but, his Bacchanalian antipathies apart, he really is an agreeable and instructive writer."

" Why, ye-es ; still there is a dash of milk-and-water throughout *Salmonia*, that nothing but its ingenious account of the affinities and natural history of fishes could compensate. Take, for example, the introduction of the Fishing-Party, and remark the colloquy between Halieus and Poietes :—

" *Hal.*—' I am delighted to see you, my worthy friends, on the banks of the Colne ; and am happy to be able to say, that my excellent host has not only made you free of the river for this day's angling, but insists upon your dining with him— wishes you to try the evening fishing, and the fishing to-morrow morning—and proposes to you, in short, to give up twenty-four hours to the delights of an angler's May-day.'

" *Poiet.*—' We are deeply indebted to him ; and I hardly know how we can accept his offer, without laying ourselves under too great an obligation.'

" *Hal.*—' Fear not : he is as noble-minded a man as ever delighted in good offices : and so benevolent, that I am sure he will be almost as happy in knowing you are amused, as you can be in your sport : and hopes for an additional satisfaction in the pleasure of your conversation.'

" *Poiet.*—' So let it be.'

" *Hal.*—' I will take you to the house ; you shall make your bow, and then you will be all free to follow your own fancies. Remember, the dinner-hour is five ; the dressing-bell rings at half-past four ; be punctual to this engagement, from which you will be free at seven.'

" Now, because a country gentleman takes heart, and invites four philosophers to dinner, Hal can scarcely find words to communicate the hospitable message, and Poietes opines that the obligation shall be eternal. After the worthy host is lauded for this generous act to the very skies, it appears that he bundles off the company at seven o'clock, and, before they had time to look around the table, quoits them out, ' like a shove-groat shilling !'—But hark ; the piper is in the hall.   *Shin suis, Cormac !* *   Pass the wine, and a fig for philosophy !"

## CHAPTER VII.

Symptoms of a coming storm—A Sportsman's Dinner—Old John—Pattigo —Gale comes on—Shawn a tra buoy—Seals—The blind Seal.

THE morning had a sullen look; *Slieve More* retained his nightcap; the edge of the horizon where the ocean met the sky was tinged with a threatening glare of lurid sunshine; the wind was capricious as a woman's love—now swelling into gusts, now sinking to a calm, as the unsteady breeze shifted round to every point "i' the shipman's card." As evening approached, the clouds collected in denser masses, and the giant outline of Slieve More was lost in a sheet of vapour.   The swell from the Atlantic broke louder on the bar; the piercing whistle of the curlew was heard more frequently; and the small hard-weather tern, which seldom leaves the Black Rock but to harbinger a coming tempest, was ominously busy; whirling aloft in rapid circles, or plunging its long and pointed wing into the broken surface of the billow. All portended a storm; the wind freshened momentarily, and at last blew steadily from the south-east.

I was at the door, engaged in speculating upon the signs of the approaching gale, when old John, my kinsman's grey-headed butler, summoned me to dinner.—Some say that a bachelor's repast has always a lonely and comfortless appearance; and it may be so.   I grant that a sprinkling of the sexes adds to the social character of the table; but this apart, with the abatement of that best society—*lovely woman*, who shall dine more luxuriously than I ?   Two hours' rabbit-shooting in the sand-hills has given me a keen and wholesome appetite.   That salmon at noon was disporting in the sea, and this kid was fatted among the heath-flowers of the mountain-glen.   *Kitchener* and *Kelly* could take no exception to the cookery; and had these worthies still been inhabitants of "this fair round globe," the Doctor would have found

* Play up, Cormac !

ample amusement for "every man's master, the stomach," and honest *Myke* might have safely ventured to dinner without his "*sauce piquante.*"

In due time the cloth disappeared; a bundle of split bog-deal was laid upon the hearth, and speedily lighted into a cheerful blaze. Old John, with the privilege of an ancient retainer, conversed with us as he extracted a fresh cork for the evening's potation. "Awful weather in July, sir. Well, that *Shawn a tra buoy** is a wonderful beast; I knew a change of weather was at hand when he rose beside the shore last night, and showed his grey head and shoulders over the water."

"Is the seal, John, a sure foreteller of an approaching storm?"

"A certain one, sir: I remember him from I was a boy in the old master's kitchen—the Lord be merciful to his soul! *Shawn a tra buoy's* features are as familiar to me as my own; I would swear to him among a thousand."

"You see him frequently?"

"Oh, yes, sir. When the salmon come in, he is every day upon the yellow strand opposite the lodge: there you will see him chase the fish into the shoal-water, catch them beside the boats, ay, or if that fails, take them from the nets, and rob the fishermen. Year after year he has returned with the salmon, spending his summer on the 'tra-buoy,' and his winter near Carrig-a-boddagh."

"How has he escaped so long, John? Has he not been often fired at?"

"A thousand times; the best marksmen in the country have tried him without success. People say that, like the *master otter*, he has a charmed life; and latterly nobody meddles with him."

Old John's narrative was interrupted by the entrance of another personage; he was a stout burly-looking man, with indifferent good features, a figure of uncommon strength, and a complexion of the deepest bronze. He is the schipper of my cousin's hooker. After a career of perilous adventure in piloting the Flushing smugglers to the coast, he has abandoned his dangerous trade, to pass an honester and safer life in future.

"Well, *Pattigo*,† what news?"

* Jack of the yellow strand.　　　　　　　† A by-name.

D

"The night looks dirty enough, sir; shall we run the hooker round to Tallaghon, and get the rowing-boats drawn up?" His master assented, and ordered him the customary glass of poteen, Pattigo received it graciously in the fingers of his right hand—for he has lost his thumb by the bursting of a blunderbuss in one of his skirmishes with the Revenue—made his ship-shape bow, clapped his *sow-wester* on, and vanished.

The storm came on apace; large and heavy drops struck heavily against the windows; the blast moaned round the house; I heard the boats' keels grate upon the gravel, as the fishermen hauled them up the beach; I saw Pattigo slip his moorings, and, under the skirt of his main-sail, run for a safer anchorage. The rain now fell in torrents; the sea rose, and broke upon the rocks in thunder; mine host directed the storm-shutters to be put up, ordered in candles, with a fresh supply of billets for the fire, and we made final preparations to be comfortable for the night.

Were I required to name the most *recherché* of my kinsman's luxuries. I should specify his unrivalled " canastre." An ample quantity of this precious *tabac*, (brought from Holland by a smuggler), with excellent Dutch pipes, was produced by honest John, who rises hourly in my estimation. There was also an *addendum* in the shape of a foreign-looking bottle, which the ancient servitor averred to have been deposited in the cellar since the time of "the master's father." If it were so, the thing is a marvel; for such liquor is rarely vouchsafed to mortals. Alas! George, while my aching head testifies a too devoted attachment to that misshapen flask, the unequalled flavour of the exquisite *schiedam* it contained will ever haunt my memory.

"I remarked," said my kinsman, as he struck the ashes from his meerschaum, " that you appeared amused with old John's history of *Shawn a tra buoy*. Although, in its wild state, the seal is always shy, and sometimes dangerous, yet when taken young it is easily domesticated, and susceptible of strong attachment to its keepers.* There is a curious story told of

* In January, 1819, in the neighbourhood of Burnt Island, a gentleman completely succeeded in taming a seal : its singularities attracted the curiosity of strangers daily. It appeared to possess all the sagacity of the dog, and lived in its master's house, and ate from his hand. In his fishing excursions, this gentleman generally took it with him; upon

one of these animals—I believe the leading incidents of the narrative to be perfectly authentic ; and it is a memorable record of enduring attachment in the animal, and exquisite barbarity in the man. The tale runs thus :—

" About forty years ago a young seal was taken in Clew Bay, and domesticated in the kitchen of a gentleman, whose house was situated on the sea-shore. It grew apace, became familiar with the servants, and attached to the house and family; its habits were innocent and gentle ; it played with the children, came at its master's call, and, as the old man described him to me, was 'fond as a dog, and playful as a kitten.'

" Daily the seal went out to fish, and, after providing for his own wants, frequently brought in a salmon or turbot to his master. His delight in summer was to bask in the sun, and in winter to lie before the fire, or, if permitted, creep into the large oven, which at that time formed the regular appendage of an Irish kitchen.

" For four years the seal had been thus domesticated, when, unfortunately, a disease, called in this country *the crippawn*— a kind of paralytic affection of the limbs, which generally ends fatally—attacked some black cattle belonging to the master of the house ; some died, others became infected, and the customary cure produced by changing them to drier pasture failed. A wise woman was consulted, and the hag assured the credulous owner, that the mortality among his cows was occasioned by his retaining an unclean beast about his habitation—the harmless and amusing seal. It must be made away with directly, or the crippawn would continue, and her charms be unequal to avert the malady. The superstitious wretch consented to the hag's proposal ; and the seal was put on board a boat, carried out beyond Clare Island, and there committed to the deep, to manage for himself as he best could. The boat returned, the family retired to rest, and next morning a servant awakened her master to tell him that the seal was quietly sleeping in the oven. The poor animal

which occasion it afforded no small entertainment. When thrown into the water, it would follow for miles the track of the boat, and although thrust back by the oars, it never relinquished its purpose; indeed, it struggled so hard to regain its seat, that one would imagine its fondness for its master had entirely overcome the natural predilection for its native element.

overnight came back to his beloved home, crept through an open window, and took possession of his favourite resting-place.

"Next morning another cow was reported to be unwell; and the seal must now be finally removed. A Galway fishing-boat was leaving Westport on her return home, and the master undertook to carry off the seal, and not put him overboard until he had gone leagues beyond Innis Boffin. It was done : a day and night passed ; the second evening closed ; the servant was raking the fire for the night; something scratched gently at the door—it was, of course, the house-dog—she opened it, and in came the seal! Wearied with his long and unusual voyage, he testified, by a peculiar cry expressive of pleasure, his delight to find himself at home ; then stretching himself before the glowing embers of the hearth, he fell into a deep sleep.

"The master of the house was immediately apprised of this unexpected and unwelcome visit. In the exigency, the beldame was awakened and consulted : she averred that it was always unlucky to kill a seal, but suggested that the animal should be deprived of sight, and a third time carried out to sea. To this hellish proposition the besotted wretch who owned the house consented ; and the affectionate and confiding creature was cruelly robbed of sight on that hearth, for which he had resigned his native element! Next morning, writhing in agony, the mutilated seal was embarked, taken outside Clare Island, and for the last time committed to the waves.

"A week passed over, and things became worse instead of better ; the cattle of the truculent wretch died fast, and the infernal hag gave him the pleasurable tidings that her arts were useless, and that the destructive visitation upon his cattle exceeded her skill and cure.

"On the eighth night after the seal had been devoted to the Atlantic, it blew tremendously. In the pauses of the storm a wailing noise at times was faintly heard at the door. The servants, who slept in the kitchen, concluded that the *Banshee** came to forewarn them of an approaching death, and

---

* The *Banshee* is a nondescript being, supposed to be attached to particular families, and to take a lively interest in their weal or misfortunes ; and there are few ancient houses in Ireland unprovided with this domestic spirit. It gives notice of impending calamity—and a death

buried their heads in the bed-coverings. When morning broke, the door was opened—and the seal was there lying dead upon the threshold !"

" Stop, Julius !" I exclaimed, " give me a moment's time to curse all concerned in this barbarism."

" Be patient, Frank," said my cousin, " the *finale* will

in the family is always harbingered by the lamentations of the ill-omened *attaché*. The sex of the banshee is usually feminine; but I knew one instance where a male familiar attended on an old house, and was known by the title of the " Far-a-crick." The banshee was contented with frightening the family she patronised with her laments ; but the Far-a-crick was a more troublesome neighbour. On one occasion he beat severely a drunken servant who was belated returning from a fair—and a quarter of mutton, which the unhappy man was bringing home, confirmed the story, for after the " Hill man's" assault, it was found to be as black as the ribs of the unfortunate sufferer.

The appearance of the banshee is variously described—as she some-times assumes the form of " a little wizened old woman," and at others takes the semblance of " a black bitch."

probably save you that trouble. The skeleton of the once plump animal—for, poor beast, it perished from hunger, being incapacitated from blindness to procure its customary food—was buried in a sand-hill, and from that moment misfortunes followed the abettors and perpetrators of this inhuman deed. The detestable hag who had denounced the inoffensive seal, was, within a twelvemonth, hanged for murdering the illegitimate offspring of her own daughter. Every thing about this devoted house melted away : sheep rotted, cattle died, 'and blighted was the corn.' Of several children, none reached maturity, and the savage proprietor survived every thing he loved or cared for. He died *blind* and miserable.

" There is not a stone of that accursed building standing upon another. The property has been passed to a family of a different name, and the series of incessant calamity which pursued all concerned in this cruel deed is as romantic as true."

It was midnight : I laid down my pipe, took a candle from the sideboard, wished my cousin " a good night, and went to bed, full of pity for the gentle and affectionate seal.

## CHAPTER VIII.

A wet day—Fly-tying—Piscatory disquisitions—The tinker—Lessons in the " gentle art"—An unexpected ally.

THE night throughout continued wild and blustrous ; the squalls which shook the casements became less frequent and violent towards morning ; the wind settled in the south, and dying gradually away, was succeeded by a heavy and constant fall of rain. To stir out of doors was impossible ; the Lodge is unprovided with a billiard-table, and it requires ingenuity to contrive some occupation for the long duration of a summer's day.

The breakfast was prolonged as much as possible ; it ended, however, and my kinsman left me to give some necessary directions to his household. I seated myself in the window ; the view seaward was interrupted by the thickness of the weather, the rain dropped from the thatch incessantly, the monotonous splash of the falling water, with the sombre influence of a dull and torpid atmosphere, gradually produced a drowsiness, and I fell fast asleep over a dull collection of sporting anecdotes. My cousin's return roused me; he placed a spider-table beside the window, and, having unlocked a box filled with angling materials, "in great and marvellous disorder," proceeded to extract, from a mass of unmentionable things, the requisites for dressing a cast or two of flies. As my own voluminous book had been sadly discomposed in the numerous interchanges I made, when vainly trying to seduce a salmon to try my "tinsel and fine feathers," I proceeded to arrange my splendid collection, while my kinsman was busied with his own simple stock. The disappointment I had endured in finding my flies so unprofitable, had made me hold the entire outfit of the London artist in disrepute; and I would have given my most elaborate and expensive fishing-rod for the hazel angle of the ancient otter-killer.

"Frank," said my cousin, "you must not undervalue what really is unexceptionable; I mean the mechanical part of your collection. Those rods are beautiful; and your reels, lines, gut, and hooks, cannot be surpassed; your flies may be excellent in an English river, so put them carefully aside, as I will supply you with some better adapted to our mountain streams. But what a size that book is! In fishing, as in literature, the schoolmen's adage holds, *Mega biblion, mega kakon.* Why, nothing but a soldier's pack would carry it! we will soon, however, render you independent of this mighty magazine, by teaching you to fabricate your own flies."

"I fear I am too old to learn; the art of tying must, I presume, be acquired early in life, and brought to perfection by after experience."

"This does not always follow; I did, when a boy, tie flies passably; but, having left off fishing when I removed from my native river, I forgot the art, and depended on others for my supply. The person who furnished my casting-lines fell sick, and it unluckily happened that his illness occurred in the best period of the season; and as the river was filled with fish, constant service soon wore out my scanty store. Necessity is the mother, — you know the proverb, — I was sadly reduced; ground blunted hooks and patched ravelling bodies, till at last my stock was reduced to half-a-dozen, and that half-dozen to perfect skeletons. What was to be done? Man is an imitative animal — I endeavoured to fabricate—produced something between a bird and a bee— tried again, succeeded better; and before my artist had recovered, by the shade of Walton! I could turn out a reputable fly."

"I believe I must make an attempt."

"You shall succeed, and, as a preliminary, I will put you under the tutelage of my worthy neighbour, the priest. Observe his style of casting, and mark the facility with which he sends five-and-thirty feet of hair and gut across the broadest pool. I fish tolerably, but have repeatedly laid aside my rod to admire the beautiful casting of this perfect master of the angle."

"He ties a very handsome fly, no doubt."

"I won't say that,—he ties a very *killing* one. I expect him presently; and as the day is wet, I'll leave the materials ready, and to-morrow, if the rain ceases soon, we shall prove the value of his flies.

"As we are on the subject of tying, I must observe, that the advantage one derives from being able to construct his own flies is wonderful; in fact, without attaining this accomplishment in the 'gentle art' no one can fish comfortably or successfully. No stock, however extensive, will afford a supply adapted for every change of weather and water; and a man may lose a day overlooking an interminable variety of kinds and colours, in a vain search after one killing fly. Not so the *artist:* the favourite insect being once ascertained, he speedily produces an imitation, and fills his basket; while his less fortunate neighbour is idly turning the pages of his overstocked fishing-book.

"I had two sporting friends, who were excellent instances of this. Colonel S——— was an ardent, and, I may add, a very tolerable angler; and no one went to more trouble and expense in procuring the most approved flies. He never tied, or attempted to tie one, and he assured me he had many hundred dozens in his possession. To find a new fly was with him sometimes the labour of a day; and when about to try another water, he would spend hours toiling through his immense collection, before he could succeed in discovering the necessary colour and description. I have seen him, with Job-like patience, labouring through endless papers and parcels, in search of a paltry insect that I could fabricate in five minutes.

"His companion, Captain B——, ran into an opposite extreme. He rarely had a second casting-line, and seldom a second set of flies. Did the day change, or the river fill or lower, he sat down on the bank, ripped wings and dubbings from his hooks, and prepared a new outfit in a twinkling. I never met an angler who was so certain of filling a basket as my friend B——. His system, however, I would totally disapprove of. Without burthening oneself with enough to furnish out a tackle-shop, a small and effective collection is desirable; and it is absurd to lose a fortunate half-hour tying on the river bank, what could be more conveniently fabricated during the tedium of a wet day within doors. An accident may rob the most discreet angler of his flies, and surely it is necessary to have a fresh relay to put up. But though I take a sufficiency along with me, I never leave home without being provided with the materials for constructing new ones. An hour may bring ephemeræ on the waters, which you must imitate, or you will cast in vain; before evening they have vanished and given place to some new variety of the insect world. Thus far, at least, the tyer possesses an advantage over him who cannot produce a fly, that no collection which human ingenuity can form will compensate.

"The best practical lesson I ever got originated in the following accidental occurrence. Some years ago I received private information, that a travelling tinker, who occasionally visited these mountains to make and repair the tin stills used by the peasantry in illicit distillation, was in the constant habit of destroying fish, and he was represented as being a most successful poacher. I was returning down the river after an unfavourable day, a wearied and a disappointed fisherman, and observed, at a short distance, a man chased across the bogs by several others, and eventually overtaken and secured. It was the unfortunate tinker, surprised by the keepers in the very act of landing a splendid salmon; two, recently killed, were discovered in his wallet, and yet that blessed day I could not hook a fish ! He was forthwith brought in durance before *my honour*, to undergo the pains and penalties of his crime. He was a strange, raw-boned, wild-looking animal, and I

half suspect Sir Walter Scott had seen him before he sketched
Watt Tinlin in the 'Lay.'   He was a convicted felon—he had
no plea to offer, for he was taken in the very fact.   But he
made two propositions wherewithal to obtain his liberty—' He
would never sin again—or he would fight any two of the
captors.'   My heart yearned towards him—he was after all a
brother—and admitting that rod and coat were not worth
threepence, still he was an adept in the 'gentle art,' although
the most ragged disciple that ever Walton boasted.   I forgave
him, dismissed the captors, and ordered him to the Lodge for
refreshment.   ' My honour had no sport,' and he looked carelessly at my flies.   ' Would I condescend to try one of his ?'
and he put a strange-looking combination of wool and feathers
on the casting-line.   There was a fine pool near us—I tried it,
and at the second cast I was fast in a twelve-pound salmon !
My ragged friend remained with me some days ; and in his
sober intervals, 'few and far between,' gave me lessons in
the art, that have been more serviceable than any I had
hitherto acquired.

"Two years after, I was obliged to attend the winter fair
of Ball to purchase cattle.   It was twilight when I left it,
and I had proceeded only a few miles towards a gentleman's
house, where I was to dine and sleep, when my horse cast a
shoe, and forced me to leave him at a smith's shop, which was
fortunately at hand.   The evening was chilly, and I determined to proceed on foot, directing my servant to follow.   I
passed a lonely *poteen-house*—several ruffian-looking fellows
were on the road beside it.   They were half-drunk and inso-
lent—I was rash—words borrowed blows, and I soon discovered that I should have the worst of the battle, and was
tolerably certain of a sound drubbing.   Suddenly, an unexpected ally came to my assistance ; he *dropped* the most
formidable of the assailants as if he had been struck down by
a sledge-hammer.   A few blows settled the contest ; and I
turned round to recognise and thank my deliverer.   ' 'Pon my
sowl, you're mighty handy, Master Julius ; it's a murder that
ye don't practise oftener !'   The speaker was my gifted friend
—the tinker."

## CHAPTER IX.

Sporting topography of Mayo—Hunting country—Fox covers—Cakes, rivers, and fish—A domiciliary visit—Revenue foray—Capture of drunken distillers—Alarm—Midnight meditations—Angling excursion —Goolamore—Salmon fishing—English and Irish hooks—Limerick preferable to all others.

To look, my dear George, at the map of Mayo, one would imagine that Nature had designed that county for a sportsman. The westerly part is wild and mountainous; alpine ridges of highlands interpose between the ocean and the interior, and from the bases of these hills a boundless tract of heath and moorland extends in every direction. To the east, the face of the country undergoes a striking change—large and extensive plains cover the surface, and as the lands are generally occupied in pasturage, and consequently not subdivided into the numerous enclosures which are requisite in tillage farming, this part of Mayo is justly in high estimation as a hunting country, and for centuries has been a favourite fixture of the neighbouring fox-hunters. *The Plains*, as this sporting district is usually denominated, afford constant opportunities for the horse to show his powers, and the rider his nerve. The parks are of immense size; the fences stiff and safe; the surface agreeably undulated, and from the firmness of the sward, affording superior galloping ground. One may occasionally ride over miles without being necessitated to take a leap; but when one does meet fences, they are generally *raspers*; and if the scent lies, and the dogs can *go*, nothing but a tip-top horse, and a man "who takes everything as God sends it," will hold a forward place upon *the plains*.

The covers in the vicinity of the plains are numerous and well supplied with foxes. Of these animals there is no scarcity anywhere in Mayo; but in the mountain districts there is, unfortunately, a superabundance. The herdsman and grouse-shooter complain sadly of their devastations; and notwithstanding numbers are annually dug out for hunting, or destroyed by the peasantry, there seems to be an anti-Malthusian property in the animal, which enables its mischievous stock, maugre traps and persecution, to increase and multiply.

While the country is peculiarly adapted for field-sports, the extensive lakes and numerous rivers offer every inducement to the angler: the streams are plentifully stocked with trout, and the rivers which communicate with the sea have a good supply of salmon. Curious varieties* of the finny tribe are to be found in the mountain loughs; and in those noble and expansive sheets of water, Lough Con, Lough Mask, and Lough Corrib, the largest and finest specimens of fish are easily obtained.

---

We have just had a domiciliary visit from the revenue police. Under cover of the night, they made a descent upon our valleys from their station, some fifteen miles off. Excepting causing dire alarm—a general abduction of stills, worms, and all the apparatus of the craft, and the concealment of malt, and the burying of kegs—the consequences of the foray have not been important. One fatal casualty occurred: a distillery had finished its brewing, (*i.e.* distilled the quantity brewed,) and principals and accessories were indulging a little after their exertions. Unluckily, the revenue stumbled upon the convivial meeting; and although the *stuff* was gone, the still, apparatus, and unextinguished fire, were proofs positive that the king—God bless him! had been wofully defrauded. Such of the party as could strike a walk escaped without difficulty; but two unhappy gentlemen who were blind drunk, and fast asleep in all security before the smouldering embers of the still-fire, were captured and conveyed to my loving cousin, to undergo the pains and penalties of their crime. He, as a matter of course, committed them to gaol; and the next going judge, as another matter of course, will discharge them. Meanwhile they are taken from their families, and supported at the expense of the county; their utility is lost when it is most requisite, and they are, during the term of incarceration, a useless burden upon the community. I cannot see the moral and legal expediency of all this; but the men who framed the revenue laws were probably more clear-sighted than I am.

When I first observed a score of banditti in blue jackets

---

* For example, the Gillaroo and Par.

and white cross-belts arranged before the Lodge, I felt particularly nervous; and old John, my refuge in perplexity, was immediately consulted. "John," said I, in a masonic whisper, "are we safe?"—"Safe! from what, Sir?"—"The gauger." —"Lord, Sir! he dines with us."—"But—but is there any *stuff* about the house?"—"Any! God alone can tell how much there is above and under."* "If any body told the gauger, John—"—"They would only tell him what he knows already. The gauger!—Lord bless you, Sir! he never comes or goes without leaving a keg or two behind him. If the master and he did not pull together, what the devil business would he have here? Don't mind, Sir; we know what we are about: *Tiggum Tigue Thigien!*"†

---

Midnight. I hope the weather has settled: the moon looks well, and, as John avers, the sun set favourably. There is, however, one solitary scintillating star;—one! there are two. Confound the *poteen!* it is the queerest, pleasantest, out-o'-the-way drink imaginable!—and the gauger told such odd stories, and sang such extraordinary songs! The sooner I am in bed the better! What a field the Temperance Society would have here for their exertions! Well, if I rise without a headache, I'll immortalize the man who first invented distillation.

---

We start under favourable auspices; a sweet, steady westerly wind is blowing, clouds and sunshine alternately prevail, the river should be in good order, and we anticipate that this will be a killing day.

We have determined to fish the sister stream; the waters of Goolamore unite in the same estuary with those of our own river, and yet the fish vary with regard to season as much as if they inhabited waters a thousand miles apart. In Goola-

---

* *Poteen* is commonly buried in the earth in small-sized vessels. This is done for the double purpose of improving the whisky and concealing it from the revenue. If detected in a dwelling-house, the owner incurs a penalty of one hundred pounds; notwithstanding which, there are few gentlemen in this part of Connaught who are not plentifully supplied with this proscribed spirit.

† An Irish proverb, literally meaning "Tim understands Teady."

more, throughout the whole year, white* salmon are found in high condition ; in Aughniss, from October till April, the fish are red, spent, and worthless. In size, in character, the streams are much alike : they unite in their debouchement in the sea, and flow, but a few miles asunder, through a flat and moory country. That the fish of these sister streams should differ so much is surprising, and can only be attributed to one circumstance : Aughniss is a union of mountain-streams, Goolamore flows from an extensive lake, and affords an outlet to the waters of Carramore. Judging, therefore, from the constant supply of white fish which Goolamore yields all through the year, one would conclude that the lake offers better food and winterage to the salmon, than the shallower and colder waters of Aughniss.

Our expectations were fully realized, and we found the pools in excellent order. Independently of a west wind being a favourite point for the angler—in these rivers it blows against the current of the stream, and consequently increases the ruffle on the surface of the water, which in salmon fishing is so favourable. My cousin, who is perfectly acquainted with the local haunts of the salmon, placed me where I seldom failed to rise or hook a fish. What splendid angling this wild country offers ! It spoils one in after-life, however. The man who has held a salmon on his line disrelishes the inferior amusements of the craft; the fox-hunter will seldom condescend to ride to beagles ; the deer-stalker will not waste time and powder in a rabbit-warren ; and the disciple of Izaac, who has once indulged in the exquisite delight of salmon fishing, will feel little satisfaction in the commoner pursuits and lesser pleasures of the gentle art.

We landed five salmon, besides taking a pannier full of sea-trouts. Had I been an adept, or better appointed than I was, we might have killed double the number of salmon. My flies were unluckily tied on London hooks, and from their defective quality and formation several fish escaped me. Repeated failures caused me to examine the hooks,

---

* By the simple appellation of white and red fish, the peasantry distinguish salmon when in and out of season. Indeed, the colour is such a perfect indicative of health and disease, that any person who has frequented a salmon river will, on seeing a fish rise, be enabled to tell with accuracy the state of his condition.

and I ascertained that they were both ill-shapen and badly
tempered. My cousin had warned me against the consequences of using them, but I believed that he was prejudiced,
and concluded that this department of my London outfit
must be unobjectionable. The event, however, proved that
I was deceived. My kinsman rarely lost a salmon, and
mine broke from me continually. I find by sad experience,
that in hook-making the Irish are far before us; our workmen either do not understand the method of forming and
tempering hooks, or they do not take sufficient pains in their
manufactory. It is strange when so much of the angler's
pleasure and success depends upon the quality of his hooks,
that more attention is not bestowed upon their fabrication.
The art of forming, and the process of tempering them,
appears simple enough; and that little difficulty is required
to attain it, is evident from the fact, that many fishermen
make their own hooks.* For my own part, however, I consider hook-making to be an unnecessary accomplishment for
the angler, as the best hooks in the world can be procured
without trouble, and at a trifling expense, from O'Shaughnessy
of Limerick.†

## CHAPTER X.

Salmon—Fishing described—Draughting—Fishing precarious—Change of
season and condition—Poaching—Private distillation—Size and weight
of Salmon—Sir H. Davy—Migration of Salmon—Natural history—
Anecdotes and experiments—Lernææ Salmoneæ.

To those unacquainted with the method of taking salmon,
a brief detail may not be uninteresting: premising that in
other fisheries different means are employed, yet the simplest
and general method is that used at Aughniss.

* " I have even made a hook, which, though a little inferior in form,
in other respects, I think, I could boast as equal to the Limerick ones."—
*Salmonia.*

† " I never use any hooks for salmon fishing except those which I am
sure have been made by O'Shaughnessy of Limerick; for even those
made in Dublin, though they seldom break, yet they now and then bend;
and the English hooks, made of cast-steel, in imitation of Irish ones, are
the worst of all."—*Salmonia.*

About March fly-fishing commences, and a strong and active spring fish will then frequently be killed, if the river is sufficiently supplied with water, and the wind brisk and *westerly*. As the season advances, the fishing materially improves ; and from the month of April, salmon in the highest condition, with red and white trout, will rise here freely at the fly.

In June, however, the regular fishing with nets commences, and then the wear is raised to stop the passage of the fish, and the river water vented through a small aperture provided with a trap, or as it is technically called, a *box*. By these traps and artificial canals, in other fisheries the salmon are principally taken ; but here, except some straggling fish, the box produces little.

The fishing is confined to the estuary, where the river meets the sea. Here, according to naturalists, the salmon undergo a probationary course, before they exchange the salt for the fresh water, as a sudden change from either would be fatal to the fish, and a temporary sojourn in water of an intermediate quality (brackish) is supposed to be requisite, before they can leave either the ocean or the river.

The draughting is carried on at the last quarter of the ebb, and during the first of flood—five or six boats, with as many men in each, are necessary. When the salmon are seen, the nearest boat starts off, leaving a man on shore, with a rope attached to one extremity of the net, which is rapidly thrown over, as the boat makes an extensive circle round the place where the fish is supposed to lie. Returning to the shore, the curve of the net is gradually decreased. Stones are flung in at each extremity, to prevent the salmon from escaping ; the net reaches the bank, the semi-circle is complete, and all within effectually secured. The fish are then carefully landed, and at a single draught five hundred salmon have been taken. This is, however, an event of rare occurrence, and unless the net were powerfully strong, and the fishers skilful, a fracture, and consequently a general escape, would be inevitable.

The fishing here is exceedingly precarious. If the season be favourable from the 1st of July to the 12th of August, the daily average would be probably five hundred salmon, exclusive of an immense quantity of white trouts. But success depends entirely upon the weather. Should the season prove rainy or tempestuous, the salmon directly leave the estuary, and remain at sea until the water clears and the storm abates ; and the time allowed by law often expires before a moiety of the fish can be secured.

It is extraordinary how much the flavour and quality of the salmon depend on circumstances apparently of trifling moment. A single day in the river will injure, and a flood spoil their condition ; and the difference between a fish taken in the nets, and one killed with a rod, will be easily perceptible.

Although in this water angling may be considered as ending in September, yet, through the succeeding months till spring, the fish rise freely at a fly. But the sport is very indifferent compared with summer angling ; the salmon now has lost his energy ; he struggles *laboriously* to get away, but his play is different from the gallant resistance he would have offered had you hooked him in July. I have landed and turned out again as many as nine salmon in one day, and their united exertions did not afford me half the amusement I have received from the conquest of one sprightly summer fish. Salmon appear to lose beauty and energy together. They are now reddish, dull, dark-spotted, perch-coloured fish, and seem a different species from the sparkling silvery creature we saw them when they first left the sea. As an esculent, they are utterly worthless—soft, flabby, and flavourless, if brought to table ; and instead of the delicate pink hue they exhibited when in condition, they present a sickly, unhealthy, white appearance, that betrays how complete the change is that they have recently undergone.

And yet at this period they suffer mostly from night-fishers. This species of poaching* is as difficult to detect as it is ruinous in its consequences. It is believed that the destruction of a few breeding fish may cost the proprietor one thousand ; such being the astonishing fecundity of the pregnant salmon !

Night fishing is carried on when the river is low, and the

---

* " When I made the tour of that hospitable kingdom in 1754, it (the Coleraine fishery) was rented by a neighbouring gentleman for £620 a year, who assured me that the tenant, his predecessor, gave for it £1600 per annum—andthat he was a greater gainer by the bargain, on account of the numberof poachers, who destroy the fish during the fence month."—*Pennant.*

E

night moonless. The poacher, with a gaff and torch, selects some gravelly ford—for there, by a law of nature, the salmon resort to form beds in the stream, wherein to deposite their ova; and they continue working on the sand, until they are

discovered by the torch-light,* and gaffed by the plunderer. Hundreds of the breeding fish are annually thus destroyed; and although the greater fisheries may be tolerably protected, it is impossible to secure the mountain streams from depredation. If detected, the legal penalty upon poaching is trifling; and, as appeals on very frivolous grounds are allowed from the summary convictions of magistrates, it too frequently happens that delinquents evade the punitory consequences attendant on discovery.

Here, too, the evils of private distillation may be traced; for most of the depredations committed upon the salmon are effected by persons concerned in this demoralizing trade. They are up all night attending to the still. The watch kept against the revenue police, enables them to ascertain when the bargers are away, and the river consequently unguarded. A light is snatched from the still-fire, the hidden

* "There are a good many pike in the river near to Trolhatten. In the course of two successive days, I once took with my rod sixty-three of those fish; they were, however, small, their aggregate weight being little more than one hundred pounds. The largest fish weighed eight pounds. Great quantities of pike and other fish, salmon amongst the rest, are speared in the vicinity of Trolhatten by torch-light, many of the people thereabouts being adepts at that amusement."—*Lloyd.*

fish-spear speedily produced, and in a very short space of time an infinite deal of mischief is perpetrated.

---

I should be inclined to question the accuracy of weight which Sir Humphry gives his salmon. Fish, of the sizes he describes, are rarely met with here, and out of one thousand taken in the nets, there will not be ten fish of twenty-five pounds weight.

The average size is from seven to fifteen pounds. Within thirty years, but one monster has been taken; he weighed fifty-six pounds. Four years ago one of forty-eight pounds was caught: but of the thousands which I have seen taken, I would say, I never saw a fish weighing more than thirty-five pounds, and not many reaching even to twenty-five pounds.

The Priest, my neighbour, who lives on the banks of Goolamore, told me he once killed a salmon of twenty-seven pounds weight, and that the feat gave him an infinity of trouble, and occupied three mortal hours. The Priest fishes with tackle of amazing strength, and is one of the best practical anglers I have ever met with. Sir Humphry Davy mentions salmon of twenty-five and thirty pounds as being commonly taken with a fly. The largest I ever killed was eighteen pounds four ounces, and it gave me abundant exercise for an hour. Either Sir Humphry overrates the weight of Scottish salmon, or in the rivers he frequented they must be immensely superior to those found in the Irish waters. In the Shannon, I believe, the largest fish are found, and I am inclined to think, that even there the capture of salmon of this unusual magnitude, is an event of very rare occurrence.

Pennant states, " that the largest salmon ever known weighed seventy-four pounds. In September 1795, one measuring upwards of four feet from nose to tail, and three in circumference, weighing within a few ounces of seventy pounds, was sold at Billingsgate, and was the largest ever brought there. The Severn salmon are much inferior as to their bulk, for one taken near Shrewsbury, in 1757, weighing only thirty-seven pounds, is recorded in the British Chronologist, as exceeding in length any ever known to be taken in that river, and being the heaviest except one ever remembered in that town. They have in many parts been caught by angling.

with an artificial fly and other baits, upwards of forty pounds in weight.''

Passing Grove's shop in Bond-street about a month ago, I remarked an immense fish extended in the window; I stopped to inquire what its weight might be, and was informed that it weighed forty-five pounds. It had been a little too long on its passage from Scotland, and I should be inclined to say, that at best it was a coarse flavoured fish, but in its present state a most indifferent one.

The migratory habits of the salmon, and the instinct with which it periodically revisits its native river, are curious circumstances in the natural history of this fish. As the swallow returns annually to its nest, as certainly the salmon repairs to the same spot in which to deposit its ova. Many interesting experiments have established this fact. M. de Lalande fastened a copper ring round a salmon's tail, and found that for three successive seasons it returned to the same place. Dr. Bloch states, that gold and silver rings have been attached, by Eastern princes to salmon, to prove that a communication existed between the Persian Gulf and the Caspian and Northern seas, and that the experiment succeeded. Shaw, in his Zoology, mentions that a salmon of seven pounds and three-quarters was marked with scissors on the back, fin, and tail, and turned out on the 7th of February, and that it was retaken in March of the succeeding year, and found to have increased to the amazing size of seventeen pounds and a half. This statement, by the by, is at variance with the theory of Dr. Bloch, who estimates the weight of a five or six year old salmon at but ten or twelve pounds.

That the salmon should lose condition rapidly on quitting the sea for the fresh water, may be inferred from a fact agreed upon by naturalists, that during the period of spawning, the fish neglects feeding. In this peculiar habit the salmon, however, is not singular, for animals of the Phocæ tribe, in breeding-time exercise a similar abstinence. On opening a salmon, at any season, no food will be discovered, and the contents of the stomach will be confined to a small quantity of yellowish fluid and tape-worms, which are generated there. Sir Humphry Davy believes that occasionally food may be found. I have seen thousands opened preparatory to being salted, and I never observed any thing but this fluid and tape-worms. Another circumstance may be stated as a curious proof of health, as well as of the period of time the salmon has been resident in a river. When the fish leaves the sea, and of course is in its best condition, insects (the Lernææ Salmoneæ of Linnæus) will be perceived firmly adhering to the skin. Immediately on entering the fresh water, these insects begin to detach themselves from the salmon, and after a short time they gradually drop off and disappear.

## CHAPTER XI.

Mullet—Preparations for mullet-fishing—Seals—Anecdotes—The Red Dwarf—His mode of killing seals—Catching a tartar—Pitching mullet nets—Excursion on the island—A wild guide—Coursing—Comparison between English and Irish greyhounds—Take of mullet—Return—Anecdotes of mullet fishing—The homicide.

EARLY this morning we received intelligence that a school* of mullet† had been seen on the preceding evening, working in a sandy bay some six miles distant from the Lodge—and as we determined to devote the day to fishing, the household were soon upon the alert, and a galley and row-boat were laden with nets, poles, and spars; half-a-dozen rifles and muskets put on board, and a stout and numerous crew, we started for the scene of action.

It was a bright and cheerful day; the sun sparkled on the blue water, which, unruffled by a breeze, rose and fell in the long and gentle undulations which roll in from the westward when the Atlantic is at rest. While pulling to the cove, we amused ourselves in shooting puffins as they passed us, or trying our rifles at a distant seal, while my kinsman's anecdotes whiled away the tedium of the voyage.

---

* Shoal.

† Although the grey mullet is common in the Mediterranean, it is in such indifferent repute that none but the lower classes use it. The red mullet is, however, held in the highest estimation, and from its scarcity and peculiar flavour is much sought after as a delicacy. It seldom exceeds a pound or two in weight, and it is dressed with the inside entire, as the woodcock is sent to table with his trail.

On our coasts it is rarely seen. At particular seasons the grey mullet visits us abundantly, and nothing can be more delicate, when *uninjured by keeping or carriage.*

"Seals are very numerous on the coast, and at this season a number may be seen any warm day you make an excursion up the sound of Achil. We shoot them occasionally—the skin makes a waterproof covering, and the fat affords an excellent oil for many domestic purposes. It is difficult however, to secure the animal, for numbers are shot and few gotten. The head is the only place to strike them, for even when mortally wounded in the body, they generally manage to escape. This fact we have ascertained, from finding them dead on shore many days after they were wounded, and at a considerable distance from the place where they had received the bullet. I shot one last autumn at the mouth of the river, and a fortnight afterwards he was taken up in the neighbourhood of Dhuhill. There could be no doubt as to the identity of the creature, for on opening him to extract the oil, a rifle-ball, such as I use, of the unusually small size of fifty-four to the pound, was found lodged in his lungs. Unless when killed outright, they sink instantly; and I have seen the sea dyed with blood, to an extent that proved how severely the seal had been wounded, but have never been able to trace him further.

"Formerly, when seal oil and skins were valuable, some persons on the coast made the pursuit of the animal a profession. There is one of these persons living near the Sound, a miserable dwarfish red-bearded wretch, whom you would consider hardly equal to grapple with a salmon, and yet he secures more seals than any hunter in the district. His method of effecting it is singular: he uses neither gun nor spear, but kills the animal with a short bludgeon loaded at the end with lead.

"Adjacent to the seal-killer's residence, there is a large rock uncovered at half-tide, and this appears the most favourite haunt for the animal to bask upon. The rock is easily approached from the main-land, and on a sunny day, when the wind favours the attempt, the hunter, undressed, and armed with his bludgeon, silently winds among the stones, and steals upon his sleeping prey. Wary as the creature is, the *Red Dwarf* seldoms fails in surprising him, and with astonishing expertness generally dispatches him with a single blow.

"The number he kills annually proves his extraordinary success. If the first blow fails, an event that seldom happens, the dwarf is in considerable danger. When attacked, and especially at such a distance from the water as renders his escape doubtful, the seal will turn with amazing ferocity on the assailant. If it be an old one, in case his first essay is unsuccessful, the dwarf declines the combat and flies from his irritated enemy; but the cubs are taken without much difficulty.

"Last summer I was witness to a curious scene. Running through the Sound of Achil in my hooker, at a short distance to leeward I observed several men, who appeared to be practising a quadrille over the thafts and gunnels of a row-boat, as they never rested for a moment, but continued jumping from stem to stern, and springing from bench to bench. Struck by the oddity of their proceedings, I eased away the sheets and ran down upon them—and I was a

welcome ally, as the result proved. It turned out, that having espied a seal and her cub sleeping on the sand, they had procured an old musket and rowed over to attack them. They were partially successful, and seized the cub before it could regain its native element, although the dam rendered all assistance possible to relieve the young one. Having placed their prize in the boat, they were returning, followed by the old seal, who kept rising beside them, attracted by the cries of the cub—till after many bootless attempts, their gun at last exploded, the ball entered the seal's head, and for a moment she appeared dying. The captors, seizing her by the tail and fins, with an united exertion dragged her into the boat—but this exploit had nearly ended in a tragedy. Stunned only by the wound, the animal instantly recovered, and, irritated by pain and maddened by the cries of her cub, attacked her captors fiercely. Every exertion they could make was necessary to save them from her tusks, and their oars were too long and clumsy to enable them to strike her with effect. I came most opportunely to the rescue, and by driving a carbine-bullet through the seal's brain brought the battle to a close. Never was the old saw of 'catching a Tartar' more thoroughly exemplified; and though we laughed at their terror-stricken countenances, the deep incisions made in the oars and gunnels by the tusks of the enraged animal, showed that *galopading* with an angry seal is anything but pleasure."

Although the mullet are generally first seen here in the month of June, from the wetness of this summer the shoals are later in their appearance than usual. Mullet are taken in draught-nets like salmon, but on this coast a different mode of fishing is pursued. The shoals in hot weather run in with the tide, and after remaining on the shores and estuaries during flood, they return with the ebbing water. The following method we employed in our fishing to-day. Being provided with a sufficient quantity of herring-nets and a number of spars and poles, we selected at low-water a sandy creek for our operations, and commenced erecting a line of poles across the entrance of the cove. The nets were then extended along these uprights, and also secured firmly to the bottom of the spars ; the lower part of the net is kept upon the bottom by a row of stones, and the remainder laid flat upon the sands. With the flowing tide the fish pass over the prostrate net, and run along the estuary : at high water the buoy-ropes are raised and secured to the upright poles—and with the assistance of a boat the whole is effected in a few minutes, and a net-work barrier effectually

cuts off the retreat of all within. When the ebb of tide commences the mullet begin to retire, and when they discover
that their egress is obstructed, their attempts to effect a passage are both constant and curious—now running down the
nets, trying for a broken mesh by which to force an aperture
—now with a bold spring endeavouring to clear the buoy-
ropes, and even after repeated failures, leaping at it again and
again. The last effort is directed to the bottom; but there
the heavy stones resist every attempt to dislodge them, and
deserted by the treacherous water, the mullet are left upon the
bare sands.

As hours must elapse from the time the nets are laid down
until the fish can be secured, I left my kinsman, who officiated
as chief engineer. Having brought two brace of greyhounds
with us, I set out to course, under the guidance of a man who
joined my cousin on the island.

There was a striking air about the stranger, joined to his
wild and haggard look, that at once riveted my attention.
His clothes were much better than those of any of the
peasantry I had yet seen, and in address and manner he was
far superior to the rest of my cousin's retainers. He was not
above five-and-twenty, his figure tall, gaunt, sinewy, and
almost fleshless,—but his square shoulders and well-knit joints
proved him to be a powerful and active man. I shall never
forget the singular expression of his countenance. It was
settled sorrow bordering on despair; the hollow cheek, the
sunken rayless eye, the wandering and suspicious glance
around him, all showed a mind fevered with apprehension
and harrowed by remorse. He shunned observation, and if
my eye met his by accident, he instantly looked another way.
He was armed with a new carbine; and his whole bearing
and appearance were so singular and alarming, that more
than once I wished my kinsman had allotted me some other
guide.

My companion was, however, shrewd and intelligent—and
he appeared fond of field sports, and perfectly conversant with
the arcana of shooting and coursing. He enumerated with
the science of a connoisseur the points, and praised the
beauty of a pair of English dogs I had brought with me;
but told me " *the master's* (my kinsman's usual title) would
outrun them *here*." I differed with him in opinion. Mine

were of distinguished breeding, the produce of a Swaffham
sire, and compared with my cousin's, appeared descended
from a giant-stock. His, certainly, were beautiful diminutives; but as I conceived, very unequal to compete with
animals of such superior strength and size as mine—yet
the result proved how correctly my wild companion judged.

Our first start was on hard, firm ground — and here my
dogs outstripped my kinsman's, although they displayed
uncommon fleetness. Being hard pressed, puss crossed a
morass and ran into an unsound bog. Then were my guide's
predictions verified. From their own weight, my dogs sank
and floundered in the swamp; while my cousin's topping
the surface with apparent ease, turned and killed the hare,
while their larger companions were struggling through the
mire.

On the second start puss left the moor, and took to the sea-
shore, always a favourite run of island hares. Rushing headlong through rocks, and running over pointed pebbles, the
English dogs were speedily disabled. But my cousin's,
accustomed to the beach, ran with caution till they cleared
the rocks, then taking advantage of the open strand, killed
without a scratch, while my unpractised dogs were rendered
unserviceable for a fortnight.

Generally speaking, the large and high-bred English
greyhound is not adapted for Irish coursing. *There* he
will encounter a soft and difficult surface, instead of the fine
firm downs he has been accustomed to in his native country.
And any plains on which he could exert his powers and
prove his superiority, are, with few exceptions, in the possession of some pack, and of course preserved as hunting-
grounds, and grey-hounds rigidly prohibited.

On returning to the estuary where I had left the fishing-
party, I found the tide had fallen, and in a little time we
were enabled to secure the spoil. We had enclosed upwards
of a hundred mullets, weighing from four to ten pounds
each. While embarking our nets and poles I observed
several boats filled with men row towards us from a distance;
and, after a short *reconnoissance*, return to the place from
whence they came. The evening breeze blew fresh, and in
our favour; the boatmen hoisted a large square sail; my
kinsman took the tiller, and with wind and tide along with

us, in an hour we crossed the bay and reached our destination, accompanied by the tall melancholy looking man, who had been my companion in the island.

We dined sumptuously. The flavour of a mullet, fresh from the water, neither injured by land-carriage* nor spoiled by exposure to the sun, is exquisite. I mentioned casually, the noble addition which this delicious fish must give to my cousin's *cuisine*. "And they are so abundant, that I presume you seldom want them?" "The contrary is the case," he replied; "a remnant of barbarous usage prevents this wild population from benefiting by the ample supply which Providence sends to the shores. Did you remark several boats approach and reconnoitre us?"

"Yes, and what of it?"

"Nothing more than that they came with the laudable design of relieving us of the produce of our fishery. The natives believe that there is a prescriptive right to rob mullet-nets; and in consequence, none will be at the trouble of laying them down, if they have not a sufficient party to protect the fish when taken. You remarked the formidable preparations made this morning; they were requisite I assure you, or we should have returned home as lightly laden as we left it. Those people are not upon my territory, and I am on bad terms with their landlord. They would spoil me of fish without ceremony, and think themselves too indulgent in permitting me and my dependants to return with undamaged heads. Last year they robbed and beat my boatmen cruelly— and on the next occasion of a mullet *chasse*, I went in person. They soon discovered us, and with three boats full of men came to despoil us. I warned them off—but they were resolutely bent on mischief. Finding them determined, I let the leading boat approach within forty yards, and having them well under my fire, threw in two barrels loaded with B.B. shot. The effect was decisive, for out of a dozen marauders

---

* The general length of the common mullet *(mugil)* is from twelve to eighteen inches. When used immediately after being taken, the fish is excellent; carriage, even for a short distance, injures it, Dr. Bloch recommends *oil and lemon-juice* to be used with it at table. Vinegar, with parsley and melted butter, is better—"probatum est." This fish is sometimes preserved by salting; and from its spawn an inferior kind of caviar, called *Botargo*, is prepared by using the common process of curing and drying.

who formed the crew, not one escaped without receiving a fair proportion of the charge. They put about instantly, and for a fortnight afterwards, a country quack had full employment in extracting my double B. I sent a *message* to their master, for which he *Benched* me; and it cost me a cool hundred before I got clear of the Honourable Justices. ' A plague upon all cowards !' as honest Jack says."

" But, Julius, who was that wild and melancholy man to whose guidance you entrusted me in the island ?"

" Oh, Hennessy, my foster-brother ! Poor fellow, he has been rather unlucky !"

" Unlucky ?"

" Why, yes—he hit a fellow a little too hard, and finished him. He is keeping close until the assizes are over, and then he will have time to settle with the friends. It would not signify a farthing, had he not been in two or three scrapes before."

" Has he been always riotous ?"

" Oh, no, quite the contrary. When sober, he is the civilest creature on earth. No, poor fellow ! they were only two homicides, and an abduction."

" And do you countenance and shelter such a character ?"

" What ! abandon my own foster-brother for an accident or two ?—Pshaw, Frank, you jest. I'll tell you the particulars another time."

It was late, and we separated.

---

## CHAPTER XII.

Angling—Fish found in Mayo—Peasantry—Their mode of fishing—The Pooka—Description and use—Pike and trout—Their size—Perch—Their fecundity—Trout destroyed—Greater lakes described—Subterraneous communication between them—Lesser lakes—Their fish—Lake of Derreens—Its trout extinct—Lake of Castlebar.

In a country whose surface is covered with numerous and extensive sheets of water like Mayo, it may be considered that the angler will find ample occupation. Independently of salmon and trout fishing, to those who will employ themselves in killing pike and perch, the lakes and rivers here offer superior amusement. In the greater waters, Lough Mask, Lough Carra, and Lough Conn, the coarser species of fishes are taken in immense numbers, and in the lesser lakes many interesting varieties of the trout tribe will be found, from the little speckled samlet to the large and curious gilaroo.*

It is true, that the scientific angler generally confines himself to the use of the fly, and for salmon and trout, he will forego the commoner department of bait and float fishing. Hence, angling for pike and perch is usually an amusement of the peasantry ; and to those contiguous to the banks of the large lakes, it yields occupation for idle hours, which might be less innocently dissipated, and occasionally supplies their families with a welcome addition to their unvarying food, the potato.

Besides the established system of bait-fishing, other and more successful methods are resorted to by the lake-fishers

* The natural history of the samlet, or par, is very doubtful. Some assert it to be a mule produced by the salmon and trout ; and as a corroboration of this theory, it is stated that the rivers where the par is found, are always resorted to by salmon. Others conjecture it to be a hybrid of the sea and river trout ; and Sir Humphry Davy mentions, that fishing in October, in a small stream communicating with the Moy, near Ballina, he caught a number of sea trout, who all proved males, and accordingly infers that " these fish, in which the spermatic system was fully developed, could only have impregnated the ova of the common river trout."

The par differs from the small mountain trout in colour, and in having additional spines in the pectoral fin. It has also certain olive bluish marks upon the side, similar to the impressions made by the pressure of a man's fingers.

Great numbers of salmon are found in the upper streams of the Ballycroy river. They will rise voraciously at a fly, provided it be gay and small enough. I remember my friend Sir Charles Cuyler and I amused ourselves on a blank shooting-day, when there was neither a sufficiency of wind nor water to warrant salmon-fishing, in angling for this hybridous diminutive. We nearly filled our basket ; we reckoned them, and they amounted to above two hundred.

Pennant says :—" In all these lakes the gillaroo is found. It varies in weight from twelve to eighteen pounds, but sometimes reaches thirty ;" and Daniel states these fish to be " esteemed for their fine flavour, which is supposed to exceed that of any other trout. Their make is similar to the common, except being thicker in proportion to their length, and of a redder hue, both before and after being dressed. The gillaroo is remarkable for having a gizzard resembling that of a large fowl or turkey." He also says :—" It is usual to dress the gizzards only, which are considered as very favourite morsels."

By mesh-nets immense numbers of pike are annually taken ; and with night-lines, and a very simple contrivance called the *pooka*, these fish, with the largest trout and perch, are constantly killed.

This latter implement is formed of a piece of flat board, having a little mast and sail erected on it. Its use is to carry out the extremity of a long line of considerable stoutness, to which, at regulated distances, an infinity of droppers *or* links are suspended, each armed with a hook and bait. Corks are affixed to the principal line or *back*, to keep it buoyant on the surface ; and from a weather-shore, if there be a tolerable breeze, any quantity of hooks and baits can be floated easily across the water. The corks indicate to the fishermen when a fish is on the dropper, and in a small punt or *curragh*, he attends to remove the spoil and renew the baits when necessary. Two hundred hooks may be used on the same line, and the *pooka* at times affords much amusement, and often a well-filled pannier.

There are no waters in Great Britain, with the exception of the river Shannon, where larger pike* are caught than those taken in Loughs Mask and Corrib. It would appear, that in these lakes the fish are commensurate to the waters they inhabit. It is no unusual event for pikes of thirty pounds weight to be sent to their landlords by the tenants ; and fish of even fifty pounds have not unfrequently been caught with nets and night-lines. The trout in those loughs are also immensely large. From five to fifteen pounds is no unusual size, and some have been found that have reached the enormous

---

* " About seventeen years since, when visiting the late Marquis of Clanricarde, at Portumna Castle, two gentlemen brought to the marquis an immense pike, which they had just caught in the river Shannon, on the banks of which they had been taking their evening walk. Attracted by a noise and splashing of the water, they discovered in a little creek a number of perch driven on shore, and a fish, which, in pursuit of them, had so entangled himself with the ground, as to have a great part of his body exposed, and out of the water. They attacked him with an oar, that by accident lay on the bank, and killed him. Never having seen any fish of this species so large, they judged it worth the observation of the marquis, who, equally surprised at its magnitude, had it weighed, and to our astonishment it exceeded the balance at *ninety-two pounds ;* its length was such, that when carried across the oar by the two gentlemen, who were neither of them short, the head and tail touched the ground.

weight of thirty. The perch tribe appear the smallest in
the scale of relative proportion. These seldom exceed a herring
size; but they, too, have exceptions, and perch of three or
four pounds weight have been sometimes seen. Within fifty
years, this latter fish has increased prodigiously, and, in the
lakes and rivers where they abound, trout have been found to
diminish in an equal ratio. If any doubt remained touching
the fecundity of the perch, some of the Mayo waters would
prove it satisfactorily. Half a century since, I have been
assured that pike and perch were almost unknown in the rivers
of Belcarra and Minola, and the chain of lakes with which
they communicate, and that these waters were then second to
none for trout fishing. Within ten years, my cousin tells me
that he often angled in them, and that he frequently killed
from three to six dozen of beautiful middle-sized red trout.
Now, fly-fishing is seldom practised there. The trout is nearly
extinct, and quantities of pike and perch infest every pool and
stream. The simplest methods of taking fish will be here
found successful, and the lakes of Westmeath will soon be
rivalled by the loughs of Mayo.*

Of the great Western lakes, Conn and Carra belong to
Mayo; Corrib to Galway; and Mask lies between both
counties. The most northerly, Lough Conn, is about nine
miles long, by two or three in breadth. Part of its shores are
beautifully wooded; and where the lower and upper lakes
unite, the channel is crossed by a bridge of one arch, called the
Pontoon; and there the scenery is indeed magnificent.

Lough Carra is smaller than Conn; but, as a sheet of water,
nothing can be more beautiful; and everything that the painter
delights to fancy may here be realized. Islands and penin-
sulas, with rich overhanging woods, a boundless range of
mountain masses in the distance, and ruins in excellent keeping
—all these form a splendid study for the artist's pencil.

Mask communicates with Carra, and their united waters
discharge themselves into Lough Corrib by a very curious

---

* Mr. Young mentions that, at Packenham, Lord Longford informed
him, respecting the quantities of fish in the lakes in his neighbourhood,
that the perch were so numerous, that a child with a packthread and a
crooked pin would catch enough in an hour for the daily use of a whole
family, and that his Lordship had seen five hundred children fishing at
the same time; that, besides perch, the lake produced pike five feet long,
and trout of ten pounds each.

subterraneous channel at Cong.* Lough Corrib is largest of all; it stretches twenty miles to its southern extremity at Galway, where, through a bold, rocky river, it discharges its waters into the Atlantic. Its breadth is very variable, ranging from two to twelve miles. Besides its singular connexion with the Mayo lakes by the underground channel at Cong, Lough Corrib produces a rare species of muscle, in which pearls are frequently discovered. Many of them are said to afford beautiful specimens of this valuable gem.

The smaller lakes, which are so profusely scattered over the surface of this country, vary in the species of fish which they respectively produce, as much as they do in their own natural size and character. Some of them afford trout, others pike only, and many are stocked with both. That this union cannot long subsist, I should be inclined to infer from one remarkable circumstance, and it is a convincing proof of the rapid destruction which the introduction of pike into a trout lake will occasion. Within a short distance of Castlebar, there is a small bog-lake, called Derreens; and ten years ago it was celebrated for its numerous and well-sized trout. Accidentally pike effected a passage into the Lough from the Minola river, and now the trout are extinct, or, at least, none of them are caught or seen. Previous to the intrusion of the pike, half-a-dozen trout would be killed in an evening in Derreens, whose collective weight often amounted to twenty pounds.

Indeed, few of the Mayo waters are secure from the encroachments of the pike. The lakes of Castlebar, I believe, still retain their ancient character ;† but I understand that pike have been latterly taken in the Turlogh river, and of course they will soon appear in a lake which directly communicates with this stream.‡

---

* " At Cong, about five miles from Ballinrobe, is a subterranean cave, to which there is a descent of sixty-three steps, called the Pigeon Hole; at the bottom runs a clear stream, in which the trout are seen sporting in the water ; these fish are never known to take a bait, but are caught with landing-nets."—*Daniel.*

† " In the lake of Castlebar, near that town, is the charr and the gillaroo trout, and it is remarked that there are no pike in this and some of the adjacent lakes."—*Daniel.*

‡ The voracity of the pike is strongly exemplified in the following extract from a *Provincial Newspaper*. Of the truth of the occurrence we presume there can be no reasonable doubt, even in the minds of the most sceptical ; but we believe there is no instance of animal ferocity on

## CHAPTER XIII.

Nineteenth of August—Preparations for the mountains—Order of march—
A cook broiled to death—Interruption of a funeral—Drowned shepherd
—Grouse shooting—Evening compotation—Morning—Locale of a
shooter's cabin—Life in the mountains—The red deer—Return to the
hut—Luxury of a cold bath.

THE nineteenth of August, that busy day of preparation
with Irish sportsmen, came at last. An unusual commotion
was evident among my kinsman's household, and there was a
wondrous packing up of camp-beds, culinary utensils, baskets
and bottles, arms and ammunition—in short, of every necessary
article for the support and destruction of life. At dawn of day
four horses set off heavily laden; shortly after, a second
division of dogs and guns moved under a careful escort; the
"otter-hunter" hobbled off while I was dressing; and the
piper, the lightest-laden of all concerned, closed the rear.
After breakfast, two ponies were brought to the door, and,
with a mounted attendant to carry our cloaks, my cousin and I
pursued the same route that the baggage had already taken.

Talk not of India! Its boasted gang of servants is far
surpassed by the eternal troop of followers appertaining to
an Irish establishment. Old John tells me that sixteen
*regulars* sit down to dinner in the servants'-hall, and that at
least an equal number of *supernumeraries* are daily provided for
besides. When I hinted to my cousin the expense that must at-

record which could parallel it, except in the celebrated case of the Kil-
kenny cats, whose respective demolition of each other is as wonderful as
authentic.

" A party angling at Sunbury, one of them sat across the head of the
boat, as a punishment inflicted on him for wearing his *spurs*. Another,
having caught a *gudgeon*, stuck it on one of the spurs, which he (the
delinquent in the bow) not perceiving, in a few minutes a large jack bit
at the gudgeon, and the *spur being crane-necked*, entangled in the gills
of the jack, which, in attempting to extricate himself, actually pulled the
unfortunate person out of the boat. He was with difficulty dragged on
shore, and the fish taken, which was of *prodigious size*."

Now, after this cautionary notice of ours, we do assert that any gentleman who goes to fish in *crane-necks*, and disposes of his legs overboard,
with *a gudgeon on the rowel*, is not exactly the person on whose life, were
we agent to a company, we should feel justified in effecting a policy of
insurance.

F

tend the supporting of this idle and useless multitude, his reply
was so *Irish*. " Pshaw ! hang it !—*sure they have no wages, and
what the devil signifies all they eat ?* My father, before the landing
of the *Paul Jones*, fed two hundred men for a fortnight, and
used to declare, that never were there such plentiful times. It
killed the cook, however, poor woman! she was literally
broiled into a pleurisy—but such a wake as she had ! I
remember it as if it occurred but yesterday. She was carried
to the old grave-yard of *Bunmore* the very evening the *Paul
Jones* landed her cargo, and although five hundred men left
the house with the corpse, the cook remained over-ground
till the following morning, for want of sufficient persons to fill
the grave. The fact was, that just as the funeral reached
the church-yard, the lugger was suddenly discovered rounding
the Black Rock. Instantly the mourners absconded, the
bearers threw down the body—the priest, who was deeply
concerned in the cargo, was the first to fly ;—and the defunct
cook was left accordingly in peaceable possession of Bunmore."

To arrive at our mountain-quarters we were obliged to
cross the river repeatedly. When swollen with rain, the
stream is impassable, and the communication between the hill
country and the lowlands interrupted, until the flood abates.
At one of the fords, my kinsman pointed out a little *cairn*, or
heap of stones, erected on the summit of a hillock which
overhung the passage we were crossing. It is placed there to
commemorate the drowning of a shepherd, and, as an incident
in humble life, it struck me as being particularly affecting.

" In 1822, when the western part of Ireland was afflicted
with grievous famine, and when England stepped forward
nobly, and poured forth her thousands to save those who were
perishing for want, a depôt of provisions was established on
the sea-coast, for the relief of the suffering inhabitants of this
remote district.

" A solitary family, who had been driven from their lowland
home by the severity of a relentless *middle-man*, had settled
themselves in this wild valley, and erected the clay walls of
that ruined hut before you. The man was shepherd to a
farmer who kept cattle on these mountains. Here, in this
savage retreat, he lived removed from the world, for the nearest
cabin to this spot is more than four miles distant.

" It may be supposed that the general distress afflicted this isolated family. The welcome news of the arrival of succours at Ballycroy at length reached them, and the herdsman set out to procure some of the *committee-meal* to relieve the hunger of his half-starved family.

" On arriving at the depôt, the stock of meal was nearly expended: however, he obtained a temporary supply, and was comforted with the assurance that a large quantity was hourly expected.

" Anxious to bring the means of sustinence to his suffering little ones, the herdsman crossed the mountain with his precious burden, and reached that hillock where the stones are loosely piled.

" But during his absence at Ballycroy, the rain had fallen

heavily in the hills ; the river was no longer fordable , a furious torrent of discoloured water rushed from the heights, and choaked the narrow channel. *There* stood the returning parent, within twenty paces of his wretched but dearly loved hovel. The children with a cry of delight rushed from the hut to the opposite bank to welcome him ; but, terrified by the fearful appearance of the flood, his wife entreated him not to attempt its passage for the present.

" But would he, a powerful and experienced swimmer, be deterred ? The eager and hungry looks of his expecting family maddened the unhappy father. He threw aside his clothes, bound them with the meal upon his back, crossed himself devoutly, and, ' in the name of God,' committed himself to the swollen river.

" For a moment he breasted the torrent gallantly—two strokes more would bring him to the bank—when the treacherous load turned, caught him round the neck, swept him down the stream, sank, and drowned him. He struggled hard for life. His wife and children followed the unhappy man as he was borne away—and their agonizing shrieks, told him, poor wretch ! that assistance from them was hopeless. At last the body disappeared, and was taken up the following morning four miles from this fatal place. One curious circumstance attended this calamity : to philosophers I leave its elucidation, while I pledge myself for its accuracy in point of fact. A herd of cattle galloped madly down the river-side at the time their unfortunate keeper was perishing ; their bellowings were heard for miles, and they were discovered next morning, grouped around the body of the dead shepherd, in the corner of a sandy cove, where there the abated flood had left it."

Every one shoots grouse ; the operation is so commonplace, that none but a cockney would find novelty in its detail. Our morning's sport was excellent. The dogs were in good working condition, and under perfect command ; but at noon the breeze died away, the day became oppressively hot, and the biting of gnats and horse-flies intolerable. Not being exterminators, we ceased shooting at three o'clock, and returned to our cabin with *two-and-twenty* brace of birds.

The particulars of the evening compotation I shall be excused in passing over. I must allow that the portion of wine allotted to sportsmen by the *Author of Salmonia* was awfully exceeded. We anointed our faces with cold cream, which speedily removed the pain and inflammation consequent on the stinging we had endured from the insects, and, after

" blowing a comfortable cloud," went to bed and slept ; but a man must exercise and carouse with a grouse-shooter, to conceive the deep and delicious repose which attends the sportsman's pillow.

This morning we were early astir. There was a mutual admission of slight headache, but coffee and fresh air will soon remove it. Having finished breakfast, and, in spite of Sir Humphry's denunciations, fortified ourselves against damp feet with a glass of *Mareschino*, we left the cabin for the moors.

Never was there a wilder spot than the dell in which we have taken up our shooting quarters. It is a herdsman's hovel, to which my kinsman has added an apartment for his accommodation in the grouse season. This is our banquet-room and dormitory ; a press in the corner contains our various drinkables, and upon a host of pegs, stuck into the interstices of the masonry, hang guns and belts, and all the unmentionable apparatus of a sportsman. The cabin itself is appropriated to culinary purposes, and to the accommodation of our dogs and personal attendants. The quadrupeds are quartered in the farther extremity of the house, and, after their fatigue, luxuriate gloriously upon a fresh bed of sun-dried fern.

In a *calliogh*\* beside the fire, the keeper and old John, who officiates as cook, are deposited at night, while the otter-hunter and piper canton themselves in the opposite den. A detachment of *boys*, or irregulars, who have followed the *master* to the mountains, *bivouac* somewhere in the vicinity of the cabin. In a sod-walled sheeling erected against a huge rock, the herdsman and his family have taken up their temporary residence, while we occupy the hut ; but its limited dimensions would be quite unequal to shelter a moiety of our extensive train. But while a mountain sheep hangs from

\* " Callioghs" are recesses built in the side walls of an Irish cabin, convenient to the hearth, and sufficiently large to contain a bed. Some of them are quite open to the fire ; while others are partially screened from view by a rude matting of bent or straw.

If you enter a peasant's hovel on a wet day, and inquire for the owner of the house, a strapping *boy* will generally roll out of one of these dark cribs, yawn, stretch his arms, scratch his head, and bid " your honour" welcome, and then inform you that he " was just *strichin'* on the bed."

"the couples"* of the cabin, and the whisky-keg continues unexhausted, those worthies matter little in what cranny they ensconce themselves at night.   To a late hour the piper is in requisition, and these careless devils dance, and laugh, and sing, until my cousin's mandate scatters them like ghosts at cock-crow; off they scamper, and where they bestow themselves till morning none but themselves can tell.   Although the quantity of whisky consumed here, in the short space of three days, appears almost incredible; yet upon these seasoned vessels its effects are so very transitory as almost to authenticate the boasted virtues of the mountain-dew—" that there is not an aching head in a hogshead full!"

While traversing a low range of moors, an incident occurred which at this season was unaccountable.  A red and white setter pointed at the top of a little glen.  The heathy banks on both sides of a mountain rivulet undulated gently from the stream, and caused a dipping of the surface; and the ground seemed a favourable haunt for grouse, and our dogs were beating it with care.  Observing the setter drop, his companions backed and remained steady, when suddenly Hero rose from his couchant attitude, and next moment a wild deer, of enormous size ,and splendid beauty, crossed before the dog and sprang the birds he had been pointing. The apparition of the animal, so little expected, and so singularly and closely introduced to our view, occasioned a sensation I had never hitherto experienced.   I rushed up the bank, while, unembarrassed by our presence, the noble deer swept past us in a light and graceful canter, at the short distance of some seventy or eighty yards.  I might have fired at and annoyed him — but on a creature so powerful, small shot could have produced little effect, and none but a Cockney, under similar circumstances, would waste a charge; and to tease, without a chance of bringing down the gallant beast, would have been a species of useless mischief, meriting a full month upon the tread-mill. I gazed after him as he gradually increased his distance; his

* The couples are the principal timbers that support the roof; they are placed at stated distances, and an Irishman describes the size of a house by telling you that it has so many "couples."

antlers were expanded as fully as my arms would extend; his height was magnificent; and, compared with fallow-deer, he seemed a giant to a dwarf. The sun beamed upon his deep bay side, as he continued describing a circular course over the flat surface of the moor, till reaching a rocky opening leading to the upper hills, he plunged into the ravine, and we lost sight of him.

What could have driven the red deer so low upon the heath was marvellous. Excepting when disturbed by a solitary hunter, or a herdsman in pursuit of errant cattle, or driven from the summit of the hills by snow and storm, those deer are rarely seen below the Alpine heights they inhabit. But the leisure pace of the beautiful animal we saw to-day, proved that he had not been alarmed in his lair, and led one almost to fancy, that in freakish mood he had abandoned his mountain home, to take a passing glance at the men and things beneath him.

At five o'clock, we left the moors, and returned to our cabin. The day throughout had been propitious; the breeze tempered the heat which yesterday oppressed us, and our

walk this morning had been only pleasant exercise.   We
were neither exhausted by an ardent sky, nor annoyed by
the dazzling glare of constant sunshine.   The gnats, which
lately had been intolerable, had vanished, and we were thus
enabled to perform our ablutions in the clear and sparkling
river; a feat last night impracticable, from the number and
virulence of the insects.   He who has bathed his limbs in the
cool and crystal waters of a mountain-stream after a busy day
upon the heath, can only estimate its luxury.   Twenty brace
of grouse, three hares, and a half score of gray plovers, was
the produce of our *chasse.*

---

## CHAPTER XIV.

Ball opens—Moonlight—Mountain scenery—Old Antony—Adventure
  with the Fairies—Ball continues—The otter-hunter's history—Ball
  concludes—The pater-o-pee.

THE moon rose in great splendour over the bold chain of
mountains which belts the valley where we are cantoned.
The piper is merrily at work, for some of the peasant girls
have come to visit us, attracted by the joyful news that a *pie-
beragh**\** was included in our suite.   The fondness of these
mountain maidens for dancing is incredible; at times of
festival, on the occasion of a wedding, or *dragging-home,*†
or whenever a travelling musician passes through these wilds,
they assemble from prodigious distances, and dance for days
and nights together.

My kinsman and I having duly executed a jig with a
brace of Nora Crinas, left the hut and strolled a short way
up the river.   The quiet of " lonely night " contrasted
strikingly with the scene of turbulent and vivacious mirth

---

\*  *Anglice,* piper.

†  " Dragging home," is the bringing the bride for the first time to her
husband's house.  An immense mob of relatives and *clevines* of " both the
houses," are collected on the occasion, and as an awful quantity of whisky
must of necessity be distributed to the company, this " high solemnity "
seldom concludes without subjecting the host's person and property to
demolition.

we had but just quitted. A jutting bank suddenly shut the cabin from our view, and its lights and music ceased to be seen or heard. A deep unbroken silence reigned around. The moon's disc appeared of unusual size, as she rose in cloudless majesty over the mountain masses which earlier in the evening had concealed her. Not a cloud was in the sky, and the unequal outline of the hills displayed a fine picture of light and shadow—and the stream rippled at our feet, as, " tipped with silver," we traced its wanderings for miles, while its sparkling current was lost or seen among the moor-land.

Just then a human figure turned the rock abruptly, and the old Otter-killer stood beside us. The rushing of the stream prevented us from noticing his approach. He had been examining his traps, and as the way was rugged, he was delayed till now. The old man's appearance in this place, and at that hour, was picturesque. His dark dress, his long white hair falling down his shoulders, the seal-skin wallet, the fish-spear, and the rough terrier his companion, all were in perfect keeping.

" Well, Antony, what sport ?"

" Little to speak of, Master Julius. I suspect the trap wants oiling, for there was an otter's spraints* every place about it. I went to the lake yonder, and while the breeze kept up the fish took well. I killed a dozen red trout."

" Did you meet any of the ' *gentlefolk*,'† friend Antony ? This is *just* the night that one would expect to find them *quadrilling* upon some green and mossy hillock."

The old man smiled and turned to me,—

" Well, well, the master won't believe in them ; but if he had seen them as I did—"

" And did you *really* see them ?"

" God knows, I tell you truth, Sir." Then, resting himself on a rock, he thus continued : —

" It will be eleven years next month, when I was hunting otters at Lough na Mucka ;—the master knows the place, for many a good grouse he shot beside it. I then had the two best *tarriers* beneath the *canopy*; this poor *crater* is their daughter," and he patted the dog's head affectionately. —" Well, I had killed two well-sized cubs, when Badger,

---

* Marks or traces left by the animal.　　　　† Fairies.

who had been working in the weeds, put out the largest
bitch I ever saw : I fired at her, but she was too far from
me, and away she went across the Lough, and Badger and
Venom after her. She rose at last ; Badger griped her, and
down went dog and otter. They remained so long under
water, that I was greatly afraid the dog was drowned ; but,
after a while, up came Badger. Though I was right glad
to see my dog, I did not like to lose the beast ; and I knew,
from the way that Badger's jaws were torn, that there
had been a wicked struggle at the bottom. Well, I encouraged the dog, and when he had got his breath again, he
dived down nothing daunted, for he was the best *tarrier*
ever poor man was master of. Long as he had been before
at the bottom, he was twice longer now. The surface
bubbled, the mud rose, and the water became black as ink :
' Ogh ! murder,' says I, ' Badger, have I lost ye ?' and I
set-to clapping my hands for trouble, and Venom set up the
howl as if her heart was broke. When, blessed be the
Maker of all ! up comes Badger with the otter griped by
the neck. The bitch swam over to help him, and I waded
to the middle, and speared and landed the beast. Well, then
I examined her, she had her mouth full of *ould* roots and
moss, for she had fastened on a stump at the bottom, and
the poor dog was sorely put-to to make her break her hold.
I mind it well : I sold the skin in Galway, and got a gold
guinea for it."

" Was that the night you met the fairies ?"

" Stay, Master Julius ; I'm coming to that. Well, three
otters were a heavy load, and I had four long miles to travel
before I could reach Morteein Crassagh's.* The master
knows the house well. The night was getting dark, and
it's the worst ground in Connaught. Well, I was within
a mile of Morteein's, when it became as black as pitch ; and
I had the shaking bog to cross, that you can hardly pass
in daytime, where, if a man missed his way, he would
be swallowed up in a moment. The rain began, and the
poor dogs were famished with cold and hunger. God !
I was sure I must stay there, starving till the morning ;
when on a sudden, little lights danced before me, and
showed me the hard tammocks as plain as if the sun was

---

* Martin with the rough face.

up. I was in a cruel fright, and the dogs whimpered, and would not stir from my foot. I was afraid to stay where I was, as I knew the *gentle-people* were about me; and I was unwilling to attempt the quagh,* for fear the light would leave me, and then I would get neither back nor forward. Well, the wind began to rise; the rain grew worse; I got desperate, and resolved to speak to the fairies civilly. ' Gentlemen and ladies,' says I, making a bow to the place where the lights were dancing, ' may be ye would be so obliging as to light me across the bog.' In a minute there was a blaze from one end of the quagh to the other, and a hundred lights were flashing over the bogs. I took heart and ventured; and wherever I put my foot, the place was as bright as day, and I crossed the swamp as safely as if I had been walking on a gravelled road. Every inch the light came with me, till I reached the *boreein*† leading to Morteein Crassagh's; then, turning about, I made the fairies a low bow : ' Gentlemen and ladies,' says I, ' I'm humbly thankful for your civility, and I wish ye now a merry night of it.' God preserve us ! The words were hardly out, when there was a roar of laughter above, below, and around me. The lights vanished, and it became at once so dark, that I could scarcely make out my way. When I got fairly inside Morteein's kitchen, I fainted dead; and when I came to, I told them what had happened. Many a time, fairy candles are seen at Lough na Mucka; but sorrow mortal was ever lighted across the quagh by the *gentle-people* but myself, and that the country knows. Well—the master is laughing at me; but I'll hobble to the cabin, or they'll think that the *good people* have carried me off at last, as they did Shamus Bollogh,‡ from Ballycroy."§

* A morass.    † A horsepath leading into bogs.
‡ James the Stutterer.
§ This gentleman's temporary sojourn with the fairies is generally credited in Ballycroy. Why the gentlefolk, who are accounted scrupulous in selecting youth and beauty when they abduct mortals, should have pitched upon Shamus, is unaccountable. His charms are of the plainest order, and he had long passed his teens before the period of his being carried away. His own account of the transaction is but a confused one—and all I recollect of the particulars is, that he crossed to Tallaghan, over an arm of the sea, on a grey horse, behind a little man dressed in green. Neither good nor evil resulted from this nocturnal gallop of " the Stutterer," if we except a sound horse-whipping which he received from

Presently we returned to the hut: the whisky had began to operate on the *corps de ballet* in the kitchen, for the pipes played louder, and the girls danced with additional *esprit*. To think of bed, with such a company beside us, would be idle : my cousin accordingly recharged his meerschaum, and, between many a puff, gave me the following memoir of the otter-hunter.

" The old man is a character. In his early days he was a travelling pedlar, a dealer in furs and Connemara stockings. He had always an unconquerable fancy for angling and otter-killing; and, with a pack upon his shoulders and a fish-spear in his hand, he traversed the kingdom in the double pursuit of pleasure and profit.

" When he disposed of his merchandize, he returned home laden with the skins he had collected in his wanderings. He has frequently brought thirty furs together to Limerick for sale ; and as they were then a valuable commodity, he acquired in a few years a considerable property.

" In one of his excursions, however, Antony managed to pick up a wife. She was young and handsome ; and, tiring of his unsettled life, persuaded the unhappy otter-killer to forego his favourite calling, and turn his fish-spear into a spigot. In short, he took a house in town, became a publican, got extensive business, gave credit, and soon was drunken and embarrassed ; his wife flirted, his property melted away, and his frail rib at last levanted with an English showman. Antony was astounded, but he bore misfortune like a philosopher. Renouncing whisky, except in limited quantities, he resumed the otter-trap, which had been rusting in a garret ; and one fine moonlight night, turned the key in the door, abandoned goods and chattels to the landlord, and disappeared, ' leaving his curse with Limerick.'

" No Bedouin returned from captivity to his parent's tent— no Swiss revisited his native valley, with more delight, than the cornuted otter-killer, when he hurried back to his beloved mountains. From that moment he forswore the town ; and, excepting on his annual visit to the furrier. Antony has avoided the busier haunts of mankind. Having added bleed-

the priest, for attempting to abuse the credulity of the peasantry, by detailing the fairy revels in which he alleged that he partiᴄipated.

ing to the number of his acquirements, he practises phar-
macy in this wilderness, and for forty years has led a
careless, migratory life, tolerated in the hall, and welcomed
in the cabin, until increasing years and bodily infirmity
confined him to his wild birth-place, where the otter can be
trapped without fatigue, and the salmon will yet reward the
old man's skill. The Lodge is now Antony's head-quarters,
and the remnant of his wandering life will probably be spent
with me.

" But it is not as a hunter and leech that the ancient otter-
killer is alone valuable. In his wanderings, he picked up
tales and traditions among the wild people he consorted with :
his memory is most tenacious, and he narrates strange legends
which, in wildness and imagination, rival the romances of the
East. In winter, when the snow falls and the fury of the
storm is unloosed, Antony is settled in his rude but comfortable chair, formed of twisted bent. The women of my
household listen to his love-stories with affected indifference,
but there is always some apology for remaining near the otter-
killer. At times, when the old man is summoned after dinner
to receive his customary glass, I, if I be ' *i'* the humour,' listen
to his wild legends ; and here, in this mountain-hut, seated in
this room, ' mine own great chamber,' while I luxuriate over
a bright bog-deal fire, an exquisite cigar, and an admixture of
pure hollands with the crystal water that falls from the rock
behind us, I listen in voluptuous tranquillity to Antony's
romances, as he recites to his attentive auditory in the kitchen
his narratives of former times.

" If the otter-hunter's tales be true, the primitive gentlewomen of the Emerald Isle were no vestals; and the judge
of the Consistorial Court, had such then existed, would have
had scarcely time to bless himself."

It was twelve o'clock, and no abatement of revelry was yet
manifest among the dancers in the kitchen. The piper's music
appeared inexhaustible, and, maugre fatigue and whisky, the
company were as fresh and effective as when the ball commenced. " I must rout them," said my cousin; " the devils
would dance till doomsday." He opened the door, but
stopped and beckoned me to approach. I looked out; the
boys and girls had left the floor, the men settling themselves
on the *colliaghs*, empty casks, and turf *cleaves*,* while the

* *Anglice*, baskets.

ladies were comfortably accommodated upon their partners'
knees.  One gentleman alone was standing.  Presently two
sticks were laid crosswise on the ground ; the pipes struck up
an unusual sort of jig, and the feat commenced.  " This,"
said my kinsman, " is called the ' pater-o-pee,' and none but
an accomplished dancer would attempt it."

To describe this dance would be impossible : it consisted
of an eternal hopping into the small compartments formed
by the crossing of the cudgels on the floor, without touching
the sticks.

Now, holding reasonable doubts whether, upon Mr. Cooney
presenting himself to Monsieur Laporte, this gentleman would
favour him with an engagement, I'll bet the manager, notwithstanding, *a cool hundred*, that, on the strength of the
King's Theatre, he has no *artiste* who will *touch* Tim Cooney
at the *pater-o-pee!*

---

## CHAPTER XV.

Moon looks suspicious—Heavy fall of rain—River flooded—Sporting
    writers—Criticism on Hawker—Originality of the Cólonel—His outfit
    of a wild fowl shooter—Samuel Singer and his gun.

WHEN we took a last look from the window of our hut,
before we retired to our respective mattresses, there was a
broad belt observable around the moon's disc, which is the
well-known token of an approaching change of weather ;
and early this morning, the constant plashing from the roof
told us that the rain was falling heavily.  The river rose
apace, and the flood thundered past the cabin, momentarily
increasing by the frequent torrents from the high grounds.
The gentle and sparkling stream, on whose moonlight banks
I had been musing at midnight, disappeared, and a fierce and
turbulent body of discoloured water rushed through its swollen
channel, bearing along huge portions of the banks, which had
yielded to its fury.

" We are fairly caught, Frank," said my kinsman.
" Hemmed in by the stream, if life depended on it, we could
not now communicate with the Lodge.  Fortunately the cabin
roof is impervious to the water ; and, thanks to the foresight

of old John, I see the backgammon box has not been forgotten.  Come, shall we have a hit; tie a fly; cut card-waddings; play écarté; or listen to one of Antony's amatory narratives, showing how a baron's lady left her liege lord for a black-eyed page, and how a holy monk proved in the end to be no better than he ought to be ?  And we have books too ; shall we speculate and star-gaze with Sir Humphry, or paddle in a punt with Hawker, after ' blue-billed curres" ' dun-birds and divers,' 'Tommy Loos and Isle of Wight parsons ?' "*

" Anything for me but Colonel Thornton ; for I am heartsick of Mrs. T—— and 'red-legged partridges.' "

" I confess I would rather wade through the mud with honest Philip, after all, than accompany the Colonel in his researches for French estates, which he never had an intention to purchase.  I own that Hawker is in many things exquisitely absurd, but he is amusing also, although in his adaptation of matter his work does not precisely exhibit the happiest specimen of good arrangement.  See, for example, page 136; here he recommends you to ' dine at one o'clock,' ' not to snore away the evening in concert with your dog,' and admits that, ' if a man likes grog, he may finish the evening with a bucket-full;' assures you that soap and water is 'the sovereignest thing on earth' for soiled hands ; and that kid gloves are sold by Mr. Painter, No. 27, Fleet-street ; concluding with the following valuable recipe :

" ' If a person is extremely nervous from hearing the report of his gun, or from the noise of the rising game, let him prime his ears with cotton, and his inside with tincture of bark and sal volatile.

" This fortification of the ears is, no doubt, an excellent precaution for a cockney, and certainly less hazardous than the aerial mode propounded by the Colonel for killing rabbits. To perch in a tree, I think, would be a sufficient punishment; and what assistance a dog would render in the branches is inconceivable.

" What say you also to the association in one sentence, of ' game, flies, rats, red-herrings, and corrosive sublimate ?'† The information, further, that mercury will kill bugs, and a nota bene, warning the King's subjects against poison ; con-

* Hawker, p. 177.                              † Ibid, p. 240.

cluding with a valuable recipe for a *sauce piquante,* that would
' tickle the gustatory nerves where fifty failed.'*

" The Colonel, indeed, may fairly claim the palm for being
as diffusive as successful. He opens up the mysteries of gun-
making in one page, and in another gives you instructions for
correcting sour beer—proves that publicans dilute spirits—
damp sheets produce rheumatisms—and draughts of air bring
on the tooth-ache; gives you a recipe for making cold punch,
' which was given him some years ago in Glasgow,' where the
said cold punch was universally drunk; and furnishes such
information upon ' game laws,' ' tartar emetic,' fleecy hosiery,'
and ' tincture of bark,' as must astound the reader, and cause
him to marvel at the astonishing capacity of the commander's
cranium."

" All these are excellent in their way. The Colonel, however, owns that he has borrowed much from others; but for
originality take him upon dress, and listen to his equipment of
a wild-fowl shooter.

" *Imprimis*—the nether extremities are to be thus gar-
nished—' one *extra* pair of coarse yarn stockings; one ditto
of the thickets *wads;* one ditto of under-stockings of the
*warmest quality;* a pair of *water-proof boots,* and a ditto
*Flushing trowsers.*' The worthy Colonel proceeds :

" ' It is needless to say, that (except the feet, which we
have already defended) *every part of the body* should be clothed
with *flannel.*

" ' With regard to further covering for the body, could
we ensure not getting wet — *leather* would, perhaps, be
*warmest;* but, at all events, the waistcoat, both *before and
behind,* should be made of *shag, or Bath-coating,* which
certainly, taking all weather, answers best, and is the most
comfortable. *Under* the waistcoat should be worn a *Flushing-
frock,* and *over it* a *sort of jacket,* of either drab cloth or
swan-skin. *The cap* may be made of the same (or any
thing that has the same appearance), and, if cold, worn
over a *Welsh wig.* Mr. Lloyd, 13, Old Bond-street, has

---

* Recipe for sauce to wild-fowl: Port wine or claret, one glass; sauce
*à la Russe* (the older the better) one table-spoonful; ketchup, one ditto;
lemon-juice, one ditto; lemon-peel, one slice; shalot (large) one sliced;
Cayenne pepper (the darkest, not that like brick-dust) four grains  mace,
one or two blades. To be scalded, strained, and added to the mere
gravy which comes from the bird in roasting.

invented an excellent, though simple *defender for the chest* (which he calls an " Anglesey,") and a *large shawl* handkerchief may be worn over the collar. A pair of *worsted wristbands* (sold by the name of " muffatees") should be worn with *cloth gloves,* and, over all, a large and' long pair of *double swan-skin cuffs.'*

" But what signify all these flannels and Flushings—shag and swan-skin—wads, water-boots, and Welsh wigs, to that immortal garment invented by one Larry Rogers, who calls it his ' *sou' wester,'* ' and gets it all for nine shillings,' of which *loquitur* the Colonel—

" Now to the point !—' Make, with an article called Russia-duck, (which, as well as swan-skin, should be previously wetted and dried, to prevent shrinking,) a loose over-all frock-coat, and a hood or cap, with a flap behind, similar to *a coal-heaver's hat*, and dress them as follows :

" ' Take three quarts of linseed oil, and boil them till reduced to two quarts and a half, the doing which will require about three hours ; and when the oil is sufficiently boiled, it will burn a feather. (The addition of some India rubber was suggested to me, but of this I did not make a trial.) When the oil is quite cold, take a clean paint brush, and work it well into the outside of the whole apparel, *and it will soon find its way to the inside.'*

" There is here a judicious and cautionary nota bene, requesting the operator *neither to burn himself nor the house*—with an admission that the savour of the garment is abominable. The Colonel concludes, that with ' *a very large old umbrella, fitted up with brown holland*—a bag full of straw, or something of the kind, *a pair of goggles*, and a sufficient supply of *Messrs. Fribourg's mixture*, the sportsman has all the necessary *covering* that can be required for *real* wild-fowl shooting.

" Nothing, indeed, can exceed the author's ingenuity, from the construction of a *hare pocket* to making *an old gun shoot straight*, and firing *two pounds of shot to the best advantage*. Not that I would ambition being the operator in the latter exploit, and would rather leave the affair to ' one Samuel Singer, of Pool, who shoots with a gun, weight 141 lbs. !' Still the Colonel is a merry soul ; and provided with his ' pocket-nightingale,' I wish we had him here. He should compound cold punch *ad libitum,* and receive the *ceade fealteagh* of our highland hut.

G

"Yes;—Frank, I'll bet my new Purday to a Queen Anne,*
that he would never have used his friends, as Sir Humphry
treated the unhappy philosophers whom he seduced into
Scotland, and shabbed off with half-a-pint of claret in a
rascally sheebein-house. No; Hawker is a worthy fellow;
one, who, as our lamented countryman, Lord L——, told
Abernethy, 'puts his trust in Providence, and takes a big
drink.' By the way, I have often wondered that any honest
gentleman, having a christian propensity for the bottle, would
venture within arms-length of that unjoyous and dispiriting
doctor,—and here comes dinner!''

---

# CHAPTER XVI.

Flood subsides—My cousin's henchmen—Their description—Post-bag
arrives—Messenger belated in the mountains—The Fairy Glen—Herd of
red deer—Their destruction by poachers—Gradual decrease—Difficulties
in continuing them—Anecdotes—Rearing the fawns—Sterility when
domesticated—Red deer in parks—The tame hind—The Tyrawly stag—
Skill requisite in shooting deer—Curious anecdote.

How rapidly the waters of a mountain river swell and
subside! Last night the steep bank before the cabin-door

---

* "Queen Anne's muskets" are in great repute among the Irish
peasantry, who assert that the barrels of these antiquated implements
are excellent. The following curious notice of these guns is extracted
from "An Appeal to the Public," by the unfortunate George Robert
Fitzgerald.

"Informant was with his said master, and in the carriage with him,
when the said George Robert Fitzgerald came up alone and unarmed, and
peaceably and politely addressed his father, the said George Fitzgerald,
who went home with his said son to Rockfield-lodge; and had he wished
not to go with his said son, he might have refused going, he having in
his carriage, in which informant was, *three bell-muzzled blunderbusses,
loaded with swan-drops, and a small ditto, and also three Queen Anne's
muskets, with bayonets, loaded as aforesaid, and three fuzees, one of
which was loaded, together with a small sword. Four powder-horns, all
filled with gunpowder, one of which contained three pounds of gunpowder,
besides several large bags of musket balls, swan-drops, and slugs*; and had
the said George Fitzgerald, this informant's master, been disposed to
make any opposition in going home with his said son to Rockfield-lodge,
informant would have made use of said arms and ammunition in his said
master's defence." Now we opine, that Colonel Hawker, and his "new
double-swivel gun," with Sam Singer at his back, would scarcely hazard
an engagement with this formidable vehicle.

was scarcely visible above the swollen and discoloured stream. The flood is gone ; the river has recovered its silvery hue, and no traces of yesterday's violence appear, save the huge masses of turf left by the receding waters on the shore, which, from their size, prove how fierce the torrent was when at its height.

We have been expecting anxiously a messenger with the post-bag, for three days have elapsed since its last arrival. There will be an accumulation of newspapers. What a treasure they would have been yesterday ! Ha ! there is a bustle in the outer cabin ; no doubt an arrival. It is the messenger.

I never saw finer samples of the mountain peasantry than this man and his brother exhibit. They are scarcely to be known asunder ; young, particularly handsome, five feet eleven inches, light, active, clean-limbed, perfect specimens of strength and symmetry combined ; good-humoured, indefatigable, and obliging, submissive to *the Master's* nod, and yet the boldest and *handiest* boys in Ballycroy. I sometimes look after my kinsman as he strides over the moors with his handsome *henchmen* at his back. He walks as if the province was his own ; bold, and careless, and confident—no wonder—those wild fellows are his *fosterers*, and they would shed the last drop of their blood for " the Master,' if he required it.

This fidelity and devotion on the one side, is requited by kindness and protection on the other. These men have lived about the Lodge from boyhood—and they come and depart as they please. At spring and harvest-times they repair to the village where their parents reside, to assist the old couple and *the girls* in getting the potatoes in and out of ground ; they tend the cattle in the mountains when requisite, and pass the remainder of the year following *the Master* to the moors or to the river, catching fish, netting rabbits, or killing wild-fowl in the winter ; and dancing, drinking, and fighting on holiday. and festivals, as becomes good men and loyal subjects.

When they marry—for Malthus and restrictions upon population are no more recognised in Erris, than the Pope is by a modern Methodist—they will obtain a patch of mountain from their patron, erect a cabin, construct a still, and setting political dogmas at defiance, then and there produce most excellent whisky, and add to the " seven millions" considerably.

The messenger presented himself with the post-bag, being anxious to render a personal account of the causes of his delay. His night's adventure is quite characteristic of the wild life, and bold and reckless spirit of these mountain peasants.

The route to the next post-town lies through the ridge of hills which I have already described, as bounding the valley where we are quartered. The usual way to reach it is by an old and rugged horse-path, which, although seldom frequented now, was fifty years since the only means of communication which Erris had with the southern baronies. This easier, but more circuitous route was abandoned by the young peasant, who hoped, by directly crossing the heights, to arrive at the cabin before the night shut in. He took this perilous direction accordingly; but the rain was still falling fast, and when he topped the ridge of the hills, the valley beneath was covered by a dense mist. Presently the mountain streams rose, the light failed—to advance or retreat was impossible; and the isolated peasant had no choice left but to seek a shelter in the rocks, and remain there until morning dawned. He easily discovered a fissure in the steep bank above the river, crept in—" *blessed himself*"—and lay down to sleep upon his cold and rugged bed.

What situation could be more desolate and heart-sinking than this? Imprisoned among savage mountains, perched in a wild rock far above the rest of mankind, separated from human help by an impassable torrent, cold, hungry, and exhausted; yet all these dejecting circumstances were unheeded by the hardy mountaineer. He had but one source of terror; the otter-hunter had often described this glen as a favourite haunt of fairies; and "what would become of him if the *gentle-people* caught him there ?"

The midnight hour passed, however, without any supernatural visitation. No fairy revelry disturbed the peasant's slumbers; the rain ceased; the flood was falling; the chough* and raven were preparing to take wing; and while the first

* Cornish chough, or red-legged crow. (*Corvus Gracilis*, Linn.—*Le Coracias*, Buff.) This bird is about the size of the jackdaw. The bill is long, curved, sharp at the tip, and of a bright red colour; the iris of the eye is composed of two circles, the outer one red, the inner one blue; the eyelids are red; the plumage is altogether of a purplish-violet black; the legs are as red as the bill; the claws are large, hooked and black.

faint light was breaking through the mountain mists, Cormac, anxious to quit his cheerless *bivouac*, crawled out from his cold retreat.

Suddenly, from above, an indistinct noise alarmed him. Feet clattered down the rocky path; a rush, a snorting, announced their near approach, and a herd of deer appeared within half a stone's cast. They traversed the narrow track in single files, and were moving rapidly down the mountain side to browse in the glen beneath.

When the leading stag discovered the startled peasant, he halted, tossed his antlers wildly, and gave a loud and peculiar neigh. The pause, though momentary, permitted the rear to come up, and the herd were clustered in a group. The panic lasted but an instant: they turned round, and with amazing speed rushed up the hill, regained the heights, and were lost in the thick mist. Cormac could not reckon them accurately, but imagined their number to be about sixteen.

It is seldom, now, that the red deer are seen in herds. Within late years they have diminished sadly, and unless vigorous means are promptly adopted to prevent their destruction by poachers, like their ancient enemy, the rough Irish greyhound, they too will become extinct. My cousin, when a boy, has often met forty deer herded together; but, from their decreased numbers, one rarely sees now more than a few brace. Since the French descent upon this coast in Ninety-eight, their destruction has been rapid. Unfortunately, many of the fire-arms then distributed among the peasantry, remain in their possession still, and in the winter months, when the severity of the season forces the deer to leave the hills and seek food and shelter in the valleys, idle ruffians, too well acquainted with the passes of the mountains, take that opportunity to surprise and slaughter them.

There are many circumstances connected with this scarce and beautiful species, that should render their preservation a matter of national interest. They are the last relic of other times ; and all besides of the once famed stock which tenanted the Irish forests have disappeared. The wolf, the morse-deer, the greyhound,* exist no longer ; and this noble creature is

---

* Captain Brown places this animal in the class of " domesticated dogs which hunt in packs or singly, principally by the eye, although sometimes by the scent."

" The Irish Greyhound.  *Canis Graius Hibernicus.—Ray.*     [" This

the sole remnant of her aboriginal animals, when Ireland was in her wild and independent condition.

"This is one of the largest of the canine race, with an air at once beautiful, striking, and majestic. He has been known to grow to the extraordinary height of four feet, although the general standard is about three feet.

"In shape the Irish greyhound somewhat resembles the common greyhound, only that he is much larger and more muscular in his formation, clumsy in all his different parts, and is quite unserviceable in hunting either the stag, fox, or hare. His chief use in former times was in clearing the country of wolves and wild boars, for which his great size and strength peculiarly adapted him.

"The colour of the Irish greyhound is a pale cinnamon or fawn. His aspect is mild, and his disposition gentle and peaceable. It is said he is greatly an overmatch for either the mastiff or bull-dog; and when he fights he generally seizes his antagonist by the back, and shakes him to death, which his great strength enables him to do with ease.

"M. Buffon supposes the great Danish dog to be only a variety of the Irish greyhound; and Mr. Pennant was of opinion that the French mâtin and the Albanian dog were also varieties of the same.

"The Irish greyhound is now rarely to be met with, even in his native country.

"The Marquis of Sligo is among the few individuals who possess that fine animal in a state of tolerable purity; he keeps a number at Westport, in the county of Mayo, Ireland, where there is a person employed to look after them. It is said that great care is necessary to preserve the breed, and keep them in good health.

"Aylmer Bourke Lambert, Esq. one of the vice-presidents of the Linnæan Society, took the measure of one of the Marquis of Sligo's dogs, which was as follows :—'From the point of the nose to the tip of the tail, sixty-one inches; tail, seventeen and a half inches long; from the tip of the nose to the back part of the skull, ten inches; from the back part of the skull to the beginning of the tail, thirty-three inches; from the toe to the top of the fore shoulder, twenty-eight inches and a half; the length of the leg, sixteen inches; from the point of the hind toes to the top of the hind shoulders, thirteen inches; from the point of the nose to the eye, four inches and a half; the ears, six inches long; round the widest part of the belly, (about three inches from the fore legs), thirty-five inches; twenty-six inches round the hind part, close to the hind legs; the hair short and smooth; the colour of some brown and white, of others black and white.'

"They seem good-tempered animals, but from the accounts Mr. Lambert received, it is obvious that they must have degenerated, particularly in point of size.

"Dr. Goldsmith says he has seen a dozen of these dogs, and assures us the largest was about four feet high, and as tall as a calf of a year old."

We are sorry to remark, that Captain Brown's statement, "that the Irish greyhound is still preserved by the Marquis of Sligo," &c. is totally

Individual exertions to continue the red deer are found to be of little use. They seldom breed when deprived of liberty, and restricted to the enclosures of a park. If they do, the offspring degenerates, and the produce is very inferior in size to what it would have been, had the animal remained in its state of natural freedom. Even when taken young in the mountains, to rear the fawns is a difficult and uncertain task. My cousin has for many seasons made the attempt, and generally failed three times for once that he succeeded. Last year one young deer that he procured throve well and grew apace until he was sufficiently stout to go out and graze with the cows. Unfortunately, a visitor brought a savage-tempered greyhound to the Lodge, the dog attacked the fawn, and it died of the worrying it received, before the greyhound could be taken off.

It is almost impossible to procure the fawns from the mountains in an uninjured state. They generally receive a blow of a stick or stone from the captor, or undergo such rough usage in conveying them to the low-lands, that death commonly ensues. A fine well-grown male was brought to the Lodge last week. For a day or two nothing could be more promising than its appearance. It began, however, on the fourth morning to pine away, and soon after died. We opened it to ascertain, if possible, the cause of its death, and discovered a gangrened wound in the side, evidently produced by a blow. The peasant who brought him declared that he was sound and uninjured; and to account for his caption swore lustily that he *caught the fawn asleep*, but it appeared that the rogue had knocked the poor animal over with a stone, and thus produced the inward bruise which terminated fatally.

It is strange that a creature of such strength and endurance when arrived at maturity, should be so very difficult to bring up. Means were resorted to by my kinsman to have the cow's assimilated to the wild deer's milk, by changing the fawn's nurse to a heathier and poorer pasturage; a lichen, indigenous to the mountains on which the deer principally feeds, was also

unfounded. No dog of this description has been for many years in the possession of the noble lord. In his father's time, there were, I believe, some descendants of this splendid stock at Westport House—but for years they have been extinct. The present Marquis introduced some double-nosed boar-hounds into the country, which possibly were mistaken for the Irish greyhound, although no animals could be more dissimilar in shape, courage, and docility.

procured, and intermixed with the cow's hay; and yet this attention and trouble were attended with but indifferent success.

When once, however, the period of infancy is passed, the wild deer is hardy, vigorous, and easily provided for. At different times, many have been located in the neighbouring parks, and lived there to a great age. In the domain of a nobleman in Roscommon, there are several brace—and in the park of Clogher, a stag and hind are confined at present; they are all vigorous and healthy, but have never continued their species.

Many curious anecdotes are recorded of the red deer. Some years since, a hind was domesticated by a neighbouring baronet; it was a fine and playful animal, and gave many proofs of extraordinary sagacity. Like many fairer favourites, she was a very troublesome one, and from her cunning and activity, a sad torment to the gardener. No fences would exclude her from the shrubberies, and if the garden gates were for a moment insecure, the hind was sure to discover the neglect, and avail herself of the opportunity to taste the choicest vegetables. This beautiful but mischievous pet met with some accidental injury, and died, to the great regret of her proprietor.

Many years ago, a stag was in the possession of a gentleman of Tyrawley. He grew to be a powerful and splendid beast, but his propensities and dispositions were very different to those of the playful and innocent hind.

The stag was bold and violent, detested strangers and women, and from his enormous size and strength, was frequently a very dangerous playfellow. He had a particular fancy for horses, resided mostly in the stable, and when the carriage was ordered to the door, if permitted, he would accompany it. A curious anecdote is told of him. He had no objection whatever to allow a gentleman to enter the coach; but to the fair sex he had an unconquerable aversion, and with his consent no lady should be an inside passenger. The servants were obliged to drive him away, before their mistress could venture to appear; and at last, he became so troublesome and unsafe, as to render his banishment to an adjoining deer-park the necessary punishment of his indocility. He did not survive this disgrace long; he pined away rapidly, avoided the fallow deer, and died, as my informant declared, of a broken heart.

In killing deer, it is necessary to select the head, or aim directly behind the shoulder. A body-wound may eventually destroy the animal, but the chances are, that he will carry off the ball. Many, when severely struck, escape the shooter ; and there have been stags killed in these mountains, who bore the marks of severe wounds, from the effects of which they had entirely recovered. The following singular and authentic instance of a bullet lodging in what is usually considered a mortal place, and failing to occasion death, is extracted from a scientific periodical.*

" A buck, that was remarkably fat and healthy in condition, in August, 1816, was killed in Bradbury Park, and on opening him, it was discovered, that at some distant time he had been shot in the heart, a ball being found in a cyst in the substance of that viscus, about two inches from the apex. The surface of the cyst had a whitish appearance ; the ball weighs two hundred and ninety-two grains, and was quite flat. Mr. Richardson, the park-keeper, who opened the animal, is of opinion the ball had struck some hard substance before entering the body of the deer. That the animal should subsist long after receiving this ball, is endeavoured to be accounted for from the instance of a soldier, who survived forty-nine hours after receiving a bayonet wound in the heart : however, the recovery from a gun-shot wound in an animal inferior to man can, in no respect, materially alter the importance of the fact, and of the great extent to which this vital organ may sustain injury from external violence."

## CHAPTER XVII.

An alarm—Deceptive appearance of the weather—A blank fishing day— Recovery of the setter—Hydrophobia—Melancholy anecdote—Loss of a kennel—Strange apathy of Irish servants—Extraordinary preservation.

A CIRCUMSTANCE to-day has given us considerable uneasiness ; one of our best setters, who had been observed to look rather dull yesterday, has refused his food, and continues listless of what is passing around him. He was a sprightly,

* The Edinburgh Medical Journal.

active-minded dog, and his torpidness is alarming. We promptly separated him from his companions, and have chained him in na adjoining cabin, under the especial observation of old Antony. The otter-killer is preparing to use his leechcraft, and I trust with good effect. Canine madness is a frightful visitation, and no caution can be too strict to guard against its melancholy consequences.

Who shall say that success in angling can be calculated upon with any thing like certainty ? If a man were gifted with the properties of a walking barometer, the weather of this most capricious corner of the earth would set his prognostics at defiance. Never did a morning look more favourable; it was just such a one as an angler would swear by; a grey, dark, sober, settled sky, without any vexatious glare of threatening sunshine to interrupt his sport. The otter-killer was not so sanguine of this happy promise of good weather as we were. He observed certain little clouds, to which he gave some Irish name. " The wind, too, had shifted a point southerly since daybreak, and the pinkeens* were jumping, as they always jump, when they expect more water." We laughed at him; but Antony was right.

We tried some beautiful pools; the fish were rising fast; they sprang over the surface of the water frequently, and no worse omen can threaten the fishermen with disappointment. If they did condescend to notice our flies, they rose as if they wished merely to reconnoître them, or struck at them scornfully with their tails.

Still hoping that a change in the temper of the fish—for a lady is not more fanciful—might yet crown our efforts with success, we proceeded down the river and pushed on for Pull-garrow. To angle here with the water clean and full, and the wind brisk from the westward, would almost repay a pilgrimage. For its extent, there is not a better salmon haunt in Christendom. The fish were rising in dozens, and where the river rushes into the neck of the pool, the constant breaking of the surface by the rolling or springing of the salmon, was incredible. The number of fish collected in this pool must have been immense, for in every part of it they were rising simultaneously. *But not one of them would touch the fly.* I hooked a salmon accidentally in the side, and after a short

---

* The usual name among the peasantry for samlets and trout fry.

and violent struggle the hold broke and I lost him, The mode of fishing attributed by Sir Humphry Davy to the Galway fishermen* must be as unprofitable as *unartistlike*. If ever it could avail, we should have succeeded to-day in Pullgarrow.

Meanwhile the breeze gradually died away, or came in gusts from the south; the sky in the same quarter grew thick and misty; large drops fell, and in a short time the rain came down in torrents. The reason why the salmon had declined our flies was now disclosed; although we had not foreseen the coming change, the fish had evidently expected it. Wearied and drenched, we returned to our shooting quarters. But we speedily forgot our fatigue and disappointment. Antony's report of the health of his canine patient was satisfactory. The animal's stomach had been disordered, and the otter-hunter's remedies were promptly administered, and successful. My cousin had a dread of madness breaking out in his kennel; and from his melancholy experience of the fearful consequences of neglect, I do not marvel that on the first symptom of loss of appetite or abated spirits, he forthwith causes the suspected dog to be removed, and places him under a strict *surveillance*.

Our conversation after dinner naturally turned upon the indisposition of the setter.— "You may think, my dear Frank," said my cousin, "that I carry my apprehensions of the slightest illness in my dogs to a ridiculous and unnecessary length; but when I tell you that I have witnessed the fatal course of hydrophobia, in the human as well as the brute victim, you may then conceive the horror I feel when any thing recalls to my memory this hopeless malady.

"During my first season at the Dublin University, I was invited to pass a short vacation with a relative of my mother. He lived in the south of Ireland, in an ancient family mansion-

---

* "In the river at Galway, in Ireland, I have seen above the bridge some hundreds of salmon lying in rapid streams, and from five to ten fishermen tempting them with every variety of fly, but in vain. After a fish has been thrown over a few times, and risen once or twice and refused the fly, he rarely ever took any notice of it at that place."

"When the water is low and clear in this river, the Galway fishermen resort to the practice of fishing with a naked hook, endeavouring to entangle it in the body of the fish; a most unartistlike practice."— *Salmonia.*

house, situated in the mountains, and at a considerable distance
from the mail-coach road.

"This gentleman was many years older than I. He had
an only sister, a girl of sixteen, beautiful and accomplished;
at the period of my visit she was still at school, but was to
finally leave it, as my host informed me, at Midsummer.

"Never was there a more perfect specimen of primitive
Milesian life, than that which the domicile of my worthy
relative exhibited. The house was enormously large—half
ruinous—and all, within and without, wild, rackety, and
irregular. There was a troop of idle and slatternly servants
of both sexes, distracting every part of the establishment:
and a pack of useless dogs infesting the premises, and crossing you at every turn. Between the biped and quadruped
nuisances an eternal war was carried on, and not an hour of
the day elapsed, but a canine outcry announced that some
of those unhappy curs were being ejected by the butler, or
pelted by the cook.

"So common-place was this everlasting uproar, that after a
few days I almost ceased to notice it. I was dressing for
dinner, when the noise of dogs quarrelling in the yard,
brought me to the window; a terrier was being worried by
a rough, savage-looking fox-hound, whom I had before this
noticed and avoided. At the moment, my host was crossing
from the stable; he struck the hound with his whip, but,
regardless of the blow, he continued his attack upon the
smaller dog. The old butler in coming from the garden,
observed the dogs fighting, and stopped to assist in separating
them. Just then, the brute quitted the terrier, seized the
master by the leg, and cut the servant in the hand. A groom
rushed out on hearing the uproar, struck the prongs of a
pitchfork through the dog's body, and killed him on the spot.
This scene occurred in less time than I have taken in relating
it.

"I hastened from my dressing-room; my host had bared
his leg, and was washing the wound, which was a jagged tear
from the hound's tooth. Part of the skin was loose, and a
sudden thought appeared to strike him. He desired an iron
to be heated; took a sharp penknife from his pocket, coolly
and effectually removed the ragged flesh, and, regardless of
the agony it occasioned, with amazing determination, cauterized
the wound severely.

" The old butler, however, contented himself with binding up his bleeding hand. He endeavoured to dissuade his master from undergoing what he considered to be unnecessary pain. ' *The dog was dead, sure, and that was quite sufficient to prevent any danger arising from the bite ;*' and, satisfied with this precaution, he remained indifferent to future consequences, and in perfect confidence that no ulterior injury could occur from the wound.

" Three months passed away—my friend's sister was returning from school—and, as the mountain road was in bad repair, and a bridge had been swept away by the floods, saddle-horses were sent to meet the carriage. The old butler, who had some private affairs to transact in the neighbouring town, volunteered to be the escort of his young mistress, and obtained permission.

" That there was something unusual in the look and manner of her attendant, was quickly remarked by the lady. His address was wild and hurried, and some extraordinary feelings appeared to agitate him. To an inquiry if he was unwell, he returned a vague and unmeaning answer ; he trembled violently when assisting her on horseback, and it was evident that some strange and fearful sensations disturbed him.

" They rode some miles rapidly, until they reached the rivulet where the bridge had been carried off by the flood. To cross the stream was no way difficult, as the water barely covered the horse's fetlock. The lady had ridden through the water, when a thrilling cry of indescribable agony from her attendant arrested her. Her servant was on the opposite side, endeavouring to reign in his unwilling horse, and in his face there was a horrible and convulsed look that terrified his alarmed mistress. To her anxious questions, he only replied by groans, which too truly betrayed his sufferings ; at last he pointed to the stream before him, and exclaimed, ' *I cannot, dare not cross it ! Oh God ! I am lost !—the dog—the dog !*'

" What situation could be more frightful than that in which the lady found herself ? In the centre of a desolate and unpeopled moor, far from assistance, and left alone with a person afflicted with decided madness. She might, it is true, have abandoned him ; for the terrors of the poor wretch would have prevented him from crossing the rivulet ; but, with extraordinary courage, she returned, seized the bridle fearlessly, and, notwithstanding the outcries of the unhappy man, forced his horse through the water, and never left his side, until she fortunately overtook some tenants of her brother returning from a neighbouring fair.

" I arrived on a visit the third evening after this occurrence, and the recollection of that poor old man's sufferings has ever since haunted my memory. All that medical skill and affectionate attention on his master's part could do to assuage his pain, and mitigate the agonies he occasionally underwent, was done. At length, the moment that was devoutly prayed for came. He died on the sixth morning.

" From this horrible fate nothing but his own determination preserved my relative : and, by the timely use of a painful remedy, *excision and cautery of the wound*, he escaped this dreadful disease.

" I have related the calamity of another ; but I, too, have been a sufferer, although, thank God ! not in person.

" A setter of uncommon beauty was presented to me by a gentleman under peculiar circumstances. He had been the favourite companion of his deceased wife; and, during her long and hopeless illness, had seldom left her chamber. He begged me to allow him a place in the Lodge, and not subject him to the restraint of the kennel. His wishes were obeyed, and Carlo was duly installed into all the rights and privileges of a carpet-dog.

" I left home on a shooting-visit, and luckily brought a brace of my best setters with me. A week after my departure, an express reached me to say that Carlo ' was very odd, would not eat,* and bit and worried every dog he met with.' I took alram instantly, and returned home without delay. I found the household in desperate alarm, and Carlo was confined in a separate out-house, but not until he had worried and torn every dog in my possession !

" I went to reconnoitre him through an iron-stanchioned

---

* Dr. Clarke, of Nottingham, relates a case in that neighbourhood, of a dog that was not suspected to labour under rabies until *ten days* after he had bitten an unfortunate man, who, in six weeks after the bite, died of hydrophobia. This dog ate and drank heartily, showed no signs of indisposition, hunted as usual, and occasionally went into a neighbour's house among children, without injuring any of them; but, on the morning of the tenth day (that is, ten days after communicating the disease by the bite, and when he had no hydrophobia) he was seen snapping at every dog in the street, and was in consequence destroyed.

window : he was in the last and frightfullest stage of confirmed
hydrophobia. I sent for a rifle and terminated the animal's
life.

" I was at first afraid to inquire into the extent of my calamity.
I mustered courage to enter the kennel, and personally investigated the state of my dogs. Every one of them, ten in number,
had been bitten, and several of them were fearfully mutilated
by the rabid animal I had despatched. Even the terriers had
not escaped ; and they, poor animals ! were necessarily included in the general order for execution that I issued to
the keeper. That noble house-dog, who has been the
subject of your admiration, was fortunately preserved, by
having been sent for by a gentleman who resided in the
next county.

" A most extraordinary insensibility to danger was evinced
by the female members of my household. Unluckily, Antony
was absent in the mountains, setting a broken bone ; the
keeper had accompanied me ; every one acquainted with the
habits and management of dogs was from home ; and the
kennel was entrusted to the kitchen-boy. On this occasion,
the disease appears to have come on gradually, and for days
the setter betrayed the customary signs of incipient madness.
Had he been tied up even when the malady was fully established, no mischief might have resulted. But until his violence
became frightful, he was actually permitted to run about the
house, and got access to the kennel, while the boy was carrying
food to his charge.

" The escape of the servants was miraculous. The day
only before my arrival, the dog, in a paroxysm of suffering,
had thrown himself across the fire-place. ' Come away from
that, Biddy,' said the old cook, with perfect *nonchalance*, to
her attendant : ' *Don't ye see the dog is mad ?*' and continued
some culinary operation, in which, at a distant corner of the
kitchen, she was engaged. The boy's preservation was unaccountable. The poor lad made many unavailing efforts to
part the dogs when fighting in the kennel, and prevent the
setters from being bitten. In this perilous attempt his
clothes were literally torn to ribbons ; but, fortunately for
himself, there was not a scratch visible on his skin."

## CHAPTER XVIII.

Preparations for visiting Achil—Embarkation and passage to Dugurth—
Fishing—Sea-fowl shooting—Meeting the lugger—Picturesque appearance of the vessel—Our landing—Coast-guard watch-house—·
Slieve More—Grouse scarce—Rabit-shooting—Interior of the watch-
house — Culinary proceedings — The Dutchman—Morning, and a
headache—A sea-bath—The eagle's aërie—Curious anecdote of these
birds — Grouse-shooting — Demolition of a pack — Rock-fishing—
Dangerous employment—Fatal accident—John Dory—A temperate
evening.

For three days it has continued raining and blowing
violently. We fortunately abandoned the mountain-hut, on
noticing the unpromising state of the weather, before the
flood rose to a height aspect would have insulated us in the
hills. We have determined on an excursion into Achil,
and wait impatiently until the wind and clouds give some
indications of amendment. The moon enters her second
quarter to-night, and we trust her ladyship's influence may
mitigate the unusual severity of the weather.

This morning my servant's report was favourable; the sky
looked settled, the wind blew from the north-west, and old
Antony was satisfied with the prognostics. My cousin was
already a-foot, and his voice at my window loudly summoned
me to "turn-out." I opened the curtains—the sun was
shining, as if he intended to keep a fair face throughout the
day, and there was a cheerful bustle in front of the Lodge
which gave "note of preparation." The main-sail of the
hooker was already *chalk up* and shivering in the morning
breeze; and the boatmen, sitting on the grass before the
window, were preparing lines and baiting spillets. The piper
looked on, stretching one arm lazily out, while with the
other he hitched up the waistband of his *unmentionables;*
and frequent visits of the dog-boy to the kennel, showed
that both bipeds and quadrupeds would be shortly in requisition. Hammocks, hampers, and gun-cases, were subsequently
embarked, and about eight o'clock we had finished our
*déjeuner* and committed our persons and fortunes to the
waves.

Never was there a lovelier day or wilder scenery; after
we had cleared the river and opened the bay, a view of

surpassing grandeur was presented. We were surrounded on every side by an amphitheatre of bold and endless hills, except where the opening to the Atlantic showed us the dark waters of a boundless ocean—the surface was clear and undisturbed—and the light breeze rippled the long and measured undulations from the sea, and bore us gently towards the island. The bay was filled with mackerel, and consequently it was crowded with sea-fowl. In clamorous groups the gulls were darting on the fish below, and an endless variety of puffins and cormorants were incessant in pursuit of the smaller fry, which had attracted the shoals of mackerel from the deep. But the wind was too scanty, and the hooker's sailing not sufficiently fast, to allow us to kill fish in any quantity. We occasionally, however, caught a mackerel, and shot among a number of water-fowls a beautiful specimen of the sea-hawk, which I shall endeavour to preserve.*

We had gradually neared Dugurth, which is the only spot on which for many miles a boat, even in moderate weather, can safely effect a landing, when a galley stood out of Elly bay and bore down upon us. Our courses nearly crossed : they were running off the wind, we close-hauled as possible. Nothing could be more picturesque than the light and elegant appearance of this "fairy frigate." At a little distance she seemed a cloud of canvass flitting across the sea, for the long low hull was not visible until her close approach revealed it. Her large lugs and topsails where of the whitest duck, and as all her sails *drew*, light as the breeze was, she

---

* Large birds should be carefully skinned, the head, tail, and feet, left entire ; the skin may then be either put into a vessel of spirits, or rubbed well on the inside with the following mixture :—One pound of salt, four ounces of alum, and two ounces of pepper, pounded together. Small birds may be thus treated. Take out the entrails, open a passage to the brain, which should be scooped out through the mouth, introduce into the cavities of the skull, and the whole body, some of the above mixture, putting it also through the gullet and entire length of the neck. Hang the bird in a cool airy place, first by the feet, that the body may be impregnated by the salt, and afterwards by a thread through the under mandible of the bill, till it appears to be sweet, then expose it in the sun, or near a fire ; after it is well dried, clean out what remains loose of the mixture, and fill the cavity of the body with wool, oakum, or any soft substance.

passed us with the velocity of a race-horse. The airy motion of this "light shalloop" as she glided through the water, might to the fancy of a poet, present a similitude of that imaginary bark, in which the spirits of departed mariners are seen flitting over the dark billows beneath which their bodies rest.

Having weathered the Ridge Point, we made a signal for a rowing-boat, and one immediately came off. Our boatmen, having ascertained by their landmarks that they were upon clean ground, prepared to shoot their spillets. We left them, taking with us our dogs and attendants, and landed on a small sandy beach.

Having established our head-quarters in the watch-house of the coast-guard, and procured an adjoining cabin for the suite, we set out to look for grouse, taking a westerly direction along the base of Slieve More. Deceived by the false report of the villagers, we found the beat we had chosen neither a pleasant nor productive one. The heath was short and withered, the side of the mountain unsheltered, and exposed to the severe and almost eternal west wind : and, with the exception of a very few banks beside the water-courses, and one or two natural ravines, there was not a spot in which a grouse could shelter. In these hollows we generally found a *stager*,* and in one rugged dell shot three old cocks. Contrary to their general caution they stood the dogs well, or, from the short cover and stunted heath, had the weather been wet and the birds wary, it would have been almost impossible to have approached them.† The peasants, while looking after cattle and cutting peats upon the

---

* An old cock grouse which has not paired.

† Against running after grouse I uplift my voice. If they are wild, and will not stand or sit, a commonplace occurrence in wet cold weather, I would recommend gentlemen to remain at home. If circumstances bring them to the moors, or they are particularly solicited (as I have often been) to procure birds, let them depend on *close-marking*, tie up every dog but the steadiest one, and quietly, patiently, and silently endeavour to come within range of their object. If the bird moves, then to *out-flank* him is the best chance. Take a considerable circuit, and the more apparent carelessness you show in striving to close with a wild grouse, the more likely you will be to succeed. If the bird observes any hurry in the approach of the shooter, he will take alarm instantly, and an immediate flight will shew that he has been perfectly on the *qui vive.*

hill, had frequently disturbed those solitary birds, and concluded from meeting them so often, that there must be some packs convenient.

Too late we found out our error; it was four o'clock, and we determined to abandon the heath for the day; and, having from a high ground examined the interior of the island, we arranged to-morrow's beat accordingly.

Quitting the hill, we walked for a mile along the beach to some bent banks, where we were told that rabbits were abundant. In an hour we shot eight pair, and two couple of whimbrels; and perceiving that the hooker had anchored off the landing-place, we gave up shooting and returned to the watch-house.

In our absence the servants had been active; they slung our hammocks, and made the necessary preparations for cooking dinner. The chief officer of the coast-guard kindly gave us his own apartment. His little cabin was crowded with every necessary requisite for one so far removed from the civilized portion of mankind, and it was amusing to remark the ingenuity with which the occupier had arranged his numerous goods and chattels; nothing could exceed the cleanliness of his cottage, and it formed a striking contrast to the filth and misery of the surrounding hovels.

The boatmen were just landing in their punt, and we descended to the beach to ascertain what addition to our *cuisine* the spillets had afforded. They produced a pair of fine soles, and a score of large plaice. These, with the mackerel taken in the morning, supplied the fish department admirably. Our purveyor had purchased a *Keim sheep*;* and at six o'clock we went to dinner. Nothing could be more delicious than our fare;—fish transferred from the sea to the kettle, and diminutive mutton, whose only fault was excessive fatness. We had a grouse, too, one of our stagers, but it was coarse and flavourless; and if toughness be a test of years, I should set him down as coeval with Saint Patrick.

The host joined us after dinner, and presented us with a bottle of genuine Inniskea. If such be the customary produce

* Keim is a mountain district of Achil, celebrated for the flavour and fatness of its sheep.

of their stills, those gifted islanders are worthy of being canonized. Although our host's flask was a true Hollander, having an amplitude of bottom that would have put two degenerate wine-bottles to the blush, I regret to say such unyielding thirst beset us, that before any of the company sought a hammock, the honest Dutchman was left without a drop!

We were astir betimes next morning. It was an excellent shooting-day; a brisk breeze had sprung up with the first of flood, and the fog rising gradually up the mountain-side, cleared the summit of Slieve More, leaving its rugged pinnacle—a disordered mass of shivered granite—sparkling in the sunshine. Our dogs were in beautiful condition; and we were gratified to hear from a water-guard patrol, that, but an hour before, he had sprung a strong pack of birds on our purposed beat.

But, alas! the departed Dutchman had left us certain twinges in the head to make us recollect him, and we felt a nervous sensibility that was anything but favourable to good shooting. An immersion in the sea was recommended as a certain remedy, and our host conducted us to a rock, from which we could plunge into water four fathoms deep, and yet clear enough to enable us to observe the shells and pebbles at the bottom. We enjoyed a delightful ablution, returned *new men* to the watch-house, and, like giants refreshed, prepared for a good day's fag.

So salutary proved our bath, that we breakfasted as if we had never drained a Dutchman in our lives. The dogs were duly coupled, and sundry disengaged gentlemen of the village, whom we found lounging at the door, were being invested with shot and game bags, when, roused by an exclamation of the keeper, we witnessed a curious scene.

In a huge and inaccessible crag, on the east side of Slieve More, and immediately above the coast-guard station, the eagles had formed an aërie;—a fissure in the cliffs beyond the possibility of being disturbed by the approach of man, afforded these birds for many years a secure retreat. Here, annually, they produced their offspring, to the sad annoyance of the islanders, and more particularly the villagers of Dugurth. This morning they had descended from their rocky habitation, accompanied by two eaglets, evidently to teach their young to stoop and lift their prey.* The old birds tore up turfs from the mountain side, rose high in the air, and dropped them. The eaglets, in turn, stooped, and took them up again. This was frequently repeated, and the course of instruction having lasted half-an-hour, the eagles mounted to their aërie, and, leaving their progeny safely in the nest, sailed off upon the rising breeze to provide for the evening meal. We viewed the proceedings of this predatory family through the telescope of the coast-guard, who gave us many curious anecdotes of those daring and destructive birds.

We took an opposite course to the barren beat we had yesterday pursued. The bogs were intersected by several mountain-streams, whose dry and heathy banks offered excellent feeding and shelter for grouse. Our success, however, was very indifferent to what we had anticipated, from the promising appearance of the ground, and we had spent an hour, hunting with two brace of prime dogs, before we saw a bird. We met numerous indications of a strong pack having recently visited the river, and left no place untried which birds might be expected to frequent. At last, we began to imagine that the eagles had been here before us, when at some distance a young setter dropped on a heathy brow that overhung the rivulet. We were advancing, but the pack, alarmed by the sudden appearance of the dog above them, took wing, and we had to content ourselves with reckoning them, as they got up bird by bird. We counted nineteen, and concluded that two broods had packed accidentally.† They all pitched in a scattered manner on the side of a neighbouring eminence, and having marked them carefully down, we took up one brace of dogs, and with the other proceeded quietly to work. I never in my sporting experience saw a pack disposed of in better style. The dogs picked up the broken birds immediately, and with one miss (mine was the deed!) we brought nine brace

* " The story of the eagle brought to the ground, after a severe conflict with a cat, which it had seized and taken up into the air with its talons, is very remarkable. Mr. Barber, who was an eye-witness of the fact, made a drawing of it, which he afterwards engraved."—*Bewick.*

† I have never known red grouse flock in Ireland. Excepting an accidental junction of two broods, I have not met with grouse in any considerable number. Broods will occasionally pack together, but it is not a commom occurrence.

to bag. The sole survivor probably *roaded off* during the
slaughter, or threw himself into a hole in the heath, for we
could not make him out.

From our opening essay, we reckoned that this would prove
an exterminating day ; but with the destruction of this pack
our sport might be said to cease. For hours we traversed hills
and crossed moors, meeting but one weak brood and a few
*stagers.* We did find another brood, but the poults were
scarcely able to leave the ground, and consequently were too
weak for shooting. From their appearance, we concluded
them to be a second progeny of birds, who had lost their first
eggs by robbery or vermin. We met, however, a number of
hares, and shot seven. These, with thirteen brace of grouse,
filled the game bags.

Our course homewards lay along the base of Slieve More.
The evening was calm and sultry, and a number of men and
women of all ages were seated on the rocks fishing for gunners,* or gaffing the horse-mackerel, which were seen in
numbers on the surface of the water.

This rock-fishing is more dangerous than productive, and
many lives have been lost in pursuing it. Descending the
precipices to reach the water's edge is attended with imminent
risk : and as sudden and terrible swells come in frequently and
unexpectedly from the Atlantic, many fishers have been swept
off the rocks, and perished. Another perilous occupation of
the female peasants is what they term " picking cranagh."
This sea-weed, which forms a favourite esculent of the
islanders, grows on the rocks that are but occasionally
covered by the sea. Exposure to sudden swells from the
ocean attends those who search for it, and loss of life has too
often occurred.

---

* The *gunner* is the common name given to the *sea-bream* by the
fishermen of the western coast. They are found near the shore, in from
five to fifteen fathom water, where the bottom is foul and rocky. The
gunners are pretty, but insipid fish, and in variety of colour differ from
each other more than any species of the finny tribe I have met with. In
size, they seldom exceed three or four pounds : but from the avidity with
hich they bite, they afford excellent amusement when the breeze is not
sufficiently stiff to allow a take of mackerel and coal-fish. The bait
generally used for gunners, is a small crab, broken, and bound about the
hook with a thread ; and two hooks affixed to a trap-stick, with a light
leaden plummet, comprise the simple apparatus requisite for this kind of
sea fishing.

One accident, which happened not long since, was truly melancholy. A woman, the mother of several helpless children, and who but a month before had given birth to twins, perished in the sight of her family. No relief in such cases can be given : the reflux of these mountainous waves bears the victims away, and, with rare exceptions, the bodies are never found, as they are either borne out to sea, or entombed in one of the many deep caverns with which the bases of these fearful precipices are perforated.

We reached home at seven, made a hasty toilet, and dined sumptuously from mountain mutton and a fine *John Dory*, which the priest had sent us in our absence. Determined to eschew temptation, we avoided engaging a fresh Dutchman, which our host pressed upon us, and put in a quiet evening. After smoking a cigar, and discussing its necessary association of *schnaps* and water, we turned into our hammocks in such grave and philosophic moderation, as might have claimed the approbation of Sir Humphry, and entitled us to a place of honour in any Temperance Society in Great Britain.

## CHAPTER XIX.

From the scarcity of grouse in Achil, we altered our original plans, and decided upon sending our dogs back to the Lodge by a rowing-boat, and going in the hooker to visit the island of Inniskea.

After breakfast we proceeded to embark our personals ; and having despatched our heavy luggage by the attendants, whom we ordered home, we ascended the hill, (while the crew were clearing and baiting their spillets,) in the vague hope of getting a shot at those predatory birds, of whose spoliations we had heard so much on the preceding evening.

On reaching the bottom of the rock in whose face the aërie stands, we discovered that the old birds were absent; and as the nest was formed in a deep fissure, we could not ascertain its situation exactly. But that the eagles' dwelling was above us was evident enough : the base of the cliff was strewn with bones and feathers, and the accumulation of both was extraordinary. The bones of rabbits, hares, and domestic fowls, were most numerous ; but those of smaller game, and various sorts of fish, were visible among the heap.

Many attempts are annually made to destroy this predatory family ; but it is impossible to rob the nest. Situated two hundred feet above the base of the rock, it is, of course, unapproachable from below; and as the cliffs beetle over it frightfully, to assail it from above would be a hazardous essay. An enterprising peasant some years since was let down by a rope and basket; but he was fiercely attacked by the old birds, and the basket nearly overturned. Fortunately, the cord was strong, and had sufficient length to allow his being lowered rapidly, or he would have undoubtedly sustained some bodily injury from the wings and talons of those enraged and savage birds.*

* The following interesting anecdote is well authenticated : " Two eagles, in the wildest part of a neighbouring county, had for some time depredated on the neighbourhood, and bore away lambs, kids, &c., for the sustenance of their young. Some peasants determined, if possible, to obtain the young birds ; and ascended the mountains, but found that the nest was in a part of the perpendicular rock, near one hundred feet below the summit, and about three hundred above the sea, which, with terrific appearances, dashed against its base. They had provided themselves with ropes, and a lad, armed with a cimetar, was by this means lowered by the rest. He arrived in safety at the nest, where, as he expected, he was attacked with infinite fury by one of the old eagles, at which he made a stroke with his sword, that nearly cut asunder the rope by which he was suspended. Fortunately, one strand of it remained. He described his state to his comrades, waiting in horrible expectation that the division of the cord would precipitate him to the bottom ; but though he might have been to die by a rope, it was not in this manner. He was cautiously and safely hauled up ; when it was found that his hair, which a quarter of an hour before had been of a dark auburn, had in that short period become perfectly white."

The village of Dugurth suffers heavily from its unfortunate proximity to the aërie. When the wind blows from a favourable point, the eagle in the grey of morning sweeps through the cabins, and never fails in carrying off some prey.

To black fowls, eagles appear particularly attached; and the villagers avoid as much as possible rearing birds of that colour.

A few days before our arrival, one of the coast-guard, alarmed by the cries of a boy, rushed from the watch-house: the eagle had taken up a black hen, and as he passed within a few yards, the man flung his cap at him. The eagle dropped the bird; it was quite dead, however, the talons having shattered the back-bone. The villagers say (with what truth I know not) that turkeys are never taken.

That the eagle is extremely destructive to fish, and particularly so to salmon, many circumstances would prove. They are constantly discovered watching the fords in the spawning season, and are seen to seize and carry off the fish. One curious anecdote I heard from my friend the priest. Some years since, a herdsman, on a very sultry day in July, while looking for a missing sheep, observed an eagle posted on a bank that overhung a pool. Presently the bird stooped and

seized a salmon, and a violent struggle ensued. When the herd reached the spot, he found the eagle pulled under water by the strength of the fish, and the calmness of the day, joined to drenched plumage, rendered him unable to extricate himself. With a stone, the peasant broke the eagle's pinion, and actually secured the spoiler and his victim, for he found the salmon dying in his grasp.

When shooting on Lord Sligo's mountains, near the Killeries, I heard many particulars of the eagle's habits and history, from a grey-haired peasant, who had passed a long life in these wilds. The scarcity of hares, which here were once abundant, he attributed to the rapacity of those birds; and he affirmed that, when in pursuit of these animals, the eagle evinced a degree of intelligence that appeared extra-ordinary. They coursed the hares, he said, with great judgment and certain success; one bird was the active follower, while another remained in reserve, at the distance of forty or fifty yards. If the hare, by a sudden turn, freed herself from her most pressing enemy, the second bird instantly took up the chase, and thus prevented the victim from having a moment's respite.

He had remarked the eagles, also, while they were engaged in fishing. They chose a small ford upon the rivulet which connects Glencullen with Glandullah, and, posted on either side, waited patiently for the salmon to pass over. Their watch was never fruitless; and many a salmon, in its transit from the sea to the lake, was transferred from his native element to the wild aërie in the Alpine cliff, that beetles over the romantic waters of Glencullen.

Nor is it to birds of prey alone that the extreme scarcity of game upon this island may be attributed. Foxes are found here in numbers that appear incredible. The sides of Slieve More, in places formed of masses of disrupted rock, afford numerous and inaccessible burrows to those mischievous animals; and the sand-banks, stocked with rabbits, offer them an easy and certain means of subsistence. Hence, their annual increase is wonderful; and the numbers on the island may be estimated from this simple fact, that one of the coast-guard, who happened to have a couple of good terriers, destroyed, in the space of a season, eighteen full-grown foxes.*

* Dr. Johnson, in his Tour to the Hebrides, remarks, "To check the ravages of the foxes in the Isle of Sky, the inhabitants set a price upon their heads, which, as the number diminished, has been gradually

The multitude of lambs lost by these depredators, has nearly deterred the islanders from keeping ewes; and there is not a spot in Great Britain so persecuted by winged and footed vermin as this wild district. Of smaller birds of prey, there is a plentiful variety; but the devastations of the greater tribe cause their minor larcenies to be unnoticed.

With a light leading breeze, we stood across the bay, passed the Island of Devilawn, and, running through a sound, which separates Tarmon from Inniskea, came to at the distance of a quarter of a mile from the landing-place. It was low water, and the boats were all hauled up upon the beach. Even in the calmest weather, the greatest caution is requisite to protect them from the heavy and sudden swells that eternally break on this wild coast; and, if left within the reach of the surf, they are frequently stove before the careless crew are aware of danger. Anxious to land, we fired a gun, and, being upon an excellent bank for spillet-fishing, the boatmen adjusted their buoys, and commenced throwing their lines overboard.

I was watching the progress made by a dozen of the islanders to launch a row-boat to the water, when suddenly, from beneath the opposite cliff, a floating substance appeared to issue from the side of the precipice. We had neared the shore considerably, and the object, of which I had previously but an indistinct view, was now more clearly seen. It was a woman sitting in a curragh, fishing for codling and gunners. Startled by the discharge of the musket, she pulled a short distance from the cliffs, and then lay-to upon her paddles, watching the hooker as she shot the spillets.

" These lazy lubbers will be half an hour getting that heavy row-boat across the sand-ridge," said my kinsman. " Hail the curragh, Pattigo, and let us get ashore."

To the shout of the skipper, a " cead fealtagh," was returned; the paddles dipped in the water, the light curragh skimmed over the surface like a sea-bird, and in a few minutes the female and her frail bark were rocking beneath the counter of the sailing-boat.

raised, from three shillings and sixpence to a guinea; a sum so great in this part of the world," adds the Doctor, " that in a short time Sky may be as free from foxes as England from wolves." The fund for these rewards is a tax of sixpence in the pound, imposed by the farmers on themselves, and said to be paid with great willingness.

I shuddered as I looked over the hooker's side at this crazy vehicle; it was but a few slight hoops, secured together by cords, and overlaid by a covering of canvass, rendered waterproof by a coating of tar and tallow. The machine was so unsubstantial, that a schoolboy could carry it easily upon his shoulders. Nor was its fragility alone that which rendered this bark so perilous; from its peculiar construction, it scarcely rested on the surface of the sea; and, consequently, the least change of position in the occupant, would inevitably capsize it; and yet in this frail vessel the young islander sat in perfect security, a couple of hand-lines coiled at her feet, and the bottom of the curragh overspread with the produce of her fishery. Without the romance of Scott's beautiful boatwoman, there was something more than interesting in the air and look of this wild female. Free from that timidity which might be expected in the inhabitant of a remote coast, on her first introduction to strangers of a different grade in society, she laughed and jested with the boatmen; and the play of her merry hazel eye, and the smile which disclosed a row of pure and even teeth, had really more in them to captivate, than the cold and regular charms of many a high-born beauty.

"We must land singly," said my cousin; "for your curragh is but a crank concern. Mind how you step in, Frank." But I had already determined against an embarkation, and accordingly declined the honour of being first adventurer. My timidity only excited the mirth of the sea-nymph; and, unwilling to be laughed at by a woman, I took courage, and cautiously committed my person to the skiff; a change of position was of course necessary on the lady's part, and this she managed with such adroitness, that the equilibrium of the coracle was undisturbed. In a moment, her sculls were flashing in the waters, and we speedily reached the strand.

The rowing-boat was now afloat, and pulling to the hooker to bring off my kinsman. My sea-nymph tossed her fish and paddles to a little boy, who was expecting her, received with a low curtsey the silver I presented as my passage-money, and, having returned her small purse to her bosom, she threw the curragh across her back, and left me, invoking "God to bless my honour."

The boat returned my cousin and our guns; and while the dinner requisites were being brought ashore, we strolled towards the side of a hill, where we observed a number of rabbits at play. They were very numerous, and exhibited a greater variety than those of the other warrens that I had as yet visited. We selected some of the gayest colour for our practice, and whiled an hour away, until a summons from the cook recalled us to the village.

The spillets had provided us sumptuously with flat-fish, and a present of shrimps and lobsters completed our *cuisine.* The best house in the island had offered us its accommodation, and there was an appearance of comfort and rustic opulence in the furniture, that we had not anticipated when we landed.

There are numerous chances and godsends incident to these islands, which the other lines of sea-coast seldom obtain. Frequent and valuable wrecks furnish the inhabitants with many articles of domestic utility. The drift timber from the Atlantic gives them an abundant supply for the building and repairs of boats and houses ; and immense quantities of sea-fowl feathers are annually collected upon the Black Rock, which is contiguous to Inniskea. The island affords excellent pasturage for sheep; and thus timber, feathers, and wool, enable the inhabitants to have domestic comforts in abundance. In winter, the take of cod, hake, and ling, is inexhaustible ; peats are excellent and plenty, and food and fuel are consequently never scarce in Inniskea.

These are, doubtless, great advantages over the interior districts, but they are barely necessary to compensate the other local inconveniences. Throughout the greater portion of the winter, all communication with the main is interrupted. The sick must die without relief, and the sinner pass to his account without the consolations of religion. Should anything beyond the produce of the island be requisite in the stormy months, it must be procured with imminent danger; and constant loss of life and property, forms the unhappy theme of the tales and traditions of this insulated people.

A calm and misty twilight had fallen on Slieve More, and abridged the almost boundless range of ocean, over which the eye passed when we first landed. At a little distance the village girls were milking, carolling those melancholy ditties to which the Irish are so partial. I strolled among the rocks, and chose the narrow path, which the full tide left between its margin and the cliffs. The moon was rising now in exquisite beauty—the water was rippling to the rocks—one

long and wavy line of molten silver undulated across the
surface of the sea—and there were wild cliffs and bolder
headlands in glorious relief. No scene on earth could be more
peaceful or romantic.

I was indulging in delicious reverie, when something like a
bird flitted hastily by—again, and there was a heavy plump in
the water. I looked up,—a wild unearthly looking creature
stood on the cliff above, in the very act of launching a huge
stone at me! Just then a female figure rose beside him, and
with threats and blows drove him from the rock. It was my
fair friend of the curragh, who seeing me take the lonely path
I did, hastened after to warn me of the danger. She told me
that the assailant was a dangerous lunatic; he was treacherous
beyond description, and his antipathy to women and strangers
was remarkable. Many accidents had occurred from his
savage disposition. He feared men and rarely attacked them;
but if he saw a female at a distance from the village, he would
lurk with malignant perseverance for hours behind a bank or
cliff to attack her unawares. Some of the island women had
narrowly escaped death from this truculent monster, and few
of the males but had at some time or other suffered injury
from his hands; a stone was his favourite missile, which he
threw with wonderful force and precision. To my inquiry
" Why this dangerous being was not removed to some
asylum?" my protectress replied with a smile, " He was but
a poor natural, after all; he was born in the island, and God
forbid that they should send him among strangers." On
conversing with my cousin afterwards, he told me that, in the
west of Ireland, the peasantry had a superstitious veneration
for idiots and madmen, and, like the Turks, believed that
insanity and inspiration were only synonymes.

The illicit whisky made in this island holds a first rank
in the estimation of the *poteein* fancier. The cause of its
superior excellency may arise from the insular situation of the
place, enabling the distiller to carry on his business leisurely,
and thus avoid the bad consequences attendant on hurrying
the process,—for to rapid and defective distillation may be
ascribed the burnt flavour, so common in whisky produced
within the range of the Revenue. The barley, also, grown in
this and the other adjacent islands, is excellent—and as the
spirit is drawn from a copper still, it has many advantages to
recommend it. The illicit apparatus in common use is, with

few exceptions, made of tin—the capture of a copper still, from the superior value of the metal, would be a serious loss, and consequently a cheaper substitute is resorted to.

*Here*, the still is considered a valuable heirloom in a family, and descends in due succession from father to son. When not in use, it is lowered by a rope into one of the deep caverns, with which the western face of the island abounds, and nothing but a treacherous disclosure by some secret enemy could enable the Revenue to discover the place where it is concealed, in any of the unfrequent visits they make to this remote spot.

That the attention of the Preventive officers is not more particularly turned to a place notorious for its inroads on the Revenue, may appear strange. In fact, this island enjoys a sort of prescriptive privilege to sin against the ordinances of the Excise. This indulgence arises, however, not from the apathy of the Revenue, but from natural causes which are easily explained. A boat may approach Inniskea in the full confidence of a settled calm, and before an hour a gale may come on, that will render any chance of leaving it impracticable, and weeks will elapse occasionally before an abatement of the storm would allow the imprisoned stranger to quit those dangerous shores. Hence, in his professional avocations, the priest is obliged to watch the weather carefully before he ventures to visit Inniskea—and it has not unfrequently occurred, that the rites of religion have been interrupted, and the celebrant obliged to embark at a moment's notice, to avoid the consequences of being caught by a coming gale. The islanders, from constant observation of the phenomena of sea and sky, generally foresee the storm before it blows; but even the oldest and most skilful inhabitant will frequently be surprised by an unexpected tempest.

There are no people on earth more punctilious in the interment of the dead, than the peasantry of this remote district. A strange and unaccountable custom exists of burying different families, resident on the main, in island cemeteries, and great difficulty, and oftentimes imminent peril, attends the conveyance of a corpse to its insulated resting-place. No inducement will make those wild people inter a body apart from the tomb of its fathers, and if a boat will live, the corpse will be transported to the family tomb. At times the weather renders this impracticable, but the

deceased is kept for many days unburied in the hope that the
storm may subside ; and only when frail mortality evinces
unequivocal tokens of decay, will the relatives consent to unite
its dust with the ashes of a stranger.

It is asserted, but with what truth I cannot pretend to state,
that the inhabitants of Inniskea are prone to litigation, and a
curious legend of a lawsuit is told upon the main, illustrative
of this their quarrelsome disposition.   A century ago, two
persons were remarkable here for superior opulence, and had
become the envy and wonder of their poorer neighbours.
Their wealth consisted of a flock of sheep, when, unfortunately,
some trifling dispute occurring between them, a dissolution of
partnership was resolved upon.    To divide the flock, one
would suppose, would not be difficult, and they proceeded to
partition the property accordingly.    They possessed one
hundred and one sheep ; fifty fell to each proprietor, but the
odd one—how was it to be disposed of ?   Neither would part
with his moiety to the other, and after a long and angry
negotiation, the animal was left in common property between
them.    Although the season had not come round when sheep
are usually shorn, one of the proprietors, requiring wool for a
pair of stockings, proposed that the fleece should be taken off.
This was resisted by his co-partner, and the point was finally
settled by shearing one side of the animal.    Only a few days
after, the sheep was found dead in a deep ditch ; one party
ascribed the accident to the cold feelings of the animal having
urged him to seek a shelter in the fatal trench ; while the
other contended, that the wool remaining upon one side had
caused the wether to lose its equilibrium, and thus the melancholy catastrophe was occasioned.    The parties went to law
directly, and the expenses of the suit actually devoured the
produce of the entire flock, and reduced both to a state
of utter beggary.    Their descendants are pointed out to
this day as being the poorest of the community, and litigants
are frequently warned to avoid the fate of  " *Malley and
Malone.*"

Notwithstanding the uncertainty of weather in Inniskea is
proverbial, we had no reason to complain.    The sun rose
gloriously from the ocean—every cloud vanished from the
rocky pinnacle of Slieve More — a stiff breeze from the
north-west blew steadily, and by nine o'clock we had embarked our goods and persons ; and with as much wind as the

hooker could carry her three sails to, we ran through the Sound of Devilawn, and bade adieu to this interesting and hospitable island.

## CHAPTER XX.

Signs of Fish—Mackerel—Spillet-fishing—Seal and Mermaids—Anecdote —The Bull's Mouth—Preservation of a Ship—The Fox and Cruiser— The Lodge in a consternation—Arrival—The Colonel's Portmanteau— Robbing, and its consequences.

It was evident that the bay was full of mackerel. In every direction, and as far as the eye could range, gulls and puffins were collected, and, to judge by their activity and clamour, there appeared ample employment for them among the fry beneath. We immediately bore away for the place where these birds were most numerously congregated, and the lines were scarcely overboard when we found ourselves in the centre of a shoal of mackerel.

The hooker, however, had too much way. We lowered the foresail, double-reefed the mainsail, and then went steadily to work. Directed by the movements of the birds, we followed the mackerel, tacking or wearing the boat occasionally, when we found that we had overrun the shoal. For two hours we killed those beautiful fish, as fast as the baits could be renewed and the lines hauled in; and when we left off fishing, actually wearied with sport, we found that we had taken above five hundred, including a number of the coarser species, known on this coast by the name of *Horse Mackerel*.

There is not on sea or river, always excepting angling for salmon, any sport comparable to this delightful amusement. Spillet and long-line fishing are generally tedious and uninteresting; and, unless` the fish take freely, it is even with moderate success a tame and spiritless employment. How different is mackerel fishing!—full of life and bustle, every thing about it is animated and exhilarating; a brisk breeze, a fair sky, the boat in quick and constant motion,—all is calculated to interest and excite. But hanging for hours above a spillet, or enduring the drudgery of lowering and

I

hauling in an almost interminable length of line over the side of a motionless boat, is an abomination. Like *mud-shooting*, this is only work for a peasant, and should accordingly be excluded from the list of gentlemanly pursuits, and consigned entirely to those with whom fishing is a trade; and profit, not pleasure, the object of their piscatory occupations. He who has experienced the glorious sensations of sailing on the western ocean, a bright autumnal sky above, a deep green lucid swell around, a steady breeze, and as much of it as the hooker can *stand up* to, will estimate the exquisite enjoyment our morning's mackerel-fishing afforded.

In following the shoal, we had crossed the bay, and got under the Achil shore. Having made sail again, we stretched over towards the Bull's Mouth, attracted by an immense play of sea-fowls. It was nearly low water, and while running past Innisbiggle, we observed several seals basking on the rocks. One was so curiously couched among the seaweed, as to render its species a subject of doubt and discussion, until the close approach of the boat obliged it to quit the rock, and thus afford a distinct view, while, to use the skipper's phrase, it *wabbled* to the water. From the strange and undefined ideas the seal's first appearance occasioned, accustomed as we were to see the animal in its varied attitudes of action or repose, it is not surprising that numerous and ridiculous extravagances have had their origin in the Phocæ tribe being seen under accidental circumstances by the wild and credulous peasantry of this remote district. To these animals, the submarine beings, who have for ages delighted the lovers of the marvellous, may, without much difficulty, be traced; and many a wonder-stricken fisherman imagined himself watching the movements of a mermaid, while all the time he was only staring at a *sea-calf*.

A whimsical instance of the credulity of the peasantry was mentioned by my kinsman. Some years ago, a party engaged in a fishing excursion on the coast, came-to in Achil Sound, and, leaving the boat, took up their quarters for the night in the priest's house, which was situated in a neighbouring village. One of the company was hunch-backed, with a face of singular and grotesque expression. Having indulged gloriously over-night in the native beverage, which the honest priest most liberally supplied. the little gentleman found himself rather amiss in the morning, and determined to try what salutary effect the cool sea-breeze might have upon the fever warmth his nocturnal revelry had raised. He left the cabin accordingly,—and the early hour, with the islanders' celebrity for a simplicity of costume, induced him to postpone the business of the toilet to a more convenient season, and to sally forth in perfect dishabille. For a time he straggled along the shore, until reaching the point of land which forms the entrance of Achil Sound, he selected a smooth stone, and deposited his person among the rocks, to meditate the hour away, before whose expiry he could not expect that breakfast would be paraded in the cabin.

It was dead low-water. Half-a-dozen row-boats, bound for the fair of Newport, and filled with men and women, were rowing merrily to the Bull's Mouth, intending to enter it upon the first of flood. Having approached close to the spot where the little gentleman was ensconsed among the seaweed, up popped an *outré* countenance, surmounted by a scarlet nightcap! The effect was sudden, for till now a rock had concealed him from the boats. Instantly the women screamed, and the men betrayed unequivocal symptoms of dismay. But when the dwarf, remarking their alarm, skipped upon the stone, and uttered a wild unearthly yell which reverberated from rock to rock, the boats put about directly, and abandoned the fair of Newport, men and women, with one consent, made off for their respective homes as fast as four oars could carry them. The awful intelligence was promulgated with incredible rapidity through Erris and Ballycroy. The same *Leprehawn* who was seen *the year before the French,*\* had reappeared, to harbinger, no doubt, some local or national calamity. To this day, the credulity of the islanders has never been disabused, and Tom's uncouth face and scarlet nightcap is often fearfully expected to rise over the rocks by the belated fisherman, as he runs through its dangerous opening to shelter for the night in Achil Sound.

The Bull's Mouth is rarely entered but with flood-water, or

---

\* The landing of the French is a common epoch among the inhabitants of Ballycroy. Ask a peasant his age, and he will probably tell you, " he was born two or three years before or after *the French*."

a powerful leading wind ; and the southern outlet of the sound
at Achil Beg is similarly circumstanced. These straits are
deep and dangerous, for through them the waters which flow
from Blacksod and Clew Bay, and fill this extensive channel
and its surrounding estuaries, rush with amazing violence ;
and the rapidity with which the tides enter and recede is
frightful. The opposing currents flow nearly north and south,
and meet and separate at the ruins of an ancient salt-house.
Here, the old mountain-road terminated, and at the *Farsett*—as
the ford across the estuary is termed—the passenger can earliest
cross to the island from the mainland. Indeed, the intercourse
with Achil was in former days limited enough. Few persons,
except those engaged in smuggling, visited this insulated district ; and many an islander lived and died without having ever
seen a town.

The fishing-boats and hookers, whose easy draught of water
will permit it, naturally prefer a passage through the sound,
when voyaging from Erris to Clew Bay, rather than the longer
and more exposed course of rounding Achil Head. To effect
it, however, requires some skill, and a strict attention to the
tides. On the *Farsett*, the depth at high-water seldom exceeds
eight or nine feet : and as the flow and recession of the
opposing waters is astonishingly rapid, the boat must enter
upon one and retire upon the other. The passage, if effected,
is consequently but very short, and the sound may be cleared
in an hour, with the same wind that would occupy an entire
day, if Achil Head were doubled.

In bad weather, both entrances, however, are dangerous in
the extreme, and care and seamanship are necessary to pass
either with safety. The peasantry are habituated to this
voyage, and comparatively little 'risk ensues. Still many
accidents have occurred—small boats have foundered in the
attempt—and large hookers, when deeply laden, have perished
in the conflicting eddies which opposite winds and tides occasion. The most cautious boatmen are sometimes overtaken
by squalls from the surrounding hills—and night and drunkenness have, alas ! been more fatal than all besides.

Yet the Bull's Mouth, like the ordeal of mortal inquietude,
leads to its haven of rest. In a gale from the westward, when
the Atlantic tumbles with mountainous fury into Blacksod
Bay, the fishing-boat, once within the sound, finds smooth

and unbroken water. Hence, when the weather breaks, the hookers seek its shelter, there to wait until the storm moderates.

Nor is it to the fisherman alone that the Bull's Mouth has afforded shelter and protection. Not many years ago, a large American vessel was driven upon the coast by a continuance of westerly winds, and unable to work off, was fairly embayed within Blacksod. Shipwreck appeared inevitable—anchor after anchor was let go, but the tremendous swell from the ocean parted the cables, and the vessel drifted rapidly towards the shore. The wild and rock-bound coast to leeward terrified the crew, and, in despair, they committed themselves to their boat, abandoning the ship to her fate. A hooker's crew, which had been caught by the gale, witnessed the desertion of the vessel, and although boarding her was a service of danger, they determined to attempt her rescue. They succeeded, and the *derelict* bark was carried safely within the sound.

To the Bull's Mouth, also, one of his Majesty's cruisers was indebted for her deliverance. During the last American war, an enemy's schooner of formidable force dragooned the coast from Arran to the Stags of Broad Haven. She landed where she pleased, and amused herself by burning every coaster that was silly enough to leave her harbour. In Achil the *Fox* was quite at home,—the crew trafficked, danced, and drank among the islanders, with as much *sang-froid* as if Paul Jones had been commander. But this could not last for ever. Some heavy sloops and brigs were ordered from the southward, and the Fox was reluctantly obliged to disappear. A revenue cruiser, that had been long blockaded in Westport Bay, took heart and ventured out. The enemy was out of sight, and, with a clear sea, old Morris rounded Achil Head. When the scarecrow vanishes, it is marvellous how rapidly one's courage is rekindled ; and too late the Nepean discovered that the odds between herself and the privateer were not so desperate. In point of men and metal the Fox was indeed overwhelming, but still, steady discipline and close fighting might do wonders. Morning dawned—and its first light showed the infernal Fox but two short miles to *windward!* Away went the cutter, and away went the privateer. With singular audacity the Fox followed into the bay, came up hand-over-hand, and gained upon the cruiser, until the long *two-and-thirty*, which the

Yankee mounted amidships, began to throw its shot to a most alarming proximity. The Bull's Mouth was before, and a rakish schooner that, to use a fancy phrase, " would not be denied," was astern ;—there was no alternative, and for the first, the most probably the last time, the King's *bunting* sought safety within the sound of Achil. Finding her water lessen—for she had actually crossed the Ridge Point before she hauled her wind—the Fox abandoned the pursuit, and left the Irish coast for America, where she duly arrived, after a daring and destructive, but a very unprofitable cruise.

---

Safely landed at the Lodge,—but all is in an uproar! Colonel Dwyer, an honoured and expected visitor, has arrived in safety, but he comes *minus* his portmanteau, which some delinquent, neither having the fear of hanging or my kinsman's wrath before his eyes, abstracted from Andy Bawn, to whom its safe delivery was entrusted. Nothing can surpass the surprise and consternation this event occasions—the women are clamorous—the men curse fluently in Irish—and, from the vows of eternal vengeance which are uttered against the spoliator of the Colonel's wardrobe, I should imagine, in case of apprehension, that the ceremony of waiting till the next assizes will be dispensed with. Antony " remembers the country these seventy years : many a robbery happened in his time, but—God stand between him and evil!—to take a gentleman's property, and he coming to the master !—If it was a stranger, why there would be no great harm," &c. &c.

Fear and poteein disturb the concatenation of ideas, and Andy Bawn's is anything but a lucid narrative. There is a confused account of the Bridge of Ballyveeney, and a dark man, and the clicking of a gun-cock. Now it appears that Andy is at feud with a Mr. Burke, who finished a relative of his with a *turf-slane*,* and in consequence has deemed it advisable to take to the mountain until terms can be arranged with the widow. Meantime, being a gentleman of active disposition, he occupies his leisure hours upon the highway, and all parties are unanimous in saddling him with the spolia-tion of the portmanteau. I am inclined to suspect, that my kinsman hitherto sported *deaf-adder* to any rumour of Burke

---

* An implement used for cutting turf, and *heads* occasionally.

being concealed within his territory—but I think now, the sooner Mr. Burke levants the better. There is a settled gloom upon my cousin's brow, and yonder consultation with his foster-brother, my island friend, bodes the present proprietor of the portmanteau little good. To intercept a visitor's effects, was indeed to

> " Beard the lion in his den,
> The Douglas in his hall.—"

But dinner is announced.

---

I wish the value of the Colonel's assets could be ascertained, and that I dared liquidate the amount. An earthquake, I think, would not have created half the sensation. My kinsman is dreadfully irate—his feudal power is shaken to the centre, and either he or Mr. Burke must leave Ballycroy. It is quite evident that he tacitly permitted the outlaw to conceal himself in this neighbourhood, and considered that he existed but by his sufferance. There is a strange dash of barbarism among the old proprietors still. To hunt a felon down, who acknowledges the supremacy of the master, would be *infra dignita tem.* The good old system would then be at an end—and, in time, even a bailiff might pass what has been the *Ultima Thule* of the law, and *live.* My cousin is aware of this. He feels that the rights and immunities of his modern Alsatia must not be lightly compromised. His rent-roll may be small, but he can boast, as Dick Martin did of Connemara, that " here, thank God! the King's writ is not worth a halfpenny." Hence the impudence\* of Mr. Burke is intolerable. An embassy will be dispatched, and if the Colonel's wardrobe be not forthwith restored, with full satisfaction for the insult, I hold the value of the outlaw's life to be not worth a pin's fee.

---

\* I remember hearing this word used in a court of justice in a most curious sense. A man was on trial, capitally indicted for murder. The chief witness on his examination detailed the leading incidents—his being awakened by cries of help, rising, striking a light, opening his door, and finding a man dead upon the threshold. " And what did you do next, my friend?" interrogated the crown lawyer. " Why," replied the witness, with amazing *sang froid*, " I called out, ' Are any of ye there that kilt the boy? By J——s, I'll give a *thirteen* to him who'll tell me who it was that had the *impudence* to murder a man at my door!'"

Indeed the whole *esprit de corps* is up—the multitudinous idlers of the Lodge are concocting schemes of vengeance. The honour of the "ancient house" is at stake; and the very women are roused to action. Old Antony himself is not supine —he does not, like Diogenes at Sinope, contemplate the general activity with indifference : while all besides are turning the secular arm against the delinquent, the Otter-killer will call in the assistance of the Church, and, by the blessing of God, he will have Mr. Burke *cursed* in two chapels next Sunday, and in a style too, that he expects shall give universal satisfaction to all concerned.

Nor am I, though unassailed in dignity or effects, upon a bed of roses.   Who shall say where this business will terminate ?   We shall exchange deer-shooting for robber-hunting ; and night and the mountains being unfavourable to identity of the person, I may be shot by mistake for an outlaw, or find myself in some ravine, *tête-à-tête* with Mr. Burke !   I plead guilty to constitutional nervousness, and for the last hour my kinsman and his visiter have been seeking a parallel case in a number of outrages, that are quite sufficient to ruin a man's rest for the winter.   What memories they have !   There has not been a house robbed for the last century with whose localities they are not as well acquainted as the builder ; and in murder-cases, they display an anatomical experience that is surprising !  Hennessey, who seldom shows, has been eternally with us since the cloth was lifted, and having received his final instructions, (I hope,) has disappeared.   Lord ! the tall, gaunt, care-worn, homicidal look of the man, as with a double gun across his arm, and a case of pistols projecting from his coat-pockets, he took the wine his patron gave him ! but, "*chacun à son goût*,"—my kinsman would not lose him for a thousand, while his very look gives me the horrors !   Even the Piper appears to have caught the general infection : he has been lilting a full hour—not a jig or strathspey, but love-lorn ditties, and the most lamentable compositions that ever issued from the bag or chanter.

Would I were in England again ! for what is matrimony to manslaughter ?   I have been for a moment out to breathe the cool sea-breeze, and passing the window peeped into that *refugium peccatorum*, the kitchen.   The keeper is flinting a blunderbuss !  There is security in Terracina contrasted with this cabin, and the Abruzzi is a land of Goshen compared with the mountains of Ballycroy ! I wish I were in bed; and why there—to dream of everything felonious ! I may as well submit with Turkish endurance—it is the will of Allah. The Colonel replenishes the fire, apportioning turf and bog deal in such scientific proportion, that it is evident he is making himself up for a *wet evening*; and the cork our host is now extracting, will be merely *avant-courier* to three flasks which I see lurking in the cooper. Oh, that a deputation from the Temperance Society would drop in ! But why complain ?— 'tis useless. The Colonel has discharged a bumper to the speedy demolition of Mr. Burke ! Nor has he forgotten to replenish again. The man is honest—a person that one might safely drink with in the dark. He clears his throat, and that cough preliminary is the prologue of a story. I must, in common courtesy, be attentive. This long and steady pinch is alarming, and we are on the brink of some desperate detail !

## CHAPTER XXI.

### The Colonel's Story—The Night Attack.

" It is thirty-five years this very month, since I was quartered with my regiment in ——ford ; I recollect the time particularly, for I got my Company in the thirty-seventh on the same day that I received an invitation from a Mr. Morden, with whom I had formed a mail-coach acquaintance, to spend a week with him, and join his nephew in partridge-shooting. This gentleman's house was fourteen miles distant from the town, and situated in a very retired part of the country. It was a wild but beautiful residence, placed upon the extremity of a peninsula which jutted into an extensive lake. To a sportsman it offered all the inducements that shooting and fishing could afford. But it had others besides these ; no man lived better than Mr. Morden—and his daughter Emily, and an orphan cousin, who resided with her, were decidedly the finest women who had attended the last race-ball. No wonder then that I accepted the old gentleman's invitation willingly, and on the appointed day put myself into a post-chaise, and reached the place in time for dinner.

" The house was one of those old-fashioned, comfortable Irish lodges, which are now extinct, or only to be seen in ruins. It was a long low building, covered with an infinity of thatch, which bade defiance to rain, cold, and storm. The tall and narrow casements reached the ground, a handsome flower-knot extended in their front bounded by a holly hedge, and woodbine and other creepers festooned the windows with their leaves and berries. At some distance a well-stocked haggard peeped over a spacious range of offices ; the lawn was studded with sheep, which appeared overburdened with good condition ; and as I drove up the avenue, 1 passed a well-featured, well-clad simpleton, urging before him from a neighbouring stubble-field, a flock of turkeys as formidable for numbers as for size. In short, everything about the place bespoke the opulence and comfort of the proprietor.

" Mr. Morden was a clever and respectable man ; he was land-agent to several large estates—noted for plain and unpretending hospitality, punctuality in business, and a character of unusual determination.

" The old gentleman received me with friendly sincerity, and his handsome daughter added a warm welcome. They apologized for not having company to meet me, but 'two families which they had expected, had been detained by some unforeseen occurrences at home.' Dinner was shortly after served. Like the host, it was excellent without display—the wines were superior—and when the ladies left us, the claret went round the table merrily.

" ' We are in trouble here,' said Mr. Morden, addressing me, ' and you have come to a house of mourning. We have just suffered a serious, I may say irreparable loss, in the sudden death of two favourite dogs. They were of the genuine breed of Newfoundland, and for size, courage, and sagacity, unequalled. Poor Emily has cried incessantly since the accident.'

" ' Were they stolen ?'

" ' Oh, no ! I wish they were, for that would afford a hope that chance or money might recover them. No, Sir, they would not follow a stranger ; alas ! they died yesterday by poison. We unfortunately laid arsenic in a meal-loft to destroy rats—and yet how the poor animals could have got to it is a mystery ; the steward declares the key never left his possession. I would give a hundred guineas the meal

had been in the bottom of the lake. By Jove! no loss,
short of the death of a friend, could have given us all so much
uneasiness. They were my daughter's companions by day,
and my protectors at night. Heigh ho!—Come, Sir, pass the
wine.' Tears stood in the old gentleman's eyes as he spoke
of his unhappy favourites, and from the valuable properties of
the lost dogs, it was not surprising that their death occasioned
so much regret to the family.

" We joined the ladies in the drawing-room. After tea Mr.
Morden took a bedroom-candle, and apologised for retiring.
'Old habits best suit old people, Captain ; but I leave you
with the ladies, who will sit up till cock-crow, if you please :'
and bidding us a good night, he departed.

" ' Emily,' said young Morden, ' you are still thinking of
your favourites ; well, I will ride the country over, till I
find you a handsome dog. Julia, hand me that violin from
the piano, and Captain Dwyer will dance a reel with you and
Emily.'

" ' Heavens ! who is at the window ?' exclaimed Miss
Morden, suddenly ; ' it looked like that nasty beggarman
who has been haunting the house and grounds these three
days. Ah, Wolf and Sailor ! had you been living, that
vagabond would not have ventured here at this late hour.'
Henry Morden had left the room on hearing his cousin's
exclamation, but soon returned, assuring the lady that the
beggar was a creature of her imagination ; he had searched
the shrubbery and flower-garden, and no mendicant was to be
found in either.

" The alarm was speedily forgotten, and we danced reels
till supper was announced. The doors were locked, the windows fastened, the ladies wished us good night, and retired to
their respective chambers.

" Henry and I remained for some time in the eating-room ;
the clock struck twelve, and young Morden conducted me to
my apartment, and took his leave.

" I felt a strange disinclination to go to bed, and would
have given anything for a book. For temporary employment,
I unlocked my gun-case, put my fowling-piece together, and
examined whether my servant had sent all necessary apparatus
along with me. I opened the window-curtains. The moon—
a full bright harvest moon was shining gloriously on the lawn
and lake : I gazed on the sparkling surface of the waters till

I felt the chill of the night-breeze; then closing the shutters, reluctantly prepared to undress.

"I had thrown my coat and vest aside, when a distant crash was heard, and a fearful noise with oaths and screams succeeded. I rushed into the corridor, and encountered a terror-stricken maid-servant running from the extremity of the passage. Miss Morden next appeared; she was in complete dishabille, and had hastily thrown on a dressing-gown. 'Good God! Captain Dwyer, what has occurred?' A volley from without prevented my reply, and the crashing of the windows, as the glass was splintered by the bullets, made it unnecessary. 'The house is attacked,' she said; and then with amazing self-possession added, 'There are always loaded guns above the kitchen fire-place.' We both ran down the corridor, she to alarm her father, and I to procure a weapon; young Morden, armed with a sword, met us. 'The attack is upon the kitchen,' he said, hastily; 'it is our weakest point; this way, Captain,'—and we both entered it together.

"There was a bright fire burning on the hearth. The large window was shattered to pieces, and the idiot I had noticed on the lawn, was standing beside the ruined case-ment armed with a spit, making momentary passes at the breach, and swearing and bellowing frightfully. I leaped upon a table to seize two muskets which were suspended in the place Miss Morden had described. I handed one to Henry, when the fire blazed out suddenly, and discovered me to the banditti without. Instantly, three or four shots were discharged. I heard a bullet whistle past my head, and felt something strike my shoulders like a sharp cut from a whip, as a slug grazed me slightly—but having secured the gun I jumped from the table uninjured. We heard Mr. Morden in the passage—his manner was calm and collected, as he ordered the servant-men to the front of the house, and dispatched his daughter for ammunition.

"Meanwhile, a dropping fire continued from without— for from within no shot had been returned, as the robbers sheltered themselves effectually behind the angles of the offices and the piers of the gates. From some hurried words we overheard they were arranging a determined attack.

"'They will make a rush immediately,' said the elder Morden coolly, 'and here comes Emily in good time; don't

come in, love !'—and he took some forty or fifty cartridges
which she had brought in the skirt of her dressing-gownd.
Notwithstanding the peril of our situation, I could but not
gaze a moment on the white and statue-looking limbs of
this brave and beautiful girl. ' Go, love, tell John to bring
the Captain's gun-case from his chamber ; and do you,
Emily, watch from the end window, and if you perceive any
movement that side, apprize us of it here.—Now, my boys,
be cool—I'll give my best horse to him who shoots the first
man. You have a good supply of ammunition, could we
but coax the scoundrels from their shelter—and I'll try a
*ruse.'* The old gentleman took the idiot's spit, placed a
coat upon it, while Henry and I chose a position at either
side of the broken window. Mr. Morden raised the garment
to the breach ; it was indistinctly seen from without ; three
bullets perforated it, and it fell. ' He's down, by —— !'
roared a robber, exultingly. ' Now, Murphy, now's your
time ; smash in the door with the sledge !' Instantly a
huge ruffian sprang from behind a gable, and his rush was
so sudden that he struck twice with shattering force. We
heard the hinges give—we saw the door yielding—and at
that critical moment young Morden's gun missed fire !
' Curses light upon the hand that loaded it !' he cried as he
caught up an axe and placed himself determinately before
the door, which we expected to be momentarily driven in.
Murphy, perceiving the tremendous effects of his blows,
called to his comrades to ' *be ready.'* He stood about five
yards from me—the sledge was raised above his head—and
that blow would have shivered the door to atoms. I drew the
trigger—the charge, a heavy one of duck-shot, passed like a
six-pound bullet through the ruffian's body, and he dropped a
dead man upon the threshold. ' Captain Dwyer,' said Mr.
Morden, calmly, ' *the horse is yours !'*

" I had now received my own double gun, and gave the
musket I had used so successfully to Henry Morden. The
death of the ruffian with the sledge brought on a heavy fire
from his comrades. Between the volleys they summoned
us to surrender, with fearful denunciations of vengeance if
we resisted longer. We were within a few yards of each
other, and during the intervals of the firing, they poured
out threats, and we sent back defiance.—' Morden, you old
scoundrel !' exclaimed the captain of the gang, ' in five

minutes we'll have your heart's blood.' 'No,' was the calm reply, 'I'll live to see you arrayed in cap and halter.' ' Surrender, or we'll give no quarter.'—' Cowardly scoundrel ! come and try your hand at the sledge !' said the old gentleman, with a cold and sarcastic smile, as he turned his eye on me, where I was watching the door, with the confidence a man feels who has his own trustworthy weapon to depend upon.

" ' Morden ! we'll burn the house about ye.'—' Will you put the coal in the thatch, Bulger ?'—' Morden, you have a daughter !' and the ruffian pronounced a horrid threat. The old man shuddered, then in a low voice, tremulous with rage he muttered,—' Bulger, I'll spare five hundred pounds to hang you, and travel five hundred miles to see the sight.'

" ' The coal ! the coal !' shouted several voices, and unfortunately the scoundrels had procured one in the laundry. ' By heaven ! they will burn us out,' said Henry, in alarm. ' Never fear !' replied his cooler uncle ; ' the firing must have been heard across the lake, and we'll soon have aid sufficient.' But a circumstance occurred, almost miraculously, that averted the threatened danger. The moon became suddenly overcast —heavy rain-drops fell—and in an instant an overwhelming torrent burst from the clouds, rendering every attempt the robbers made to ignite the thatch abortive. ' Who dare doubt an overruling Providence ?' said the old gentleman, with enthusiasm : ' surely God is with us !'

" The storm which came to our relief appeared to dispirit our assailants, and their parley recommenced. ' Morden,' said the captain of the banditti, ' you have Lord ——'s rent in the house ; give us a thousand pounds, and we'll go off and leave you.'

" ' All I promise I'll perform" said the old gentleman, coldly. ' Bulger, for this night's work you have earned a halter, and I'll attend and see you hanged.'—' Dash in the door,' exclaimed the robber in a fury ; ' we'll have the old rogue's heart out !' A volley of stones rattled against the door, but produced no effect, and again the robber parleyed. ' Will you give us a hundred, Morden ?' ' Not a sixpence,' was the laconic answer. Once more stones were thrown, shots discharged, and threats of vengeance fulminated by the exasperated villains. At last, the demand was reduced to ' Twelve

guineas—a guinea for each man.' 'They'll be off immediately,'
said the old gentleman; 'they know assistance is at hand:
would that we could amuse them for a little longer!' But the
ruffians were already moving, and Miss Morden presently
announced that they were embarking, twelve in number, in a
boat. 'Now for a parting shot or two,' said Henry Morden.
We picked up a dozen cartridges, and sallied from the house
as the banditti were pulling hard across the lake. We opened
a quick and well-directed fire, which they feebly and without
effect replied to. While a musket-ball would reach them, we
plied them liberally with shot; and, as we learned afterwards,
mortally wounded one man, and slightly injured two others.
As we returned to the house, we met some fifty countrymen,
armed with all sorts of rustic weapons coming to our relief.
Without a moment's delay, we launched boats, and set off to
scour the country, and at noon, so prompt and vigorous had
been the pursuit, that six of the gang, including the wounded
robbers, were secured.

"We reached '*the Wilderness*' completely exhausted by the
exertions of the morning, and the fatigue of the preceding
night. We refreshed ourselves, and went to bed—but previous
to returning to my room, I visited the scene of action.
Another blow, even a very slight one, must have driven in the
door; and in the rush of twelve desperate ruffians, the chances
would have been fearfully against us. Murphy lay upon his
back—he was a disgusting object. The ground was saturated
with blood, for the charge of heavy shot made as large a
wound as a cannon-bullet would occasion. He was the
strongest brute I ever saw; not more than five feet eight
inches in height, but his limbs, body, and arms were a giant's;
he was a blacksmith,—a man of infamous character, and most
sanguinary disposition.

"Our escape from robbery was fortunate indeed; Mr.
Morden had seven thousand pounds that night in the lodge,
for he had just received the rents of two estates. It was
almost entirely paid in specie—and this was of course known,
and induced two desperate bands, who had kept the adjoining
counties in alarm since the rebellion was suppressed, to unite
for the purpose of robbing 'the Wilderness,' and securing this
immense booty.

"The body of the smith was sent away, and buried in the
jail-yard of the neighbouring town; and having brought the

battle to a close, I shall explain some matters connected with
this daring outrage.

" A man named Mitchell originated the intended robbery,
and arranged the method of attack.   He was a slight, low-
sized person, but his activity was amazing, and no attempt
was too hazardous for his desperate courage to undertake.
On the morning of his execution—(he, with the three others,
was hanged the subsequent assizes)—he gave us a cool detail
of his plans.

" The dogs were to be destroyed, and the premises recon-
noitred.   In the disguise of a beggar he effected both ; laid
meat prepared with arsenic for the poor animals ; then made
his way into the kitchen, and ascertained that the fastenings
of the back-door were defective.   He purposed surprising the
family at supper, or forcing an entrance when they were
asleep.   The first attempt he made at the drawing-room, but
quickly perceiving that he had been observed by Miss Morden,
he retired hastily.   A council was held by the robbers, and it
was fortunately determined to postpone the attack until the
family had gone to rest.

" Nothing could be bolder, or more likely to succeed, than
Mitchell's desperate resolution.   It was to leap feet foremost
through the window, and, armed with a dagger, to fight his
way, if opposed, and open the back door for his associates.
He made the attempt, and providential circumstances alone
prevented its being successful.   That very morning a small
iron bar had been placed across the window ; it caught the
robber in his leap, threw him back with violence, and the
noise, united to the outcries of the idiot, alarmed the family
instantly.

" Circumstances, they say, will often make men courageous.
In this case it had the same effect on two beings of a very
different description—a lovely girl and an idiot boy.   Miss
Morden, throughout the trying scene, displayed the coolest
courage ; and the poor simpleton, who commonly would avoid
the appearance of a gun, armed with his spit, defended the
breach like a hero.

" We met at dinner.   Julia, Miss Morden's cousin, would
hardly venture to join us, for her brother rated her timidity
severely.   When the alarm was heard, the fearful girl buried
her face beneath the bed-coverings, and remained in pitiable
agitation until the contest ended.   Mr. Morden took her from

his daughter's arm, kissed her, and congratulated her on their delivery from the last night's danger.

" ' You little coward !' said the old man jocularly; 'you must give your deliverer one kiss at least for your preservation.' The blushing girl received my salute. Miss Morden took my hand. ' You, too, Emily, will you not reward your protector ?' Without coquetry, she laid her lips to mine, and that kiss was a sufficient recompense for twice the peril I had encountered.

" But for me no praises seemed sufficient : the successful defence was attributed to my exertions ; and the fortunate shot that killed the villain smith was never to be sufficiently commended.

" My visit ended. *I was in love with Emily;* but then I had little chance of succeeding to the property which afterwards, by a chapter of accidents, fell to me ; and a company of foot was all my earthly riches. She was an heiress ; and would it be generous to take advantage of a casual service to press a suit that would be as painful to refuse as unlikely to be granted ? I mean (so says vanity) by Mr. Morden. No ! I overcame the temptation of risking a trial, and returned to ——ford, possessing the esteem and good wishes of every inhabitant of ' the Wilderness.'

" I was on parade some mornings after I rejoined the regiment, when a horse, splendidly accoutred with a superb tiger-skin, holsters, saddle, and every housing fit for a field-officer, was led into the barrack-yard by a groom. The animal was a perfect picture of symmetry and strength ; a dark chestnut, sixteen hands high, and worth at least two hundred guineas. The groom presented me a letter ; it was from Mr. Morden— the horse was a present.

" Emily and her cousin married most happily, and we have often met since. They treat me as sisters would a brother ; and we frequently talk of the night attack upon ' the Wilderness.'

" Three years passed away ; the gang had been incessantly followed by Mr. Morden, and were extirpated with the solitary exception of Captain Bulger. Dreading the sleepless vengeance of that determined old man, this ruffian fled the country, and established himself in a disaffected district of the south.

" In the interim I got a majority in the Seventieth, then

K

quartered in Cork. Soon after I joined, I happened to be field-officer of the day on which a notorious criminal was doomed to suffer. The regiment had given a guard, and curiosity induced me to attend the execution.

" I entered the press-room. In a few minutes the malefactor appeared in white grave-clothes, attended by two priests. It was ' mine ancient enemy,' Bulger! Suddenly the sheriff was called out, and after a short absence returned, accompanied by a plain, vigorous country gentleman, enveloped in a huge driving-coat, and apparently like one who had travelled a considerable distance.

" I looked at the criminal; he was the ruin of a powerful man, and the worst-visaged scoundrel imaginable. He was perfectly unmoved, and preserved a callous sort of *hardiesse*; and as the priests hurried over their Latin prayers, made a careless response whenever they directed him. The door leading to the drop was open, and the felon looked out upon the crowd most earnestly. ' *He is not there*,' he murmured : ' *he caused my apprehension, but he will not see me die ;*' and added, with a grim smile, ' *Morden, you neither kept your word, nor proved your prophecy!*' The muffled stranger stood suddenly forward : ' *I am here, Bulger ! I paid for your apprehension, and have come some hundred miles to witness your execution !*'

" ' Morden,' said the dying felon, solemnly, ' if a ghost can come back again, *I'll visit you !*'

" The person addressed smilded coldly : ' I found you unable to execute your threats while living; and, believe me, I apprehend nothing from you when dead.'

" The clock struck—the sheriff gave the signal—Bulger advanced to the scaffold—the drop fell, and in two minutes he was a corpse."

## CHAPTER XXII.

Conversation—A Brave Resistance—The Contrast—The Burglary.

" WELL, I like a man to keep his word," said my relative ; " and I admire your friend Morden prodigiously for his punctual attendance on Mr. Bulger, when he made his parting bow to an admiring multitude, and, as the song goes, ' died with his face to the city.' "

" There is little danger, after all," said the Colonel, " to be apprehended from ruffian force, if a man's nerve and coolness desert him not at the pinch. In house attacks, the odds are infinitely against the assailants. The attempt is generally made in the dead of night ; a robber-party are never sufficiently organized to combine their efforts judiciously, and two men within, if properly armed and plentifully supplied with ammunition, are in my opinion an overmatch for a dozen outside the doors."

" Calm and steady courage does wonders, certainly ; and, even when surprised and unprepared, a cool man will rarely be left without some means of defence. The Scotch proverb is a true saw—' A gleg (ready) hand never wanted weapon.' "

" There never was a better illustration of that truth than the heroic resistance offered by an aged gentleman in the south to a band of ruffians, under most discouraging circumstances. I knew him intimately," continued the Colonel ; " and I'll briefly give you the story.

" Several years ago, when the south of Ireland was, as it has ever been within my memory, in a disturbed state, a gentleman advanced in years lived in a retired country-house. He was a bachelor ; and whether trusting to his supposed popularity, or imagining that the general alarm among the gentry was groundless, he continued in his lonely mansion long after his neighbours had deserted theirs for a safer residence in town. He had been indisposed for several days ; and on the night he was attacked had taken supper in his bedroom, which was on the ground-floor, and inside a parlour with which it communicated. The servants went to bed ; the house was shut up for the night ; and the supper-tray, with its appurtenances,

K 2

by a providential oversight, forgotten in the old man's
chamber.

"Some hours after he had retired to bed, he was alarmed
at hearing a window lifted in the outer apartment; his
chamber-door was ajar, and the moon shone brilliantly through
the open casement, rendering objects in the parlour distinct
and perceptible to any person in the inner room. Presently a
man leaped through the window, and three others followed
him in quick succession. The old gentleman sprang from
his bed, but unfortunately there were no arms in the apartment. Recollecting, however, the forgotten supper-tray, he
provided himself with a case-knife, and resolutely took his
stand behind the open door. He had one advantage over the
murderers—they were in full moonlight, and he shrouded in
impenetrable darkness.

"A momentary hesitation took place among the party, who
seemed undecided as to which of them should first enter the
dark room; for, acquainted with the localities of the house,
they knew well that there the devoted victim slept. At last
one of the villains cautiously approached, stood for a moment
in the doorway, hesitated, advanced a step—not a whisper was
heard, a breathless silence reigned around, and the apartment
before him was dark as the grave itself. ' Go on, blast ye!
What the devil are ye *afeerd* of.!' said the rough voice of an
associate behind. The robber took a second step, and the
old man's knife was buried in his heart! No second thrust
was requisite, for, with a deep groan, the villain sank upon
the floor.

"The obscurity of the chamber, the sudden destruction
caused by that deadly thrust, prevented the ruffians in the
outer room from knowing the fate of their companion. A
second presented himself, crossed the threshold, stumbled
against his dead associate, and received the old man's knife in
his bosom. The wound, though mortal, was not so fatal as
the other: and the ruffian had strength to ejaculate that he
was ' a dead man !'

"Instantly several shots were fired, but the old gentleman's
position sheltered him from the bullets. A third assassin
advanced, levelled a long fowling-piece through the doorway,
and actually rested the barrel against the old man's body.
The direction, however, was a slanting one; and, with ad-

mirable self-possession, he remained steady until the murderer drew the trigger, and the ball passed him without injury. But the flash from the gun unfortunately disclosed the place of his ambush, and then commenced a desperate struggle. The robber, a powerful and athleti ruffian, closed and seized his victim round the body : there was no equality between the combatants with regard to strength ; and although the old man struck often and furiously with his knife, the blows were ineffectual, and he was at last thrown heavily on the floor, with the murderer above him. Even then, at that awful moment, his presence of mind saved this heroic gentleman. He found that the blade of the knife had turned, and he contrived to straighten it upon the floor. The ruffian's hands were already on his throat—the pressure became suffocating —a few moments more, and the contest must have ended ; but an accidental movement of his body exposed the murderer's side : the old man struck with his remaining strength one desperate blow—the robber's grasp relaxed—and, with a yell of mortal agony, he fell dead across his exhausted opponent !

" Horror-struck by the death-shriek of their comrade, the banditti wanted courage to enter that gloomy chamber which had been already fatal to so many. They poured an irregular volley in, and leaping through the open window, ran off, leaving their lifeless companions behind.

" Lights and assistance came presently—the chamber was a pool of gore—and the old man, nearly in a state of insensibility, was covered with the blood, and encompassed by the breathless bodies, of his intended murderers. He recovered, however, to enjoy for years his well-won reputation, and to receive from the Irish Viceroy the honour of knighthood, which never was conferred before upon a braver man."

" I know a melancholy contrast to this gallant story," said my cousin ; "it occurred not many years ago in an adjoining county. I heard it detailed in a court of justice as well as privately from the lips of the unfortunate gentleman, and I never shall forget his nervous agony, as he gave me a partial narrative of the outrage."

" Oh ! let us have the particulars, Julius ; next to a good ghost-story, a cruel burglary is delightful."

" In 181—," said my kinsman, " a gentleman with his family left Dublin, and removed to an extensive farm he

had taken in the wild and troublesome barony of ————.
There was no dwelling-house procurable for some time, and
the strangers took up their residence in a large cabin upon
the road-side, about a mile distant from the little town of
————ford.

"It was naturally supposed, that coming to settle in a
strange country, this gentleman had brought money and
valuables along with him; and a gang of robbers who infested that lawless neighbourhood under the command of
the notorious Captain Gallagher, marked the stranger for a
prey.

"This new settler had been married but a few months, and
his wife was a young and very lovely woman. On the third
night after their arrival they retired at their customary hour to
rest—he slept upon the ground-floor, and the lady and her
female attendants occupied some upper chambers.

"It was past midnight; the unsuspecting family were buried
in deep repose, when Mr. ——— was fearfully awakened by a
stone shattering the window and breaking the looking-glass
upon the table. He was unhappily a nervous timid man; he
was aware the house was being attacked; a loaded carbine
lay within his reach, but he appears to have abandoned all
hope or thought of defending himself;—he heard the crashing
of the cabin windows—he heard the appalling sound of
women's shrieks—but, trembling and agitated, he had not
power to leave his bed.

"Never did a more dastardly gang attack a house than
Gallagher's. After every window was driven in, more than
half an hour elapsed before one of them would enter, although
no show of resistance had been offered by the inmates of the
house. The cowardly villains would occasionally peep through
a shattered casement and instantly withdraw.

"A single blow struck with good effect, one shot from the
loaded carbine, would have scattered the scoundrels, and saved
the family from plunder and a dreadful insult. But the unhappy man, paralyzed with terror, lay in helpless imbecility
upon his bed, and the banditti, satisfied that no resistance
would be offered, at last made good an entrance.

"They lighted candles, bound the unfortunate gentleman,
left him half dead with terror, and proceeded to ransack the
premises. Soon after, shrieks from the lady's chamber an-

nounced their being there. They drank wine, and broke every place and thing in the expectation of plunder.

" But unfortunately they were disappointed; I say *unfortunately*, for had they found money, it is possible the lady would have been preserved from insult. Maddened by liquor, and disappointed in their expected booty, the helpless women were subjected to savage insult.

" What must have been that wretched man's sufferings, as he listened to the supplications of his beautiful wife for pity ? Some of the villains were ' of milder mood' than their fellows, and a partial protection was afforded to the miserable lady.

" After a dreadful visit of three hours, the ruffians left the house. Their apprehension was almost immediate. I was present at the trial, and the testimony of that beautiful woman, who sat on the bench beside the Judge, with the evidence of the wretched husband, was melancholy.

" Conviction followed, and I attended at the place of execution. Gallagher, the most horrible-looking scoundrel imaginable, came out. The buzz among the crowd subsided into muttered prayers and compassionate ejaculations. He, the felon, was unmoved ; his deportment was desperately hardened ; he looked without emotion on the multitude, and from amid the mass recognised some acquaintances, and acknowledged them with a demoniac grin. He was turned off in savage callousness — but his life was miserably prolonged.

" From his immense weight — for the ruffian was of Herculean proportions—the rope gave way, and he fell with violence to the ground. His thighs were badly fractured, and he was carried to the scaffold again, a maimed and trembling wretch. All his hardihood had forsaken him, and if it were possible for a man to undergo the agonies of death a second time, assuredly they were twice endured by that loathsome criminal—Captain Gallagher."

## CHAPTER XXIII.

Midnight Reflections—A good Story-teller—The affair of Ninety-eight.

WE separated for the night, and I retired to my well-appointed dormitory; every thing bespoke cleanliness and comfort, from the snowy coverlet to the sparkling fire of brilliant bog-deal. The room was papered with caricatures, and crowded with prints on sporting subjects. This was cheerful and bachelor-like. I looked at the mantelpiece; a brass blunderbuss and a case of pistols were there suspended in most effective order. This brought on a train of thought, and all the pleasant narratives of my kinsman and his visiter rushed back to my recollection.

I have, God help me! no fancy for what the Irish call *active amusements*. I would have no ambition to hold a nocturnal colloquy with Mr. Bulger—nor would it afford me satisfaction to listen to solemn assurances of his determination to cut my throat. I would not give one farthing, to spend half-an-hour in a dark closet with three robbers and a case-knife. I love uninterrupted repose, and it would annoy me to have my window dismantled at midnight, and my entire toilet annihilated by a well-directed volley of paving-stones. On earth there is not a more enchanting object than the exquisite symmetry of a woman's well-formed leg; but Miss Morden's would have no charms for me, if *preluded* by a discharge of musketry. There is moreover a murderer quietly cantoned within a room or two of mine; and though the man may be "honest," as my loving cousin believes and verifies, yet one feels nervous in being within a dozen yards of a man who has thinned the population for the third time.

Your stupid Englishman retires to bed after his daily labour is ended—your livelier Milesian then only lays himself out for pleasure, and betakes himself to shoot at a Justice of the Peace, or still better, amuse himself with a *too-roo among the Peelers*. Do you go out to dinner?—Calculate at being fired at when returning. Do you require a physician?—The odds are, that the honest doctor is qualified for a patient himself, before he leaves your lawn. Do you delight in hunting?—You will find the monotonous

period of waiting at the cover-side, agreeably diversified by
the occasional whistle of a musket-bullet from some am-
bushed *Rockite ;* and if you venture to send a horse out
to exercise, your groom returns *solus,* to acquaint you that
the quadruped is no more, and that the gentleman who
despatched him, sent you his regrets that he was so
unlucky as to miss yourself, but, by the assistance of the
Blessed Lady—for they are a pious and religious race—he
hoped to be more successful on a future opportunity.
Are you fond of a quadrille ?—Ascertain before you attempt
your first *chassez,* that the ball-room windows are *bricked-
up,* and a guard of honour stationed at the door. Are you,
*unfortunately,* a parson ?—Insure your life to the uttermost
farthing you can raise—arrange your affairs—perfect your
will — and, if you be curious in posthumous renown, pre-
pare your epitaph ; then demand one *thirtieth* of your
tithes—*you are a dead man to a moral*—and your heirs,
executors, and assigns, secure of opulence within a fortnight.

All this is pleasant and exciting, but I, as I premised,
"have no ambition." In spite of female persecution, I will
return to England (if my life be spared) before the "morrow
of All Souls," a day for ever ingrafted on my memory, it
being the appointed period that a rascally tailor (when I was
in the Blues) allotted for producing my body before his
Majesty's Barons of the Exchequer.

Thus resolved I went to sleep. Next morning my cousin
rallied me at breakfast. " I think, Colonel Dwyer, we
gave my friend Frank enough of robber narratives last night.
Confess, was your couch visited by any of the departed
heroes, whom illiberal enactments consign to the gallows,
while lesser men are sent in state to Westminster ? Dreamed
you

> Of cutting foreign throats ;
> Of breaches, ambuscadoes, Spanish blades ?"

" Ah no," said the Colonel, " our dull tales require the
seasoning of good story-telling to render them impressive.
I wish my quondam acquaintance, Mr. ——, had been here,
and, by the shade of Munchausen, he would have embellished
a simple burglary to such superlative perfection, that I am

persuaded your kinsman could not have counted on a second night's sleep for a fortnight."

"Is the gentleman happy in description ?" I inquired.

"Inimitable. 'He lies like truth.' I shall never forget the first evening I met him." The Colonel took a preparatory pinch of brown mixture, and thus proceeded :

"Before I retired from the army, I was ordered to Castlebar to attend a court-martial. It was then a most hospitable town, and during our stay I and the other members of the Court had more invitations than we could possibly accept of.

"At a large dinner-party, the conversation turned on circumstances connected with the disgraceful defeat of the King's troops here, in Ninety-eight, by Humbert. An elderly gentleman, opposite to me at table, favoured us with a striking and spirited account of the affair, and none could give it with more effect, for he had been a prominent actor in the scene.

"It was really the most soul-stirring narrative I had ever listened to,—and when in course of the detail the fortune of the day threatened to become disastrous, the individual exertions of this gallant gentleman appear to have been incredible. He flew through every arm of the Royal Forces— objurgated the militia, lauded the artillery, encouraged the irregulars, and d—d the carbineers ;—held momentary consultation with three field officers, and the Lord only knows how many subordinates besides—and traversed the line from one extremity to the other with such rapidity, as proved that he must have been mounted on a race-horse, or possessed of the gift of ubiquity itself.

"When the panic became general and a rout inevitable, it was melancholy to hear this veteran mourn over blighted glory and blasted renown. He was forced away at last, it appeared, by the remnant of the combatants ; but still, 'in the ranks of death you'd find him,' retiring reluctantly through the town, a sort of intermediate speck between his own rear-guard and the French advance. How the deuce he escaped the cross-fire of both, I never could comprehend.

"I looked at him with wonder and respect—no truculent traces of war lined a harsh and merciless countenance—no 'token true of foughten field' disfigured him with scar or blemish; but there was a quiet tradesman sort of simper eternally mantling over his features, which would have been worth a hundred a-year to any city dealer in ladies' mercery. Surely, thought I, he has at all events the true military enlargement on the *occiput*, and I'll warrant it a *splendid development*. In short, I was astonished, and marvelled how well such apparent benignity concealed a heart, that only throbbed with rapture amid the roar and blaze of battle.

" How long this train of thought might have continued is uncertain; it was broken by a twitch upon the elbow from my neighbour.—' Curse him,' he said in a whisper that paralyzed me, ' his story is nothing to-night, he forgot to kick down Humbert's aide-de-camp.'

"' *Kick down an aide-de-camp!* that would indeed be an unusual feat.'

" ' Well, Sir, that very feat is worth the remainder of the battle. It happened that our fat friend opposite had a horse that never could endure a crupper; the rider was disabled in a charge, broke his sabre, and was, or rather any other man would be, completely *hors de combat*. What did he do in this dilemma?'

" ' Call out lustily for quarter, I presume.'

" ' The farthest thing from his intentions. No, he slipped his hand slily over the croup, and with the first fling knocked out the brains of Humbert's principal aide-de-camp. There was a simple and ingenious method of making a vacancy in an enemy's staff! Oh, the story is nothing, wanting it! Had I not better make him tell it over in the new?'

" Just then we were summoned to the drawing-room, and whether the narrative was again given to the company, with the interesting addendum of the kick, I cannot take on me to say."

" Was the man even present at the battle?" I inquired.

" As much, my friend, as you were at Camperdown; and I have reason to believe, that that affair was transacted before you were born. He absconded the moment it was known the French had landed at Killala, and never appeared in the county afterwards until the rebellion was suppressed, and the country as quiet as it is at present."

" Heaven protect us !" I exclaimed. " It is a lying world that we live in."

---

## CHAPTER XXIV.

Spring tides—Hennessey and the portmanteau—Spillet-fishing—Coal fishing—Mackerel — Sea-fowl—A failure — Preserving gunpowder— An explosion—Another accident—A house burned—The dinner signal.

THE springs have commenced, and the gray and lowering atmosphere which the influence of these tides occasion has set in. Ailhough the darkness would intimate a change, the fresh breeze and sky appearances portend, as they tell me, good weather.

We are bound for the bay to lay down spillets ; and during the tedious interval which of necessity occurs before they can be lifted, we shall kill coal-fish, shoot sea-gulls, smoke cigars, and no doubt, have a further detail of atrocities from the Colonel, which would put the Newgate Calendar to the blush.

The mainsail is *chalk-up*, — the hooker has slipped her cables, and hangs by a single end to the pier,—and we are waiting for a row-boat, which four sturdy peasants propel with might and main from the opposite shore. There is a man in the stern-sheets who engrosses the undivided attention of my cousin and his followers. The boat approaches, and "Blessed Mary ! can it be ?" there sit Hennessey and the Colonel's portmanteau ! The embassy has succeeded, the bustle of the boatmen is commensurate to the importance of the freight, and they *give way* in the full consciousness, that they carry " Cæsar and his saddle-bags."

Mr. Burke has made the *amende honorable* ; my cousin looks two inches taller, and hints slily that feudal power in Bally-croy is not yet extinct ; and well he may, for the Colonel's chattels are uninjured—no rude hand has undone a buckle— not a shirt is wanting, or even the fold of a neckcloth disar-ranged. There is a mysterious whispering between the ambassador and Pattigo ; the commander rejoices over his wardrobe ; my kinsman looks " every inch a king ;" and I am probably the happiest of all, for I trust that the pleasant narratives which for two nights robbed me of my rest, like " the thousand and one" of Scheherazade, have at last drawn to a close.

Did a man wish to moralize upon the unrealities of human expectations, let him hang over a spillet, and be interested in its success. Conceive an eternity of line with a thousand hooks at given distances—as every snood is placed a fathom apart, a person less conversant with figures than Joe Hume, may guess *the total*. This endless continuity of hemp must be carefully taken up. Do it slowly, and the thing is worse than a penance to Lough Dergh; and if you attempt rapidity, the odds are that the *back-line* breaks, and a full hour will scarcely remedy the mischief.

It would puzzle a philosopher to determine the state of affairs in ten-fathom water; and if you *shoot* in *foul ground*, you will probably lose the spillet, or with a world of labour disentangle a moiety from rocks and sea-weed. Should it, however, have escaped those casualties, after a two hours' probation, while you listen to a *Drimindhu** from the skipper, and the exact state of the herring-market from the crew, you proceed to raise it. Up it comes—that vibratory motion announces that a fish is fast upon the snood; conjecture is busily at work, and there is a difference of opinion, whether " the deceived one" be a codling or red-gurnet. It appears— a worthless, rascally, dog-fish! A succession of line comes in—star-fish, and " few and far between," some solitary plaices and flounders—at last *a victim*—heavy and unresisting. An indistinct glance of a dark object broad as a tea-tray, brings the assistant *spilleteer*, gaff in hand, to the quarter. Alas! *the turbot* in expectation, turns out to be *a ray!* Often have I shot a spillet under favourable circumstances and in approved ground, and lost time, hooks, and snoods, and my whole reward was a boat-load of skates and dog-fish.

We ran quickly with a leading wind, to the fishing-bank, and having shot the spillets—a tedious thing enough—stood for a rocky part of the coast, where the coal-fish are always abundant. This water-sport (viz., coal-fishing) is unknown " to the many," and yet to him whose hands are not unac-

* A melancholy Irish ditty.

quainted with rope and oar, it affords at times an admirable
amusement.

The coal-fishing requires a stiff breeze, and if there be
a dark sky it is all the better. In its detail, it is perfectly
similar to mackerel-fishing, only that the superior size of the
coal-fish makes stronger tackle and a heavier lead indispen-
sable.

An eel of seven or eight inches long is the bait. The head
being removed, the hook is introduced as in a minnow, and
the skin brought three or four inches up the snoud. This
latter is a fine line of two or three fathoms length, affixed to
the trap-stick and lead, the weight of which latter is regulated
by the rate of sailing.

The coal-fish, in weight, varies from two to fourteen
pounds; it is finely shaped, immensely rapid, uniting the
action of the salmon with the voracity of the pike. If he miss
his first dash, he will follow the bait to the stern of the boat,
and I have often hooked them within a fathom of the rudder.

Four or five knots an hour is the best rate of sailing for
killing coal-fish, and upon a coast where they are abundant,
the sport at times is excellent.

Like the pike, the coal-fish is very indifferent to the tackle
used, which is generally very coarse. Not so the mackerel;
he requires much delicacy of line and bait to induce him to
take.

In light winds, or when the fish are out of humour, I have
killed mackerel by substituting a salmon casting-line of single
gut, for the hempen snoud commonly employed by fishermen,
which with a newly-cut bait of phosphoric brilliancy commonly overcame his resolve against temptation. But there
are times when a change of weather, or some inexplicable
phenomena of sea or sky, render these fish dull and cautious:
for usually it requires but trifling art to kill them.

A little experience is necessary. The bait must be cut
from the freshest mackerel, and assimilated in size and shape
to the herring-fry, which they generally follow; and the *way*
of the boat must be so regulated, as to preserve the deception
by a sufficient velocity, without breaking by its *rapidity* the
mackerel's hold. The mouth of this fish is particularly
tender; and if care be not taken, many will drop from the
hook, before they can be secured on board.

Unaccustomed to the painful effects which friction and salt water occasion hands unused to *hemp*, I transferred my line to an idle boy, who proved a much more fortunate *coal-fisher* than I, notwithstanding the instructions of my friend Pattigo.

We were bearing down to a glorious play of sea-birds, and I got a gun *uncased* to practise at the gulls. It was a curious and bustling scene. Above, thousands of these birds were congregated in a small circle, screaming, and rising, and dipping over a dense mass of fry, which appeared at times breaking the surface of the water, while grebes and puffins of many varieties were persecuting those unhappy sprats underneath. As we bore down, I fired at a few straggling puffins. Some were missed, some disabled, but not a *clean-killed* bird! The great body of sea-fowl appeared so much engrossed with their predatory pursuits, as to neither attend to the reports of the gun, or notice the approach of the hooker until the boat's bolt-sprit seemed almost parting this countless host of floating and flying plunderers.

Bent on destruction, I waited until we cleared the ball, and reached that happy distance when the charge should open properly. Pattigo estimated the shot would, *moderately*, produce a stone of feathers. I fired; a solitary gull dropped in the water, and half-a-dozen wounded birds separated from the crowd, and went screaming off to sea. The failure was a melancholy one. I sank immeasurably in the estimation of the crew as an *artiste*. Pattigo's bag of feathers was but an unrealized dream—while my kinsman muttered something about *the best single* he ever possessed—and I, to cover my disgrace, occupied myself with reloading.

"I can't congratulate you on your gunnery," said my cousin, "although I must admit, that it required some ingenuity to avoid accidents among the crowd. But give me the gun,—and here comes a victim," he continued, as a huge grey gull, reckless of danger, wheeled as they will do round and round a wounded companion.

"I would not be in his coat for half the hooker," said Pattigo, in a stage whisper.

"The Lord look to him!" exclaimed another boatman, "if it be not a sin to pray for a bird."

"He shall not carry his life to the water," rejoined the Master, as he laid the barrel to his eye.

But, notwithstanding prayer and prophecy, the gull merely

parted a few feathers, and flew off to all appearance with little
injury.

"By every thing blind!" exclaimed my kinsman, "the
gun must have been charged with sawdust.   Ha! let's see the
flask!   Frank, Frank, thou art a careless gunner; the powder
is not worth one farthing."

It was true.   I had forgotten my flask in the pocket of a
wet *cota more*,* and consequently the powder was spoiled.

Nothing puzzles me more, with the exception of keeping
the Sheriff at a distance, than preserving gunpowder, and
preventing my arms from rusting; and it is incredible how
soon the humidity of this climate spoils the one, and causes
the other.†

* *Anglice*, great-coat.

† Gunpowder is composed of very light charcoal, sulphur, and well-
refined saltpetre.   The powder used by sportsmen in shooting game, is
generally composed of six parts of saltpetre, one of charcoal, and one of
sulphur; but these proportions, as well as the introduction of other
ingredients, and the sizes of the grains, are undoubtedly varied by the
different manufacturers in the composition of the powders of the same
denomination, and are always kept profoundly secret.

The materials are put into a wooden trough, where they are ground
together, to render the contact of the nitrous and combustible particles
intimate and equal throughout the whole mass.   The mixture is occasionally sprinkled with water, to form an amalgam, which is afterwards
granulated, and to prevent the finer particles of the sulphur and the
charcoal from flying off, which would necessarily alter the proportion of
the composition.   The powder-makers employ more or less time in the
operation of grinding, in proportion to the quantity and quality of the
saltpetre.   When they conceive that the ingredients are properly mixed
together, they from the paste form those little grains, which, being dried,
obtain the name of gunpowder.

There are two general methods of examining gunpowder; one with
regard to its *purity*, the other with regard to its *strength*.

Its *purity* is known by laying two or three little heaps near each
other, upon white paper, and firing one of them.   For if this takes fire
readily, and the smoke rises upright, without leaving any dross or feculant
matter behind, and without burning the paper, or firing the other heaps,
it is esteemed a sign that the sulphur and nitre were well purified, that
the coal was good, and that the ingredients were thoroughly incorporated
together; but if the other heaps also take fire at the same time, it is
presumed, that either common salt was mixed with the nitre, or that the
coal was not well ground, or the whole mass not well beat or mixed
together; and if either the nitre or sulphur be not well purified, the paper
will be black or spotted.

To determine the *strength* of powder, dry it perfectly, and ascertain
how many sheets of paper it will drive the shot through at the distance

" My grand magazine is a sort of basket, secured with a lid and padlock, and covered with a sheep-skin, which, like the coffin of Mahomet, hangs suspended between sky and earth, from the couples of the kitchen. This disposition secures it alike against damp and accident. My arms give me an infinity of trouble, but by a weekly inspection, I manage to keep all in order.

" It is marvellous how quickly, even with moderate care, powder spoils. With my attention I experience little inconvenience, as I always warm my flask by plunging it in boiling water before I take the field. This renders the powder sufficiently dry, without deteriorating from its strength, which exposure to a stronger heat will inevitably occasion.

" By the way, I have had more actual experience in this necessary article than was exactly agreeable. Come, we will bear away for the Lodge, and as the Colonel is immersed in ' The Packet,' and deep in the debate, I will give you the particulars. In powder I am not *' ignarus mali,'* for I blew myself up, or made an excellent attempt,—and burned a cabin to the very ground.

" Both tales are briefly told. We were on a Christmas visit, when, a slight fall of snow having taken place overnight, the host proposed that I, and Captain H—— of the 7th dragoons, should go out and shoot snipes among the numerous drains by which his lawn was irrigated. Guns were procured but only *one* powder-flask was attainable, and it was to be a part-

of ten or twelve yards. In this trial we should be careful to employ the *same sized shot* in each experiment—the quantity both of the shot and the powder being regulated by exact weight; otherwise we cannot, even in this experiment, arrive to any certainty in comparing the strength of different powders, or of the same powder at different times.

To protect guns from rust in the humid climate I have been latterly accustomed to, I found nothing answer well but *strong mercurial ointment*. On the western coast, oil, no matter how good in quality, is useless, but for cleaning. Those who are acquainted with the localities of that country know that *turf* is of trifling value. No limit is consequently placed upon its consumption; it is calculated only by the *stack* or the *boatful*, and hence more fuel was wasted in my lodge than would supply three moderate houses. Yet so penetrating is the damp from the ocean breeze, that the house-arms rusted above the fire-places, and the pistols I kept upon my table would spot if not frequently examined, and dry-rubbed with a flannel cloth.

nership concern. For this purpose it was large enough in all
conscience, being an old-fashioned horn, bound with brass,
and capable of holding a pound of powder. *We filled it to the
top.* At a short distance from the house, a snipe sprang unexpectedly—I killed it—and in attempting to reload, the charge
ignited in the barrel, and the horn blew up in my hand. My
clothes were reduced to tinder, my hat scorched, my hair and
eyebrows burned off, but excepting a slight cut in my hand,
otherwise I was perfectly uninjured. *Not a fragment of the
flask, but one shattered piece of horn, could be found upon the
unbroken surface of the snow.* H——, who was about one
hundred yards distant from me, described the explosion as
louder than the report of a nine-pounder; yet, to me, the
noise seemed trifling. Was not this escape miraculous?

"The second explosion, in which I perpetrated *arson,*
occurred some ten miles up the river. By some uuhappy
mischance, I took out a flask of condemned powder, and
the accident was not discovered until it was too late to be
remedied. To dry the powder was the alternative; and we
repaired for this purpose to the only house within four miles
of the place, a *shieling* occupied by an old herdsman and his
wife.

"The powder was spread upon a wooden platter, and laid at
a sufficient distance from the fire; and while I stirred it with
a ramrod at a distance, one of my attendants conceived it a fit-
ting opportunity to roast *a cast of potatoes* in the embers. Both
operations went forward successfully. The powder was almost dry
—the potatoes nearly roasted, when my follower ingeniously
contrived to introduce a coal into the loose powder. This incident, though trifling in itself, made an immediate alteration
in affairs. The roof of the cabin was dry as tinder, while tow,
flax, and other combustible matters, were stored immediately
above the hearth. In a moment all was in flames—the potato-
roaster blown into the corner, and I, either by fear or gunpowder, *capsized* in another direction.

"The agony of the poor old woman, who fortunately was
outside the hovel when the explosion took place, was pitiable.
In five minutes her cabin was a ruin—and to her that
wretched *shieling* was worth a marble palace. For a time
she could not be pacified. In vain she was assured 'that the
master would build her a new house, *wider, and bigger, and*

*warmer,* ay, and that should have *a wooden door!*' but, like another Rachel, she mourned, and refused to be comforted.

" Two or three days removed her sorrow. I sent assistance, and, progressing, like another Aladdin, the cabin rose, Phœnix-like, from its ashes. It is now the envy of the passing travel-ler; and as the old couple close their *wooden door* at night, they pray for *the Master's* long life, and bless God that ' a pound of powder blew up at their fire-side.'

" But see ! old John's signal flies at the flag-staff. In with that endless spillet, Pattigo! Pshaw! red gurnets, codlings, flat-fish, with skates and rays eternally. Now, *out reefs*—on with the *big jib*—nay, my dear Colonel, I am commander. *Ease away the sheets.* Ha ! she stoops to it ! Hish! she travels *Carry on,* Pattigo—the Colonel is aboard, ' *Cæsarem vehis !*' *She does scrape the sand a little ;* but we are fairly over *the bar*—John's dinner signal would make any man a hero."

## CHAPTER XXV.

A calm night—Sand-eel fishing—Dangerous to the fair sex—Cockles—Crabs—Scallops—Oysters—Punt adrift—My brother's shoes—Seal sur-prised—Incident—Gun burst—Birmingham guns—Percussion locks—London makers—Barrel-making—Gun-making—Inferior guns—Shoot-ing accident.

It was nearly dark, but the night was calm and warm. I stole from the heated room to indulge in a luxurious smoke *al fresco ;* and seated upon the wall of the little pier, puffed away in Turkish indolence. The swell upon the bar was par-ticularly distinct, as, in successive falls, the wave burst upon the sands, and ran hissing up the beach, till its volume of water broke and subsided. The tide was almost out, and the river which forms the channel of the estuary, would hardly reach beyond the knee ; and I thought of the singular con-trast that existed between the quiet stream, now scarcely a stone's throw over, and the fierce and lowering water which a westerly gale forces in, rushing every moment with in-creased violence from the ocean, and threatening to burst over bank and rock that opposed a barrier to its rage. My musings were, however, speedily interrupted; voices came to-wards me from opposite directions, and loud and frequent laugh replied to rustic badinage and youthful romping. My cousin joined me, and from him I ascertained that the jolly parties who seemed every were scattered over the sands beyond the river, where the village girls assembled to collect sand-eels, an employment they would pursue till the return-ing tide filled the estuary again. A little flat punt, which the servants use for bringing spring water from the bent banks, was speedily placed upon the river, and we pushed over to the opposite strand, and found ourselves surrounded by several hundreds of the young villagers of both sexes, who were busily engaged in this curious species of night-fishing.

The sand-eels are generally from four to nine inches in length, and lie beneath the surface seldom deeper than a foot. The method of taking them is very simple; it is effected by passing a case-knife or sickle with a blunted edge, quickly through the sands; and by this means the fish is brought to the surface, and its phosphoric brilliancy betrays it instantly. At the particular times during the summer months when these eels run in upon the estuary, quantities sufficient to fill several barrels have been collected during a night. When dressed the fish is reckoned by the peasantry a great delicacy, but to my taste it is much too strong. But they are sought after for other purposes : from the particular brilliancy of the skin they make an admirable bait for flat-fish ; and hence a spillet-settee prefers them to every other kind, as they are much more durable than the lug,* and infinitely preferable to eels of a coarser size.

In speaking of this nocturnal fishery, if a search in the sands may be so termed, my cousin said that it was a source of considerable trouble to himself and the priest in their res-pective vocations : for accidents of a delicate description were occasionally to be lamented, and many an unhappy calamity was traced to "the returning from the sand-eels." Whether the danger of this curious pursuit enhanced its enjoyment is questionable ; but, regardless of the frequent mishaps, which prudent mothers would of course duly enumerate, the fair por-

* The sand-worm used by fishermen.

tion of the peasantry waited anxiously for twilight, and then, fortified by maternal advice and female resolution, set off in troops to the strand to share the pleasures and the perils of this interesting but dangerous amusement.

A crowd of a more youthful description of the peasantry, are collected every spring-tide to gather cockles on the same sands by daylight when the tide answers. The quantities of these shell-fish thus procured would almost exceed belief; and I have frequently seen more than would load a donkey, collected during one tide by the children of a single cabin. They form a valuable and wholesome addition to the limited variety that the Irish peasant boasts at his humble board; and afford children, too young for other tasks, a safe and useful employment.

Indeed, its plentiful supply of shell-fish may be enumerated among the principal advantages which this wild coast offers to its inhabitants. Along the cliffs, whether in the islands or on the main, lobsters are found in abundance; and, if the peasantry possessed the necessary means for prosecuting the fishery, it might at times afford them a lucrative employment. But, simple as the apparatus is, they do not possess it; and the lobsters obtained by sinking pots and baskets in the deep sea, are taken by strangers, who come for this purpose from a considerable distance. Those killed by the islanders are only procurable at low springs, when the ebbing of the water beyond its customary limits, permits caves and crannies in the rocks being investigated, which in ordinary tides could not be entered.

Crabs are found on this coast of considerable size and sufficiently numerous. Like the lobsters, they are only accidentally procured; but there is no doubt but a large supply could be obtained if proper means were employed to take them.

The most esteemed of all the shell-fish tribe by the western fishermen is the scallop, which here is indeed of very superior size and flavour. They are commonly found by the oyster-dredgers in deep water; and are estimated so highly as a luxury, as to cause their being transferred to the next gentleman who may have been serviceable to the peasant who finds them, or whose future favour it may be advisable to propitiate. Indeed, in former days, and those too not very distant from our own times, to approach a justice of the peace without

" a trifle for his honour," would be an offence of passing
magnitude; a basket of chickens, a cleave of scallops, or an
ass-load of oysters, harbingered the aggriever and the aggrieved.
If these formulæ were not duly attended to, the fountain of
law was hermetically sealed ; and a house functionary—for all
the servants on the establishment were " four pound con-
stables"—announced that " his honour would do no justice,"
and bundled off the applicant to some one more approachable
of his Majesty's numerous and poor esquires.

The oysters found in the bays and estuaries along this coast
are of a very superior quality ; and their quantity may be
inferred from the fact, that on the shores where they are
bedded, a turf-basket large enough to contain six or seven
hundred, can be filled for a sixpence.  A couple of men will
easily, and in a few hours, lift a horse-load !—and, notwithstanding the numbers carried off by sailing-boats from Clare
and Munster, the stock appears to be little reduced by the
constant dredging.    There are besides these, other shell-
fishes greatly prized by the peasantry, but which I had never
had the curiosity to eat, such as razor-fish, clams, and various
kinds of muscles.    These occasionally make a welcome change
in the otherwise unvarying potato diet ; and, better still,
employ the idler members of the family, whose youth or age
unfits them for more laborious exertions.

We dallied so long among the fairer portion of the sand-eel
fishers, that the tide insensibly rose; and when we reached the
place where our punt had been secured, we discovered that the
water had crept up the sands, and floated the frail skiff away.
To hail and get a boat from the Lodge, from the calmness of
the night, was readily effected; and while it was being
launched down the beach, my kinsman told me that it was
not the first time that the treacherous punt had played truant
to its crew.

" On a stormy evening, one of the boatmen was ordered to
cross the estuary for spring-water, and set out accordingly for
a supply, accompanied by a wild-looking and nondescript
animal who infests the premises, who is known to the
establishment by the name of ' Achil.'   The river was flooded,
the evening stormy, and Peeterein, after leaving his coadjutor
in strict charge of the skiff, set off to fill his water-vessels,
and to return, if possible, before the dusk had fallen into
darkness.   Achil, as the evening was chilly, lay down in the

bottom of the skiff to shelter himself from the piercing east wind; and, in place of keeping watch and ward like an able mariner, composed himself to sleep. Meanwhile the river rose fearfully; the breeze freshened into a gale; and when Peeterein hurried back with his water-vessels, he had the satisfaction of seeing the punt half a mile down channel, hurrying as fast as a flooded river and a freshening storm could urge it to the bar, which now broke in thunder. I had been shooting on this side, and reached the strand while Peeterein was hallooing for assistance. A boat was rapidly despatched —the skiff, when its destruction appeared inevitable, was overtaken, and *Achil* found as comfortably asleep as if he were in his accustomed crib in the barn. The ebullitions of Peeterein's sorrow, while the fate of skiff and boy was still uncertain, astonished me; and when I saw the punt in tow, I observed that, as the boy was recovered, he might now cease his lamentations.—' The Lord be blessed! there she is: another minute would have made noggin-staves of her! Arrah! and did ye think it was *Achil* I was frettin after—the devil pursue him for an unlucky member! No, faith—I was in sore distress, for *my brother's shoes were aboard!*'"

We were assembled round the breakfast-table this morning, and it was a questionable affair whether we should pass the forenoon in the warren, or shoot a spillet on the banks, when the conclave was dissolved by one of those incidental alarms that diversify the rustic monotony of our common-place existence. The spring-tide had left the channel nearly dry, and, except in some deep pools, the water was but ankle-deep. Into one of these an unlucky seal had been seduced in pursuit of a salmon, and his retreat was cut off before he was aware that his ill-timed chassé would cause his ruin. On his being discovered, a host of cockle-gatherers formed across the neck of the hole, while a breathless courier brought the tidings to the Lodge. Instantly all was bustle; a salmon-net was procured, and the whole of the " Dramatis Personæ," even to the Colonel and the Priest, were speedily armed with divers and deadly implements. Old Antony had hobbled off at the first alarm, and, by the prudent plan of taking time by the forelock, managed to be the first man at the scene of action. It was a deep and rather an extensive pool, and the unfortunate seal absconded to the place most likely to afford concealment till the flood-tide should liberate him from the hand of his enemies. But, alas! they were many and malignant; and, driven from his deepest and last retreat, to avoid being meshed in the net, he was forced upon the shoal, when an otter-spear, struck to the socket of the grains by the vigorous arm of Hennessey, killed him without a struggle. When the net was brought ashore, the moiety of a large salmon remained in the meshes, and told the errand which.induced the defunct seal to commit himself to the faithless shoals which proved so fatal to him.

---

This is, indeed, a day of incidents. Dinner was just removed, when, on the top of flood, a coast-guard galley ran in with a leading breeze from the westward. The very elegant proportions of the boat, the happy attitude, the snowy whiteness of her large lugs, as with the favourable light which a sunless but clear blue sky gave, she rounded the headland, and came up like a race-horse to the pier, had called our undivided attention to her arrival. While conjecture was busy as to what her business might be, we observed a man with his arm slung in a handkerchief, and apparently in considerable pain, leave her. The cause was soon ascertained, for a serious accident had occurred, and we all adjourned to the kitchen, where Antony was already occupied with the wound.

It appeared that a gun, with which the poor fellow had been shooting rabbits, had burst and shattered his hand; and when I saw the whole of the palm sadly lacerated, and the thumb attached by a small portion of the muscles, I really feared to save it was a hopeless task. But Antony and my kinsman thought differently. The old man bound the wound up with a professional neatness that I could not have expected from him; the patient was accommodated in the Lodge, and in a fortnight the galley again returned, to bring him, thoroughly convalescent, to his station.

I had some curiosity to examine the unlucky gun that caused the mischief. There was a longitudinal rent along the barrel, of seven or eight inches, terminating where the left hand usually grasps the stock. There had, no doubt, been a deep flaw in the inside of the metal; for the wounded man declared that he had not loaded the gun beyond the customary charge.

It proved to be one of those wretched affairs which are constantly smuggled into Ireland, and sold under the denomination of London guns, but which, it is well known, are fabricated in Birmingham; and the extent to which this dangerous imposition upon public safety is carried, would scarcely be credited. There is a constant demand in this unhappy country for fire-arms; the well affected and disaffected seek them for very different purposes;—one wants them for defence, the other requires them for aggression; and every steamer that arrives from Liverpool has generally some stands of contraband arms on board.

That our times should be as far distinguished for increased effect and superior elegance in the formation of fire-arms, as for any other mechanical improvement, will be admitted by all but the most prejudiced of the old school. Antique gunners may still be found, who are obstinate in preferring the flint to the percussion plan; but any person who has suffered the disappointments that the best guns on the former principle will entail upon those that carry them, and particularly in wet and stormy weather, will freely admit the wonderful advantages that simple and effective invention, the copper cap, confers upon the modern sportsman. The misery entailed upon the man who in rain and storm attempts to load and discharge a flint gun, may be reckoned among the worst upon the human catalogue; and if he who has suffered repeated disappointments of eternal misses and dilatory explosions, from a thick flint and a damp pan, tried the simple and elegant improvement now in general use, he would abandon the stone gun for ever.

It has been said that gun-making is only brought to perfection in London, and that the Irish are not able to compete with their English rivals. I am of this opinion, I confess, and decidedly partial to a London gun; and while I admit that I have occasionally met with excellent fire-arms produced by Dublin makers, yet they are, in finish and elegance, far behind those which one gets from any of the leading artists in the great metropolis. To point to any particular name, among the host of London makers, would be absurd. From any of a dozen a person will be certain of obtaining a first-rate implement; and from the Mantons, Purday, Egg, and many others, guns of the most efficient qualities and beautiful finish will be procured.

Some sportsmen are partial to such makers as forge their own barrels, and who thus afford them an opportunity of seeing their gun in progress from its commencement to its finish; and I acknowledge that I like to see my barrels fabricated; not but that I believe the greatest pains are bestowed upon proving his barrels by every gunmaker of character, and that none will be permitted to leave the shop of any reputable artist that have not been faithfully tested as to strength and safety.

So much depends on individual fancy, as well as the personal formation of the shooter, that no two persons will exactly select the same gun. He who has long or short arms, or any peculiarity in the formation of neck or shoulders, will require, according to circumstances, a differently shapen stock. Every man knows the gun best suited to his taste and figure, and few can shoot with one that differs materially from that which he has been accustomed to. To tell an experienced sportsman the qualities a finished gun should possess, would be giving him unnecessary information; and should the neophyte on this head wish for ample instructions, let him consult Colonel Hawker, and he, honest man, will open up all the arcana of the craft;—and though he may not teach him " the cunning trick of shooting;" he will, if his advice be attended to, enable him to thoroughly comprehend the requisite qualities of an efficient and well-finished fowling-piece.

Indeed, it is a miserable species of economy for a sportsman to purchase an inferior gun. To expect that the low-priced ones which are manufactured in country towns will be either safe or durable, is an absurdity. No doubt the charges of some fashionable makers are exorbitant; and from more moderate tradesmen, of excellent repute, an equally good gun may be procured at a considerably less price. But if a London maker be expensive, he certainly gives you the best article that improved machinery and the first workmen in the world can produce. With common care it will nearly last a life-time; and the small consideration between a warranted, and a flimsy and hastily-formed fowling-piece, will be too contemntible for a person to place in competition with personal security and sporting comfort.

When a gun begins to exhibit symptoms of having done its work, the sooner a man discards it the better. An injured barrel, or enfeebled lock, may prove fatal to the owner or his associates. Accidents every day occur, and very lamentable consequences arise from a culpable neglect, in retaining arms that should be declared unserviceable, and of course disused.

I had once a favourite gun, which, from constant wear and tear, exhibited unequivocal weakness in the lock, and which I had been earnestly recommended by a veteran sportsman to discard. On a cold and rainy day I was with my friend, O'M——, shooting woodcocks in the heath, and having sprung several, which, from the severity of the weather, were as wild as hawks, we marked them into a ravine, and determined to tie up the dogs, and endeavour to steal upon them. To keep my gun dry, I placed it under the skirt of my jacket, with the muzzle pointing downwards. My companion and our attendant were busy coupling the dogs, when the gun exploded, and the charge passed between O'M——'s bosom and the back of a dog he was in the act of securing, buried itself at the foot of the keeper, covering him with mud and gravel. From the close manner in which we were all grouped, how the shot could have entered the ground, without killing men or dogs, or both, was miraculous. I was desperately frightened, and from that moment forswore, for ever, the use of weakened locks and attenuated barrels.

---

## CHAPTER XXVI.

Bad roads—Native horses—Carins—Bridge of Ballyveeney—Our beat—Midday on the Moors—Hints to grouse-shooters—Finding game—Wild scenery—The ruined chapel—The well—Act of penance—Storm in the mountains—The deserted burying-place—Our return—The Colonel's method of rabbit-shooting—A disappointment.

I VERILY believe that no people upon earth are more easily satisfied in roads, than the natives in Ballyveeney. A narrow strip of rough gravel along the sea-beach—a mountain water-course, tolerably disencumbered of its rocks, or practicable passage across a bog, provided it be but fetlock deep, are considered by the inhabitants of this wild peninsula to be excellent horseways.

That accidents do not more frequently occur is marvellous. But the horse is born in the wilderness, and if there be a practicable path, he appears to know it by intuition. Hence, the rider traverses with impunity a morass in which Colonel Thornton would have been ingulfed, and skirts a dizzy precipice, with no more apprehension than a cockney wayfaring upon a turnpike trust. " Use lessens marvel," quoth Sir Walter Scott,—and I, who formerly witnessed the accoutrement of these Calmuck-looking coursers, with a lively anticipation of broken bones, now stumble through a defile, or cross a bog, with all the indifference of a native.

Having despatched the dogs and keeper, we arranged our beat, and started after breakfast. The road by which we reached our shooting-ground, is the sole means by which this, our *terra incognita*, is connected with the rest of Christendom. It is rough and dangerous in the extreme, and impracticable to every quadruped but the ponies of the country. In place of mile-stones, which mark better frequented roads, heaps of irregularly-sized pebbles meet the eye, and a stranger will be at a loss to assign their uses. They are melancholy memorials of uncivilized society, and either mark the scene of murder, or the place where a corpse has been rested in the progress of a funeral. These tumuli are numerous—and many a wild and fearful record of former violence is associated with them. The greater portion of these *cairns* record loss of life, consequent upon drunkenness ; and the stone, at present, appears as fatal as the *middoge*\* in former days.

---

\* This weapon, I believe, was almost confined to the west of Ireland, and at this time is rarely met with. Yet some centuries back, it was as constantly borne by the Milesians, as the dirk in the Highlands, and the stiletto in Italy. All the legendary tales of blood usually employ it as the means of violence ; and old Antony says, that in his youth the old people shuddered when they named it. I never saw but one ; it was a broad-bladed dagger, about fifteen inches long, of clumsy workmanship, and hafted with a piece of deer's horn. From the formidable figure the *middoge* cuts in ancient chronicles, the temper of the blade was supposed to be superior to any weapon forged in these degenerate days ; and I heard an old man assert that he had seen one, which, when held up and let fall perpendicularly but a few feet, would pierce through *three half-crown pieces—Credat Judæus !*—This interesting and valuable implement,

We left our horses at the old bridge of Ballyveeney, and proceeded to make an extensive circle of the moors, skirting, as we went along, the bases of the ridge of hills, which shuts out Erris from the interior.

It was eleven o'clock when the dogs were uncoupled. The breeze was brisk and warm, and the ground was either undulated into hillocks, or intersected by rivulets, whose broken banks were thickly covered with luxurious heath. It was a beat, on which a grouse-shooter would risk a kingdom,—it realized our expectations, and we found game abundantly.

Hunting for grouse during the basking hour of the day, is rigidly prohibited by all gentlemen who compile sporting directories; and yet every shooter knows, that at these proscribed hours, himself is commonly on the moors. Morning and evening, when the birds are on foot in search of food, is undoubtedly preferable to the duller portion of the day, when they are accustomed to indulge in a *siesta*. But generally some considerable distance must be travelled before the sportsman can reach his beat from his quarters. The morning is consumed on horseback or in the shooting-cart; the same road must be again accomplished before night; and hence, the middle of the day is, of necessity, the portion devoted to the pursuit of game.

To find the birds, when, satisfied with food, they leave the moor to bask in some favourite haunt, requires both patience and experience; and here the mountain-bred sportsman proves his superiority over the less practised shooter. The packs then lie closely, and occupy a small surface on some sunny brow or sheltered hollow. The best-nosed dogs will pass within a few yards, and not acknowledge them; and patient hunting, with every advantage of the wind, must be employed to find grouse at this dull hour.

But if close and judicious hunting be necessary, the places to be beaten are comparatively few, and the sportsman's eye readily detects the spot, where the pack is sure to be discovered. He leaves the open feeding-grounds for heathery knowes and sheltered valleys—and, while the uninitiated wearies his dogs in vain over the hill-side, where the birds, hours before, might have been expected, the older sportsman profits by his experience, and seldom fails in discovering the dell

according to his account, was lost "during the French," that is, at the period of the French invasion in '98.

or hillock, where, in fancied security, the indolent pack is reposing.

We had been upon the moors some hours—our walk was enlivened by success, and the time had arrived when the commissariat was required, and old John's supplies were ordered from the rear. A rivulet was reported to be *just round the hill,* and thither our course was directed.

We turned a rugged brow suddenly, and never did a sweeter spot present itself to an exhausted sportsman ; and resting on the bank of a ravine, where a small stream trickled over a precipice, forming beneath its brow a basin of crystal water, we selected this for our " *bivouac.*" Wild myrtle and shrub-like heather closed the opposite sides, and one spot, where the rivulet *elbowed* back, was covered with short green moss, that seemed rather an effort of human art, than a piece of natural arrangement.

Here we rested—and while baskets were unpacked, and the cloth extended upon the velvet surface we reposed upon, I looked with feelings which I cannot describe, upon the wild and melancholy scene below.

It was a ruined chapel and deserted burying-place—one gable of the building alone was standing, and, from beneath the ivied wall, a spring gushed out and united itself with the rivulet I have described. A stone cross, whose rude work-manship showed its antiquity, was erected beside the fountain; and although the cemetery had long since been deserted, a circle round the well* was freshly worn in the turf, and a

---

* The following passage is quoted from " *The Minstrelsy of the Border :*"—" Many run superstitiously to other wells, and there obtain, as they imagine, health and advantage ; and then they offer bread and cheese, or money, by throwing them into the well." And again : " In the bounds of the lands of Eccles, belonging to a lineage, of the name of Maitland, there is a loch, called *the Dowloch,* of old resorted to, with much superstition, as medicinal both for men and beasts, and that with such ceremonies as are shrewdly suspected to have begun with witch-craft, and increased afterwards by magical directions. For bringing of a cloth or somewhat that did relate to the bodies of men and women, and a shoe or tether belonging to a cow or horse, and these being cast into the loch, if they did float it was taken for a good omen of recovery, and a part of the water carried to the patient, though to remote places, without saluting or speaking to any they met by the way ; but if they did sink, the recovery of the party was hopeless. This custom was of late much curbed and restrained ; but since the discovery of many medicinal fountains near the place, the vulgar, holding that it may be as medicinal as these

woman at the moment was performing an act of devotion, on her bare knees, making an occasional pause, to offer up a prayer and drop a bead from her rosary.

The valley had a solemn and imposing character; everything about it was lonely and desolate. No traces of human visits were discernible; no pathway led to the ruin,—all was deep unbroken solitude; a hallowed and melancholy spot, where the living seldom presumed to approach the mansions of the dead.

The breeze fell, the air became unusually oppressive, the hill behind robbed us of the little wind that still partially cooled the sultry atmosphere; a distant muttering among the mountains was faintly heard, and a sound like a rising stream, was audible. Suddenly, a black cloud rose like magic upon the summit of the mountain, and a flash of light succeeded. "The storm is on," said my kinsman, and leaving the attendants to discuss the fragments of the feast, where they might best obtain shelter, we hurried down the hill, and couched beneath the ruins of the chapel.

There is more grandeur in an Alpine storm, than can be imagined by those who have not witnessed its effect. As the thunder crashes over the hills, and miles away is reverberated from the opposite mountains, the loneliness of the wilderness is in fine keeping with the anger of the elements. The rain-drops now fell faster—quick and vivid flashes burst from the southern heavens, and roll after roll succeeded, like sustained discharges of artillery. The dogs, in evident alarm, cowered at our feet, soliciting mortal protection from what, instinct told them, were the visitations of an awful power. Suddenly, one prolonged and terrific crash burst overhead— a deluge of rain descended—and rapidly as it came on the storm passed away—the peals became fewer and more distant, and in five minutes died in sullen murmurs among the distant hills.

"Is not this, indeed, sublimity?" said my kinsman, as he broke a silence of some minutes. "To convey ideas of the grand and terrible, give me a storm in the mountains, and let it be viewed thus: sheltered by the ivied walls of

are, at this time begin to reassume their former practice."—*Macfarlone's MSS.*

a ' toppling' ruin, and surrounded by the dwellings of the dead."

" How comes it," I inquired, " that, contrary to the known attachment of the lower Irish for ancient places of interment, this seems to be neglected and disused ?"

" You are right," he replied; "although it was once the only burying-ground to which the inhabitants of this district conveyed the dead for interment, more than two centuries have elapsed since it has been abandoned.    There is a curious tradition connected with its desecration, which Antony will be too happy in narrating, and as the clouds appear collecting on the hills, I propose that we retreat in good time, for it is rare to find such shelter on the moors, as that afforded us by the ruins of Knock-a-thample."*

Even the sublime and beautiful may be enjoyed to satiety, and we agreed that one thunder-storm is sufficient for the day. The game-bags, upon examination, produced twenty brace of grouse, and a leash of mountain hares.    For moderate men we had done enough, and we could dispense with the evening shooting.    Accordingly, we left our attendants to follow at their leisure, and mounting our Cossack cavalry, set off at a killing pace, " over bank, bush, and scaur," nor drew bridle until we reached the sand-banks, where the boat, with Pattigo and his companions, was awaiting our arrival.

Nor have we been the only denizens of the lodge whose exertions have this day been successful.    The Colonel has spent the forenoon in the sand-banks, much to his own satisfaction, in slaying rabbits, and studying the Morning Post. To unite the sportsman and politician, may at first sight seem difficult—but, ensconcing himself in a good position, the commander waits patiently for a shot, and, confiding loading and look-out to *Andy Bawn*, whose attentions since the unfortunate affair of the portmanteau have been redoubled, he coolly proceeds with *the debate*, until a rabbit is reported within range of the favourite *Spanish barrel*,† by his assistant

* *Anglice*, The church of the hill.

† *Spanish barrels* have always been held in great esteem, as well on account of the quality of the iron, which is generally considered the best in Europe, as because they possess the reputation of being forged and bored more perfectly than any others.    It should be observed, however, that of the Spanish barrels, those only that are made in the capital are accounted truly valuable; in consequence of which, a great many have

gunner. This mode of shooting the Colonel recommends, provided the day and the debate be *warm*. In winter, he may be induced occasionally to take the side of a sunny cover, but gout and rheumatism are ever present to his imagination, and he would not "wet a foot for all the birds upon Brae Mar."

After dinner, I reminded my kinsman of the promised legend of Knock-a-thample, and the otter-killer was ordered to the presence. But on inquiry, Antony had been professionally called off to a distant village upon the coast, to minister to a broken head, and had taken his departure in a four-oared boat, with as much ceremony as though he had been *surgeon-general*. I felt, and expressed my disappointment. "And are you really curious about this wild tradition?" asked our host. "I believe this is one of many legends, which, during a terrible winter, I amused myself by transcribing." Opening a drawer he took out a common-place book, and marked the page. Finding no inclination to sleep when I retired for the night, I heaped more bog-wood on the fire, and, before I slept, read the following specimen of the "wild and wonderful."

---

## CHAPTER XXVII.

### THE LEGEND OF KNOCK-A-THAMPLE.

In the valley of Knock-a-thample, beside a ruined church and holy well, the shattered walls of what had been once a human habitation, are still visible. They stand at a bow-shot distance from the fountain, which, instead of a place of penance for ancient crones and solitary devotees, was visited two centuries since for a very different purpose.

The well, although patronised by St. Catharine, a lady of as determined celibacy as ever underwent canonization, had one peculiar virtue, which, under her especial superintendance,

---

been made at other places in Catalonia and Biscay, with the names and marks of the Madrid gunsmiths; they are also counterfeited at Liege, Prague, Munich, &c., and a person must be a good judge not to be deceived by these spurious barrels.

M

it might not have been expected to possess. Indeed, in everyday complaints, its waters were tolerably efficacious; but, in cases of connubial disappointments, when the nuptial bed had been unfruitful, they proved an absolute specific; and in providing an heir for an estate, when "hope deferred had made the heart sick," there was not in the kingdom of Connaught, a blessed well that could hold a candle to that of Knock-a-thample.

Numerous as the persons were, whom the reputation of the fountain collected from a distance, few returned without experiencing relief. Occasionally, a patient appeared, whose virgin career had been a little too protracted, and to whom the rosary, rather than the cradle, was adapted.—And so thought St. Catharine—though her water was unequalled, yet she had neither time nor inclination to work miracles eternally; consequently, those ancient candidates for the honours of maternity returned precisely as they came: to expend holy water on such antique customers was almost a sinful waste—their presumption was unpardonable—it was enough to vex a saint, and even put the blessed Patroness of Knock-a-thample in a passion.

Holy water, like prophecy, appears to be of little value at home, and hence the devotees usually came from some distant province. The soil, indeed, might then have possessed the same anti-Malthusian qualities for which it is so remarkable at the present day. Certainly, the home consumption of Knock-a-thample was on a limited scale—and the herdsman and his wife, who then occupied the ruined cottage near the church, owed their winter comforts to the munificence of the strange pilgrims, who during the summer season resorted in numbers to the well.

It was late in October, and the pilgrimages were over for the year—winter was at hand—the heath was withered, and the last flower had fallen from the bog-myrtle—the *boollies*\*

---

\* The *Boolies*, in the mountain districts, are an interesting remnant of antiquity; and refer evidently to that period when Ireland was in its wild and unsettled state. They are simply one or more temporary *sheilings*, or huts, constructed with rude materials, in spots the most convenient for attending to the cattle in the summer and autumn, when they are allowed to depasture on the mountains.

According to the usual leases granted by the landlord to the tenant in this wild country, villages in the lowlands, or on the coast, have a reserved

were abandoned, and the cattle driven from the hills.   It was
a dark evening; and the rain which had been collecting on the
mountains began to fall heavily, when a loud knock disturbed
the inhabitants of the cabin.   The door was promptly unbarred,
and a young and well-dressed stranger entered, received the
customary welcome, with an invitation to join the herdsman's
family, who were then preparing their evening meal.   The
extreme youth and beauty of the traveller did not escape the
peasant's observation, although he kept his cap upon his head
and declined to put aside his mantle.

An hour before the young stranger had arrived, another,
and a very different visiter, had demanded lodging for the
night.   He belonged also to another country, and for some years
had trafficked with the mountain peasantry, and was known
among them by the appellation of *the Red Pedler*.   He was
a strong, under-sized, and ill-visaged man; mean in his dress,
and repulsive in his appearance.   The Pedler directed a keen
and inquisitive look at the belated traveller, who, to escape
the sinister scrutiny of his small but piercing eyes, turned to
where the herdsman's wife was occupied in preparing the
simple supper.   The peasant gazed with wonder at her guest;
for never had so fair a face been seen within the herdsman's
dwelling.   While her eyes were still bent upon the stranger,
a fortuitous opening of the mantle displayed a sparkling cross
of exquisite beauty, which hung upon the youth's bosom; and
more than once, as it glittered in the uncertain light of the
wood fire, she remarked the rich and sparkling gem.

When morning came, the Pilgrim took leave of the hospitable peasants, and as he inquired the road to the holy
well, slipped a rose-noble into the hand of the herdsman's

right of pasturage on particular portions of the adjacent hills; and in some
cases the distance from the tenant's habitation to this mountain pasturage
will exceed a dozen miles.   Hence it is impossible to pay the requisite
attention to the cattle, without residing on the spot; and a part of the
family, generally the young girls, are detached to *bivouac* in the hills,
and attend to the herding and milking of the cows.

These huts are always erected in lone and beautiful valleys, generally
on the bank of a rivulet, and placed beneath the shelter of a cliff.
When the season closes, they are deserted until the following year; and
a few hours' work suffices to render them habitable when the returning
summer obliges the fair villagers to resume their wild and pastoral
employment.

wife. This was not unnoticed by the Red Pedler, who proffered his services as guide, which the youth modestly, but firmly, declined. The Pilgrim hastened to the fountain, performed the customary ceremonies before noon, and then took the mountain path, leading through an opening in the hills, to a *station*,\* which, though particularly lonely, was usually selected by good Catholics for a last act of devotion, when returning from visiting at the blessed well. The Pedler, who, on various pretences, had loitered near the place, soon afterwards departed in the same direction.

That night the herdsman's family sought repose in vain :— wild unearthly noises were heard around the hovel; and shriek and laughter, awfully mingled together, were borne upon the breeze which came moaning from the mountains. The peasant

barred his door, and grasped his wood-axe; his wife with trembling fingers, told her rosary over again and again.

\* A place of penance frequented by Catholic devotees.

Morning broke, and, harassed by alarms, they sunk to sleep at last. But their slumbers were rudely broken—a gray-haired monk roused them hastily—horror was in his looks, and with difficulty he staggered to a seat. Gradually he collected strength to tell his fearful errand—the young and lovely devotee lay in the mountain glen, before St. Catharine's cross, a murdered corpse.

The tidings of this desperate deed flew through the country rapidly. The body was carried to the herdsman's cabin. For many hours life had been extinct, and the distorted countenance of the hapless youth bespoke the mortal agony which had accompanied the spirit's flight. One deep wound was in his side, inflicted evidently by a triangular weapon ; and the brilliant cross and purse of gold were gone.

The women from the adjacent villages assembled to pay the last rites to the remains of the murdered Pilgrim. Preparatory to being laid out, the clothes were gently removed from the body, when a cry of horror burst from all—*the Pilgrim was a woman !* Bound by a violet ribbon, a bridal ring rested beside her heart ; and, from unequivocal appearances, it was too evident that the fell assassin had committed a double murder.

The obsequies of the unhappy lady were piously performed ; the mountain girls decked her grave with flowers ; and old and young, for many a mile around, offered prayers for the soul of the departed. The murder was involved in mystery— the peasants had their own suspicions, but fear caused them to be silent.

A year passed—the garland upon the stranger's grave was carefully renewed—the village maidens shed many a tear as they told her melancholy story ; and none passed the turf which covered the murdered beauty, without repeating a prayer for her soul's repose.

Another passed—and the third anniversary of the Pilgrim's death arrived. Late on that eventful evening, a tall and noble-looking stranger entered the herdsman's cottage. His air was lofty and commanding ; and though he wore a palmer's cloak, the jewelled pommel of his rapier glanced from beneath the garment, and betrayed his knightly dignity. The beauty of his manly countenance forcibly recalled to the peasants the memory of the ill-starred stranger. But their admiration was checked by the fierce, though melancholy, expression of the handsome features of the stranger; and if they would have been inclined to scrutinize him more, one stern glance from his dark and flashing eye imperiously forbade it.   Supper was prepared in silence, until, at the Knight's request, the herdsman detailed minutely every circumstance connected with the lady's murder.

While the peasant's narrative proceeded, the stranger underwent a terrible emotion, which his stern resolution could not entirely conceal.   His eyes flared, his brows contracted till they united; and before the tale was ended, he leaped from his seat, and left the cabin hastily.

He had been but a few minutes absent, when the door opened, and another visiter entered with scanty ceremony, and, though unbidden, seated himself upon the stool of honour.   His dress was far better than his mien, and he assumed an appearance of superiority, which, even to the peasants, appeared forced and unnatural.   He called authoritatively for supper, and the tones of his voice were quite familiar to the herdsman.   With excited curiosity, the peasant flung some dried flax upon the fire, and, by the blaze, recognised at once the well-remembered features of the *Red Pedler* !

Before the peasant could recover his surprise, the tall stranger entered the cottage again, and approached the hearth. With an air which could not be disputed, he commanded the intruder to give place.   The waving of his hand was obeyed, and, with muttered threats, the Pedler retired to the settle. The Knight leaned against the rude walls of the chimney, and remained absorbed in bitter thought, until the humble host told him that the meal was ready.

If a contrast were necessary, it would have been found in the conduct of the strangers at the board.   The Knight ate like an anchorite, while the Pedler indulged his appetite largely.   The tall stranger tempered the *aqua vitæ* presented by the host copiously with water, while the short one drank fast and deep, and appeared anxious to steep some pressing sorrow in the goblet.   Gradually, however, his brain felt the influence of the liquor, and, unguarded from deep and repeated draughts, he thus addressed the host :—

" Markest thou a change in me fellow ?"

" Fellow !" quoth the peasant, half affronted ; " three years ago we were indeed *fellows* ; for the *Red Pedler* often sought shelter here, and never was refused."

" *The Red Pedler !*" exclaimed the tall stranger, starting from his reverie, as if an adder had stung him ; and fixing his fiery glance upon the late visiter, he examined him from head to foot.

" You will know me again, I trow," said the Pedler, with extraordinary assurance.

" *I shall*," was the cold reply.

" Well," said the new-comer, " though three years since I bore a pack, I'll wager a rose-noble that I have more money in my pouch than half the beggarly knights from Galway to Athlone. There !" he exclaimed, as he flung his cloak open, " *there* is a weighty purse, and *here* a trusty *middoge*, and a fig for knighthood and nobility !"

" Slave !" said the stranger, in a voice that made the peasants tremble, " breathe not another word until thou hast satisfied my every question, or, by the Mother of Heaven ! I'll cram my rapier down thy false throat ;" and, starting on his feet, he flung his mantle on the floor.

Though surprised, the Pedler was not discomfited by the dignity and determination of his antagonist.

" Yes !" he sullenly replied, " I wear no rapier—but this *middoge* has never failed me at my need," and drawing from his bosom a long triangular weapon, he placed it on the table.—" Sir Knight," he continued, " the handle of my tool is simple deer-horn ; but, by the mass ! I have a jewel in my breast, that would buy thy tinselled pommel ten times."

" Thou liest, slave !" exclaimed the Knight.

" To the proof, then," said the Pedler ; and opening a secret pocket, he produced a splendid cross.

" Villain !" said the tall stranger, under deep emotion, " surely thou hast robbed some hapless traveller !"

" No !" replied the Pedler, with a cool smile ; " I was beside the owner of this cross when his last sigh was breathed !"

Like lightning the stranger's sword flashed from its scabbard.

" Murderer !" he shouted in a voice of thunder, " for three years have I wandered about the habitable earth, and my sole object in living was to find thy caitiff self; a world would not purchase thee one moment's respite!" and before the wretch could more than clutch his weapon, the Knight's sword passed through his heart—the hilt struck upon the breast bone, and the Red Pedler did not carry his life to the floor.

The stranger for a moment gazed upon the breathless body, and having with the dead man's cloak removed the blood from his blade, replaced it coolly in the sheath. The Pedler's purse he flung scornfully to the peasant, but the cross he took up, looked at it with fixed attention, and the herdsman's wife remarked, that more than one tear fell upon the relic.

Just then the gray-haired Monk stood before him; he had left his convent to offer up the mass, which he did on every anniversary of the pilgrim's murder. He started back with horror as he viewed the bleeding corpse; while the Knight, having secured the cross within his bosom, resumed his former cold and haughty bearing.

" Fellow!" he cried to the trembling peasant, " hence with that carrion. Come hither, Monk—why gapest thou thus? hast thou never seen a corpse ere now? Approach, I would speak with thee apart"—and he strode to the further end of the cottage, followed by the churchman.—" I am going to confide to thee what—"

" The penitent should kneel," said the old man, timidly.

" Kneel!" exclaimed the Knight, " and to *thee*, my fellow mortal! Monk, thou mistakest—*I am not of thy faith*, and I laugh thy priestcraft to derision. Hearken, but interrupt me not. The beauteous being whose blood was spilled in these accursed wilds, was the chosen lady of my love. I stole her from a convent, and wedded her in secret; for pride of birth induced me to conceal from the world my marriage with a fugitive nun. She became pregnant, and that circumstance endeared her to me doubly, and I swore a solemn oath, that if she brought a boy, I would at once announce him as my heir, and proclaim my marriage to the world. The wars called me for a time away. Deluded by the artifice of her confessor, my loved one was induced to come hither on a pilgrimage, to intercede with thy saint, that the burden she bore might prove a son. Curses light upon the shaveling that counselled that fatal journey! Nay, cross not thyself, old man, for I would execrate thy master of Rome, had he been the false adviser. Thou knowest the rest, Monk. Take this purse. She was of

thy faith, and thou must say masses for her soul's health.
Yearly shall the same sum be sent to thy convent; see that all
that prayers can do, be done, or by my hopes of grace, thy hive
of drones shall smoke for it.   Doubt me not.—De Burgo will
keep his word to the very letter.   And now, farewell! I hurry
from this fatal spot for ever; my train are not distant, and
have long since expected me."

As he spoke, he took his mantle from the floor, and wrapped
it round him carelessly; then, as he passed the spot where the
body of the murderer lay, he spurned it with his foot, and
pausing for a moment, looked at the Monk—

" *Remember !*" he said in a low voice, which made the old
man shudder, and passing from the cabin, he crossed the
heath, and disappeared.

But the terror of the herdsman's family did not abate
with his departure; a dead man lay before them, and the
floor was deluged with his blood.   No human help was nigh;
before daylight assistance could not be expected; and no
alternative remained, but to wait patiently for the morrow.
Candles were lighted up, the hearth was heaped with fuel,
and a cloth thrown over the corpse, which they lacked the
courage to remove.   To sleep was impossible, and in
devotional acts they endeavoured to while the night away,
Midnight came; the Monk was slumbering over his breviary,
and the matron occupied with her beads, when a violent
trampling was heard outside, and the peasant, fearing the
cattle he had in charge were disturbed, rose to ascertain the
cause.   In a moment he returned.   A herd of wild deer
surrounded the cabin, and actually stood in threatening attitude within a few paces of the door!   While he told this
strange occurrence to the Monk a clap of thunder shook the
hovel to its centre—yells, and shrieks, and groans succeeded
—noises so demoniac, as to almost drive the listeners to
madness, hurtled through the air—and infernal lights flashed
through the crevices of the door and window.   Till morning
broke, these unearthly terrors continued, without a moment's
intermission.

Next day the villagers collected.   They listened to the
fearful story with dismay, while the melancholy fate of the
gentle pilgrim was bitterly lamented,   To inter the Pedler's
corpse was the first care; for the Monk swore by his patron
saint, that he would not pass another night with it overground

to be made a " mitred abbot." A coffin was forthwith prepared, and, with " maimed rites," the murderer was committed
to the earth.

That masses were requisite to purify the scene of slaughter
was indisputable—and with the peasants who had flocked
from the neighbouring villages, the Monk determined to pass
that night in prayer. The blood-stains were removed from the
floor—the corpse had been laid in consecrated earth—and the
office had commenced at midnight, when suddenly, a rushing
noise was heard, as if a mountain-torrent was swollen by the
bursting of a thunder-cloud. It passed the herdsman's cabin,
while blue lights gleamed through the casement, and thunder
pealed above. In a state of desperation, the priest ordered
the door to be unclosed, and by the lightning's glare, a herd of
red deer was seen tearing up the Pedler's grave! To look
longer in that blue infernal glare was impossible—the door
was shut, and the remainder of the night passed in penitential
prayer.

With the first light of morning, the Monk and villagers
repaired to the Pedler's grave, and the scene it presented
showed that the horrors of the preceding night were no
illusion. The earth around was blasted with lightning, and
the coffin torn from the tomb, and shattered in a thousand
splinters.—The corpse was blackening on the heath, and the
expression of the distorted features was more like that of a
demon than a man. Not very distant was the grave of his
beautiful victim. The garland which the village girls had
placed there was fresh and unfaded ; and late as the season
was, the blossom was still upon the bog-myrtle, and the
heath-flower was as bright and fragrant as though it were
the merry month of June. " These are indeed the works
of hell and heaven," ejaculated the gray friar. " Let no hand
from this time forth pollute itself by touching yon accursed
corpse."

Nightly the same horrible noises continued. Shriek and
groan came from the spot where the unburied murderer was
rotting, while by day the hill-fox and the eagle contended who
should possess the body. Ere a week passed, the villain's
bones were blanching in the winds of heaven, for no human
hand attempted to cover them again.

From that time the place was deserted. The desperate
noises, and the frequent appearance of the Pedler's tortured

spirit, obliged the herdsman to abandon his dwelling, and reside in an adjacent village. The night of the day upon which he had removed his family and effects, a flash of lightning fell upon the cabin, and consumed the roof; and next morning nothing remained but black and rifted walls. Since that time the well is only used for penance. The peasant approaches not the desecrated burying-place if he can avoid it. The cattle are never known to shelter underneath the ruined walls—and the curse of God and man have fallen on *Knock-a-thample*.

## CHAPTER XXVIII.

Visit to the mountain hut—The Colonel—An argument and a wager—No honesty among anglers—State of the river—Mogh-a-dioul—Father Andrew's flies—Splendid scenery—Its effect upon me and my companion—Beautiful pool—The otter—A curious scene—The Colonel's troubles—Wager decided—A new bet—A salmon killed—Conversation—The Colonel outmanœuvred.

THE Colonel has girded up his loins for the mountains, and with the assistance of Mogh-a-dioul, a pony of unhappy name, but good and enduring qualities, he purposes to favour us with his company during our sojourn at the cabin in the hills. While we traverse the moors, the commander will infest the river; or, if the day be questionable, like honest Sancho, he will patiently remain beside the flesh-pots. To him the "meminisse juvabit" will apply. Thirty years ago, with his lamented contemporary, our host's father, the soldier, who was then a keen and accomplished sportsman, spent many a happy hour upon the heath. To his memory every dell and hillock is still green; and hence our evening details will recall to him those happier recollections of youthful pastime, which, when "life was new," he had once delighted to indulge in.

The Colonel fishes well! and I, at least my vanity believes it, have improved marvellously—I really *can* throw a line, and this the priest avers upon the word of a churchman. I begin also to have what the Scotch call a *gloamin'* of what forms the composition of a killing fly. But my pride has sadly abated. Last night, during a stormy controversy, touching the comparative merits of Pull-garrow and Pull-bouy, upon which the host and commander held opinions opposite as the an-

tipodes, to prove that I belonged to a "thinking people,"
I raised my voice in favour of the *yellow pool*. Our host in
dudgeon having premised that one of us was blind, and the
other a botch, declared by the shade of Walton, that on any
given day he would kill more than we both could produce
together. This, as every Irish argument ends in a duel or
bet, has terminated, *fortunately*, in the latter : and though the
wager be not so deep as Hamlet's "Barbary horses" to
"French rapiers, poniards, and their assigns," yet the
respective parties appear deeply interested in the result. To-
morrow will decide the question, and settle the doubtful point
of scientific superiority between the rival artists.

It strikes me forcibly, that among Irish anglers the doctrine
of *meum et tuum* is but indifferently understood. My kinsman
and the commander are constantly lamenting a loss of property,
and certainly they do not indulge in these *jeremiads* without
good reason. I never observe the Colonel's huge book
forgotten for a few minutes, but it is unmercifully plundered
by the host—and if the key of the latter's fly-drawer can be
procured, the commander unlocks it without ceremony, and
having explored its *arcana*, adopts liberally such articles as find
favour in his sight. The housemaid has been suborned to
abstract the Colonel's casting-lines from his dormitory ; and, as
the host generally hides a favourite fly or two in the lining of
his hat, I never pass the hall without finding the commander
fumbling about the hat-stand. It was clearly stipulated and
understood that the flies with which to-morrow's match should
be decided, were to be *bona fide* the handy-work of the respective parties ; yet the colonel privately informs me that he has
despatched a trusty envoy to the priest, to implore that gifted
churchman to furnish him, *sub sigillo*, with a *cast* or two for
the occasion ; and the said envoy has covenanted to be at the
commander's window with an answer, "before a *mother's soul*
is stirring."

The thunder-storm produced a considerable fresh in the
river, as the rain fell abundantly in the hills. The stream,
however, had sufficient time to clear after the flood, and we
found it in beautiful order. The wind is steady at north-
west ; and as the drafting has long since been discontinued,
and the wears lowered to permit the fish to enter from the sea
without obstruction, old Antony declares that, as a fishing-day,
nothing could be more favourable. We tossed for choice, and

lost it. My kinsman commences his work three miles up, at
his favourite Pull-garrow, while we fish from the mouth of
the river. At five we meet at the cabin, and the party then
producing the greater weight of fish is conqueror. These
preliminaries being adjusted, our opponent went off like an
Arab, to join his aide-de-camp, Mr. Hennessey, who has all
in readiness for his commencement, and, I suspect, a salmon
or two already in the pannier.

The opening of our campaign is every thing but satisfactory
—Mogh-a-dioul seems possessed with the demon of obstinacy;
any advance towards the river is his aversion, and, as Pattigo
expresses it, "the beast will neither *wear or stay.*" The
commander's seat has been more than once perilled by his
gambadoes ; and, as we are informed that he is caparisoned
with a bit, which is his abomination, there is but little chance
of amendment in Mogh-a-dioul. This appears very like a plot
against the Colonel's person ; and I fear that the midnight
embassy to the priest will be more than countervailed, by the
manœuvres of our abler antagonist.

Both adepts made excellent professions of good faith at
starting ; but, as my kinsman left us, there was a "lurking
devil in his eye," that augurs us no good fortune. The commander, too, talked in good set terms of "honourable conduct;" but precept and practice, I lament to say, are somewhat irreconcilable.

"*Andy,*" he said, in his most insinuating manner, to our
attendant; " *Andy Bawn,* you were always an obliging boy,
and very handy with the gaff. Just keep your eye about the
banks as we go along ; and if you can *snaffle* a salmon or two,
why, the pannier will tell no tales, and weigh all the better."

To me there never was a more delightful expedition ; but
my companion was cold to all the romance of nature, and engrossed with one consideration—to win his wager. While I
was enraptured with the splendid scenery that each new point
presented, the colonel was cursing his flies, and pouring
anathemas on the priest. " How beautiful !" I exclaimed, as
the sunshine fell upon a mountain valley, through which a
little rivulet was winding, and whose waters, in the glare of
light, danced downwards like a streak of molten silver. " How
damned provoking," responded my brother fisherman, " that
the only decent fly in that cursed priest's collection, should be
tied upon a hook with no more point upon it than a hobnail !

Ah, Father Andrew! was this treatment for an old acquaintance—a man who would have trusted his life to you, and drink
with you in the dark ? Here, *Andy Bawn*, give me my book,
and fling this most villanous assemblage of faded wool and
ragged feathers into the next bog-hole. And now, my friend
and fellow-labourer, leave the mountains alone, and think more
of filling the fishing-baskets, or we are beaten men !"

We followed the course of the river for a distance of ten
miles, stopping at the pools as we went along, but leaving the
streams and shallows without a trial. As we proceeded up
the hills, the scenery became wilder and more interesting ;
here and there, the moors were sprinkled with green hillocks,
and the range of mountains behind was splendidly picturesque.
The pools alone had beauty in my companion's eyes, and some
of them were indeed magnificent. One was particularly romantic—it was a deep natural basin, formed by a sudden
turning of the river, where the banks on either side were
nearly perpendicular, and rose to a considerable height, and, to
the water's edge, were thickly covered with hollies and hardy
shrubs. At the upper end of the pool, a rock of immense
magnitude reared its naked front, and shut out every other
object. Round its base, the river forced its waters through a
narrow channel, and at the other extremity, falling over a
ledge of rocks, turned sharply round a hillock, and was lost
sight of. There were but two points from which the angler
could command the pool, for elsewhere the banks and underwood prevented his approach : one was a sand-bank about the
centre, to which, by a narrow goat-path, the fisher could descend ; the other, a small space immediately beneath the rock,
of green and velvet-looking herbage. At this point the shep-
herds had erected a hut for occasional shelter, and never was
a sweeter spot selected, wherein to dream away a summer
night. No human dwelling was in sight—deep and undisturbed solitude breathed around—the blue and lucid pool
before the cabin danced in the moonlight, or glittered in the
first rays of morning—while the rushing waters of the river
produced such melancholy and tranquillizing sounds, as would
lull to rest any bosom untortured by mortal passions.

" Julius has been here before us, and has left some mementos
of his visit," said the Colonel, pointing to foot-marks in the
sand, and blood and fish-scales upon the pebbles ; " I fear our
be is in jeopardy ; verily, our worthy relative will never shame

the proverb, that ' De'il's bairns have de'il's luck !' But what can the matter be among the salmon ? in faith, the pool appears bewitched."

As he spoke, I remarked the occurrence which the commander noticed. The fish, which upon our first arrival had risen merrily at the natural flies, ceased on a sudden altogether —now they rushed confusedly through the water, or threw themselves for yards along the surface. It was not the sullen plunge at an insect, or the vertical spring, when sport, not food, brings the salmon over water; but it was evident there was some hidden cause of alarm, and we were not long left in doubt. Near the neck of the pool, an otter of the largest size showed himself for a moment, then darting under water, the same commotion ensued again. Before a minute elapsed, *Andy Bawn* pointed silently to a shoal beneath an overhanging bush, and *there* was the spoiler, apparently resting himself after his successful exertions, and holding a *four-pound* white trout in his mouth. Either he noticed us, or had some more favourite haunt to feed in, for he glided into the deep water, and we saw no more of him.

Although we found out that the otter and ourselves could not manage to fish in company, we ascertained that the pool was abundantly stocked with salmon; during the period of the greatest alarm, at least a dozen fish were breaking the surface at the same time.

We reached the cabin after a day of excellent sport; but every thing on earth has its alloy, and two circumstances appear to cloud the sunshine of the commander's bosom. One is the inexplicable conduct of the priest; the other the repeated misconduct of Mogh-a-dioul. We have, to be sure, four fine salmon, and a score of good-sized sea-trouts; but the Colonel swears, that he lost his best fishing until he discarded the priest's flies; and it is probable, if their defects had been apparent at an earlier period, our baskets would have been considerably benefited by the discovery.

As we ascended the bank before the cabin door, our rival met us. He had left off fishing for some time, and had changed his dress entirely—" Come, brush up, or dinner will be spoiled. Colonel, I trust that you and Mogh-a-dioul are on pleasing terms with each other. You stole my bridle, but, no apologies—I can ride *Crughadore* with a hayband. Come, —to scale at once, or dinner is not worth a gray groat.

Hennessey, the steel-yard—produce—despatch—*one, two, three, four*. You killed *one* apiece, I presume, and Andy gaffed the other *two*; nay, commander of the faithful, look not so ferocious. What, no more! and is this paltry *creel* of fish the produce of the day? Colonel, I blush for you. Barely *forty pounds*. Turn that *clave** over, and put these gentlemen of the angle out of pain." As he spoke, the attendant emptied the contents of the pannier, and *nine well-sized salmon*, with a multitude of sea-trouts, rolled out upon the sward.

"By my faith!" exclaimed the commander, "these fish were never fairly killed; you drafted a hole or two, as surely as I am a sinner."

"The latter part of your remark I admit," said my kinsman, "the former I deny. By this virgin hand! every fish before you was killed by hook and line. Come, are you for

* A horsebasket.

another bet? For five pounds, and *within five minutes*, I'll kill another salmon, and make the number *ten !*"

"Done!" we exclaimed together.

"Hennessey, the rod; wet the flies below the pool, and in in twenty seconds, yon cloud will be over the sun."

Before the cabin there is a tolerable hole, deep, but narrow. Where the stream runs in, the ripple is considerable, and between it and the bank, the deepest water lies. If there be a salmon in the pool, *there* is the spot to find him. My cousin sent the casting line in such masterly style into the opposite eddy, as proclaimed him at once an adept, and the second cast a salmon rose and took him.

He was but a light fish, and in less than three minutes was bounding upon the grass, beside his dead companions. My kinsman handed the rod to the attendant.—"Gentlemen," he said in mock heroics, "in your memories be all my bets remembered! And now to dinner, with what appetite you may."

"Well," said the commander, "*this beats Bannagher.*\* I would have given my corporal oath the knave had swept the river. His flies are absolute perfection! There's villany somewhere; but come along. The dinner must not cool, and the wine shall pay for it!"

---

"Julius," said the commander, as he extracted the third cork, "thy star predominated; a villanous combination of circumstances, with infernal flies, and an intractable pony, destroyed me. *Andy Bawn* (we are *beaten*, and the truth may be told) for the first time in his life was taken with a fit of conscience, and actually refused to gaff a salmon. The very otters were combined against us, and disturbed the best pool upon the river but *Pull-buoy*. I had no time to tie fresh flies."

"Or even send to Goolamere, to *borrow*," said my kinsman, drily.

"Ah, hem," and the colonel appeared a little *bothered* —"I want no man's flies; my own, I find, will generally answer."

\* An Irish phrase synonymous with "this exceeds everything."

"And yet," said the host, "the priest, when he pleases, can tie a *killing one*."

"Why—ye—es, he does—a *leetle* coarse—but let me see your casting-lines; I fear, my friend, that we had not the right colours up."

"*I fear so too*," said our host, with much expression.

"By my conscience!" exclaimed the colonel, as he scrutinized the casting-lines that were wound about my kinsman's hat, "I would have taken my oath on a bag-full of books, that this *mallard's wing* was tied by Father Andrew."

"And by *my* conscience," returned the host, "you would not have been very far astray."

"And was this fair, Julius—to fish with any but your own?"

"Why, really, they looked so beautiful, that for the life of me, I could not but put them up. But, my friend, the next time you despatch a midnight messenger, select a trustier one than *Currakeen*\*—and take a better opportunity to praise young Alice's '*black eyes*,' than when issuing your secret instructions. Nay, I will respect those blushes. The fact is, Currakeen was at your window before 'a *mother's soul was stirring*'—but, my dear Colonel, he did me the favour to *first* call at *mine*. I merely took the liberty of exchanging a few flies—you fished with some old acquaintances, while I tried experiments with *Father Andrew's*. Come, the bets are off—we both violated treaties, and thus, I renounce my victory, though my opinion of *Pull-garrow* is unalterable."

"Julius," said the commander solemnly, "you'll be on the highway next. Breaking a letter open, I think is an excellent preparative for stopping his majesty's mail."

"And in that case, I trust that you will be an accomplice. If one must swing, good society is every thing. Your demeanour at 'the fatal tree.' I am persuaded, would be exemplary. And yet, my dear Frank, although I treated Father Andrew's despatch with scanty ceremony, I never came within the clutches of the law but *once*, and that was, as old Jack says, through *villanous company*."

---

\* A bye-name given to one of the endless tribe of *Malley*.

" Was that the time you stole the snuff-box ?" asked the commander.

" *I steal a snuff-box*! No—I deny the *theft*—I was only *an accessary* after all. But, to clear my character, I must tell the story to my cousin."

## CHAPTER XXIX.

### THE GOLD SNUFF-BOX

It was the spring before my father's death. A vacation was at hand, and for some college irregularities, I had been deprived of my chambers as a punishment, and turned upon the town to shift as I best could. I fixed myself at the *Wexford Hotel* for the short time I intended remaining in the capital, and there formed my first acquaintance with Colonel B—— and Lieutenant K——, both of the —— Militia.

They arrived at " The Wexford" late one evening from Naas, where the regiment was then quartered, and were on their route to visit, on private business, " the realms beyond the Shannon."

I was alone in the parlour when the strangers arrived. They cast a wistful eye at a choice haddock, then in the very act of being served up as exordium to the dinner. The waiter in a whisper assured the belated travellers that he was convinced the young gentleman, meaning me, would share his fish and table-cloth. The request was very politely made, very politely granted, and down we sat, as if we had been bosom friends for a twelvemonth.

The colonel was an overgrown bombard — a vessel full-charged with good-humour and old port. He said odd things, and did them too. The subaltern was a squab-built snub-nosed strange sort of merry fellow, having a rich brogue and racy wit ; and while the corpulent commander believed that he was humbugging the short lieutenant, the short lieutenant, all the while, was playing the devil with the corpulent commander. No two persons were ever better constructed

N 2

to elicit reciprocal amusement ; and they were, though
opposites in every thing, as necessary to each other, as
" sheath to sword."

But there was a circumstance that united the strangers
and myself directly. My friend, Lord L———, had just
got a majority in the colonel's regiment; and the said
colonel and his companion were going that very night to a
ball at the dowager's, who then lived in Rutland-square.

We finished a formidable portion of *Page's best**—retired
to dress, and afterwards set off in a hackney-coach to the
scene of our evening's amusement.    I was three deep in
dancing engagements, and my first partner was already in the
room—of course I separated from my companions directly,
of whom, however, I caught a distant glance as they were
formally presented to his aunt, by Lord L———.

It was a crowded ball. I was dancing busily, and how
my companions employed themselves, never occasioned me
a thought.    At last supper was whispered to be on the *tapis*.
Miss Carden and I—she was then a very pretty girl—had
quietly slipped away from *the set*, to be in readiness for the
crush, when we stumbled upon a snug whist-table in an
unfrequented corner, and there I discovered my gallant
friends actively engaged.

The unhappy men were partners.    They had, moreover,
been delivered into the hands of the dowager and Mrs. P———,
an antiquated commoner.    Both ladies were notorious for
extraordinary luck, and a fortunate arrangement of always
*cutting together*.    It was further believed, that both were
given to the good old rule of winning, *honestly if they could*—
but *winning*.

It was evident at first sight that the soldiers were no
matches for the gentlewomen.    The rubber game was on
the point of being decided just as we reached the table—
the soldiers had it by honours, but, by a barefaced revoke,
that would have been detected by any but the buzzards
they were playing with, the ladies gained the point required,
and had their claim allowed.    " Supper is served," said
Mrs. P———, with a satisfactory grin ; " had we not better
stop, Lady L——— ?"    The gentlemen simultaneously popped

* A celebrated wine-merchant, some thirty years ago.

their hands into the pockets of their nether garments. " In
how much have I the honour to be your ladyship's debtor ?"
inquired the colonel, with a gracious smile. Mrs. P——
instantly mumbled, with the rapidity of a barmaid, " Ten
points — three rubbers — *only nine guineas.*" The colonel
started and stared. " *Nine devils!* — I mean, *guineas* !"
exclaimed *the Sub,* in awful consternation. But the decree
had gone forth. " They never played *higher*—deep play
was detestable." The money was accordingly doled out,
and I observed that the contents of the lieutenant's purse,
after rendering this sweeping subsidy, were reduced to a
solitary guinea.

At this moment the supper-rooms were thrown open, and
away went the crowd. The Dowagers were left to scramble
up their winnings, and the soldiers, I presume, to execrate
their own bad luck. Miss Carden and I, who witnessed the
impudent revoke perpetrated by Mrs. P——, and passed
over by my Lady L———, mutually decided, that in common
justice, both ladies should have been consigned for a month to
the house of correction.

Supper, as all suppers have done, ended. I placed my
handsome partner in her mother's carriage, and was then
depositing myself in a hackney-coach, when I espied my
military friends upon the steps, hailed them immediately, and,
embarking in the same vehicle, we were duly landed at " the
Wexford."

" Waiter !" cried the colonel, in a voice of thunder, " some
brandy and *red hot* water. I wore my *thin tights,* for the first
time these six months," addressing me, " and, by St. Patrick !
my limbs are icicles. I drank two glasses of execrable
Teneriffe ! and, God knows *one* would be a sufficient dose of
poison for a gouty man like me. Arrah ! waiter, have you it
in the house ? If you have not, say so, and I'll run out and
save my life at the next tavern." But the waiter was prompt,
and the *house honest.* Up came the brandy and *materials ;*
and the colonel, relieved from the anticipated attack in his
stomach, " breathed again."

I looked at my unfortunate friends, and never did
men bear their misfortunes so differently. While the
subaltern was in a phrensy, the commander was calm as a
philosopher.

"Well, if the devil had his own," exclaimed the irritated lieutenant, "my lady L—— would fry."

"Rowland," said the colonel, solemnly, "what the deuce tempted you to play? You don't understand the game, and I often told you so."

"But," said I, interrupting him, "the rubber was yours. Mrs. P—— made a scandalous revoke. How could it escape your observation? The young lady, who was leaning on my arm, was horrified at such barefaced cheating."

"I remarked it," said the lieutenant; "but I was ashamed to speak. I thought we were playing half-crown points!"

"I wish I had seen it," said the colonel. "Ah, Rowly, you're no wizard!"

"Well, no matter; I have suffered enough," said the subaltern, testily. "If I have a rap left, after these swindling jades, but one solitary guinea to carry me to Connemara!"

"Pshaw! *beg*, man, *beg!* You have a face for any thing. I wonder how *I* stand upon the night's play."

"Nine guineas *minus*," said the subaltern, "unless you managed to fob off a light piece, or pass a counterfeit."

"That would be impossible," remarked the colonel; "for though the crush was desperate, and I thought, and I wished, that the table would be overturned, the dowager thumbed every guinea over as if she had played with a pick-pocket. It was just then that I managed to secure a keep-sake;" and he produced a huge snuff-box of fine gold and antique workmanship from his side-pocket. I stared with wonder, while the subaltern ejaculated, "What a chance! Ah, colonel, you are the jewel! The box will pay our losses beautifully."

"I beg to be excused from co-partnership," said the colonel, drily. "Rowly, you might have stolen for yourself. I saw a pair of gold-mounted spectacles upon the table, and a *vinaigrette* of silver device lay beside you. No, no, Rowly! rob for yourself."

"And," said I, "my dear colonel, might I ask what may be the ultimate design which you harbour against the dowager's snuff-box!"

"Why, faith, my young friend, my plans are simple

enough. I'll give you and that *ommadawn*,"* pointing to his lieutenant, " an early dinner, and bring you to the play afterwards. Well, it will be tolerably dark by that time. We'll pass St. Andrew's church, call next door, and get a worthy man who lives convenient, and who is very liberal in lending money to any body who leaves sufficient security behind him,—" we'll get him, in short, to take the box at his own valuation."

" And if it should be discovered?"

" Oh, little fear of that. No, my friend, before you and I are in the boxes, *this box* will be in the melting-pot. The man is a considerate and conscientious dealer. No, no, all's safe with him."

We parted for the night. At noon, next day, we met at breakfast. I, although pretty conversant in odd adventures and mad freaks, was dying to see the conclusion of the snuff-box affair. We, of Trinity, often touched upon street-robbery in poles and rattles; and, as far as public property went, were nowise scrupulous. I had once achieved a petty larceny, by running off with a pine-apple from a fruiterer's, for which, however, I had the grace to send payment in the morning. Still the colonel's *coup* was so superior to all this, that I was so much interested in the *dénouement*, as if I had been a principal concerned. At the appointed hour we regularly met in Dawson-street. Our host gave us the best dinner in Morrison's *carte*, and we had champagne, liqueurs, and a superabundant supply of the primest claret in the cellar.

Pending dinner, the parties made an amicable arrangement touching the disposition of the booty.

The field-officer was to share the surplus produce over the payment of the tavern bill; and the subaltern was to be the vender of the spoil.

It was nearly eight o'clock when we left Morrison's, and directed our course to the civil gentleman who lent money on good security. We entered an outer hall, and thence advanced into one encompassed by a tier of compartments, like confession-boxes. Rowly stepped into a vacant stall, and we stood close behind, to "aid, comfort, and counsel."

The money-dealer left an unfinished bargain with a trades-

† *Anglice*, an idiot.

man's wife, to attend upon his better-dressed customer. "Ah!
hem—hem!" said the subaltern, rather *bothered* to open
the negotiation—but the *Lombard* gave an encouraging simper,—" A small advance wanted, I presume?" " Why, no
—ah, hem!—wish to dispose of a trifle—a present,—no
use for it,—but would not for the world it was known."
The pawnbroker instantly presented his finger and thumb,
to receive watch, ring, or jewel, according as the case
might be.

The snuff-box was promptly displayed, and the happy eye
of the money-dealer turned rapidly from the box to the pre-
senter : " Well, sir, pray what be the value?"

" Really, can't say—a present—and—"

" Oh! ye-e-e-s—old gold—mere drug now-a-days—about
three pound ten an ounce—once valuable—bullion then scarce
—a year ago it would have been a very pretty *swag*."

" *Swag*! What do you mean?" cried the alarmed seller.
" Zounds! do you think I stole it?"

" Oh, dear, *no-o*!—beg pardon—meant present. Here, the
scales, John. Ah! ah! let me see—ay—standing beam—
ah!—say fifteen pounds—full value, I assure you—the price
to a pennyweight."

" Very well; I'm content : but if my friend discovered that
I would part with his present—"

The broker raised his forefinger to his nose, and dropped
his left eyelid with a striking expression—the look would have
done honour to an Old Bailey practitioner. The money was
told down upon the counter :—" The hammer, John!" A
lean, ill-grown, ill-visaged dwarf, produced a weighty one.
There was a small anvil affixed to the bench; my Lady
L——'s box received one mortal blow, and the attending imp
swept the shattered fragments into a crucible.

What was the exact disposition of the assets, I cannot pretend to say; but I believe they were fairly partitioned between
the parties concerned.

About six months afterwards, when passing through the
city, after my father's death, I met Lord L——, and he
received me with his customary kindness. " You must dine
with me to-day," he said. I pointed to my mourning coat.
" Oh, you *must* come—the very place for one wishing to avoid
the world. Since you left Dublin, my poor aunt has undergone such a change!—an infernal gang has got round her

entirely; and she, who once only lived for whist, cannot be persuaded to touch a card. By Jove, the good lady is bewitched. But I have arranged with her, that the first crop-eared scoundrel, or female ranter, I meet in Rutland-square, shall be the signal for my final abdication to Kildare-street—and she knows that I am positive. Do come: not a soul dines with me, but that good, fat fellow, my Colonel." I smiled as I recollected our last visit to the square, and promised to be punctual.

I arrived some time before Lord L——, and found the dowager and my fat friend, the Colonel, *tête-à-tête*. Beyond the customary interchange of civilities, I did not interrupt them, receiving, however, from the commander a warm squeeze, and an inexpressibly comic look, that recalled a volume of adventure. The old lady resumed the conversation which my entrée had suspended :—

"And you are six months absent, Colonel!—Protect me! how time passes!—it should be a lesson—a tacit monitor, as Mr. Hitchcock happily expresses it. Well, there was a carnal-minded, noisy crowd here; and I remember you lost three rubbers. How such vain imaginations will push aside the better seeds! Your partner was a well-meaning gentleman, but never returned a lead. Oh, me! that these vanities should be remembered. That very night, Colonel, I met with a serious, I may say distressing loss. My cousin, General Pillau's Indian snuff-box was stolen! I suspected—but judge not, as Mr. Heavyside said at the chapel yesterday. It was in my partner's hand the last time I ever saw it; the rush to supper came—she—but we must be charitable. But here's my nephew—O that he was awake to Gospel truth! Well, my dear George, what news since ?"

"None, madam: only that our old friend's over—dead as Julius Cæsar. Mother P—— will never cut out another honour."

"Oh, George! do stop—for once be serious. Mrs. P—— dead! and, I fear, not prepared. Ah, me! poor Mrs. P——! Many a rubber she and I have played—she knew my system so well—finessed a *leetle* too much—but where am I running? —Well, *I hope* she was prepared, *but she stole the General's box* !"

"Phew! if she stole snuff-boxes, she'll fry for it now," said
the Colonel, taking share in the lament; "I hope, madam, it
was merely a pretty toy, something not valuable?"

"*A toy!* my dear sir; fine pale gold—invaluable for weight,
age, and workmanship. Had you ever held it in your hand,
you would never have forgotten it."

"Faith! and likely enough, my lady."

"George, love, if you would just speak to the executor.
Put it on the score of a mistake."

"I speak! Madam, do you want to have me shot?"

"No, no, it's useless. Her nephew is an attorney. 'Do
men gather grapes?' as Mr. Heavyside says."

"Damn Heavyside!" exclaimed the peer, "I must go see
about some wine;" and he left the room.

The old lady recommenced with a groan—"What a memory
Mrs. P—— had! she would remember cards through a rubber, and never omitted marking in her life. *She took the
General's box;* she had always a fancy for knickknackeries,
and wore ornaments very unsuitable to her years—forgetting
the lilies of the valley. I wish Miss Clarke was here, a
worthy comely young woman, Colonel, recommended to me as
a spiritual assistant by Mr. Wagstaff, of the Bethesda. My
nephew can't bear her, because she was bred a dress-maker,
and a vile dragoon officer told him some nasty story to her
disadvantage. Oh, Colonel, I wish George was awakened—
you go to church regularly?"

"I cannot assert that I do *regularly;* not that I see any
harm in it."

"Very prettily remarked, Colonel; and you often, no
doubt, reflect upon the place you're going to?"

"Yes, indeed, madam; one must join one's regiment sooner
or later."

"Ah, Colonel, I wish George had your serious turn; and,
between ourselves, he is by no means *a safe whist player.*
His game is very dangerous. Ah, if I could have had Mr.
Wagstaff to meet you! but my nephew's prejudice is so
violent. He is a sweet, spiritual-minded young man—comes
often to sit an evening with me; and he is so obliging!—takes
*Miss Clarke* home at midnight to save me the expense of
coach-hire, although she lives beyond the lamps. Poor Mrs.
P——! I wonder who will get her card counters. They

were superb. Well, *she stole the box, however;* but as the inspired psalmist—I mean penman, says—Ah, me! I have no memory; I wish *Miss Clarke* was here.—Well, George, any appearance of dinner?"

"So says the butler, madam, and here he comes."

"Colonel, take down my aunt;" and thus ended Lady L——'s lamentation over *sin, snuff-boxes, and Mrs. P——*.

---

## CHAPTER XXX.

The Otter-killers return—Craniology—Superstitions—Sea-horse—Master-otter—Anecdotes of it—Ghosts and fairies—Their influence upon man and animals—Cure of witchcraft—Holy lakes—Lough Keirawn—Its butter fishery—The Faragurta—Its causes, imaginary and real—Cures and cases—Swearing—Comparative value upon the book, the vestment, and the skull—The clearing of Miss Currigan—An uncatholic cook.

THE otter-killer arrived here last evening, after having, according to his own account, worked wonders upon a damaged head. From the specimens I have seen during my short sojourn at *Ballycroy*, I have come to a conclusion, that the skulls of the natives are fabricated of different materials to those of all the world besides. Their endurance is miraculous—a fellow who was reported as "beaten to a jelly, and anointed by the priest," last week, actually cleared a fair with an unpronounceable name, yesterday, after qualifying for admission to the next infirmary some half-score of his Majesty's liege subjects. This is an every-day exploit; and of all the corners of the earth that I have visited, I would name this as the place wherein to establish a resident craniologist.

Like all wild people, these aborigines are absurdly credulous, and open to the grossest superstitions. Charms, as they believe, are employed with decided success, in every disease you name. The existence of ghosts and fairies is universally acknowledged; and animals of extraordinary formation, and strange virtues, are supposed to inhabit lakes and rivers. Among these the *sea-horse* and *master-otter** are pre-

* There is a strange coincidence between the master-otter of the Irish and the Jungunus crocodile of the Japanese.

eminent.  By a singular anomaly, the first is said to be found
in certain inland loughs, and his appearance is imagined to be
fatal to the unfortunate person who encounters him.  The
latter, however, should be an object of anxious research, for
he is endued with amazing virtues.  Where a portion of his
skin is, the house cannot be burned, or the ship cast away,
and steel or bullet will not harm the man who possesses an
inch of this precious material.  Antony, indeed, confesses,
that in the course of his otter-hunting, he has never been
fortunate enough to meet this invaluable brute ; but he tells a
confused story of one having been killed "far down in the
north," by three brothers called Montgomery, who, from
poverty, became immensely rich, and whose descendants are
opulent to this very day.  He says, the master-otter was seen
twice in this neighbourhood.  At Dhu-hill, he appeared about
sixty years ago, attended by about one hundred common-sized
animals, who waited upon " the master," like loyal and duti-
ful beasts.  He was also observed by one of the O'Donnel
family, whilst passing through Clew Bay in a sailing-boat.
Requiring a supply of fresh water, O'Donnel landed on an
island for the purpose of filling his keg, but found the spring
already occupied by a strange and nondescript animal.  After
his first surprise had subsided, he returned to the boat, and
procured a gun.  This he loaded carefully with five fingers
and a half*—for Antony is minute in all his narratives—and
then, and within a dozen yards, levelled at *the master*.  Thrice
he drew the trigger, and thrice the gun missed fire.  The
otter wisely determined not to give him a fourth chance, and
left the well for the ocean.  Mortified at his failure, O'Donnel
tried his gun at a passing gull; it exploded without trouble,
and finished the unfortunate bird—thus proving, beyond a
doubt, that the gun was faultless, and the preservative qualities of the animal were alone to blame—" And, indeed,"
quoth Antony, " he might have snapped at *the master* to
eternity ; for if an inch of skin can save house, ship, and man,
what a deal of virtue there must be in a whole hide !"

The legendary tales touching the appearance of ghosts, and
the exploits of fairies, are endless.  The agency of the former
appears directed principally to men, while the latter exercise

* The lower class of Irish describe the charge of a gun, not by
quantity of powder and shot, but by *long measure*.

their powers upon children and cattle. Indeed, the sinister influence of the "faëry race" appears to fall almost exclusively upon the brute creation in Ballycroy ; and through it many an unhappy cow comes to an untimely end, and if she escape loss of life, she suffers what is nearly as bad, loss of butter.\* For the *first* calamity, Antony acknowledges there is no cure ; but

* While staying at a gentleman's house, I heard, when passing the porter's lodge, that the gate-keeper's cow was ill. As she was a fine animal, the loss would have been a serious one to the family, and hence I became interested in her recovery. For several days, however, the report to my inquiry was more unfavourable, and at last the case was considered hopeless.

The following morning, as I rode past, I found the family in deep distress. The cow, they said, could not live many hours ; and the gate-keeper had gone off to fetch " the charmer," who lived some ten miles distance. I really sympathised with the good woman. The loss of eight or nine guineas to one in humble life is a serious calamity ; and from the appearance of the cow I concluded, though not particularly skilful, that the animal would not survive.

That evening I strolled out after dinner. It was sweet moonlight, and I bent my steps to the gate-house to inquire if the cow still lived.

The family was in great tribulation. " The charmer had arrived—had seen the cow—had prepared herbs and nostrums, and was performing some solitary ceremony at an adjacent spring-well, from which he had excluded every member of the family in assisting." I was most curious to observe the incantation, but was dissuaded by the gate-keeper, who implored me " to give the conjuror fair play."

In five minutes the charmer joined us—he said the case was a bad one, but that he thought he could *bring round* the cow. He then administered the " unhallowed potion," and I left the lodge, expecting to hear next morning that the animal was defunct.

Next day, " the bulletin was favourable ;" and " the charmer" was in the act of receiving his reward—I looked at him : he was as squalid and heart-broken a wretch in appearance as ever trod the earth. The cow still seemed weak, but " the charmer" spoke confidently of her recovery. When he left the lodge and turned his steps homewards, I pulled up my horse and waited for him. He would rather have avoided an interview, but could not. " Well, fellow, you have humbugged that poor family, and persuaded them that the cow will recover ?"—" I have told them truth," said the charmer, coldly.—" And will your prophecy prove true ?" I asked, in a tone of scornful incredulity.—" It will," said he ; " but, *God help me! this night I'll pay dearly for it!*" I looked at him—his face was agonized and terror-stricken ; he crossed the fence, and disappeared.

When I passed the gate-house on my return, the cow was evidently convalescent ; and in a few days she was perfectly well.

I leave the solution of the mystery to the learned ; for in such matters, as they say in Connaught—*Neil an skeil a gau maun.*

for the *second*, there *is* "balm in Gilead," and certain holy
loughs afford an antidote to this elfin visitation.

The cow, I believe, should be present at the operation,
which is performed by committing her tether and some butter
to the waves, with (of course) a due proportion of prayers for
her recovery. Whether the animal be benefited or not, there
be others who reap sure and solid advantages. At the proper
period, some saint's day, no doubt, when Lough Keirawn is
frequented by the proprietors of bewitched cattle, many of the
poor of the neighbourhood congregate on the lee-side of the
lake, and a lively and profitable fishing of fresh butter continues, until the oblations to the saint or saintess of the lake,
on the part of the afflicted cows, have ended.

Among the human diseases ascribed to supernatural causes,
the *faragurta* is the principal. Conjectures touching its
origin are numerous and contradictory, and it is attributed to
everything but the true cause. The *faragurta* comes on suddenly—a general weakness precedes the attack—the sufferer's
strength is prostrated in an instant—he sinks down, and, if
assistance be not at hand, perishes. Many persons are lost
through this disease, while crossing the extensive wilds around
us, where human relief is generally unattainable.

The causes, to which in popular belief it is ascribed, are
many. Some assert that it is brought on by treading upon
a poisonous plant; others, that it is occasioned by fairy
influence ; while more affirm, that it is produced by passing
over the place where a corpse has been laid down. But this
mystified disorder is, after all, nothing but exhaustion consequent upon hunger and fatigue. The lower classes are particularly obnoxious to its attack. They eat but seldom, and at
irregular seasons ; and commonly labour for many hours before
they break their fast. Want of food produces faintness and
exhaustion ; and a supernatural cause is sought for a simple
malady, which is only the natural consequence of dyspepsia
and an empty stomach.

One would imagine that the specific for *faragurta* would
at once point out its origin. Bread, or even a few grains
of corn, are believed to cure it instantly; but any kind of
food is equally efficacious. "I have seen," said my kinsman, "many persons attacked with *faragurta*, and have
myself een patient and physician. Some years ago, a fine

active boy, called *Emineein*,* commonly attended me to the moors, and one day he was suddenly taken ill, in the very wildest part of the hills. He lost all power of limb, and lay down upon the heath unable to proceed a step. We had no grain of any kind to administer, and in this emergency tried that universal panacea—a glass of whisky. After he had swallowed the cordial, the boy rather got worse than better, and we were obliged to carry him to a still-house, at nearly two miles, distance. On our arrival, fortunately for *Emineein*, we found the operators collected round a *skibb*† of potatoes. After eating one or two, the patient was able to join the party, and next morning proceeded stoutly home.

"In my own case, the predisposing cause was no enigma. I had been one of a knot of foxhunters who, on the preceding night, had indulged in a desperate jollification. Finding a disinclination for breakfast, I repaired, contrary to my general habit, without it to the mountains. I had exercised severely for several hours, when at once I became helpless as an infant, and sank upon a bank incapable of motion. My pony and some food were speedily obtained, and the *faragurta* banished. But assuredly, if unassisted, I must have lain upon the heath, for I could not make the slightest exertion to get forward."

---

It is a lamentable fact, that the obligation of legal oath is *here* of trifling importance. Cases of determined perjury occur every day; and an adjuration upon the evangelists, is considered as being far inferior in solemnity to one upon the *priest's vestment*. Whether there be any regular formula to be observed in this comparative swearing, I know not; I say *comparative*, for in Ballycroy, oaths, like adjectives, have three degrees of value. First, that upon the evangelists; the second, upon the vestment; and the last upon the *skull*. Nothing is more common than to hear a fellow, who had just laid down the book, offer to fortify his doubtful evidence, by taking *number two*. But even the *vestment* is not always conclusive; and the following anecdote will best describe the value of comparative swearing:

* Synonymous to *Neddy*.                                   † A basket.

Andy Bawn has felt the arrow of " the villain," and believed, " fond wretch !" that he was beloved again.  The night of the portmanteau affair will ever be chronicled upon his memory ; for while he was under fear and terror at the bridge of Ballyveeney, she, the lady of his love, was at a *prinkum** at Latrah, performing "apples for gentlemen,"† with another suitor.  Nay, more, the quondam lover, as was reported, had actually *cecisbeo'd* Miss Biddy Currigan across the bogs ; and dark and dangerous inuendoes arose from this imprudent escort. Andy Bawn was unhappily a man " who doubts, but dotes ; suspects, yet fondly loves."  Alas ! what was to be done ? Could Miss Currigan become Mrs. Donahoo, after suffering a *regular blast,* as they call it, in the kingdom of Connaught ?  Impossible ! her character must be cleared, and Andy satisfied.

The magistrate was proposed—well, that was good enough, if it were the identity of a strayed sheep, or the murder of a man ; but in a nice case, like Miss Currigan's, it was totaly inefficient.  " The vestment would be taken," —still better ; but the world was censorious : and, after all, Biddy Currigan was a giddy girl to cross a couple of miles of moorland, after midnight, with a declared lover, and him *hearty* ;‡—and so thought Andy Bawn.  At last the suspected virgin volunteered to " take the skull," dispel the fears of her liege lord, and put calumny to the blush for ever.  Andy Bawn " breathed again ;" and the otter-killer was directed to provide the necessary articles for the ceremony.

A skull was accordingly procured from a neighbouring burying-ground ; and Andy's mother, anxious for the honour of the family, threw into the relic a bunch of keys—for iron, they say, adds desperately to the solemnity of the obligation.  The apparatus being paraded, Antony explained, in the mother tongue, that the sins of the lady or gentleman to whom the skull had once appertained, would be added to Miss Currigan's, if she, Biddy, swore falsely ; and Mrs. Donahoo jingled the old iron, and showed that she was " awake

* A Ballycroy ball, on the " free and easy" plan, where much whisky and no ceremony, is used.
† A favourite *contre danse* a the above assemblies.
‡ *Anglice,* half drunk.

to time," and had left nothing on her part undone, that could give effect to the ceremonial. Miss Currigan, with a step and bearing that might silence slander, advanced under the direction of the otter-killer:—like a maid "in the pride of her purity," she devoutly placed her hand upon the skull—and Andy Bawn was made a happy man for ever!

That the saints are often and scandalously overreached by sinners, is a fact which must be admitted and lamented. One case of base dishonesty has but recently occurred in the establishment of my cousin. A cook, whom he had procured through the agency of a friend, has proved a heavy defaulter, and, as Antony says, "scandalized the family." For a considerable time her conduct was unquestionable : she went regularly to mass, gave half-a-crown at Easter, never missed confessions, and, better still, conducted the culinary department with excellent propriety,—so much so, that Father Andrew declared from the altar, that she was an exemplary *artiste*, and a capital Christian. "Frailty, thy name is woman !" This paragon of cooks levanted one frosty night with a travelling pedler ? Then, and not till then, was the dark side of her character exhibited. "She did not value *Lent* a *traneein*—had *shared a rasher* with Sir Charles's man upon a blessed Friday—and, if a skillet went astray, she would promise a pilgrimage to *the Reek* for its recovery, without the least intention of ever laying a leg upon that blessed hill."

The morning after her disappearance, her sins were freely canvassed in the kitchen. "The Lord forgive her !" said the keeper, "for I can't ; she treated the young dogs abominably. *Spot* will lose a claw; and I am sure it was Sibby, the devil speed her ! that scalded him."

"She could hide a quart of spirits, and it would never show upon her," cried Pattigo.

"She was mighty dangerous in a house," exclaimed the black-eyed chamber-maid ; "I never settled the master's room, but she was sure to pass the window."

"She's gone," said the otter-killer ; "there's worse in the north than Sibby. Many a good bowl of broth she gave me. *Tho she mur tho she ; agus neil she gun lought.** She was

---

* *Anglice*, "She is as she is ; but she's not without her fault."

no *great Catholic* it is true! for she owned to me last Saint John's—and she *hearty* at the time—that she was in debt *four stations at Ball, and three and twenty at Croagh Patrick!* She was, the crature, a fine warrant for a promise, but the worst performer under the canopy of heaven—She'll never," said the old man, with his own peculiar chuckle, " clear scores with the Reek and Father Nolan. In troth, I think it would almost puzzle *Bobby*!"\*

## CHAPTER XXXI.

Fresh arrivals—The priest's reception—The lodge alarmed—Preparations for deer-stalking—State of the garrison—The mountain lake—The peasant's adventure—The ravine and red-deer—A Highland ambuscade —The catastrophe.

IF a man were obliged to chronicle with brevity the leading events of our *terra incognita*, I would advise him to reduce them to " arrivals and departures." As the door is never locked, the stream of visiters is incessant. Every man coming from " the corners of the earth " drops in with a " God save all here !" This is the *Shibboleth* of Ballacroy ; the accredited letter of introduction, and, better for the traveller still, a full acquittance for meat, drink, and lodging.

This morning we have had an illiterative arrival—a piper, a pedler, and a priest. Although I place them according to their order of approach, I need scarcely say that the last,

\* This extraordinary being lived at the foot of Croagh Patrick, and was the first performer (religious) of his day, in Connaught. He generally resided at the house of a neighbouring gentleman ; and when a pilgrim visitor was discouraged by the acclivity of the hill, or the quantity of prayers to be got over, Bobby, *for a consideration*, undertook and executed the task. He was not only a harmless, but, as may be well imagined, a very useful personage ; and his death has left a blank which has never yet been filled.

The remains of poor Bobby, at his own request, were transported to the summit of the mountain, and deposited on the apex of Croagh Patrick, where he had so often and so usefully performed. As he was laid where no other body rested, the line intended for Sir John Moore, would be probably more applicable to the hermit :

" They left him *alone* with his glory! "

our respected friend, has given unexpected pleasure.   For me,
the visit is delightful, for I hope to obtain another lesson in
the "gentle art."   The Colonel has embraced this "Walton
of the wilderness;" a man on whom four bottles would not
show, and to whom, in woodcraft and theology, in the commander's opinion, the clerk of Copmanhurst himself was little
better than a bungler; and, notwithstanding my kinsman's
delinquency in intercepting the despatches, and abstracting the
enclosure, he has escaped with a tap or two upon the cheek;
for, as Antony declares, "Father Andrew dotes upon *the
Master.*"

But a shepherd in breathless haste has rushed into the cabin.
By expressive signs, and a few words, he has conveyed the
intelligence to Mr. Hennessey, that three outlying deer are at
this minute in a neighbouring glen.   He saw them in a valley,
as he crossed the brow above.   Nothing short of the landing
of a French army, or a smuggler, could occasion such confusion.   The chamber of state is invaded, rifles are uncased, shot
exchanged for bullets, a basket with refreshments packed: all
is hurry and preparation, and in an incalculably short time we
are ready for the fray, and in full march for the mountains.
Shakspeare, or he is belied, was in his youth a deer fancier,
and he would probably describe this busy scene by "loud alarum,
*exeunt omnes.*"

The day is particularly favourable, the sun shines brilliantly,
the sky is without a cloud, and if we even miss the deer, I
trust that the prospect from the mountain-top will more than
repay our labour in ascending it.   The party comprises three
guns, and some ten or twelve drivers, with our guide.   My
kinsman and Hennessey have rifles; I am no marksman with
a bullet, and I declined to take one, and therefore must put
my trust in honest John Manton.   We bend our course directly to the mountain cleugh, where the deer were seen by the
peasant; but when we reach the base of the hills, we must
diverge to the left, and make a considerable *détour*, and judging from the appearance of the heights to be surmounted, we
have work cut out, which, before our return to the hut, will
tell what metal we are made of.

Nor is the garrison during our absence left without protectors.   The colonel, the priest, the otter-killer, and old John,
*there* keep watch and ward.   The former twain appear to

o 2

have sworn eternal friendship over a three-legged table, and are settled *tête-à-tête* at either side of the cabin window, with all the requisites for fabricating flies displayed before them. Antony is greasing his otter-trap beside the fire. He still indulges the vain hope, that his rheumatism may be cured, and that he will once more revisit the remoter loughs, where otters are abundant, and where many of his happier days were "lang syne" spent. Poor fellow! his hunting is ended, and his trap, like a warrior's sword, must be laid aside, for age has come heavily upon its master. Old John, "the last and trustiest of the four," has assumed his culinary apron, and from the strength and array of his "*matériel*" it is clear, that he calculates little upon the red-deer venison we shall bring home.

A smart walk of some three miles over an undulating surface, of gentle but regular ascent, brought us to the deep and circular lake which lies at the base of Carrig-a-binniogh; it seems the boundary between the hill-country and the moorlands. Here we halted, and held with the peasants a council of war, on the course of operations to be pursued.

The situation of this mountain lough is extremely picturesque; on three sides it is embosomed in the hills, which rise boldly from the water's edge, and for many hundred feet appear to be almost perpendicular. Its depth is considerable, and hence, bright as the day is, the waters have a dark and sombre look. It abounds with trout of moderate size and excellent flavour. They were rising fast at the natural fly, and appeared generally to be herring-sized.

While resting here, preparatory to attempting to ascend the heights, Cooney, the guide, related a very apposite adventure.

Late in the autumn of the preceding year, the peasant had visited the lake with his fishing-rod. The trouts took well, and Cooney had nearly filled his basket, when he was startled by the report of a gun, at no great distance up the hill. While he looked in the direction from whence the shot appeared to have been discharged, a fine full-grown stag crossed the brow above him, tottered downwards for some twenty steps, and then falling into a steep and stony ravine, rolled lifelessly over, until he reached the very spot where the astonished fisherman was standing. Before his surprise had time to abate, a man, armed with a French gun,* leaped upon the bank over which the deer had fallen, and was joined immediately by a companion, armed also with a fowling-piece. Then, for the first time, they observed the startled angler. The discovery was anything but agreeable; for, after a momentary pause, they rushed down the hill together, and presenting their long guns at Cooney's breast, ordered him to decamp, in terms that admitted of no demur. The angler absconded forthwith ; for, as he reasoned fairly enough, " a man who could drive an ounce of lead through a stag's skull, would find little trouble in drilling a Christian." On looking round, he saw the deer-stealers place the carcass on their shoulders, and ascend the heights, over which they quickly disappeared. The feat is almost incredible, and it required an amazing effort of strength and determination to transport a full-grown red-deer over a precipitous mountain, which we, in light marching order, and with no burden but our guns, found a difficult task enough to climb.

From its very base, Carrig-a-binniogh presents a different surface to the moorlands which environ it ; heath is no more seen, and in its place the mountain's rugged sides are clothed with lichen and wild grasses. The face of the hill is broken and irregular, and the ascent rendered extremely disagreeable by multitudes of loose stones which, being lightly bedded in the soil, yield to the pressure of the traveller's foot, and of course increase his difficulties.

After the first hundred yards had been gallantly surmounted, we halted by general consent to recover breath. Again we resumed our labour, and, with occasional pauses, plodded on " our weary way." As we ascended, the hill became more precipitous, the grass shorter, and the hands were as much employed as the feet. The halts were now

* When the French, under Humbert, landed at Killala in the autumn of 1798, they brought with them a large qua tity of arms and military clothing, to equip the numerous partisans they expected to have found in the country. After the French general was defeated, and the insurrection had been put down, many of the guns which had been distributed among the peasantry were buried, or effectually concealed ; and they have been used in poaching and wild-fowl shooting to the present time. The French barrels are said to throw shot much better than those of English muskets. I have never seen their relative merits proven, but imagine that the superiority of the former is owing to their greater length.

more frequent; and each progression towards the summit shorter after every pause. "To climb the trackless mountain all unseen," is very poetical, no doubt, but it is also, I regret to add, amazingly fatiguing, and a task for men of thews and sinews of no ordinary strength. But we were determined and persevered—" *en avant*," was the order of the day; on we progressed, slowly but continuously; the steepest face of the hill was gradually overcome, and a wide waste of moss and shingle lay before us, rising towards a cairn of stones which marks the apex of the mountain. We pressed on with additional energy; the termination of our toil was in view: in a few minutes we gained the top, and a scene, glorious beyond imagination, burst upon us at once, and repaid tenfold the labour we had encountered to obtain it.

We stood upon the very pinnacle of the ridge, two thousand feet above the level of the sea; Clew Bay, that magnificent sheet of water, was extended at our feet, studded with its countless islands: inland, the eye ranged over a space of fifty miles; and towns and villages, beyond number, were sprinkled over a surface covered with grass, and corn, and heath, in beautiful alternation. The sun was shining gloriously, and the variety of colouring presented by this expansive landscape, was splendidly tinted by the vertical rays of light. The yellow corn, the green pasturage, the russet heaths, were traceable to an infinite distance, while smaller objects were marked upon this natural panorama, and churches, towns, and mansions occasionally relieved the prospect. We turned from the interior to the west; there the dark waters of the Atlantic extended, till the eye lost them in the horizon. Northward, lay the Sligo islands; and southward, the Connemara mountains, with the noble islands of Turk and Boffin—nearer objects seemed almost beneath us; Achil was below—Clare Island stretched at our feet—while our own cabin looked like a speck upon the canvas, distinguished only by its spiral wreath of smoke from the hillocks that encircled it. There was an indescribable loneliness around, that gave powerful effect to all we saw. The dreariness of the waste we occupied was grand and imposing: we were far removed from every thing human; we stood above the world, and could exclaim with Byron, " this, *this* is solitude!"

How long we might have gazed on this brilliant spectacle is questionable. Hennessey, less romantic than we, reminded us that it was time to occupy the defile, by which the deer, if found, and driven from the lowlands, would pass within our range. Thus recalled, we looked at the immediate vicinage of the cairn. It was a wilderness of moss and bog, and granite, barren beyond description, and connected with the upper levels of the Alpine ridge, which extended for miles at either side, by a narrow chain of rock, which seemed more like the topping of a parapet than the apex of a line of hills. Indeed, a more desolate region could not be well imagined ;— no sign of vegetation appeared, if scathed lichens, and parched and withered flag-grass be excepted. The mountain cattle were rarely seen upon these heights, and the footmarks upon the softer surface were those of the deer and goats. Hennessey discovered the tracks of a herd of the larger species, which, from his acute observations, had evidently crossed the ridge since sunrise, and must, from their numerous traces, have amounted to at least a dozen.

While we still cast a "longing lingering look" at a scene, which, I lament to say, I shall most probably never be permitted to view again—a boy rose from the valley towards the south, and hastened at full speed to join us. His communication was soon made, and, like the shepherd's at the cabin, pantomime rather than speech conveyed its import. His tidings were momentous; the deer had moved from the place in which they had been first discovered, and were now within one thousand yards of the place where we were resting. Hennessey and the *gossoon*\* advanced in double quick, and where the ridge is steepest between the highlands and the valley, we observed them make a sudden halt, and creep gingerly forward, to what seemed the brow of a precipice. We followed more leisurely, and adopting a similar method of approach, stole silently on, and looked over the chasm.

The precipice we were on forms the extremity of a long but narrow ravine, which gradually rising from the lowlands, divides the basis of Carrig-a-binnoigh and Meelroe. It was a perpendicular rock of fearful height. At either side the valley was flanked by the sides of the opposite hills ; and

---

\* *Anglice*, boy.

they sprung up so rugged and precipitous as to be quite impracticable to all but " the wild flock which never needs a fold ;" and yet the cleugh below was like a green spot upon a wilderness. To the very bases of the ridges it was covered with verdant grass and blooming heather while, at the upper end, streams from several well-heads united together and formed a sparkling rivulet, which wandered between banks so green and shrubby, as formed a striking contrast to the barren heaths below and the blasted wilderness above.

We put our bats aside, and peeped over. The wave of Hennessey's hand proved the boy's report to be correct, and we were gratified with a sight of those rare and beautiful animals which formed the objects of our expedition. They were the same leash which the peasant had noticed in the lower valley—an old stag, a younger one, and a doe.

The great elevation of the precipice, and the caution with which we approached the verge, permitted us, without alarming them, to view the red-deer leisurely. They appeared to have been as yet undisturbed, for, after cropping the herbage for a little, the younger stag and the hind lay down, while the old hart remained erect, as if he intended to be their sentinel.

The distance of the deer from the ridge was too great to allow the rifle to be used with anything like certainty; and from the exposed nature of the hills at either side, it was impossible to get within point-blank range undiscovered. Hennessey had already formed his plans, and drawing cautiously back from the ridge, he pulled us by the skirts, and beckoned us to retire.

We fell back about a pistol-shot from the cliff, and under a rock, which bore the portentous name of Craignamoina,* held our council of war.

There were two passes, through one of which the deer, when roused and driven from the glen, would most likely retreat. The better of these, as post of honour, was, more politely than prudently, entrusted to me—my kinsman occupied the other ; and Hennessey having ensconced us behind rocks which prevented our ambush from being discovered, crossed to the other side of the ridge, and I lost sight of him. Meanwhile the boy had been despatched to apprize the *drivers* that the deer were in the ravine, and to notify the spot where

---

* *Anglice*, the rock of slaughter.

we were posted, to enable them to arrange their movements according to our plans.

I will not pretend to describe the anxious, nay *agonizing* hour that I passed in this highland ambuscade. The deep stillness of the waste was not broken by even the twittering of a bird. From the place where I lay concealed, I commanded a view of the defile for the distance of some eighty yards, and my eye turned to the path by which I expected the deer to approach, until to gaze longer pained me. My ear was equally engaged ; the smallest noise was instantly detected, and the ticking of my watch appeared sharper and louder than usual. As time wore on, my nervousness increased. Suddenly a few pebbles fell—my heart beat faster—but it was a false alarm. Again, I heard a faint sound, as if a light foot pressed upon loose shingle—it was repeated. By Saint Hubert, it is the deer ! They have entered the gorge of the pass, and approach the rock that covers me, in a gentle canter !

To sink upon one knee and cock both barrels was a

moment's work. Reckless of danger, the noble animals, in single file, galloped down the narrow pathway. The hart

led the way, followed by the doe, and the old stag brought up
the rear. As they passed me at the short distance of twenty
paces, I fired at the leader, and, as I thought, with deadly aim;
but the ball passed over his back, and splintered the rock
beyond him. The report rang over the waste, and the deer's
surprise was evinced by the tremendous rush they made to
clear the defile before them. I selected the stag for my
second essay; eye and finger kept excellent time, as I
imagined—I drew the trigger—a miss, by everything unfortunate! The bullet merely struck a tyne from his antler, and,
excepting this trifling graze, he went off at a thundering pace,
uninjured.

Cursing myself, John Manton, and all the world, I threw
my luckless gun upon the ground, and rushed to the summit
of a neighbouring rock, from which the heights and valleys
beyond the gorge of the pass were seen distinctly. The deer
had separated—the hart and doe turned suddenly to the right,
and were fired at by my cousin, without effect. The stag
went right ahead; and while I still gazed after him, a flash
issued from a hollow in the hill, the sharp report of Hennessey's piece succeeded, and the stag sprang full six feet from
the ground, and tumbling over and over repeatedly, dropped
upon the bent-grass with a rifle-bullet in his heart.

I rushed at headlong speed to the spot where the noble
animal lay. The eye was open—the nostril expanded, just as
life had left him. Throwing his rifle down, Hennessey pulled
out a clasp-knife, passed the blade across the deer's throat, and
requesting my assistance, raised the carcass by the haunches,
in order to assist its bleeding freely.

Having performed this necessary operation, and obtained
the assistance of two of our companions from the valley,
whence they had been driving the deer, we proceeded to
transport the dead stag to the lowlands. It was no easy
task, but we accomplished it quickly; and perceiving some
horses grazing at no great distance, we determined to press
one for the occasion. A stout pony was most unceremo-
niously put in requisition, the deer laid across his back, and
after emptying flask and basket joyously beside a stream of
rock-water, we turned our faces to the cabin, where the news
of our success had already arrived.

## CHAPTER XXXII.

Deer brought home—Dinner—Gastronomic reflections—Grouse soup—
Roasted salmon—Cooking *pour et contre*—Carouse commences—
Symptoms of inebriety—Night in the hills—Coffee *al fresco*—Temperance society—A Bacchanalian group—Auld lang syne—Borrowing
a congregation—The company dispersed.

WONDERFUL are the inventions of man ! The slaughter of
an unhappy stag has been made good and sufficient cause
for all the idlers of the community assembling at our cabin.
They are squatted round the fire like Indians in a wigwam—
and old John, no bad authority in such matters, declares
in a stage whisper to his master, " that a four-gallon cag
will scarcely last the night, there is such a clanjamfry of
*coosherers*\* in the kitchen—the devil speed them, one and all !"

It was twilight when we got home. The deer had arrived
before us, and was already hanging up, suspended from the
*couples*. A cheerful fire blazed in the room of state, while
exhilarating effluvia from the outer chamber told that John's
preparations were far advanced. We had scarcely time to
make our hurried toilet before the table was covered, and

---

\* This phrase is used in Ireland to designate that useless and eternal
tribe, who are there the regular *attachés* of families of ancient lineage.
Nurses, fosterers, discharged servants, decayed sportsmen, and idlers of
every sex, age, and calling, come under this description.

There was a higher class of nuisance under the title of *poor relations*
who formerly wandered over Connaught, and from the interminable
ramifications of the old families, there were few houses into which these
worthies had not a right of *entrée*. The last one I recollect when a boy,
traversed the country upon a white pony, dressed in dingy black, and
arrayed in a cocked-hat ; a certain number of houses were under annual
requisition, and such was the influence of annual custom, that none would
venture to refuse this forced hospitality, although the man was latterly a
sad bore. Some gentlemen, when their " loving cousin was expected,
had his approach observed, and stopped him in the avenue with an excuse
that the house was full, and a subsidy of a few guineas. The money was
always acceptable—and whoever unluckily happened to be next number
on the visiting list, was favoured with one week additional from my
" Cousin Mac."

" Mac," with his brigadier wig and white pony, has gone the way of all
flesh, and by travestying a line of Sir Walter Scott, one could add,

" The last of all the *bores* was he."

Father Andrew, at the Colonel's especial solicitation, favoured us with a *Latin* grace.

No one merits and relishes a good dinner better than a grouse-shooter. It delights me to see my companion eat like a traveller ; and to please me, he should possess sufficient *acumen* to enable him to appreciate the fare. I despise the man who is cursed with a Spartan palate, and who hardly knows the difference between beef and mutton; and yet, in equal ratio, the *gourmand* is my abomination. There is a limit in culinary lore beyond which, as I opine, the sportsman should never travel. Like a soldier, he will sometimes find it serviceable to be able to direct the broiling of a steak and the combination of a stew. To fabricate a curry, or even regulate a hash, may be tolerated ; and in a wild country like Ballycroy, or the Scottish highlands, this knowledge will frequently be " worth a Jew's eye;" but everything beyond this in kitchen accomplishments is detestable. With one who composed omelets, and talked scholarly of the *matériel* of a plum-pudding—and I once had the misfortune to fall into a shooting party afflicted with such a personage—I would consort no more upon the heath, than I would shoot with a cook, or draw a cover with a confectioner. And yet, with these antipathies, I recommend the neophyte to make himself in everything as independent as he can. A few practical lessons are worth a world of precept : one week's cooking on the moors will render him for life an adept; and if gun and angle fail him not, he will be able to command a dinner, without owing to the devil the compliment of a bad cook.

Did I wish to elucidate my opinions, I would stake them upon two items in our bills of fare. The soldier compounded the soup—and such soup !—and yet it was the simple extract of a mountain hare, and five broken birds, which had been too much injured to permit their being sent away. Shade of Kitchener ! one spoonful of that exquisite *potage* would have made thee abandon half thy theories, and throw thy " cunningest devices" to the winds !

The Priest superintended the fish—an eight-pound-salmon, crimped, split, subdivided, and roasted upon bog-deal skewers before a clear turf-fire. All the sauces that Lazenby ever fabricated, could not produce that soup, or emulate this broil.

Let him, whose jaded palate a club-house cook connot accommodate, try the *cuisinerie* of our cabin. He shall walk to the mountain lake, and on his return, the Colonel will compose a soup, and the Priest supply a salmon : if eating like a ploughman be to him a pleasure—

> " If *these* won't make him,
> The devil take him !"

But lest my theories be mistaken, I must say, that I hold cooking and " creature comforts" as very secondary indeed to sport. If all can be had, so much the better ; and when I recommend the tyro to learn the art and mysteries of the broiling iron, it is precisely on the principle that the knowledge how to cook a dinner may, at times, be as necessary for him, as to know how to wash a gun. No man, I presume, will do either, who can manage to have them done by a deputy. But a sportsman, a keen straightforward sportsman, will of necessity be often left dependant upon his own resources, and hence he should be prepared for the contingency. It is the abuse I cry out against. A man who on the mountains counts the minutes until dinner-hour shall come, who is seeking an appetite rather than amusement, and instead of game is dreaming of *gourmanderie*—him I totally reject, and implore to lay aside his gun for ever, and exchange the powder-flask for the pepper-box. The latter he will find more useful, and not half so dangerous.

It was clear, from the very start, that this was to be among the *wettest nights* of the season. The Colonel settled himself for a comfortable carouse ; the Priest was not the man to desert his *buon camarado* ; and Antony declared that there was good cause for a general jollification, as he properly observed, that " it was not every day that Manus kills a bullock," by which old saw, I presume the defunct deer and ourselves are typified. No wonder, then, that the revel commenced with all the members of the body politic ; and whilst the contents of the " four-gallon keg" were invaded in the kitchen, the wine circulated rapidly in the chamber of state. In truth, during my short but chequered life, civil and military, I never saw a party evince an honester disposition *to drink fair*. No coquetry about filling ; no remonstrances touching " heeltaps and skylights ;"—round went the bottle, until the juice of the grape appeared too cold a fluid for such mercurial souls, and a general call for a more potent liquid was given and obeyed.

Now came "the sweet hour i' the night," and old Care might, if he pleased, have "hanged himself in his own garters." The Priest, whose voice must once have been remarkably fine, and who certainly never impaired it much by "hallooing psalms," sang national melodies, or joined the Colonel and my cousin in glees and catches, which, as, Wamba says, were not "ill-sung." "Fast and furious" the mirth proceeded, while, "every pause between," clouds of tobacco rose like a mist-wreath, and overspread the company with a canopy of vapour.

For my own part, every prudential resolution vanished with the first catch; and it was not till a certain unsteadiness of vision discovered that I had reached that felicitous state when no twelve honest men, upon oath, would certify my sobriety, that I mustered courage to retreat. I felt that, had I remained much longer, I was likely to become *hors de combat*; and, lighting a cigar, left the cabin to breathe the fresh air, which long since had been superseded in the banqueting-room by an atmosphere of genuine *cannastre*.

It was a mild, calm, dark night, and such a one feels delicious in the hills. Two or three solitary stars were feebly twinkling in the sky, though, were the truth told, probably there was but *one*. I took the pathway leading to the river, and sat down upon the banks, to "blow my cloud" in solitude. I was not, however, permitted to muse alone; my kinsman immediately joined me, and settling himself upon one of the masses of turf, which the floods tear from the banks of the stream, and leave, when their violence subsides, upon the verge of the river, replenished his *meerschaum*.

"How refreshing," he said, "to exchange that mephitic air within, for this mild but bracing night-breeze! I saw you pass the glass, and I desired John to bring us out some coffee. It is a queer place, too, for a Mocha fancier to indulge in; but this is the charm that binds me to the mountains. In life, locality is everything; it is not the *what* one does, it is the *where*. Venison at a city feast is an every-day concern; and the best haunch in England would not have the *gusto* of the red deer's that hangs from the roof within. Common comfort, in a wildeaness like this, from the barrenness of all around, receives a zest, which nothing in civilized society can realize, and ' *voilà l'exemple.* ' "

Lighted by a peasant with a bog-deal torch, that emitted more light than forty candles together, the old man approached us with his tray. Coffee taken in the open air, " in darkness palpable," into which the powerful blaze of the torch which our bare-legged attendant held could but feebly penetrate, associated with the place and company, made an impression on my fancy that will not be readily obliterated.

" Next to modern fanaticism, nothing stirs my choler more," said my kinsman, " than that silly bubble, yclept *the Temperance Society,* To prevent men from occasionally indulging, no matter what their grade in life may be, is perfectly Utopian. The more you inhibit what the world calls pleasure, the more you urge mankind to the pursuit. Hence, in water-drinking, more as in religion, there is the grossest hypocrisy practised; and I would as soon trust a denouncer of wine with the key of my cellar, as allow my cat to have the *entrée* of the dairy. Then, upon the score that health and longevity are interrupted by even a moderate attachment to the bottle, I deny the position altogether ; and for my proof I would point out the group within. The otter-killer says that he is eighty —we at the Lodge, from certain data, know him to be at least five years more ;—his life has been one of much severity, with constant exposure to heat and cold : and he has, as he admits, been always a free drinker. The Colonel, for thirty years, has been attached to the most dissipated regiments in the service, and excepting that he suffered from gout, which is hereditary in his family, and rheumatism occasioned by a neglected wound, where is there a more vigorous sexagenarian ? But the Priest is probably the best example of them all. Exposed to all the annoyances of his profession, brought constantly within the sphere of contagion, called out of bed at midnight, and obliged to brave weather, when, as it has been happily expressed, a man would not reject an enemy's dog, he exercises hospitality freely; and is there a panado-maker among the whole water-drinking gang who could *rough it* with him for a fortnight ? But hark ! he pitches that manly and melodious voice—he strikes up poor Burns' inimitable lyric, ' *Then are we met.*' That matchless song was surely written for such a voice and such a company !"

Under cover of the Priest's melody we approached the window. There sat a party, who might well put the Temperance Society to the blush. For their years, I suspect there was not a healthier, and I will swear not a happier, trio in the King's dominion. It was just the scene a Flemish artist would select to employ his pencil on. For effect, the light was excellent: the candles having been removed to the extremity of the apartment, the bacchanalian group were revealed by the red and mellow blaze of a brilliant wood-fire. Separated by a table provided with every requisite for a deep carouse, sat the soldier and the churchman. The back of the latter was turned to the window, but his amplitude of shoulder and bull-neck at once bespoke the strength for which he was remarkable, while the partial baldness of his head told that he had passed life's meridian. The tall and martial figure opposite contrasted well with the churchman's. Older by some half-score years, he might, like Jack Falstaff, be "some fifty, ay, or, by the mass, threescore!" but his age was green; and notwithstanding the wear and tear that a military life and its occasional excesses had caused, his cheerful countenance and merry eye showed that he loved yet to hear "the chimes at midnight." The otter-killer completed the group: sitting on a low stool, from time to time he regulated and supplied the wood-fire; his silver hair collected in a long cue, seal-skin pouch, singular dress, and venerable air, made him the most striking figure of the party. A little terrier bitch, who never left her master, lay at the old man's feet, while an indulged black setter luxuriated before the blaze, with his intelligent head and pendulous silky ears rested on the Colonel's knee.

"Is not that indeed a picture?" whispered my cousin. "What heads they have? John placed yonder bottle before them as I went out, and two parts of it are gone already. But hush! let us hear the conversation. I think if there be strength in poteen, the Colonel has reached the moralizing point."

"Andrew," said the commander. ("The Colonel," said my kinsman, aside, "is generally *hard screwed* when he calls the priest Andrew.")

"Andrew, fill the glass: the boys are ruminating beside the river; their young blood is hotter than ours, so we'll stick to the *ingle-side* and the tumbler. There was a day when **we**

could bring a stag to the ground, and scramble up Carrig-
a-binniogh as stoutly as the best of them,—but that day's
gone : we have changed for the worse, and so has everything.
Andrew, in our youth it was a merry world. But who succeeded old Markham ? He was as honest a divine as ever
finished a *magnum*. They talked—for virtue has always its
enemies—of his smuggling a little, and having a private still
in the stable ; but it was all hospitality. Andrew, the poteen
is sweet, but weak—help it man, for these glasses scarcely
hold a thimbleful!—at our age water-drinking won't do.—
Not a drop of brandy, you say, inside the Mullet ?"*

"Not an anker in the barony!" returned his companion
with a heavy sigh. "There was a time when my poor cabin
could not be taken short for Nantz and Hollands; but if I
can keep a bottle of *the native* now, it is the most. Would you
believe it, Colonel ? the *revenue people* searched my house a
month ago."

The Colonel looked indignant. "Search your house ?
profane a priest's own dwelling ? why, after a while, they'll
look into the Lodge. Did you curse the scoundrels from
the altar ?"

"Not I," said the churchman. "They are all northmen†
and foreigners, who would not care a brass button whether I
banned or blessed them for a twelvemonth. There is a
ruffian of the flock‡ that acts as a spy and guide, and I
suspect he sent them."

"Excommunicate him !" exclaimed the commander, with
drunken solemnity.

---

* The grand boundary of the wild peninsula of Erris, separating it
from the interior counties. It is used in a general sense to describe the
district—as "within or without the *Mullet*."

† *Northmen* is a phrase not only applied to recent settlers from the
north of Ireland, but even to families who have been located here for
centuries. In point of fact, few of the tribes here are purely aboriginal ;
for Ennis and Connemara being the *Ultima Thule* of the land, every
wanderer for private and political offences fled to these havens of refuge,
and in course of time amalgamated with the native proprietors of the soil.
Hence to this day, their descendants are not unfrequently taunted with
being *novi homines ;* and when a delinquency is committed by one of
these unhappy hybrids, an aboriginal will probably observe, " Sure, after
all, what could be expected from him, considering that his great great-
grandfather was *from the North !*"

‡ The flock—a Roman Catholic congregation is so termed in Connaught.

"I did that last Candlemas. He brought a girl out of Achil, on *book oath,* and he with his three decent wives in the parish already. I quenched the candles on him, and then he took to the revenue—*Nemo repente fuit turpissimus.*"

"And how do you and the new minister get on?"

"Poorly enough," answered the Priest. "This reformation work has put the country clean asunder."

"No good will come of it," said the Colonel. "I mind the time in Connaught when no man clearly knew to what religion he belonged ; and in one family, the boys would go to church and the girls to mass, or may be, both would join and go to whichever happened to be nearest. When I entered the militia, I recollect, the first time I was ever detached from head-quarters, I went with the company to Portumna. Old Sir Mark Blake, who commanded the regiment, happened to be passing through, and the night before he had had a desperate drink with General Loftus at the Castle. When I left Loughrea, I forgot to ascertain where I should bring the men on Sunday, and I thought this a good opportunity to ask the question. I opened his bedroom-door softly. 'Sir Mark,' says I, 'where shall I march the men?' 'What kind of a day is it?" says he. 'Rather wet,' was my answer. 'It's liker the night that preceded it,' said he. 'Upon my conscience, my lad,' he continued, 'my head's not clear enough at present to recollect the exact position of church and chapel ; but take them *to the nearest.*' That is what I call," and the Colonel shook his head gravely, "real Christian feeling."

"Real Christian feeling," said the Priest, with a groan, "is nearly banished from the world. When I went first to Castlebar, to learn Latin from Dan Donovan, my uncle Martin, God be merciful to him! was parish priest, and Jack Benton was the minister. They agreed like sworn brothers, and no one dared say a word against either in the presence of his friend. Where the priest dined, the curate was sure to be also. They lived in true brotherhood ; and when one happened to be the worse of liquor, why the other would not leave him for a bishopric. The town was the most peaceable place in Connaught ; and how could it be otherwise with such an example? Many a night I went before them with a lantern, when they carried Carney, the lame fiddler, round the streets, to serenade the ladies. There they would walk, like humble Christians, with the cripple in the middle, and neither caring a *traneein*, whether popery or protestantism was at the head of the barrow.     These were blessed days, Colonel.—I'll thank you for the canister,—that tobacco is excellent, and I'll try another pipeful."

"Och hone!" exclaimed the otter-killer, "isn't it a murder to see the clargy making such fools of themselves now! When I was young, priest and minister were hand-and-glove.     It seems to me but yesterday, when Father Patt Joyce, the Lord be good to him! lent Mr. Carson a congregation."

"Eh! what Antony?" said the Colonel.  " A congregation appears rather an extraordinary article to borrow."

"Faith," said the otter-killer,  "it's true.  I was there myself, and I'll tell you the story.  It was in the time of Bishop Beresford,  that beautiful old man,—many a half-crown he gave me, for I used often to bring game and fish to the palace from the master's father.  He was the handsomest gentleman I ever laid my eyes on ; and, och hone! it was he that knew how to live like a bishop.  He never went a step without four long-tailed black horses to his carriage, and two mounted grooms behind him.  His own body-man told me, one time I went with a haunch of red-deer and a bittern to the palace, that never less than twenty sat down in the parlour, and, in troth, there was double that number in the hall, for nobody came or went without being well taken care of.

" Well, it came into old Lord Peter's* head, that he would build a church, and s ttle a colony of *northmen* away in the west.  Faith, he managed the one easy enough ; but it failed him to do the other, for devil an inch the *northmen* would come ; for, says they, " Hell and Connaught's bad enough, but what is either to Connemara ?'

" Well, the minister came down, and a nice little man he was, one Mr. Carson.  Father Patt Flyn had the parish then, and faith, in course of time they two became as thick as inkle-weavers.

" Everything went on beautiful, for the two clargy lived together.  Father Patt Flyn minded his chapel and the flock,

---

* Grandfather to the present Marquis of Sligo.

and Mr. Carson said prayers of a Sunday too, though sorrow
a soul he had to listen to him but the clerk—but sure that
was no fault of his.

"Well, I mind it as well as yesterday, for I killed that
very morning two otters at Loughnamuckey, and the smallest of them was better to me than a pound note. It was
late when I got down from the hills, and I went to Father
Patt's as usual, and who should I meet at the door but the
priest himself. 'Antony,' says he, '*ceade fealteagh*, have ye
anything with you, for the wallets seem full?' 'I have,'
says I, 'your reverence;' and I pulls out two pair of gra-
ziers,* and a brace of three-pound trouts, fresh from the
sea, that I caught that morning in Dhulough. In these days
I carried a ferret, besides the trap and fishing-rod, and it
went hard, if I missed the otters but I would net rabbits,
or kill a dish of trout. 'Upon my conscience,' says the
priest, 'ye never were more welcome, Antony. The minister
and myself will dine off the trouts and rabbits, for they
forgot to kill a sheep for us till an hour ago; and you know,
Antony, except the shoulder, there's no part of the mutton
could be touched, so I was rather bothered about the
dinner.'

"Well, in the evening, I was brought into the parlour, and
there were their reverences as *cur coddiogh*† as you please.
Father Patt gave me a tumbler of *rael* stiff punch, and the
divil a better warrant to make the same was within the province of Connaught. We were just as comfortable as we
could be, when a *currier*‡ stops at the door with a letter,
which he said was for Mr. Carson. Well, when the minister
opens it, he got as pale as a sheet, and I thought he would
have fainted. Father Patt crossed himself. 'Arrah, Dick,'
says he, 'the Lord stand between you and evil! is there anything wrong?' 'I'm ruined,' says he; 'for some *bad member*
has wrote to the bishop, and told him that I have no congregation, because you and I are so intimate, and he's coming
down to-morrow, with the *dane*, to see the state of things.
Och, hone!' says he, 'I'm fairly ruined.' 'And is that all
that's frettin' ye?' says the priest, 'Arrah, dear Dick'—for
they called each other be their *cristen* names,—'is this all?

---

* Young rabbits.                            † *Anglice*, comfortable.
‡ *Alias*, courier.

If it's a congregation ye want, ye shall have a decent one to-morrow, and lave that to me;—and now we'll take our drink, and not matter the bishop a fig.'

"Well, next day, sure enough, down comes the bishop, and a great retinue along with him; and there was Mr. Carson ready to receive him. 'I hear,' says the bishop, mighty stately, 'that you have no congregation.' 'In faith, your holiness,' says he, 'you'll be soon able to tell that,'—and in he walks him to the church, and there were sitting threescore well-dressed men and women, and all of them as devout as if they were going to be anointed; for that blessed morning, Father Patt whipped mass over before ye had time to bless yourself, and the clanest of the flock was before the bishop in the church, and ready for his holiness. To see that all behaved properly, Father Patt had hardly put off the vestment, till he slipped on a *cota more*,\* and there he sat in a back *sate* like any other of the congregation. I was near the bishop's reverence; he was seated in an arm-chair belonging to the priest.—'Come here, Mr. Carson,' says he; 'some enemy of yours,' said the sweet old gentleman, 'wanted to injure you with me. But I am now fully satisfied.' And turning to the dane, 'By this book!' says he, 'I didn't see a claner congregation this month of Sundays!' "

"*He said no such thing*," exclaimed my kinsman, who, tired with the prolixity of the otter-killer, had interrupted the finale of the tale. "How dare you, Antony, put such uncanonical and ungentlemanly language in the mouth of the *sweet old man?* Here, John, clear the kitchen. Out with the piper, and chuck the *keg* after him. We'll disperse *this congregation*; and they may dance outside if they please, while pipes and poteen stand them. And now ventilate the cabin, open door and window, and sling our hammocks as soon as possible."

Agreeably to this mandate, the kitchen company were ejected with scanty ceremony; the Colonel and the Priest retired to their respective beds with wonderful steadiness: while we took possession of our marquee, which, under existing circumstances, was Paradise itself compared with the cabin, which smoking, drinking, and cooking, had rendered everything but agreeable.

\* *Anglice*, a great-coat.

## CHAPTER XXXIII.

Dancing kept up—Effects of poteen on the company—Ball ends—Rainy night—Morning—Pattigo—A long swim—Breakfast—An incident—Fox-catcher bitten by a wild cat—Ferocity of that animal—Anecdotes of them—House-cats frequently run wild—Destructive to rabbit-warrens—Cat-killing extraordinary—The deer-skin—Snow fatal to the red deer—Anecdote of a hind and fawn—Blistered foot—Simple remedy—My descent by " the mother's side."

For a considerable time after we had retired to our cots, the ball was kept up with unabated spirit, upon a piece of level sward beside the river. The whisky appeared to affect the company differently, and individual propensities were strikingly developed. Some of the boys were particularly amative, and the rude love-making we overheard at times amused us much; others betrayed a pugnacity of spirit which nothing but the master's propinquity repressed. By degrees the company began to separate : the piper, whose notes for the last half-hour had been exceedingly irregular, now evinced unquestionable symptoms of his being " *done up.*" Instead of the lightsome and well-sustained jig, strange and dolorous noises issued from the chanter,* and, as one of the fair sex observed, who, by the way, in passing, tumbled over the tent cords,—" Martin was totally *smothered with spirits,* and a body could no more dance to his music, than do *the Patre o'pee* to a *coronach* at a wake."

It was well that this failure in the orchestral department brought the ball to a close, for at midnight the rain began to fall, and towards morning it came down in torrents. We were obliged to rise and slack the tent-cords ; but the marquee was a double one, and perfectly water-tight, and, as the cots were slung from upright posts at least a foot from the ground, we suffered no inconvenience from the rain, except the noise it made in rattling on the tense canvas. This, however, we soon became accustomed to, and slept till eight o'clock, as sound as watchmen.

Long before we turned out, the Colonel and Priest were afoot, and we heard a prayer and supplication from the commander to old John, for a cup of strong coffee, while an idler

---

* The principal or finger-pipe of the set.

was despatched to the next well by the churchman, for a jug of cold spring water. Pattigo, who had rambled up the hills with a basket of fish and scallops, remarked, "that the gentlemen's *coppers*, he guessed, were rather hot this morning, and," as he eyed the empty bottles which were being removed, "to judge from the number of the *marines*, it was little wonder."

From Pattigo's *parlance*, I suspected that he had seen more of the world than usually falls to the lot of an ordinary skipper of a fishing-boat—nor was I wrong. I learned from his master, that for some good conduct, no doubt, he had been accommodated with board and lodging in a king's ship for upwards of two years, and that his sojourn there would have been much longer, had he not managed to abridge the visit, by slipping one dark night over the vessel's side, and swimming to the shore, a distance of two miles. On this Byronian feat, however, the honest navigator seldom plumes himself, and it is only when he is "a bit by the head," that this exploit is mentioned.

We found the household fully occupied in the cabin ; John in regulating the chamber of state, which, notwithstanding open doors and windows, still retained the miasma of tobacco-smoke, and Hennessey in skinning and breaking up the deer. If I had been yesterday delighted with his superior execution with the rifle, I was now surprised at the masterly manner in which he dressed and dismembered the venison. He is certainly a clever fellow, and, could I but forget that he has finished a few of "the finest peasantry upon earth," the man would stand as high in my estimation, as he does in his foster brother's, "our loving cousin."

When breakfast was ended, at which, to do them justice, the Colonel and the Priest did their *devoir* most gallantly, and were occupied in debating what should be the order of the morning's amusement, and to fish, or not to fish, appeared the question, an incident such as in this wild and sylvan state of things every day produces, occurred. It was the arrival of a young lad, who brought an otter-skin of unusual size as a present to "the master," and a wounded hand, whereon Antony was required to exercise his leechcraft. He had been bitten by a wild cat, and I had the curiosity to examine the wound. The hand was already in a state of high inflammation ; and the ferocity of the creature must indeed have been extraordinary, to judge from the extent of the injuries it had inflicted. The flesh was sadly lacerated, and in two places the bone was completely exposed.

The sufferer, it appeared, was not unknown to Antony, and, from the free-masonry which passed between them, I discovered that he is of the same craft, and the person upon whom the otter-killer's mantle is likely to descend, when he, Antony, shall have gone the way of all flesh. The chief occupation of the wounded man is digging out foxes in the mountains, which he brings afterwards for sale to the interior, and disposes of at a good price to the masters of hounds. This morning he had gone to a cover in the hills, in his usual avocation, when, from some traces he observed beneath a rock, he concluded that an animal was earthed there. Having put a terrier in, his suspicions were confirmed, as the dog came out severely torn, and, assisted by a shepherd-boy, he laid rabbit-nets round the den, commenced digging' and, before he had proceeded far, a cat of immense size bolted. She was breaking through the rabbit-net, when the *chasseur*, with more gallantry than prudence, seized her by the neck. The fierce animal instantly attacked him in turn, and, fastening upon his hands with teeth and talons, held her desperate grasp until the boy, with the edge of the spade, broke her back. They brought the dead beast along with them; it was of a dirty gray colour, double the size of the common house-cat, and its teeth and claws more than proportionately larger.

These animals fortunately are scarce, and generally frequent the neighbourhood of rabbit-warrens, where they prove amazingly destructive. Hennessey, two winters since, disco-covered a den in a cleft of a rock upon the shore, and adjoining the sand-banks, which are numerously stocked with rabbits. It cost him immense trouble to penetrate to the *form*, where he killed a male and female wild-cat, the latter being large with young. Hennessey's patience and ingenuity were sorely taxed to effect their destruction, having been obliged to resort to gunpowder, and blow up a large portion of the rock, before he could dislodge his dangerous game. In size and colour, they were precisely similar to the animal killed in the mountain by the fox-catcher; and had they been permitted to continue their species, in a very short time the abjacent burrow would have been devastated.

Besides this large and ferocious species, the warrens upon the coast suffer much from the common cat becoming wild, and burrowing in the rabbit-holes. They are sometimes surprised and shot in the sand-banks, or taken in traps; but they are generally too wary to be approached—and hunting only by night, during the day they sleep in their dens, and are rarely met abroad.

Some estimate of their numbers may be formed, from the circumstance of five males having been killed in a herdsman's out-house which joined the warren. They had been attracted there by one of their own species, and the noise having alarmed the peasant, he guessed the cause, and cautiously managed to stop the hole, by which they gained entrance, with a *turf-cleave*. Knowing the value of the capture, he kept guard upon the prisoners till morning, and then despatched information to the Lodge. My cousin, with his followers, promptly repaired to the place, and, surrounding the barn with guns and greyhounds, bolted the wild cats successively, until the whole number were dispatched. This *chasse* was not only novel, but profitable. After the death of their persecutors, the rabbits increased prodigiously; but fears are entertained that these destructive animals are become once more abundant in the sand-banks.

When the dressings were removed, we found that the poor lad had been so much injured, that apprehension of lock-jaw induced us to send him directly to the infirmary. There is a belief, and one more reasonable than many popular opinions in Ballycroy, that a wild cat's bite is particularly venomous. My cousin remembers a case which terminated fatally with a servant of his father's; and the Priest mentioned another of a country girl, who, finding one of these animals in a barn, rashly attempted to secure it: the cat wounded her slightly in the leg, and for six months she was unable to use the limb.

When the unfortunate fox-catcher was leaving us, in return for a trifling donation, he pressed upon me the acceptance of a fine deer-skin which he produced from his wallet. "He had another for the master," he said, "and he would bring it to him, when he returned from the hospital."

" And pray, my friend, how did you get these skins?"

The question puzzled the wounded man. "I found them *dead,* after the great snow last year."

" After a lump of lead," quoth the otter-killer, " had made a fracture in the hide ;" and he pointed to the orifice in the skin, where evidently a ball had perforated.

" Alas !" said the Priest, " the snow is always fatal to the red deer. They are obliged to leave the upper range and come down the villages :* and there are, unluckily, too many of the old French guns in the country still, and *then* they are unfortunately busy."

By the by, speaking of the snow, a very curious circumstance occurred, during its long continuance in 1822.

A fine hind, accompanied by a stout fawn, travelled across the lowlands in search of pasturage, which the deep snow had rendered unattainable in the mountains. Pressed by the severity of the weather, she at last established herself in a green field which was within sight of the windows of the Lodge. For four weeks, during which the storm continued, she remained there in safety ; for the wild visiters were protected by the commands of "the Master" : and from being undisturbed, continued in the place they had first selected.

Thinking that they would be a valuable addition to Lord Sligo's park, my kinsman determined to have them captured, and the following Sunday was appointed for the attempt. This day was selected, because the number of persons collected at the chapel would materially assist the execution of the plan.

The day came, and the whole population of the parish was employed. The place was surrounded by a multitude of people, who gradually reduced their circle, until the deer and fawn were completely enclosed, and a *cordon* of living beings was formed, two deep, around them. The hind had remarked the preparations, and more than once attempted an escape ; but, embarrassed by the fawn, her efforts were abortive. She appeared determined to share its fate, and affection was paramount to timidity. At last, when totally surrounded, her courage and address were almost incredible. She eyed the circle attentively, made a sharp peculiar noise, as if to warn her offspring of its danger, then charging the ranks where they appeared weakest, bounded over the heads

* By *a village* a very few houses are denominated, and a stranger would be sadly disappointed if he formed his ideas of their extent on the English scale.

of her opposers, and escaped. The confusion occasioned by this extraordinary proceeding, favoured the deliverance of the fawn, who, profiting by the accident, galloped off unhurt, and, with the dam, succeeded in regaining their native wilds.

The whole of the *dramatis personæ*, with the exception of the otter-killer and myself, have gone off to fish some three or four lakes, situate in a hollow in the mountains, and which are said to be remarkable for the number and flavour of their trouts. I have been prevented by an accident from accompanying the party; and though my wound be "not so deep as a well, nor so wide as a church-door," it still renders me *hors de combat*. I blistered, or rather neglected a blistered heel: and the fag of yesterday has so excoriated the surface, as to make it imperative upon me to lie by for a little. Antony engages to effect a perfect cure by to-morrow; and here I remain *tête-à-tête* with the otter-killer.

The old man proceeded skilfully enough; he lanced the

blisters, and then applied the cuticle which covers a sheep's kidney, and which is very similar in appearance and effect to what we call "gold-beaters' leaf." This application prevented the heel from being frayed by the stocking. To the remainder of the foot he rubbed a hot mixture of tallow and whisky; and his remedy was "the sovereignest thing on earth," for in twelve hours the cure was effected.

While he operated on my infirm foot, he amused me with one of his interminable stories. He says, by the "mother's side," that I and my cousin are descended from a lady called *Rose Roche*. When his leech-craft was ended he retired "to stretch upon the bed."—John was too deeply engaged in culinary affairs to favour me with his company, and having no resource besides, I have been obliged to amuse myself by transcribing the *legend of Rose Roche*, and become thus a chronicler of the otter-killer.

## CHAPTER XXXIV.

### THE LEGEND OF ROSE ROCHE.

At sixteen Rose Roche was the loveliest maid in Ulster. In infancy she was found exposed at the gate of the Ursulines, and her beauty and destitution recommended her to the charity of the sisterhood. Educated, accordingly, for a conventual life, she had never passed the boundary of the garden-walls, and accident discovered the existence of beauty, which else had faded unseen and unadmired within those cloisters, to which from childhood it had been devoted.

Cormac More, lord of Iveagh, was the patron and protector of the community at Balleek. At primes and vespers a mass was celebrated for his soul's weal. His Easter-offering was ten beeves and five casks of Bordeaux wine; and on the last Christmas vigil he presented six silver candlesticks to the altar of *Our Lady*. No wonder that this powerful chief was held in high honour by the sisterhood of Saint Ursula.

One tempestuous night in October, wearied with hunting, and separated from his followers by darkness and the storm, Cormac More found himself beneath the walls of the convent of Balleek. Approaching the gate, he wound his horn loudly, and begged for shelter and refreshment. Proud of this opportunity of affording hospitality to so noble and munificent a protector, the wicket was unbarred, the Lord of Iveagh admitted, and received in honourable state by the Lady Superior, and inducted with due form into the parlour of the Ursulines.

There a plentiful repast was speedily prepared, and the tired hunter was ceremoniously seated at the table. His morning's meal had been despatched before the sun had topped *Slieve Gallion*, and a long day's exercise had given him a keen relish for the evening banquet. The Lady Abbess feasted the patron of her house right nobly—he was attended on assiduously by the novices—dish after dish succeeded in luxurious variety, until the chief requested the tables to be drawn, and with knightly courtesy entreated permission to pledge the holy mother of the Ursulines in a deep draught of Rhenish wine.

Then, for the first time, the novice who presented the cup, attracted the good Knight's attention. The folds of her thick veil could not conceal the matchless symmetry of her form ; and, as she filled the chalice from the flagon, the exquisite proportions of her hand and arm struck Cormac More with wonder. At this moment her drapery became entangled with the jewelled pommel of the Knight's rapier ; a hasty attempt to disengage it was unsuccessful—the veil fell, and disclosed to the enraptured view of the Lord of Iveagh the loveliest features he had ever seen. Covered with blushes, which heightened her surpassing beauty, the novice caught her veil hastily up and retired from the parlour, while the Knight, despite the evident displeasure that the accident had caused the Lady Abbess, gazed after the retiring girl until she disappeared among the cloisters. In vain the proud Superior introduced costlier wines of rare and ancient vintages : in vain she enlarged upon the piety of her order, and enumerated the number of the Ursulines who had been canonized :—the Knight's whole thoughts were engrossed with one lovely object—his courtesy and converse were feeble and constrained, until, piqued by his neglect, the Abbess wished him a fair repose, and retired in full state from the apartment, preceded by a crucifix and taper, and followed by her attendant nuns.

Although the Knight lay upon the Bishop's bed, and

occupied that honoured chamber where none of a less degree
than a mitred abbot had hitherto been permitted to repose,
no slumber sealed his lids, nor was the beautiful novice for
a moment absent from his thoughts. Cormac More had
declined many a splendid alliance ; the Lord of Offaly proffered him an only sister, with a princely dower ; and O'Nial
himself courted him for a son-in-law, and promised him
the barony of Orier, and Blanche, his fairest daughter. But,
till now, Cormac had never loved : the beauteous cup-bearer
seemed to him a being of another world ; the more he dwelt
upon her image, the more his passion was excited ; alliances
with lords and princes were overlooked, disparity of rank and
fortune was forgotten, and, ere the morning sun had lighted
the storied window of the Bishop's chamber, the Knight's
determination was formed, and matins were scarcely over when
he demanded an audience of the Lady Abbess.

Never was there greater surprise than that, with which
the holy mother heard Cormac More express his passion for
the novice of the Ursulines. Joy sparkled in her eyes as
the noble Lord of Iveagh confided the secret of his love,
entreated her powerful intercession, and begged for her
sanction to his nuptials. As Rose was still unprofessed, there
existed no spiritual barrier to her marriage. Flattered by the
high honour conferred upon her house by the proudest Baron
of the Pale selecting a bride from the holy sisterhood, the
Superior willingly acceded to his request ; his offers were
accepted, and, ere the vesper-bell had tolled, the preliminaries
were completed, and the fair novice had consented to become
the bride of Cormac More.

But, alas ! the wild ardour of the good Knight, and the
carnal motives of the Abbess, caused both to neglect consulting another personage, namely, the blessed Ursula herself,
in thus disposing of one devoted to her service from the
cradle ; and the saint felt the oversight. That night the
Abbess was tormented with fearful and portentous dreams ;
the Lord of Iveagh tossed restlessly upon the Bishop's bed ;
and, if the novice closed an eye, her slumbers were broken
with strange and incoherent visions. In vain, next day,
the Knight hunted from sunrise to curfew — his hounds
were eternally at fault, and his followers appeared besotted
or bewitched ; the deer, when pressed to the utmost, vanished on the bare moor ; and knight, squire, and yeoman

unanimously agreed, that the several parties interested in the chase, were under the immediate influence of the prince of darkness.

Nor did the holy Superior of the Ursulines fare better than the persecuted Knight and his afflicted companions. Everything about the convent went astray, and the culinary preparations for entertaining the Lord of Iveagh were awfully interrupted by accident and forgetfulness. The sister who presided over the pastry, and whose conserves, throughout a long and blameless life, had been pronounced unique and irreproachable, now actually omitted the necessary ingredients; the soup, when uncovered for a second, was invaded with such a discharge of soot, as reduced it, in colour, at least, to an equality with the broth of Sparta. The nun at the organ, instead of a "*jubilate*," struck up a "*nunc dimittis* ;" the very bells were "jangled out of tune ;" and the Lady Abbess was horrified by a succession of prodigies that, from her novitiate to her promotion, had never before visited the quiet residence of the sisterhood of Saint Ursula.

What were the nocturnal visitations inflicted upon the lovely novice, have not been exactly handed down. One thing alone is certain,—she visited the Lady Abbess with the first dawn, and in her maternal bosom the bride elect deposited the causes of her sorrow.

In this perplexity, the Knight and the Superior held secret counsel in the parlour of the convent, and long and difficult was the conference. The result was, that Cormac More vowed a golden chalice to the offended virgin ; and the Abbess, not to be outdone in liberality, agreed to double *aves* and *credos* for a fortnight. But with Rose Roche herself the chief difficulty was found to lie. All measures proposed by the holy mother were inefficacious ; and, in this desperate dilemma, it was deemed advisable to add to the number of counsellors, and the Prior of the Dominicans was summoned to the assistance of the conclave.

To that holy man the exigencies of the respective parties were intrusted. The Prior was sorely disturbed with doubts, but after a night's deliberation, during which he discussed a capon single-handed, and fortified his stomach with a second scoup of Rhenish wine, he decided, that the Lord of Iveagh should add a flagon to the chalice ; the Abbess should double her penitentiaries for a month; and Rose Roche undergo a private penance, which he, the Prior, should communicate to the lady alone.

Never had such an alarming predicament a happier termination! The Knight had scarcely laid himself upon the Bishop's bed, until a sweet and refreshing slumber, blessed with the happiest visions, sealed his eyes; the Lady Abbess slept like a watchman; and, since she had first gathered wild-flowers in the convent-garden, never did the fair novice enjoy more delightful dreams!

At last the bridal day arrived. The Lord of Iveagh was attended by a splendid following. The bells rang out a joyous peal, and the *élève* of the Ursulines left the home of her youth, escorted by three hundred horsemen, the consort of the proudest baron of the Pale. No lover could be more gallant than the noble husband of Rose Roche. Fête succeeded fête, and feasting continued in the castle of Cormac More from Michaelmas till Advent.

Months passed away, and honeymoons cannot be expected to last for ever. Cormac More by degrees resumed his hunting, and again involved himself in the endless feuds and warfare of these restless times; and Rose Roche was often deserted for the chase or the field. She still was passionately loved; but in the bosom of a martial baron, other and sterner feelings held a predominance. It is true, that the young bride bore these frequent absences with wonderful resignation; and page and tirewoman confessed in secret, that Dhu Castle was gayer and merrier when Cormac and his stern companions were away.

A year wore on. The Lord of Iveagh was pensive and thoughtful; a cloud would often gather on his brow, and his bearing to his beautiful wife became chilling aud repulsive. It transpired that two circumstances occasioned his anxiety. His lady wore a curious-fashioned coif, which concealed her tresses as effectually as if she never laid aside her night-cap; and the cherished hope of an heir to his ancient line now faded in the heart of Cormac More. Dhu Castle became duller and more gloomy—the fair Baroness was more and more deserted—the chase and banquet were preferred by the moody Knight to soft dalliance in his "lady's bower,"—and any pretext was gladly resorted to, which offered an excuse for being absent from his joyless home.

Gentlewomen, in these perilous days, acquired and possessed an astonishing portion of philosophy. No baron's lady " in the Pale,"* submitted to a frequent separation from her lord with more laudable submission than Rose Roche. The customary resource of "wives bereaved," appeared any thing but consolatory to the dame. She determined to avoid crying, as being an unchristian waste of beauty—and, instead of useless lamentations, she wisely substituted mirth and minstrelsy.

There was not a more accomplished bard in Ulster than Connor O'Cahan, and for seventy years he had resided with the lords of Iveagh. No tale or tradition connected with this puissant race was unknown to this gifted minstrel: yet, by some strange infirmity of taste, young Rose preferred the light romances of her lord's English page, to all the legendary lore of the grey-haired harper; and listened with more delight to a merry roundelay from Edwin's lute than to the deeds of Cormac's grandfather, as set out in song by Connor O'Cahan. The bard, it is true, was blind, and the page had the blackest eyes imaginable.

This unhappy predilection was not concealed from her lord. His jealousy instantly took fire, and the handsome page was suddenly removed, and none knew whither. The absence of an heir had now become matter for serious complaint: it was whispered among the Baron's followers that there was no cause for hope, and maliciously insinuated, moreover, that the close coif adopted by the dame was worn to conceal some natural deformity. Cormac, a slave to suspicion, and instigated by his rude companions, insisted that the hood should be discarded, or that Rose Roche should retire in disgrace to the convent from whence she came.

On the alternative being proposed, the lady proved posi-

* The Pale was the line of demarcation drawn by the English settlers between their acquired possessions and the remoter districts, which were still permitted to remain with the ancient proprietors. As this boundary was the "debatable land" of Ireland, it was the scene of constant raid and skirmish: and the *locale* of many a wild tradition is placed beside this dangerous border.

Q

tive, and the coif was peremptorily retained. Cormac, irritated by opposition to his commands, was obstinate in his determination, and Rose Roche left the castle of her lord a repudiated wife, and once more returned to the convent of the Ursulines.

From the hour of their separation, the Baron seldom smiled. To part from his wife was a trifle ; but unluckily, he had embroiled himself with the church. The Abbess espoused the lady's quarrel fiercely, and *ave* and *credo* were no longer offered up for Cormac More !  Notwithstanding past largess, beeves and wine-butts were forgotten; the candlesticks upon the altar no longer elicited a prayer; and his soul's health was no more attended to by the community than the lowest horse-boy's of his train.

Thus matters stood, when one dark evening, returning from the chase, Cormac and his followers were surprised by a band of Catterans, and a fierce and desperate skirmish ensued. The outlaws were defeated, but the Lord of Iveagh was shot clean through the body with a three-foot arrow : and how could he have better luck ?

Then it was that the sinful Knight was tortured with remorse and unavailing sorrow.  He cursed the evil counsellors who tempted him to insult Saint Ursula and her adopted daughter, and, determining to be reconciled to his wife and the church together, directed his followers to carry him to the abbey of Balleek.  His orders were obeyed, and the Lady Abbess consented to admit the dying noble.  He was laid before the altar, and his injured wife, forgetting past resentment, was the first to rush from her cell, and minister to his relief.   In the fatal emergency, coif and veil were left dehind ;  her raven tresses fell below her shoulders, and reached to her very waist, and Cormac was convinced too late, that his ill-used consort had the finest hair in Christendom. Alas ! those ebon locks had been the admiration of the whole sisterhood ; and, for penitential purposes, the Dominican had enjoined their concealment for three years, when he gave spiritual counsel, in their hour of tribulation, to the abbess, the baron, and Rose Roche.

To make atonement for his former unkindness, he willed his rich domains to his beautiful widow.  The Prior of the Dominicans indicted the deed, which disposed of his possessions ; and the church, of course, was not forgotten.  Surrounded by all the emblems of religion, and with a splinter of the true cross in his right hand, the penitent Baron breathed his last. He lay for three days and nights in the chancel, in great state; and was interred on the fourth morning, with all the ceremonies that both Ursulines and Dominicans could bestow.

The days of mourning passed over: Rose Roche exercised her resignation; and Dhu Castle became a different place to what it had been during the latter days of the defunct Baron, and mirth and music were exchanged for the rude revelry of Cormac More. Her hall was filled with guests; at the board she did the honours nobly; and when she visited the green wood, with her gold-belled hawks and gallant retinue, she looked as if she had been ennobled from the Conquest, and in bearing and attire seemed " every inch a queen."

But amid all this splendour and magnificence, poor Rose had her own secret causes of inquietude. Beauty, accompanied by broad lands, could not but induce suitors without number to come forward, and never was woman, not excepting Penelope herself, more vigorously besieged. From past experience, Rose was not ambitious to exchange wealth and liberty for becoming the wife of some doughty baron, who would probably undervalue her charms, just as much as he would over-estimate his own great condescension in giving her his name. A tender recollection of one, long since lost, would cross her mind occasionally; and in her solitary hours the black-eyed page haunted her imagination. Accordingly she eschewed all offers for her hand with excellent discretion. Few were offended, she managed her rejections so prudently: and through the first year of widowhood neither lands nor liberty were lost.

The consort of the wise Ulysses herself could not have held out for ever. Rose was severely pressed; for, finding themselves foiled by her ready wit and good discretion, when they attacked her singly, her lovers, from necessity, agreed to coalesce, and determined that one should be accepted, and the remainder be pledged to support the acquired rights of the fortunate candidate, as report said King Henry had resolved to gift a favourite noble with the person and estates of the beautiful widow.

This agreement of her suitors was politely but decisively

Q 2

intimated to Rose Roche, and the Prior declared, " by the
vestment," that to evade matrimony longer was impossible.
" She had," the holy man said, " an ample list to choose
from : there were eleven suitors in the neighbourhood, besides
the *Big Man of the West*," for so the Thane of Connaught
was entitled.

In this extremity, the lady resolved to exercise, at least,
the privilege of free choice.  The Prior was directed to ingross
a bond, by which the respective candidates for her hand bound
themselves to grant an uncontrolled right of selection to the
widow, and covenanted, moreover, neither to molest, nor
permit her to be molested, when her choice was made.  The
deed was duly executed—the day for her decision was named
—and a reasonable time allowed for " the Big Man of the
West" to attend and try his fortune.

O'Connor was surprised when the determination of the fair
widow was communicated.  He had only time for a hurried
preparation, as his rivals, from their vicinity to the lady, had
never taken the remoter situation of " the Big Man" into
their consideration, when they named the day.  O'Connor,
however, was no sluggard ; he collected his " following"
with all haste, and every department was complete, when,
alas ! the chief harper fell sick without a cause, and no other
was procurable for a distance of sixty miles.  In this dilemma
a Saxon youth, who two years since had been shipwrecked
beneath the castle walls, was recollected.  He could not, it
is true, " strike the bold harp," but he had a sweet and
mellow voice, and his skill upon the lute was admirable.  In
wordcraft he was a thorough proficient, and with lance and
brand had more than once proved himself a man.  O'Connor
had no alternative, and the stranger was selected to fill a
place that " Cathwold O'Connor of the harp" should have
more worthily occupied.

Although the Thane of Connaught and his gallant company
pushed forward with all the speed that man and horse could
make, from bad roads and flooded rivers, they were unable to
reach the heights above Dhu Castle until the sun of the
eventful day had set.  In vain knight and squire pressed on
their jaded steeds—evening fell ; all the candidates besides
had been in the hall for hours, and, as " the Big Man" had
not appeared, according to modern parlance he was voted
present by the company, and the banquet was served.

Never with such heavy heart did Rose Roche assume the place of honour. Though her hall was lighted splendidly, and her table crowded with the proudest nobles within "the Pale"—though rich wine flowed, and the most skilful harpers in the province poured forth their lays of love and war—yet one heart was heedless of gaiety and grandeur ; and that one was hers on whom every eye was bent, in deep expectancy awaiting her decision.

The curfew rang—and in another hour the happy Lord of Dhu Castle would be proclaimed. As the moments flew, the beautiful widow became paler and more dejected ; and breasts which had never quailed amid the roar of battle, now throbbed as nervously as a maiden's, when she listens to the first tale of love. The harps were mute, the revel became less loud, for all were deeply interested in that event which a brief space must determine. At this embarrassing moment, a loud blast was heard at the grand gate, and the seneschal rushed in, to announce the arrival of the Thane of Connaught, attended by a noble following of, at least, one hundred horse.

The sudden and opportune appearance of him of the West, seemed to affect the company variously. His rivals heard the news with mingled feelings of jealousy and alarm, which was in no way abated when the number of his attendants was announced, which exceeded that of their united followings. Rose Roche felt a secret pleasure at his coming ; not that her sentiments towards O'Connor were more favourable than to her suitors generally, but his late arrival must necessarily occasion some delay, and postpone, though but for brief space, that dreaded moment when she should surrender a hand, without a heart, to her future lord.

While O'Connor, as the greatest stranger, was placed beside the lady of Dhu Castle, his bard stood behind his master, and his train bestowed themselves where they could best find room. As Rose Roche looked carelessly around to see that the band were fitly accommodated, her eyes met those of the young minstrel :—the blood rushed to her brow ; for, excepting those of her own loved page, she never looked upon a pair so black and sparkling as the stranger's.

When the Thane of Connaught had feasted to his heart's content, the Prior of the Dominicans produced the parchment,

to which his rivals had affixed their signatures already.
The "Big Man" listened attentively as the monk read it.
"'Tis all fair," he said, as he placed his sign manual to the
deed, "that lady should choose her lord ; and thus I bind
myself, faithfully to abide the intents of this parchment."
Then turning to Rose Roche, he thus proceeded : " It
grieves me, that through accident I have unwittingly
occasioned some delay; therefore, in pity to my gallant
competitors, I beg you, lady, to terminate their suspense, and
declare to this noble company the happy object of your
choice.—Nay, blanch not so, fair dame," for the lady
became pallid as the white marble of a warrior's tomb :
" exercise your own pleasure leisurely ; and while I pledge
thy matchless beauty in a cup of muscadine, Aylmer, my
bard, shall sing a Saxon roundelay." As he spoke, O'Connor signed to the minstrel, who, rising at his lord's bidding,
struck with a rapid hand the prelude of a light romance,
which, with a tremulous, but powerful voice, he thus gave
words to :—

> " Lady, farewell !—the fatal hour
> Has sped, for thus thy tyrant wills,
> When he, who loves thee, leaves this tower,
> Deserts gay hall and wood and bower
> Of her, for whom his heart's pulse thrills ;
> And thou art she—Ladye—sweet Ladye."

When the minstrel touched the prelude, Rose Roche
became visibly affected ; but when the words fell from his
lips, a burning blush dyed her cheeks and brow, and her
heart throbbed almost to bursting. Alas, it was the very
roundelay the poor page had sung beneath her casement on
that melancholy night when her defunct lord had expelled
him from the castle ! She turned hastily round to see who
the strange youth might be who thus recalled her absent
love in look and voice so forcibly. Blessed Ursula ! it was
he, the long lost page ! The minstrel, as he caught her
eyes, suddenly ceased his melody — the lute fell from his
nerveless grasp, and, overcome by feelings that could not
be controlled, he sank upon the bench behind him. It was,
indeed, young Aylmer. The well-remembered features
could never be forgotten although the boy had ripened into
manhood—the thick down upon the lip had changed to a

dark moustache—and the belt which once held a hunting-blade, supported now a goodly brand.

The strange effect of the melody upon the lady, and the minstrel's sudden indisposition, could not escape remark; a startling suspicion flashed across the minds of the company, and, after a painful silence of some minutes, Hubert de Moore rose from his seat, and bowing to the very table, thus addressed the lady of the castle:

"Wilt thou forgive the humblest but most devoted of thy suitors, if he presume to remind you that the hour has long since passed when your election should have been made? Far be it from me, noble dame, to seem importunate; but suspense is irksome to those that love, and I and my brother nobles pray to you to signify your pleasure, and end uncertainty at once."

While De Moore was speaking, Rose Roche appeared to recover her self-possession wonderfully; her eye brightened, her colour came again, and the compression of her lips proved that she was nerving herself for some determined effort. She rose slowly and gracefully, while a dead silence pervaded the hall; faint and tremulous as the first words were, they were distinctly heard by those remotest from the dais.*

"Noble lords," she said, "I own and thank your courtesy: I ask this holy churchman if I am to exercise free choice in this affair, unshackled with bar, or condition, save my own leasure: and if he whom I shall place here," and she pointed to the vacant seat beside her own, which had been reserved for the successful wooer, "shall be supported in all the rights and properties which he shall obtain through me?"

"All this," said the Prior, "is fairly stipulated in the intents of this scroll."

"Then will I not trespass on your patience, noble lords —*there* stands the object of my choice; and thus do I install him in this seat, as lord and master of Dhu Castle!"

She turned to the astonished minstrel as she spoke, and ere her words were ended, the youth was seated at her side.

A scene of wonder and wild confusion followed—most of the barons protested loudly aganst her choice; angry looks

* The place of honour in a Baronial Hall.

and threatening gestures were directed at the minstrel, and more than one sword was half unsheathed. O'Connor seemed thunderstruck—and the lady herself was the most collected of the company.

"How is this, Sir Knights!" she cried. "Is lordly word and written pledge so lightly held among you, that thus ye violate their sanctity? Thane of Connaught," she continued, as she addresssed herself to the "Big Man,"—"thy faith was never questioned, and thy word is held to be sacred as a martyr's vow. When the English King, under pain of confiscation, ordered thee to deliver the stranger up, whom thou hadst resetted—although five hundred marks were upon his head, what was thy answer? 'The lands may go, but plighted faith must stand!' The ink with which you bound yourself to the conditions of yonder bond, is not yet dry upon the parchment, and wilt thou break thy word?"

"It is a trick," cried De Moore.

"The selection rests with ourselves alone," exclaimed Mandeville.

"We will never brook that page or minstrel should hold the lands and castles of Cormac More," said both together: and they laid their hands upon their swords; the attendants followed the example of their lords, and a scene of violence and discord was about immediately to ensue.

O'Connor slowly rose—he waved his hand to command silence, and his wishes were promptly obeyed.

"This is, indeed, an unexpected choice," he said: "Sir Prior, read thy parchment aloud, that all may hear, and read it carefully, line after line, and syllable by syllable: see that a letter be not omitted." The monk obeyed. "The document is a plain one," said "The Big Man," "and by it the lady has good right to choose whom she listeth for her consort.—Lady of Iveagh" he continued, as he turned to the blushing widow, "is this youth the husband of thy choice?"—"He and none besides, so help me saints and angels!" was the solemn answer. "Then, by my father's ashes," and a knight's word that never yet was questioned, thou, Aylmer Mowbray, shalt this night possess thy bride! And why, my lords, chafe you so at this?" for the storm was again about to burst forth: "Is it because the monk was but a sorry lawyer, and the lady took advantage of a loose parchment, which should have bound her better? Is it that the Lord of Dhu Castle was once a page? What was thy ancestor, De Moore, (I mean not to offend thee,) but usher to the Lord Justice? and thine, Mandeville, but chamber-groom to Strongbow? Aylmer, I love thee too well to envy thee thy good fortune:— thy lute has won the lady—thy lance must keep her lands. Kneel down, minstrel no longer—rise up, my own knight banneret! And now, Lords of the Pale, Henry himself could not confer a nobler dignity; for O'Connor's knight is standard-bearer to the King of Connaught! Does any here gainsay his rank and dignity? The sword that conferred the honour is ready and able to maintain it!" And O'Connor, as he ended, flung belt and rapier on the table.

But none seemed disposed to quarrel with him : and gradually they followed his example, and admitted the lady's right of choice. The mirth and feasting were resumed; and each, after reasoning with himself, finding that the chances of individual success were greatly against him, became reconciled to lose the lady and her lands. Before midnight struck, the Prior performed the marriage ceremony; and while O'Connor bestowed the beauteous bride, De Moore himself attended upon the fortunate minstrel.

Nor did Sir Aylmer Mowbray disappoint his patron's expectation. As his lute was sweetest in the bower, his plume was foremost in the field. He held the possessions he gained by his lady against every claimant; sons and daughters blessed his bed, and transmitted his titles and estates to posterity : and thus, more than one powerful house traces its lineage back to an "*élève*" of the Ursulines and the *black-eyed Page*.

---

## CHAPTER XXXV.

THE fishing party had been successful, and returned late in the evening with two baskets of trout, which, although of small size, were remarkable for beautiful shape and excellent flavour.

It is a curious fact, that the loughs where the party angled, though situate in the same valley, and divided only by a strip of moorland not above fifty yards across, united by the same rivulet, and in depth and soil at bottom,* to all appearance, precisely similar, should produce fish as different from each other as it is possible for those of the same species to be. In the centre lake, the trout are dull, ill-shapen, and dark-coloured; the head large, the body lank, and, though of double size, compared to their neighbours, are killed with much less opposition. In the adjacent loughs, their hue is golden and pellucid, tinted with spots of a brilliant vermilion. The scales are bright, the head small, the shoulder thick, and from their compact shape, they prove themselves, when hooked, both active and vigorous. At table they are red and firm, and their flavour is particularly fine—while the dark trout are white and flaccid, and have the same insipidity of flavour which distinguishes a spent from a healthy salmon. The red trout seldom exceed a herring-size, and in looking through the contents of the baskets, which amounted to at least twelve dozen, I could only find two fish which weighed above a pound.

The dark trout, however, from their superior size, are more sought after by the mountain fishermen. They rarely are taken of a smaller weight than a pound, and sometimes have been killed, and particularly with a worm, or on a night-line, of a size little inferior to that of a moderate salmon.

The fishing party determined that Antony's account of the otters being very numerous about those lakes, was perfectly correct. Their paths between the waters were much beaten, and the *spraints** of the animal fresh and frequent.

* I never observed the effect of bottom soil upon the quality of fish so strongly marked as in the trout taken in a small lake in the county of Monaghan. The water is a long irregular sheet, of no great depth—one shore bounded by a bog, the other by a dry and gravelly surface. On the bog side, the trout are of the dark and shapeless species peculiar to moory loughs—while the other affords the beautiful and sprightly variety, generally inhabiting rapid and sandy streams. Narrow as the lake is, the fish appear to confine themselves to their respective limits; the *red* trout being never found upon the bog moiety of the lake, nor the *black* where the under surface is hard gravel.                † Traces.

There is a lake still farther up the mountains, and some hundred feet above the level of these loughs, which produces trout not more remarkable for size than for their peculiarity in never rising at a fly, or taking a bait; and yet they are frequently observed by the herdsmen who frequent the valley where the lake is situated, rising over the water, or, to use their own phrase, "tumbling about like dogs." From the known attachment of the lower classes of this country to indulge in "the wild and wonderful," their size or existence might be doubtful, were it not that they run like eels in the latter part of a harvest, and at that season are taken, after a flood, in the pools of the little river, which communicates directly with the lake. These trout have been found to weigh upwards of *twelve* pounds, and are said to be in shape and colour like large gillaroos, and of superior flavour when brought to table.

The otter-killer declares that he fished this lake repeatedly, and while he exhausted all his piscatory skill, he never could induce a trout to rise. He recollects, however, hearing "when a boy," that there was formerly an old man, who resided contiguous to the lake, who caught trout most plentifully near the centre of the water, by floating lines across it, their ends being attached to the legs of geese ; but he admits his belief that this was but a popular conceit, and wisely comes to a conclusion, "that there is a sea-horse, or some such devil in the lough, which prevents the fish from taking fly or worm."*

Three days have passed, and the weather has been wet and boisterous. The moors have become soft, and are now very distressing to traverse. The grouse have deserted their customary haunts, are found with difficulty, and, from their wildness, will hardly stand the dogs. Winter is fast approaching, and the time is close at hand when the cabin must be abandoned for the more substantial comforts of the Lodge.

And I shall leave this hut and these hills with sincere regret. Palled with the pleasures of the world, I found here that rude, but real happiness, which for years before I had sought in vain. *Here* I associated with a new order of beings.

* In the neighbourhood of Minola, there is a lake called Carramore, where the trout are said to be equally large, and in refusing baits and flies equally refractory. I have never fished the water, or seen the trout ; but they are taken during harvest floods, in a mill-race, which runs directly from the lough ; their size is from four to ten pounds.

I compared them with the artificial society I had consorted with, and found among them some traces of natural virtues, which ultra civilization has banished from the rest of mankind. There may be here, no doubt, much ignorance and superstition to be regretted, and false opinions and falser modes of action to be corrected—but even for their vices I can find an apology, and their worst crimes will appear, upon examination, to be either consequent upon moral neglect, or arising from rude and barbarous notions of what appears to them nothing but retributive justice.

The grave offences with which these wild people are principally charged, appear to be abduction and murder; and both are of frequent recurrence. The first, indeed, is so prevalent, that any lady bent upon celibacy had better avoid Ballycroy, and particularly so if she has obtained the reputation of being opulent. This crime, however, is seldom of a dark character, and is generally traceable to local causes, and the very unceremonious mode in which parents conclude matches between their children without consulting the inclinations of the parties most concerned in the affair. Probably the whole matter is arranged between the fathers during an accidental meeting at a fair, or likelier yet, over an *egg-shell** drinking-bout in a poteen-house. The due proportions of cattle and *dry-money*† which are to be given and received are regularly specified; and the youthful couple who are to be united by the silken bond of Hymen are first acquainted with their purposed happiness after the priest has been sent for to solemnize the nuptials. No wonder, therefore, if the lady have another *liaison*, that she intimates her feelings to the fortunate man. He finds no difficulty in enlisting a sufficient number of his faction to " hoist away" the intended bride, and carry her to some distant hill or island. Then a wonderful series of bargain-making commences : upon the lady's side it being insisted that the abductor shall forthwith make her " an honest woman :" while the gallant usually demurs to the "*amende honorable*," until the " consideration" for doing the same is propounded and guaranteed. Now it is that the *priest* engages deeply in the negociation. He assumes the first

* It may be easily imagined that *glass* is a scarce article in Ballycroy. Accordingly, in the still and drinking houses, an egg-shell is used as a substitute.

† " Dry money" is synonymous with " hard cash."

place in the *corps diplomatique*, and becomes prime minister. In the conduct of the affair, no doubt himself is interested; he is anxious to effect hymeneals, for hence arises his principal revenue, and matrimony is the best feather in his wing—and, independent of the nuptial fee, contingent christenings and increased *house-money** are in prospective. But the lover has it all his own way. A week's residence in the mountains has perilled the lady's reputation beyond recovery; as she has gotten *a blast,* her matrimonial market is spoiled, and nothing remains but an amicable arrangement. Terms are accordingly made—the parties become one flesh—the priest is considered for his great and valuable services by "both the houses," and " one raal *rookawn* of a runaway match," is better to *his reverence* than thrice the number of weddings perpetrated by general consent.

This milder class of abduction is unfortunately not the only one; girls having property, or who are likely to possess it, are oftentimes forcibly carried off. Secreted in the mountains, they are not easily recoverable by their friends, and left at the mercy of the ruffian and his confederates, they are at last obliged to become the legal property of the despoiler. As the abductor is generally some idle dissipated blackguard, the fate of the ill-starred being who is united to him under such circumstances for life, is truly lamentable.

The second and worst description of crime, of which this ⹁emote district unhappily affords too many instances, is murder. Many circumstances tend to encourage it. The system of clanship, and the imperfect administration of the laws, are chief causes. A strange infatuation prevents these people from surrendering a culprit; and to conceal or abet the escape of a criminal from punishment, is felt to be a sort of moral obligation not to be got over. Hence, the feudal system prevails in Ballycroy of repaying injury by injury! rather than submit the offender to the ordinary course of justice; violences committed by one faction are fearfully returned by the other; and in a country where ardent spirits are easily procured, and where ancient customs, and the end-

* The revenues of the Roman Catholic clergy are derived from certain fees payable for marriages and christenings, with an annual tax of two shillings upon every honse in the parish. These, with Christmas and Easter offerings, presents, and legacies. amount, in populous parishes, to a very considerable sum.

less number of holy days enjoined by the Church of Rome bring the parties into frequent collision, it is not wonderful that disastrous consequences ensue. Maddened by whisky, the national pugnacity bursts forth, old injuries are remembered, the worst passions are called into action, and loss of life is too commonly the result.

That any competent moral remedy· can be employed to check these barbarisms, is hopeless, while the present destructive system of private distillation is encouraged by the landlord and abetted by the revenue. The landlord is the chief delinquent—for owing to abominable *jobbing*, the monies taken from the public purse, and intended to open a communication between this wild country and the more inhabited districts, have been scandalously malversated, and lavished upon useless works, merely to reward favouritism, or benefit agents and dependents. No serviceable attempts have been made to facilitate the transport of grain from the mountains to those towns from whence it could be sent abroad ; and hence, the only markets which could be legitimately and beneficially resorted to by the peasantry, are, from want of means of egress from the highlands, *embargoed* to these hapless people. Left to their own resources, what can this wretched population do ? At the mercy of hireling drivers and cold-hearted agents, they are required on a given day to produce the rent—honestly if they can—but to produce it. To convey their miserable grain crop to a distant market, would greatly abate the amount of the sale, by the expence and difficulty attendant upon the carriage. An easier mode of disposing of it is presented. The still is substituted for the market ; and hence, three parts of the corn grown in these bogs and hills are converted into whisky.

At first sight, the advantages of private distillation appear immense. The grain will realize nearly three times the price that it would have produced if sold for exportation; but when the demoralization, and waste, and ulterior risk are considered, the imaginary profits are far overbalanced by the certain or contingent losses which attend it.

From the moment that the grain is first *wetted* to the time the spirit has been *doubled*, the ordinary habits of the peasant are interrupted. Night and day, he must be on the alert—and if there were no greater penalty beyond the unbidden visits of every idle blackguard who drops in to taste the " barley bree," it would be a sufficient punishment for the offence. But this is the smallest tax upon the produce of the still; when the process is complete, much of the produce is expended in drunken hospitality. If, after all these drawbacks, the residue be disposed of in the town, or sold to some itinerant whisky-dealer, the adventure is prosperous; but the chances of detection, seizure, fine, and imprisonment, are so multitudinous, as to render the vending of this pernicious article a ruinous trade. To succeed encourages him to continue in this hazardous manufacture; and then upon him who night and day parches in a still-house, certain drunkenness is entailed, with sooner or later a loss of property, from the casualties incident to the adventure; and hence, more people have been beggared by this demoralizing traffic, than all the misfortunes which bad seasons, bad crops, and worse still, bad landlords could accomplish.

Difficult as the task is found of conveying grain from the highlands, the denizens of the coast possess little advantage from their own locality. Want of harbours renders the voyage hazardous, and the arrival of the grain at market an uncertainty; and many a peasant, from rough seas and contrary winds, has been ruined. One instance of this was mentioned, and it so forcibly exemplifies the misfortune, that I shall transcribe it.

A person of comfortable means, having suffered severe loss from private distillation, determined that he would never " *wet a grain* during his natural life." He shipped his corn accordingly in a *hooker* for Westport, it being the nearest place where a purchaser could be found. Bad weather and contrary winds came on, and during eight days, for so much time was occupied in the passage, the grain was exposed to rain and spray eternally, and when it reached its destination, was found to be so much damaged, as to be rendered unfit for sale. The unlucky owner was eventually obliged to bring it back, and in self-defence to *malt and distil it*. The process was completed, and the spirits safely brought to the town of Castlebar. There it was seized by the Revenue, the proprietor imprisoned for four months, and his cattle and furniture at home *canted* to pay that rent, which the corn, had it been marketable, would have more than realized. By this accumulation of misfortune, the unhappy man was reduced to the greatest misery, and from having been once an opulent landholder. he is at this moment a *cottier* upon what was formerly his farm, with nothing to support a wife and seven children, but a limited potato-garden, and occasionally *sixpence a day*, when he is lucky enough to obtain employment at that price.

## CHAPTER XXXVI.

Day fixed for our departure—Party separate—Last day's shooting—The secret valley—The fishers—Curious incident—Di ner—An alarm—Night-search for the otter-killer—The old man found—His recovery—Narrative of the accident.

THE day for our departure is fixed, and the order for breaking up our bivouac has issued ; we leave the cabin to-morrow, and some of us, in course of mortal changes and chances are never fated to visit it again, and " breast the keen air" of these extensive mountains. We have all devoted this, our last day, to separate pursuits. I with my kinsman take to the hills, while the Colonel and the Priest descend the river, thus embracing sports by " fell and flood." Old Antony, encouraged by the report of the fishing-party, has hobbled off at day-break with his trap and terrier, determined, as he expressed it, " to try his fortune once more before he died." A shepherd-boy accompanied him, and when the distance and difficulty of the ground is considered, the old man's courage is surprising, and nothing but that master-passion, which through a long life has been remarkable, could nerve the otter-killer to the enterprise.

Our last day's sport, during its forenoon, was most unpromising. The birds were scarce, unsettled, and " wild as hawks." From the extreme steadiness of the dogs, we sometimes succeeded in surprising them ; but generally, the cock took alarm, and gave the signal for escape, and the brood got off with a random shot or two. At last, when almost weary of following birds who appeared determined not to stand a point, accident did for us what neither art nor local experience could achieve.

On a narrow strip of heather, which fringed the banks of a little rivulet, one of our youngest and wildest setters stopped in his career as if he had been shot. The suddenness of his check, and the steady point he stood at, intimated that the birds were immediately beside him; and while my cousin, who happened to be at a little distance, hurried up, Hennessey observed a splendid pack of fifteen birds stealing off across the bare bog. It was a brood of very unusual number to meet with at this advanced season, when the strongest packs have generally been reduced by gun or vermin. The moor that adjoined the banks on which the grouse were found, was a barren soft surface, without either heath or broken ground to cover our approach; and when we attempted to close up, the cock took wing, and the pack rose instantly and crossed the flats, continuing their flight over a small hill, until we lost them altogether.

We were very doubtful whether we should follow them, as the hill was particularly steep and barren, and the ground beyond it, to judge from appearances, as bare as the exposed moorlands the birds had quitted. At this moment of indecision, Hennessey recollected that there was a little valley beneath the brow where the grouse had left our view; but my kinsman, often as he had been on these hills, had never before been aware of its situation. Hennessey's information determined us to proceed; we accordingly clambered up the ascent, and when we reached the brow of the height, discovered immediately below one of the sweetest glens I ever looked at, stretching between the basis of the hill we occupied and the higher ridge beyond it. It was an admirable retreat for grouse—several rivulets trickled through the hollow, and everywhere it was covered with thick tall heath, in rich blossom, and the cranberries, of which these birds are particularly fond, were growing all around in great abundance. Delighted with our new discovery, we determined to investigate this land of promise closely, and our expectations, though excited by the appearance of this beautiful glen, were amply realized. We found the pack that escaped us in the low grounds, and they paid dearly for the long walk they had given us in the pursuit. The valley produced two other broods; and soon after some hours of capital shooting, we found our game-bags, when we left the glen, increased by twenty-three of the finest birds I ever saw. We might have thinned the packs still more, but my kinsman was anxious to leave this secret valley with a sufficient stock, to render it a sure resource when grouse could not be otherwise obtained. This was indeed a good wind-up to our highland-shooting: and as we sprang several scattered birds during our return, we decided that this was our best day throughout the season, and worthy of the brightest page of the game-book, in which all our failures and successes were duly and faithfully chronicled since we took to the hills.

A curious incident, supplied us with an excellent *white* fish. The servant who brought the post-bag, when in the act of crossing the river, which, in his route from the Lodge, he was obliged to do repeatedly, most unexpectedly encountered a large otter carrying off a salmon he had just seized. The postman attacked the poacher vigorously, who, dropping his prey, glided off into the deep water at the tail of the ford. The spoil proved to be a fresh salmon not twenty hours from the sea, and consequently in prime condition. The otter showed himself the best artist of the day; for while the Colonel and his companion returned with empty baskets, the little animal managed to secure the finest and freshest salmon in the river.

To give *éclat* to our parting feast, a red-deer haunch had been reserved, and in its roasting, John, as poor Napoleon would say, "covered himself with glory." Dinner passed as such a dinner should pass. The Colonel and the Priest appeared bent upon conviviality. We too prepared for a jovial carouse; and it was generally determined that our parting banquet should be the "merriest, *as* the last."

Evening passed quickly—there was no moon visible till after midnight, and the wind, which had hitherto been unheard, began to make that mournful noise around the cabin, which generally indicates an approaching change of weather. The otter-killer's absence was now, for the first time, remarked, and I observed that my kinsman rose frequently from the table, to look long and anxiously from the window. Another hour passed, and our alarm was fearfully increased, for, aware of the feebleness of the old man, we apprehended that he would be unable to make good his journey; and, if benighted in the moors, the probability was great that he would perish of cold before the morning.

While we remained in painful suspense, each feeling an unwillingness to interrupt the comfort of the evening by expressing fears that haply might only be imaginary, a squall rushed up the river, and showed us that the wind had

chopped round to the westward several points since twilight.
At that moment a commotion was heard outside—the pipes
ceased—loud and earnest whisperings succeeded—the door
opened, and John, with a pale face and hurried voice, told
us that the otter-killer was missing, and the boy who had
accompanied him in the morning to the lakes, had now
returned without being able to give any tidings of old
Antony, from whom it appeared that he had separated
several hours before.

"Get lights instantly," exclaimed my cousin. "Away all
of you! disperse right and left across the bogs. Come, Frank,
on with the brogues. I fear our poor otter-killer is but 'a
lost priest.' No, Colonel, your services would be useless—"
for the commander, forgetting gout and rheumatism, and
alive only to the danger of his ancient associate, had prepared to accompany the party.

In a few minutes every effective member of our body-politic
was in motion. The scene was uncommon and picturesque.
It being pitch-dark as the respective parties dispersed across
the moor upon their different routes to the mountain lakes,
the stream of torch-light falling upon the figures, as they
were revealed and hidden by the inequalities of the ground
they traversed, was really imposing. Their wild shouts died
gradually as the distance increased; and presently nothing
was heard by our party but the rushing of the stream and the
moaning of the blast.

Obedient to Hennessey's advice, we followed the river-
path, as the likeliest one which the otter-killer would select
in his unfortunate attempt to return to the cabin. On either
side of the moorland the peasants were extended, and occasionally we caught a glimpse of their fading lights, as they
glanced and disappeared among the hillocks. Our own path
was so rough and difficult, that the torch could not secure us
from many and severe falls; and from the extreme darkness
of the night, it was too evident that Antony could never
make good his way. We almost despaired of being enabled
to render assistance to the unfortunate object of our search.

Suddenly, Hennessey, who led the party, halted. "By
heaven!" he exclaimed, "I heard either a fox's *whimper*, or
the cry of a dog."

He put his finger to his lips and whistled shrilly, and
instantly a long-sustained howl answered to the signal.

"It is *Venney's* cry," said our leader. "God grant that her master be still alive!"

We pushed forward rapidly for several hundred yards in the direction the noise was heard from ; and the whining of a dog, broken now and then by a long and piercing howl, continued to guide us. We reached the place, and on turning a rock which elbowed into the river abruptly, found the old man extended on the ground, cold and motionless. The trap was bound across his back, and a large otter lay at some yards distance from the place where he had fallen.

We raised him up, while the faithful terrier frisked about us, and testified sincere delight at the promised recovery of her master. The old man's eyes feebly opened when the torch-light flashed upon his face. This symptom of existing life encouraged us, and, as his extremities were cold and powerless, his master and I rubbed them briskly between our hands, while Hennessey poured some brandy down his throat.

"We want instant help," said my cousin ; "jump upon the bank, and see if anybody is near us."

His foster-brother rushed up the brow, and whistled loudly, but the signal was unheard or unheeded. Again he exerted himself, but ineffectually, to make the flanking parties hear him : there was no reply.

"This may be heard," he muttered, and, drawing a pistol from his breast, the loud report was answered by a distant halloo. Next moment lights appeared, and our shouts and whistles directed the torch-bearers to the place.

We disencumbered the dying man of the iron trap, and our attempts to restore suspended animation appeared to be partially successful. But the Priest, who led the party coming to our relief, gave us still better hopes, by ascertaining that the old man's pulse was beating.

From the assistance we received, the unfortunate otter-killer was transported quickly to the cabin. A bed was already heated, and John had abundance of warm water to bathe his chilled limbs. Our unabated efforts were crowned with ultimate success ; for before midnight, he had recovered his speech, and was enabled, though with some difficulty, to give us the particulars of his unlucky excursion.

He reached, it appeared, the loughs soon after daylight, and discovered the numerous footmarks which the fishing-party had already observed. One trace he particularly followed, and, from the *spraint,* concluded the animal would cross the path again before evening; and after setting his trap, Antony retired to a distance, whence, himself unseen, he could watch the event.

At twilight, as the old man had conjectured, the otter, on his return, crossed the path, and was secured, and the hunter and his terrier made good the capture. Proud of his success, which to the old man seemed a proof that his energies were not yet gone, he foolishly endeavoured to carry this trophy of his skill along with him, instead of leaving it with his trap, for some *gossoon* to bring in the morning to the cabin. He turned his steps homeward; but the trap and the otter, with the soft and harassing ground he had to traverse, speedily exhausted his feeble strength; the light faded away, the wind rose, and before he crossed the swamp, and gained the firm but rugged path beside the river, the darkness rendered it almost impossible for even a young person to have proceeded safely. After feeble and slow efforts to get forward, he stumbled over a stone, his energies were totally exhausted by fatigue, and he was unable to rise again.

His faithful dog couched herself beside her fallen master, and the last sounds that the despairing otter-killer heard, were the long and mournful howls with which Venom mourned over his calamity.

Guided by the torch-light, we carried the rescued sufferer to a place of refuge. Everything that kindness could suggest was done to effect his restoration; and the old man owned it as a consolation, that he was saved from perishing in the desert; and that, in death, he should have those around his bed, who, in life, had possessed his love, fidelity, and veneration.

## CHAPTER XXXVII.

The otter-killer carried to the lodge—Fishing homewards—Angling closes for the season—Remarks—Feelings on the occasion—Smuggler appears—Landing a cargo—Captain Matthews—The Jane—Cutter stands out to sea—Hooker on a rock—Traveller alarmed—Anecdote of an Englishman.

THE illness of the old otter-killer has clouded our moorland excursions at their close, and we leave with melancholy forebodings our mountain bivouac. Antony, at his own

request, was carried to the Lodge to-day ; and when the
difficulty of the ground, and the frequent crossing of the
river is considered, it was an arduous undertaking.  The
camp-followers arranged a rude litter ; and as works of mercy
are highly estimated by pious Catholics, there were more
volunteers to assist in transporting the dying man than could
well find employment.

During our progress down, we had some hours' superior
sport with the eagle.  Pullgarrow, that inimitable hole, has
more than realized what the Colonel and our kinsman have
said and sung in its commendation.  In Christendom it could
not be surpassed, and of this best of pools may be said, that
" none but itself can be its parallel."

In the minor streams we killed more red trout this morning
than we do generally.  Indeed, from the character of this
river, I have been puzzled to account for the evident scarcity
of this species in a water that appears so especially adapted
for them.  The clearness of the stream, the gravelly soil it
flows over, its pools and rapids, all seem calculated to produce
red trout plentifully.  But they are not numerous ; and as
the flies we invariably use are formed for the other species,
it is not surprising that we find but few red trout in the
baskets.

With this day's fishing our river sports terminate.  Rods
and lines, and all the *matériel* of the craft, will now be laid in
ordinary, and till spring comes round again, other sports must
occupy the idle hours.  I have learned more—although I
acknowledge, with all humility, my unworthiness as an angler
—by a few days' practical experience, than I could have
almost considered possible ; and I have ascertained how inade-
quate theory is to instruct a neophyte in the art.  In angling,
however, like other manly exercises, men are constituted by
nature to succeed or fail.  We know that there are persons
who, though born in a *preserve*, could never shoot even
tolerably, while others, with less advantages, speedily become
adepts.  One man can never learn to ride ; and another, in a
short time, can cross the country like " a winged Mercury."
The same rule holds good in angling ;—A. in a short period
becomes perfect master of the arcana of the gentle science ;
while B. will thresh a river to eternity, dismissing flies, breaking tops, losing foot-links, and perpetrating every enormity
with which a tyro is chargeable.

Yet to a man naturally *handy* and observant, little is required to acquire the art, but a good stream and tolerable attention. He will soon gain more practical information and mechanical science than any book can inculcate. And it will be only when, by practice, he has acquired a knowledge of the science, that he will be able to comprehend what written theories profess to teach.

We had fished the deep hole above the river, and our rods are, for the *last time*, handed to the attendants. And shall I never while my idle hours away beside that beautiful stream in the intervals of unfriendly sunshine, stretched beneath a bank, turning the light pages of a book, or watching in dreamy indolence the rushing of a river? Shall I no more watch the eddying of the pool, with its sparkling surface broken by the bold and glorious spring which marks the salmon rejoicing, like a returned prodigal, in his native river? No, my foot will never press that bank again; nor shall I beside that glassy water enjoy those tranquillizing feelings, which the slave of passion, the creature of society, can neither know nor estimate!

We had scarcely left the river, when a man, who stood upon an eminence that commanded an extensive view seaward, gesticulated with great energy, and made, what appeared to me, some momentous communication in the *mother tongue*.

" It is *the Jane*!" exclaimed my kinsman, as he bounded up the bank to gain the summit of the hillock. I did not comprehend exactly what the affair was which created such powerful emotions among my companions; but when I reached the height, a scene of extreme interest was presented.

Between the Black Rock and the island of Devilawn, a cutter was opening the bay, and standing from the westward under a press of canvass. She carried a spanking breeze in, and, as her course was too points off the wind, her sails drew, and she came up " hand over hand." The approach was evidently expected, for from every nook and inlet rowboats were being launched—the whole population poured forth from the mountain villages—and the coast, as far as the eye could reach, was in marvellous commotion. Nothing could be more beautiful and picturesque than the appearance of the smuggler. The sunshine fell upon her snowy canvass, a private signal fluttered from the mast-head, and a union-jack was flying at the peak, while, occasionally, a sheet of broken foam sparkled round her bows, as she held her onward course gallantly,

" And walked the water like a thing of life."

In a few minutes after her having been first discovered, boats were pulling from the shore in all directions, while the cutter closed the land fast.    When abreast the Ridge Point, she suddenly rounded-to, handed her gaff top-sail, hauled up the main-tack, and waited for the boats.

" I cannot go on board," said my kinsman, with a heavy sigh, " being, alas! like Master Robert Shallow, ' a poor esquire of this county, and one of the king's justices of the peace ;' but though I shall not pay my personal respects, yet will not my old friend Jack Matthews forget me ; but you shall board *the Jane,* and witness a bustling business.    I'll promise you a hearty welcome from the Skipper—and see, you are just in time, for the *gig* is on the water."

As he spoke, he hailed the boat, which, returning to the beach, took me on board, and then pulled off for the vessel, which, in a quarter of an hour, we reached.

It was, indeed, a bustling scene ; a hundred boats were collected round the smuggler, who, to use nautical parlance, had already " broken bulk," and was discharging the cargo with a rapidity, and yet orderly and business-like system, that was surprising.

I was immediately recognized by Captain Matthews, and politely invited to his cabin.    Aware of the hurry consequent upon this dangerous traffic, on the plea of his presence being requisite upon deck, I would have declined the honour ; but the gallant Captain remarked, with great indifference, " that he left the delivery of his cargo to the agents and purchasers, and could not spend an hour or two more to his satisfaction, than in entertaining, in his own way, the kinsman of his respected friend."    And, calling for the steward, he stepped forward to order some refreshments.

While he was thus engaged, I had ample time to satisfy my curiosity, and observe the conduct of this illicit traffic. There appeared no confusion attendant on the delivery of the tobacco to its respective proprietors, who had already engaged certain proportions of the cargo, which they received upon the production of small tickets, specifying the quantity and description of the goods ; the business having been previously arranged on shore, before the arrival of the smuggler, facilitated the dangerous trade.

When I found myself in the cabin with the bold outlaw —for Matthews had been legally denounced for many daring and successful contests with the Revenue—I could not but admire the thorough indifference to possible consequences which this singular personage exhibited. He knew that several men-of-war were at that moment cruising on the station, and that they had been apprised he had sailed from Flushing, and that this coast was the spot selected by the owners to effect the landing—yet he laughed and drank as gaily as I should in a club-house, and despatched the messages which were occasionally brought down with perfect *nonchalance*. He spoke principally of his own exploits; and the scene was admirably in keeping. Around the cabin, muskets, pistols, and blunderbusses, were secured in arm-racks, and cutlasses and tomahawks were suspended from the bulk-heads. His had been a wild career ; and though not past the middle-age, his life teemed with " perilous adventure." I was so much amused with his varied narratives of brave attempts and desperate successes, that the second hour slipped away before I rose and took my departure. On regaining the deck, the hurry of the business was over. The contraband cargo had been replaced by stone ballast; for by previous arrangement, each boat brought a quantity of *shingle* from the beach, and hence the smuggler was already in trim, and ready to stand out to sea.

This notorious vessel was considered in size and sailing superior to any of a similar class, and her voyages had been numerous and successful. Her armament was formidable; sixteen heavy carronades were extended along the deck, with two long brass guns of smaller calibre, and every other appurtenance of war was in perfect efficiency. But the most striking object was her ferocious-looking, but magnificent crew; they seemed only formed for "the battle and the breeze ;" and well justified their commander's boast, "that he could thrash any cruiser of his own size, and land his cargo in six hours afterwards."

We left the vessel—and, to judge by the kegs and cases stowed away in the gig, my cousin had not been forgotten

in the general distribution. The outlaw stood upon a carron-
ade, and waved his hand as we pulled from the ship's side;
and in a short time set his head-sails, and stood off to sea
with the ebb tide and a spanking breeze, which carried him
out of sight directly.

This was fated to be the last landing of *the Jane,* and
the last exploit of her commander; she foundered on her
next voyage, and every person on board perished with the
vessel.*

We had nearly reached the bar, when we observed a large
sailing-boat strike on the tail of Carrig-a-boddagh, and as the
tide was falling fast, she was in momentary danger of falling
over. Every exertion of the crew to get her off was ineffectual; and on our nearer approach they evinced such unequivocal symptoms of inebriety, as accounted for the disaster. A
solitary passenger was on board, who appeared in desperate
alarm; and, at his own earnest solicitation, we received him
and his personal effects, which were extremely limited, into
our boat. The crew remained with the hooker, which they
calculated upon floating off the following tide.

I was much struck with the appearance of the stranger.
His voice and bearing told that he was not indigenous to
the soil: low in stature, delicate in form, with a timid and
suspicious bearing, I was greatly puzzled to account for his
being a passenger in a Connemara fishing-boat. Although
nervous as a woman before we reached the pier, I had tran-
quillized him so far as to find out generally that he had left
the Galway coast, in the expectation of being landed on the
shores of Sligo; but that the crew, having boarded the
smuggler, managed to get gloriously drunk, and, diverging
totally from their course, ran the hooker on a reef, from which
they should have been several leagues distant.

The stranger was an Englishman. He met from my kinsman a hospitable reception—and the Colonel and I united
our attentions, and in a great degree restored his confidence.
Nothing, however, could persuade him that the hooker had
not been run designedly upon the rock, and that he and his
travelling-bag would have been victimized by what he termed

* *The Jane* went down in a tremendous gale off the north-west coast
of Ireland. Her consort, *The Blue-eyed Maid*, witnessed the melancholy
event, without being able to render any assistance.

"desperate pirates," but for our seasonable rescue. My cousin smiled. "The conduct of the drunken scoundrels," he said, " was unpardonable ; but he doubted whether they harboured those nefarious designs. Strangers were frequently led away by appearances, and it was no uncommon thing for travellers to suffer unnecessary alarm from groundless causes." And he related an anecdote of a gentleman being put in fear and terror, in a neighbouring county, by mistaking a *fish* for a *weapon*.

"Soon after the rebellion of Ninety-eight, an English merchant was necessitated, by urgent business, to visit the kingdom of Connaught.  Having provided himself with a servant, who professed an acquaintance with the language of the country, he made his will, and took a place in the Westport mail.   He reached the post-town of —— in safety, and from it proceeded to cross that wild and picturesque mountain-chain which bounds the beautiful shores of Lough Corrib.

"It was late in autumn : the weather had been wet, and owing to the difficulty of the bridle-roads, the traveller was benighted some miles' distance from the house that he had calculated upon reaching.   Unable to proceed farther, he reluctantly took up his quarters at a *shebeine-house*.   It was but a sorry caravansera—but nothing could surpass the apparent kindness of the family.   Supper was prepared ; the best bed was sheeted, and when the belated stranger had sufficiently refreshed himself, he was conducted to an inner room, where, at his own request, the servant was also accommodated with a pallet.

" Yet, notwithstanding the marked civility of the family, the stranger could not overcome a secret apprehension of impending danger.   It was a wild place—a wilder family ; he feared that treachery lurked underneath this studied kindness; and, as he tossed upon his restless bed, he listened with painful anxiety to every sound.   Midnight came ; the outer door was opened cautiously—several men entered the kitchen with stealthy pace—they conversed in their native language, his name was mentioned, and himself was beyond doubt the subject of this nocturnal *conversazione*.   Crawling in an agony of apprehension to the pallet where his attendant lay, he awoke the sleeper, intimated his suspicions in a whisper, and desired him to report faithfully the midnight colloquy in the outer chamber.'

" ' What's that they say ?' quoth the traveller.

" ' They want another pint, for they have not had such a prize for the last twelvemonth.'

" ' That's me !' groaned the querist.

" ' They have *five pikes* already, and expect more before morning,' continued the valet.

" ' Truculent scoundrels !'

" ' The largest is intended for yourself !

" ' Lord defend me !' ejaculated the stranger.

" ' They wonder if you are sleeping.'

" ' Cold-blooded monsters ; they want to despatch us quietly.'

" ' The owner swears that nobody shall enter this room till morning.'

" ' Ay, then they will have daylight, and no difficulty.'

" ' And now he urges them to go to bed.'

" ' Heaven grant they may ! for then, escape from this den of murder might be possible.'

" Listening with a beating heart until unequivocal symptoms of deep sleep were heard from the kitchen, the unhappy Englishman, leaving his effects to fortune, crawled through the window half-dressed, and, with a world of trouble and perilous adventure, managed early next morning to reach his original place of destination.

" Never, however, was man more mortified than he, when he related his fearful story. His tale was frequently interrupted by a laugh, which *politesse* vainly endeavoured to control.

" ' Zounds !' cried the irritated Englishman, no longer able to conceal his rage, ' is my throat so valueless, that its cutting should merely raise a horse-laugh ?'

" ' My dear friend,' replied the host, ' you must excuse me—it is so funny, I cannot, for the life of me, be serious. The cause of all your fears lies quietly in the outer hall. Come, you shall judge upon what good grounds you absconded through a window, and skirmished half the night over hill and dale, with but the nether portion of your habiliments.'

" As he spoke he uncovered a large basket, and pointed to

a huge pike of some thirty pounds weight, which was coiled around the bottom.

" ' The stormy weather,' continued the host, ' having interrupted our supply of sea-fish, the peasants who alarmed you had been setting night-lines for your especial benefit. The *petka more*,* which you heard devoted to your services in the *shebeine*-house, was not an instrument of destruction, but, as you shall admit at six o'clock, as good a white fish as ever true catholics, like you and I, were doomed wherewithal to mortify the flesh upon a blessed Friday.' "

The stranger smiled.

" I may have wronged my late companions," he said, " but I have of late been under such constant and painful excitement, that I often wonder that reason held her seat. I have this evening not only been delivered from considerable danger, but I have fallen most unexpectedly upon persons and a place which, on this remote coast, and among these wild hills, appear miraculous. Your accents are different from those I have lately listened to : and could I but find courage to tell my story, you would own that I have lately undergone sufficient trials to unnerve a stouter frame than this feeble one of mine."

After some time, the stranger felt the cheering effect of my kinsman's claret, and in a strain which might be termed serio-comic, he thus narrated his story.

### MEMOIR OF A GENTLEMAN WHO WOULD NOT DO FOR GALWAY.

" I AM descended from a line of traders, and by birth as genuine a cockney as ever listened to Bow-bells. My mother's nonage was passed in St. Mary Axe, and my father was a dry-salter in Tooley-street. He was third of the same name that there had dwelt and prospered. They were a thrifty and punctilious race ; and it was a family boast, that, for seventy years, a bill bearing the acceptance of Daniel Dawkins had never been in the hands of the notary. There is virtue in a good name, 'tis said, and theirs was current for ten thousand.

---

* The large pike.

" I was an only child, and from the cradle evinced an indolent and dreamy temperature, which was ill adapted to withstand the worry of trade, and all the annoyances entailed on traffic. I hated trouble; hardly knew the difference between pearl-ashes and pearl-barley; could never comprehend tare-and-trett, and had, moreover, literary propensities. How one in whose veins the blood of the Dawkinses circulated, could be so deplorably uncommercial, is a puzzle; but I was, I suppose, 'foredoomed my father's soul to cross,' and an unhappy tutor ruined me beyond recovery.

" My Gamaliel was a Scotch gentleman of unblemished lineage, remarkable for soiled linen and classical research, who had emigrated from a highland valley with an unpronounceable name, to hold a secondary situation in a city academy, where the progeny of Love-lane and Little Britain received the rudiments of polite letters. The extra hours of the gifted Celt were, for the consideration of ten pounds' annual fee, 'to be paid quarterly, and in advance,' devoted to my accomplishments. Never had man more profound contempt for trade and traders than he at whose feet I was indoctrinated. He turned his nose up at the wealthiest grocer in the ward; and was barely civil to a tobacconist who had a villa at Pentonville, and was, moreover, first favourite for an aldermanic gown. Such delinquency could not be overlooked, and for his heretical opinions touching commerce, he was eventually ejected from Tooley-street. But, alas! the mischief was done—the seed was already sown—and, as after-experience proved, none of it had fallen upon the wayside.

" 'In brevity I shall emulate the noble Roman,' quoth Jack Falstaff; and so shall I, so far as the autobiography of my youth is concerned. I abominated business—was an admirer of the Corsair and Lallah Rookh—was generally given to inflammatory poetry—wrote fugitive pieces, and vainly endeavoured to get them a corner in the periodicals—quarrelled with my parents—was supported in my rebellion by a romantic aunt—and when my disinheritance was actually in legal train, was saved by my parents quitting this world of care, which they did within one short month, by the agency of a typhus fever and two physicians.

" Thus was I thrown upon the world at two-and-twenty,

with thirty thousand pounds. Need I say, that I abjured business instanter, and that the honoured name of Dawkins disappeared from the list of dry-salters? For some years, none led a more peaceful and literary life; and though this may appear a solecism, nevertheless it is positively true. The rejection of my early *fugitives* had chilled the metrical out-breakings of my imagination. I had almost Cowper's sensi-bility—the *lethalis arundo*, as my Scotch tutor would term it, was deep within my bosom—I swore I would never lucubrate again; never again perpetrate a stanza; and, like Mr. Daniel O'Connell's, I presume that my vow was duly registered in heaven.

" This sunny portion of my life was, alas! but transitory. Mine, sir, is a tragic tale. I date the origin of my misfor-tunes on board a Margate steamer, and this melancholy epoch I shudder to recall. Was there no tutelary sprite, no sus-picious spinster, to whisper a cautionary advice? No; with-out a single fear I embarked in the Nereid steamer; and, as the papers stated, ' left the Tower-stairs with a select party, and a band of music, on Friday, the — of June, 182—.'

" I must here observe, that my blue-stocking aunt, who had actually come out in Leadenhall-street with one small and admired volume, called ' Pedrilla, a Tale of Passion,' had been latterly urgent with me to enter into matrimony. ' Something told her,' she would say, ' that the name of Daw-kins was not doomed to be forgotten, like that of Wood, and Birch, and Bagster. Men of tarts and turpentine might perish, while— could I but procure a talented companion; could I but unite myself to a congenial soul, God knows what the result would prove!—a gifted progeny might honour me with their paternity; little Popes and diminutives Landons would thus be given to the world, fated to be glorious in their maturity, and lisping in numbers from their very cots.'

" The company on board the Nereid were generally known to me. They were exclusively *Eastern*; and there were beauties from the Minories, and nice men from Bishopsgate Within and Without. I was no swain, and as Antigallican in my dancing as Bob Acres. The old women admitted, that, though a good catch, I had no spirit; the young ones ' ad-mired the money, but disliked the man;' and as I did not form one of the *coryphées,* who were quadrilling upon the quarter-deck, I was likely enough to be left to meditative solitude.

"But there was another person who appeared to hold no communion with the company. One lady seemed a stranger to the rest. Accident placed me beside her, and thus she became more intimately my *compagnon de voyage.*

"She was certainly a fine-looking woman ; her face was comely, but somewhat coarse ; her hair and brows black as the raven's plumage, her nose rather too marked for a woman's —but then her waist and legs were unexceptionable. She evidently possessed a sufficiency of self-command ; no *mauvaise honte,* no feminine timidity oppressed her. She looked bravely around, as if she would assert a superiority ; and accepted my civilities graciously, it is true, but with the air and dignity of a duchess. She was, from the start, no favourite with the company, and there was no inclination evinced by any of her own sex to make approaches to familiarity. The cockney beaus looked upon her as a fine but formidable animal ; and to me, unworthy as I was, the honour of being *cavalier serviente,* was conceded without a contest. Indeed, at dinner, my fair friend proved herself too edged a tool for civic wit to touch upon. When, with ultra-elegance, an auctioneer, whose assurance was undeniable, pressed ' the *Hirish* lady to *teest* a roast *fole,*' she obliterated the accomplished appraiser, by brusquely replying, ' that no earthly consideration could induce her to eat *horse-flesh !*'

"And yet to this woman I was irresistibly attracted. I sate beside her on the deck, and I ministered to her coffee-cup ; and when the Nereid disembarked her crowd, and a stout, red-whiskered, do-no-good looking gentleman presented himself upon the chain-pier, and claimed his ' gentle cousin,' a pang of agony shot across my breast, and for the first time I felt the curse of jealousy. And yet, God knows, she was not the person from whom ' little Popes' might be expected ; her tender pledges would be better qualified for rangers and riflemen than denizens of the world of letters. But marriage is decreed elsewhere, and mine had been already *booked.*

" ' What's in a name ?' observed somebody. I assert— every thing. Will any body deny that ' Drusilla O'Shaughnessey' was not sufficient to alarm any but a Shannonite ? Such was the appellative of the lady, while her honoured kinsman favoured me with an embossed card, on which was fairly engraven, ' Mr. Marc Antony Burke Bodkin, Bally-broney House.'

" On minor matters I will not dilate. It appeared that Miss Drusilla O'Shaughnessey had come to London, in hope-less search after a legacy she expected in right of her great-uncle, Field-Marshal O'Toole; that the Field-Marshal's effects were undiscoverable; and no available assets could be traced beyond certain old swords and battered snuff-boxes; and consequently Drusilla, who had been an heiress in expect-ancy, was sadly chagrined. Furthermore, it appeared that Mr. Marc Antony Bodkin formed her escort from Connemara, and, being a 'loose gentleman,'* and a loving cousin, he ' bore her company.'

" If ever the course of love ran smooth, which I sincerely disbelieve, mine was not the one. I shall not attempt a description of the progress of my *affaire du cœur*; for I sus-pect that I was the wooed one, and that Drusilla had marked me for her own, and Marc Antony aided and abetted. He, good easy gentleman, was formed for Cupid's embassies. He ' could interpret between you and your love,' as Hamlet says; and to one with my sensibilities, his services were worth a Jew's eye. If woman ever possessed the cardinal virtues united, that person was Drusilla. She was what Marc called ' the soul of honour;' yet she had her weak points, and he hinted darkly that myself had found favour in her sight. As a thing of course, I muttered a handsome acknowledgement; a rejoinder was promptly returned, *per* same conveyance, as my father would have said—and before six days I was made the happiest of men, and levanted to Gretna with the lady of my love, and formally attended by that *fidus Achates*, Marc Antony Bodkin.

" What a whirligig world this is! I recollect well the evening before the indissoluble knot was tied, when I strolled into the little garden at Newark. My thoughts were ' big with future bliss,' and my path of life, as I opined, strewed knee-deep with roses of perennial blossom. I heard voices in

---

* No attempt is made here to insinuate aught against the morality of Miss O'Shaughnessey's protector. " A loose gentleman," in the common *parlance* of the kingdom of Connaught, meaneth simply a gentleman who has nothing to do, and nineteen out of twenty of the aristocracy of that truly independent country may be thus honourably classed.—ED.

the summer-house,—these were my loved one's and her relative's.    To use his own *parlance*, the latter, in the joy of his
heart, had taken a sufficiency of wine ' to smother a priest ;'
and as the conversation was interesting to the parties, and
mine was not the stride of a warrior, my approach was not
discovered by either.  The conclave, however, had terminated, and though but the parting observation reached me,
it is too faithfully chronicled on my memory to be forgotten
—' *The devil is an ommadawn*, no doubt ; but he has money
*galore*, and we'll make him do in Galwày !'   As he spoke
they rose, and passed into the house without observing me.
    " What the observation of Marc Antony meant, I could
not for the life of me comprehend.    Part of it was spoken,
too, in an unknown tongue.    Was *I* the devil ? and what was
an *ommadawn ?*   Dark doubts crossed my mind ; but vanished,
for Drusilla was more gracious than ever, and Marc Antony
squeezed my hand at parting, and assured me, as well as he
could articulate after six tumblers of hot *Farintosh,* ' that I
was a lucky man, and Drusilla a woman in ten thousand.'
    " Well, the knot was tied, and but for the *éclat* of the
thing, the ceremony might have been as safely solemnized at
Margate.    On the lady's side, the property was strictly *personal.*    Her claim upon the estates of the defunct Field-
Marshal was never since established, for the properties of that
distinguished commander could never be localized.    Marc
Antony had been a borrower from the first hour of our intimacy ; and on the morning of her marriage, Drusilla, I have
reason to believe, was not mistress of ten pounds—but then
she was a treasure in herself, and so swore Marc Antony.
    " The private history of a honeymoon I leave to be narrated
by those who have found that haven of bliss which I had
pictured but never realized.    If racketing night and day over
every quarter of the metropolis, with the thermometer steady
at 90 ; if skirmishing from Kensington to the Haymarket,
and thence to Astley's and Vauxhall, with frequent excursions
to those suburban hotels infested by high-spirited apprentices,
' and maids who love the moon :'—if this be pleasure, I had
no reason to repine.    In these affairs ' our loving cousin' was
an absolute dictator, and against his decrees there was no
appeal.    To me, a quiet and nervous gentleman, Marc's arrangements were detestable.    What he called life, was death
to me—his ideas of pleasure were formed on the *keep-moving*

plan—and to sleep a second night in the same place, would be, according to his theories, an atrocity. I found myself sinking under this excessive happiness; and when I ventured a gentle protest against being whirled off in a thunder-storm from the 'Star and Garter' to the 'Greyhound,' I received a cross fire that silenced me effectually. From that period I submitted without a murmur; my days were numbered; another month like that entitled the honey-one, would consign me to my fathers; the last of the Dawkinses would vanish from among men, and a mural monument in St. Saviour's record my years and virtues. But accident saved my life, though it annihilated my property.

"Years before I led Drusilla to the altar, a Connemara estate, which had belonged to her progenitors, and had been ruined in succession by the respective lords, was utterly demolished by a gentleman whom she termed her 'lamented father.' The property had been in chancery for half a century, and advertised for sale beyond the memory of man; but as it was overloaded with every species of encumbrance, no one in his senses would have accepted the fee-simple as a gift. But my wife had determined that Castle Toole should be redeemed, and rise once more, Phœnix-like, from its embarrassments. It owed, she admitted, more than it was worth, twice told—but then, *sure*, it was the family property. *There*, for four centuries, O'Tooles had died, and O'Shaughnesseys been born; and if she could only persuade me to repurchase it with my wealth, she would be the first lady in the barony. To Marc Antony this project was enchanting. Ballybroney had been roofless for the last twenty years, that being about the period when the last of the " dirty acres," which had once appertained to the mansion, had slipped from the fingers of of the Bodkins; therefore, to establish himself at Castle Toole, would suit my kinsman to a hair. In short, the battery was unmasked; and whether over-persuaded by the eloquence of my wife, the arguments of her cousin, or driven to desperation by a life of pleasure, I consented in due time; and having accompanied my honoured counsellors to Dublin, found no competitor for Castle Toole—proposed for the same—paid a large sum of money, and was declared, by the legal functionaries, a gentleman of estate, and that too in Connemara.

" In my eyes, the value of the purchase was not enhanced
by a personal investigation. It had its capabilities, it is
true; the house being a ruin, might be repaired; and as
the lands were in their primeval state, it was possible to
reclaim them. Still, when one looked at a huge dismantled
building of that mixed class in architecture between a
fortalice and a dwelling-house, with grey-flagged roof, lofty
chimneys, embattled parapets, and glassless windows, it was
ill-calculated to encourage an English speculator in Irish
estates. On every side a boundless expanse of barren
moorland was visible, with an insulated portion of green
surface on which the castle stood, and a few straggling trees
remained from what had once been a noble oak wood. That
some savage beauty did exist in the wild highlands, a fine
river, and an extensive lake, is certain ; but to me, the
scenery and the place were dreary and disheartening. In
vain, therefore, did my friend Mark Antony dilate upon its
advantages. The river boasted the best salmon fishing in
the country—What was it to me, who had never angled for
a gudgeon ? The mountains abounded with grouse—Who
but a native could escalade them ? The bogs were celebrated for game—And would I devote myself like another
Decius, to be engulfed, for all the wild ducks that ever wore
a wing? But then *The Blazers* were only a few miles
distant, and their favourite fixture was on the estate.
Really the proximity of that redoubted body produced a
cold perspiration when I heard it. *The Blazers!* the most
sanguinary fox-club in Connaught—a gang who would literally
devastate the country, if it did not please Heaven to thin their
numbers annually by broken necks and accidents from pistol
bullets. Yet, with me, the Rubicon was crossed—Castle
Toole was mine with all its imperfections, and I determined
to exert my philosophy to endure what it was impossible to
undo.

"To restore the decayed glories of the mansion, you
may well imagine was a work of trouble and expense. It
was done, and Drusilla slept again under the roof-tree of
her progenitors. Hitherto I had indulged her fancies
without murmuring, and some of them were superlatively
absurd. I hoped and believed that when the hurry of re-
establishing the ruin I had been fool enough to purchase

was over, the worry and confusion of my unhappy life
would terminate. While the repairs proceeded, we resided
in a small house in a neighbouring village, and were not
much annoyed by unwelcome visitors. But no sooner was
the castle completed and the apartments reported habitable,
than the country for fifty miles round complotted, as I
verily believe, to inundate us with their company. A sort
of *saturnalia*, called the house-warming, I thought destined
to continue for ever ; and after having endured a purgatorial
state for several weeks, and the tumult and vulgar dissipa-
tion had abated, swarms of relations to the third and fourth
generation of those that loved us, kept dropping in, in what
they termed *the quiet friendly way*, until 'the good house
Money-glass'\* was outstripped in hospitality by my devoted
mansion. Although ten long miles from a post-town, we
were never secure from an inroad. Men who bore the
most remote affinity to the families of O'Shaughnessey or
O'Toole, deserted the corners of the earth to spoliate the
larder ; and persons who, during the course of their natural
lives, had never before touched fishing-rod or fowling-piece,
now borrowed them 'for the nonce,' and deemed it a good
and sufficient apology for living on me for a fortnight.
Pedlars abandoned their accustomed routes ; friars diverged
a score of miles to take us on 'the mission ;' pipers infested the premises ; and even deserters honoured me with
a passing call, 'for the house had such a name." All and
every calculated on that cursed *ceade fealteagh*. An eternal
stream of the idle and dissipated filled the house — the
kitchen fire, like the flame of Vesta, was never permitted
to subside—and a host of locusts devoured my property.
I lived and submitted, and yet had the consolation to know
that I was the most unpopular being in the province. I was
usually described as a 'dry devil, or a ' *dark*,† dirty little

\* This once celebrated mansion is immortalized in the old ballad, called
"Bumper Squire Jones," which chronicles the princely hospitalities of
that puissant and hard-headed family. Like "the Kilruddery Foxchase,"
it was a mighty favourite with the stout old sportsmen in those merry
days. More popular airs have caused these popular and soul-stirring
lyrics to be disused, and, like those whose feats they recounted, they are
now almost forgotten.

† "Dark," in the kingdom of Connaught, is frequently used synony-
mously with "unsocial."

man ;' while upon Drusilla blessings rained, and she was admitted to be 'the best sowl that ever laid leg below mahogany !'

"I was weary of this state. Marc Antony was in regular possession of an apartment, which was duly termed by the servant's 'Mr. Bodkin's room.' Summer passed, and so did autumn and its host of grouse shooters. I foolishly hoped that, considering the locality of Castle Toole, my locusts would banish with the butterflies ; but the only difference a rainy day made was, that the visitor who arrived, never dreamed of departing till the morrow, and the numbers by no means abated. Some heavy bills came in, and I seized that opportunity of remonstrating with Drusilla. I told her my health was breaking, my fortune unequal to my expenses ; that common prudence required a certain limitation to our irregular hospitality ; hinted that, though an occasional visit from Mr. Marc Antony Bodkin would be agreeable, yet that an everlasting abode would rather be a bore. I would have continued, but my lady had listened, she thought, too long already. She fired at the very idea of retrenchment ; and as to Mr. Marc Antony Bodkin, we were, it appeared, too much honoured by his society. He, a third cousin of Clanricarde, condescended to take my place, and entertain my company. He rode my horses and drank my wine, neither of which feats, as she opined, nature had designed me for doing in proper person ; in short, by Herculean efforts on his part, he enabled me to hold my place among gentlemen. As to the paltry consideration of his residence, what was it ? 'God be with the time, when,' as her 'lamented father' said, 'a stranger remained for eighteen months in Castle Toole, and would probably have lived and died there, but that his wife discovered him, and forced the truant to abdicate ; and yet,' she added, proudly, 'none could tell whether he was from Wales or Enniskillen ; and some believed his name was *Hamerton*, while others asserted it was *Macintosh*. But,' as she concluded, 'when her kinsman Mr. Bodkin was turned out, it was time for her to provide a residence,' and she flung from the room like a Bacchante, making door and window shiver.

"Well, Sir, you may pity or despise me as you will ; from that day my wife assumed the absolute mastery, and I calmly

submitted. The house was now a scene of wild and unre-
stricted extravagance. Tenants ran away, cattle were depre-
ciated, and worse still, claims made upon the property that
had never been foreseen, and in nine months I was engaged
in as many lawsuits. I must have sunk beneath these calamities, but a domestic event gave a new turn to my hopes.
No heir had yet been promised, when happily it was whispered that this blessing was not an impossibility. Day after
day confirmed the happy news, till at last it was regularly
announced in the ' Connaught Journal,' that Mrs. Dawkins,
of Castle Toole, was ' as ladies wish to be who love their
lords.'

" Of course, from that moment any contradiction would
have been death to my dear Drusilla. She never reigned
lady-paramount till now, and her will was absolute. Rela-
lives trooped down in scores, and Mark Antony was doubly
cherished. Notwithstanding my nerves thrilled at their
arrival, *the Blazers* were honourably feasted ; and, at the
especial request of Mrs. Dawkins, on that occasion I determined to make a character. I really was half a hero ;
presided at the head of my own table like its master, gave
divers bumper toasts, and sat out the evening, until I was
fairly *hors de combat*, and tumbled from the chair. Drunk
as I was, I recollected clearly all that passed. As but a
couple of bottles a man had been then discussed, my early
fall appeared to create a sensation. ' Is it a fit he has ?'
inquired an under-sized gentleman with an efflorescent nose,
who had been pointed out to me as a six-bottle customer. ' Phoo !' replied my loving cousin, ' the man has
no more bottom than a chicken. Lift him ; he has a good
heart, but a weak head, *He'll never do for Galway* ! But,
come, lads,' and Marc hopped over my body, as I was
being taken up by the servants, ' I'll give you that *top-
sawyer*, his wife, and long may she wear the breeches !'
It was gratifying to find that the toast was generally ad-
mired, for the very attendants that ' bore the corpse along,'
stopped at the door, and shouted ' hip, hip, hurra !' from
the staircase.

" Every day from this period I became more unhappy
and contemptible. My blue-stocking aunt, who, for reasons
unnecessary to explain, had been since my marriage totally
estranged, was now officially informed, that the name of

Dawkins would be continued. She had the true leaven of
family affection in her, and my past neglect was pardoned,
and the kindest letter returned to my communication. One
passage of her epistle ran thus—'Though I felt acutely at
your selecting a wife without even consulting one, of whose
attachment you must be well convinced, I forgive all, from
the personal description you give of your consort. May the
heir of our line be like his mother, is my prayer! For, oh,
Daniel, my predilection for dark beauty is the same, and my
conviction unalterable, that even

> ——'Genius a dead loss is,
> With dark brows and long proboscis.'

" Poor woman! no wonder she thus considered : a sergeant
in the Guards, with a countenance of the true Kemble character, had, in early life, almost turned her brain ; and Tooley-
street was kept in an uproar, until he was fortunately drafted
off to join the Duke of York upon the Continent, and there, in
due time, rested in the bed of glory.

" It is a lamentable thing for a man of sensibility to wed
a woman whose conduct he considers irreconcilable to his
ideas of what female delicacy demands—and such was my
case. Drusilla not only assumed the mastery within doors,
but she extended her sway to the farm and the horses. One
day, at the head of a hundred paupers, she was planting trees ;
the next, with Marc Antony Bodkin, making a radical reform
in the stables. On these occasions, arrayed in a man's hat,
with her limbs cased in Hessian boots, she looked, as Tom
the Devil said, ' blasted knowing.' I occasionally was permitted to attend, as a sort of travelling conveniency to hang
her cloak upon ; and I never returned without some indignity
from strangers, or personal disrespect from herself. It was
death to me to hear her addressed in the coarse language of
the stable, and allusions made to her altered figure, which
appeared too vulgar even for the servants' hall ; and when a
fellow of forbidding countenance, with a scarlet coat and white
unmentionables, whom the rest of the gang distinguished as
' Long Lanty,' crooked up the bottom of her dress with his
hunting-whip, exclaiming, ' Bone and sinew, by the holy !
what a leg for a boot !' I could have knocked the ruffian
down, had I been able, although for the exploit I should be

taxed with my false delicacy, and the usual wind-up, ' *It will never do for Galway*!'

" Shy from my cradle, and accustomed to city formality, I was not likely to become at once inhabited to Irish manners. But in Connaught there was a laxity of form—a free-and-easy system of society, that exceeded all belief, and to a distant person like me was intolerable. People on a half-hour's acquaintance called you by your christian name; and men whom you had never even heard of, rode to your door, and told you coolly they ' would stay a fortnight.' Introductions in Connemara, I believe, are reckoned among the works of supererogation. If I took a quiet ride, expecting upon my return to meet none at dinner but my wife and the eternal Marc Antony, I probably found half a score already seated at the table, and might learn the appellatives of perhaps a couple of the gang, by the announcement of ' Mr. Dawkins, Tom the Devil,' ' Mr. Dawkins, Smashall Sweeney.'

" I remember upon the day on which I was so fortunate as to make the acquaintance of the above gentlemen, in the course of the evening they differed about the colour of a race-horse, and, after bandying mutual civilities, concluded by interchanging the lie direct and a full decanter. The latter having grazed my head, induced me to abscond immediately ; and when I recorded to my loving helpmate the narrow escape from demolition I had just experienced, instead of tender alarm and connubial sympathy, her countenance betrayed irrepressible disappointment and surprise. ' And have you, Mr. Dawkins, really deserted your company, and that too at a period when two gentlemen had disagreed ? Do return immediately. Such inhospitality, I assure you, *will never do for Galway*.' I did return ; but I had my revenge, and dearly it cost me, though neither of the rascals were shot upon my lawn. *Smashall* rode off my lady's favourite mare in mistake, and sent her back next morning with a pair of broken knees —and *Tom the Devil* set fire to his bed-curtains the same night, and nothing but a miracle saved the house. Every thing in the apartment, however, was consumed or rendered unserviceable.

" As I became more intimate with my wife's relatives, I found that nothing but the lamp of Aladdin would meet their multifarious demands. Castle Toole, like the cave of Adullam, was the certain refuge of all gentlemen who happened to be in debt and difficulty. All that came here were, what is called in Connemara, 'upon the borrowing hand;' and when the sum appeared to be too large to be forthcoming in cash, nothing could be more accommodating in their overtures,— They would make my acceptance answer; they would *wish* it at sixty-one days; but *if it obliged me particularly,* they could contrive to extend it to three months. It was, of course, a matter of mere form; it would be regularly provided for; it would, 'upon honour!' If, after all this, I hesitated, I did it on personal responsibility; and sooner than be perforated upon my own lawn, actually suffered myself to be made liable for some hundreds. When I complained bitterly of these spoliations to my wife, I received the usual comfort, 'Dear me, how narrow your ideas are! If my uncle Ulic had asked you for the money, it would have been a different affair. And so, all he wants is the accommodation of your name! Ah! if my 'lamented father' was alive, how would he be astonished! Many a time he and poor Ulic assisted each other. Indeed, the dear old man used to mention an amusing anecdote. They once purchased a pipe of port, paid for it with a two months' bill, and when the time expired, the wine was drunk, and the note protested. They had consumed so much from the wood, that it was not worth while to bottle the remainder. Do, Mr. Dawkins, at once oblige my uncle Ulic. Get rid of these narrow ideas. Believe me, *they will never do for Galway.'*

"There was another thing that added to my miseries, and yet to my honoured helpmate it was a subject of unmeasured pride. It so happened, that the geographical position of my ill-omened estate was nearly on the boundaries of Galway and Mayo—counties no less remarkable for their extent than the truculent disposition of the inhabitants. From time immemorial, my lawn was the chosen *fixture* for determining affairs of honour; and hence, more blood had been shed there than on any similar spot in Christendom. If the civil authorities were so ungentlemanly as to interrupt the combatants, the latter merely crossed the adjacent bridge, and finished the affair to their satisfaction. It is right, however, to say, that the magistracy seldom interfered; and if a functionary was forced out by some mean-spirited relative, though the fears of the Lord Chancellor might deter him from refusing his intervention, he still contrived to miss the road, cast a shoe, be run away with, or meet some unhappy casualty, that one of the parties might be defunct, and the survivor in a place of safety, before he, the justice, appeared upon the battle-ground. Hence, not a week elapsed but my nerves were tortured by the arrival of a *shooting-party,* and probably further agonized by hearing Mr. Bodkin hallooing to the butler, ' Michael, (*sotto voce,*) *devil speed ye, Michael* ! the *mistress* desires ye to keep back dinner till the gentlemen have done, and to present her compliments, and say, that she expects the company of the survivor.'

" All this was horrible to me ; in the evening to be suddenly disturbed with pop ! pop ! and an outcry ; or awakened before daylight by my lady's maid opening the curtains with a curtsey, to know ' where the dead men would be *stritched.*' It was, moreover, a desperate tax upon my finances ; vagabonds, known and unknown, lay for weeks together in my house, while their broken bones were being reunited—not a month passed but there was some dying man in the state-room —doctors came and went as regularly as the post-boy—and once in each quarter the coroner,* if he had any luck, empanelled a jury in our hall.

" Nor were we less tormented with *the Blazers.* We always had a lame horse or two in the stables ; and from the time cub-hunting commenced, till the season ended, of that redoubted community who hazard

> ——' Neck and spine,
> Which rural gentlemen call sport divine,'

we never boasted fewer than a couple on the sick-list. Once, when an inquest was holding in the house, *a Blazer* in the best bed-room, a dying earth-stopper in the gate-house, and four disabled horses, ' at rack and manger,' I insinuated what a nuisance it was to have one's house made a ' *morgue,*' and the offices an hospital.—' Do, Mr. Dawkins, have done,' exclaimed my lady—' If you have no humanity, pray conceal it. Believe me, your feelings *will never do for Galway.*'

" But Drusilla had her reward. What though we kept a lazaretto for lame horses, and a general wakehouse for gentlemen of honour who left the world without sufficient

* In Connaught this useful officer is paid by the job, and the number with which he occasionally *debits* the county is surprising.

assets to procure a grave ; our lights were not hidden, nor
our charities unrecorded.    There was not a man shot, or
an arm broken, but my lady wife was dragged neck and
crop into the columns of the Connaught Journal — as for
example :

"'THE LATE CAPTAIN MACNAB.—*Further particulars.*—
When the lamented gentleman fell, his second, Mr. Peter
Brannick, raised the body in his arms. Life, however, was
totally extinct, as the ball had fractured the fifth rib, and
passed directly through the pericardium.    In its transit, the
fatal bullet shattered a portable tobacco-pipe, which the deceased invariably carried in his right waistcoat pocket.    The
body was immediately removed upon a door to Castle Toole,
where every attention to the remains of a gallant soldier was
given by the accomplished mistress.    Indeed it is but right
to say, that this estimable lady superintended in person the
laying out of the corpse.    At midnight three friars from
Ballyhownis, and a number of the resident clergy attended,
and a solemn high mass was celebrated in the great hall.
The reverend gentlemen employed upon this melancholy
occasion, have expressed their deep sense of the urbanity of
the lady of the mansion.

"'We understand that, at the especial request of Mrs.
Dawkins, the body will remain in state at Castle Toole, until
it is removed to its last resting-place, the family burying-
ground at Carrick Nab.'—*Connaught Journal.*

"'The friends and relatives of Mr. Cornelius Coolaghan
will be delighted to hear that he has been pronounced
convalescent by Dr. M'Greal.    A mistake has crept into
the papers, stating that the accident was occasioned by his
grey mare, Miss Magaraghan, falling at a six feet wall.
The fact was that the injury occurred in attempting to ride
in and out of the pound of Ballymacraken, for a bet of ten
pounds.    As the village inn was not deemed sufficiently quiet,
Mr. C. C. was carried to the hospitable mansion of Castle
Toole.    It is needless to add, that every care was bestowed
upon the sufferer by the elegant proprietress.    Indeed, few
of the gentler sex so elegantly combine the charms and
amiabilities of the beautiful Mrs. Dawkins.'—*Ibid.*

" Well, sir, I submitted to my fate with more than mortal
fortitude.    I saw that in rashly marrying one in taste, feeling
and sentiment so totally my opposite, I had wrecked my

happiness for ever, and that I must submit. My pride would sometimes fire at the slights I suffered from my very underlings, and the cool contempt of those locusts who lived only upon my bounty. I was reduced to utter dependency, and yet I never murmured a remonstrance. Presently, my wife took possession of my banker's book — yet I did not rebel—for my nerves were weak, my spirit humble;—fate made my own conduct punish me, and I had philosophy to bear it patiently. But one thing reconciled me to much misery—it was a darling hope—a cherished fancy—this was left when all besides had fled, and I clung to it with the tenacity of a wretch who seizes the reed to support him while he drowns. That hope, that sole dependence, was in my unborn child; on that being, haply, I might lavish my love ;—and when nothing else remained on earth whereon to rest my affections, I turned to a visionary thing, a creature not in existence, as an object on which to fix my heart. You smile ; but ah, sirs, remember I had not nerves and feelings like the multitude. I am a poor helpless wretch, unfitted to withstand the villany of mankind, and struggle through a world where the boldest will often blench, and the wisest hold their course with difficulty."

He became deeply agitated, and though, poor fellow, I had laughed heartily at the faithful picture he gave, in the course of his narrative, of all concerned, I could not but respect his griefs. He soon continued—

" At times I felt a misgiving in my bosom, and pangs of jealousy tormented me. I saw much culpable familiarity between my wife and her relative : and for some trifling cause, she and I, for some time past, had not occupied the same apartment. Could she forget herself and me so far? Oh, no, no, she could not ! She would not do a being like me, who submitted to her command, and sacrificed every thing to her fancy, so base, so cruel an injury ! I never harmed a worm willingly ; and surely she would not wrong one so totally her thrall—her worshipper as I ?

" I considered that between the parties there existed a near relationship, and national habits and early intimacy might warrant what was certainly indelicate, but still might not be criminal. God help me ! At times my brain burned —my senses were almost wandering ; and had this state of torture long continued, I must, ere now, have been the inmate of a madhouse.

"The time of her trial came, and at that awful hour, I am told women like to have their husbands near them, for those they love can sometimes whisper hope, and rouse the drooping courage of the sufferer. But I was specially excluded from the chamber of the patient, although constant messages passed between the lady and her kinsman. The trial ended happily—a boy was born—the servants flocked round me, to offer their rude congratulations; but the nurse cast on me such a look of mingled pity and contempt as almost struck me lifeless. I asked affectionately for my wife—I inquired tenderly for my child. 'It is a fine boy,' said a young, wild, light-hearted creature, the housemaid; 'it has the longest legs I ever saw; and, Holy Mary! its hair is as *red* as Lanty Driscoll's jacket!'—God of Heaven! *red hair*. It was killing—murderous. Then I was the wretch my worst fears had whispered, and a child was born—*but not to me.*"

He paused, completely overcome. I felt my eye moisten at the deep though simple pathos of the story-teller. There was a sorrow, an agony, in his melancholy detail, that touched the heart more sensibly than calamities of deeper character and greater men.

After a short pause, he thus continued:

"The day the most eventful of my life, if my wedding one be excepted, at last arrived, and had it been nominated for my undergoing the extreme penalty of the law, it could not have brought more horror with it. I felt the fulness of my degradation. I was a miserable puppet, obliged to pretend a blindness to disgrace, of which my conviction was entire; and automaton as I was considered, and little as my looks or feelings were consulted, the deep melancholy of my face did not escape my conscience-stricken partner. She became pale and agitated, while with affected indifference of manner, she taxed me with rudeness to my company, and more especially to herself. What would the world say, if on this high festival, when the heir of Castle Toole was to be presented to his relatives, I should appear like a monk at a death-wake than a happy parent? 'Lord! Mr. Dawkins, this moping is so unmanly. Here will be the O'Tooles and the O'Shaughnesseys, Blakes and Burkes, Bellews and Bodkins: they will feel it a personal insult. If you, encourage these humours, I assure you, Mr. Dawkins, *you will never do for Galway.*' Before this jobation ended, carriage-wheels grated on the gravel, and men, women, and children commenced and continued pouring in, as if another deluge had begun, and Castle Toole was an ark of safety.

" While the house was crowded within, the space before it appeared to be in the possession of numerous banditti. The tenants, of course, had flocked hither to do honour to the christening. For their refreshment a beeve was roasted whole, and beer and whisky lavishly distributed. I never saw a scene of waste and drunkenness before, although I had hitherto believed that my residence was the veriest *rack-rent* in the world. In every corner pipers played, women danced, men drank, and swearing and love-making was awful. There, while dinner was being served, I had stolen forth to vent my agony unnoticed. I am not, sirs, gifted with that command of nerve which can exhibit hollow smiles while the bosom is inly bleeding. To affect gaiety so foreign to my heart, I felt would break it ; but the desperate misery that I endured would spur the dullest soul to madness. I viewed the rude revelry with disgust. I was the master of the feast, but the savages barely recognised me. Generally they spoke in their native language ; and though I did not exactly comprehend all that they said, I heard enough to assure me of my utter insignificance in their rude estimate of character. Under a gate-pier two old women were sitting ; they did not notice me, and continued their discourse.

" ' Ally, *astore*, did ye see the child ? They say it's the picture of Marc Bodkin.'

" ' Whisht, ye divil !' was the rejoinder, as the crone proceeded, with a chuckle ; ' *it has red hair*, any how : but *Neil an skil a gau maun*,* and ye know best.'

" But the further humiliation of assisting at the ceremony was saved me. In the hurry consequent upon the general confusion, the post-bag was handed to me instead of my lady-wife, who lately had managed all correspondence. Mechanically I opened the bag, and a letter, bearing the well-known direction of my aunt, met my eye. That, under circumstances, it should have reached me, appeared miraculous, and, seizing an opportunity, I examined its

* *Anglice*, ' I have no skill in it.'

contents in private. My kind relation had received my detail of misery, and, in reply, she implored me to abandon the scene of my degradation, and share her fortune, which was more, she said, than sufficient for us both. My heart beat with conflicting emotions—all unworthy as she was, I could not bring myself to abandon Drusilla thus. I actually hesitated, when curiosity prompted me to peruse a letter which was addressed to her, and marked *immediate*. Its contents were these :—

" ' Dear Madam,

" ' I have by this post received the two writs, as expected. I settled the *Ex.* against Mr. M. A. B., and he may come to town any time till further notice. With respect to those against Mr. Dawkins, it is ɛs well to let things take their course. He is a gentleman of retired habits, and a little confinement, particularly *as he don't hunt*, will be quite immaterial. I received the bullocks, but, as cattle are down, there is still a balance due.

" ' A Dublin wine-merchant has just handed me an *Ex.* for £613, and insists upon accompanying me to Castle Toole. I have therefore named *Wednesday,* on which day you will please to have *the doors closed.* As the plaintiff may again be officious, I would recommend his being *ducked,* when returning, and a city bailiff, whom you will know by his having a scorbutic face and yellow waistcoat, should for many reasons be corrected. Pray, however, take care *the boys* do not go too far, as manslaughter, under the late act, is now a transportable felony.

" ' The sooner Mr. D. renders to prison the better. Tell your Uncle Ulic I have returned *non est* to his *three last* ; but he must not *show.* You can drop me a line by bearer when you wish Mr. D. to be arrested ; and after we return *nulla bona* on Wednesday, I will come out and arrange matters generally.

" ' Believe me, dear Madam, truly yours,

" ' JOHN GRADY, Sub-sheriff, Galway.
" ' Mrs. Dawkins, Castle Toole.'

" ' P.S. What a blessing it is for poor Mr. Dawkins that he has such a woman of business to manage his affairs ! He is a well-meaning man, but *he'll never do for Galway.*

' J. G.'

"Had I been ten times over the tame wretch I was, I could not be insensible to the deep treachery of this worthless woman, who had ruined my property, and would now incarcerate my person. In spite of remonstrances upon its apparent inhospitality, I abandoned the 'impious feast,' and while my absence was neither missed nor regarded, I stole from the accursed spot, and by bribing a wandering stocking-man, was enabled to make my way to the coast, and procure a fishing-boat to place myself beyond the power of arrest. The same bad luck appeared to follow me: the drunkenness of the scoundrels threatened to interrupt my escape, and even place my life in peril. From these mishaps you have delivered me, and by your prompt assistance I shall effect my retreat from a country I must ever recollect with horror. When I reach England, I will seek reparation for my injuries; and though all besides is gone, I shall at least endeavour to liberate myself from the worthless woman who abused a weak and too confiding husband.

"Alas! gentlemen, what a stream of misfortunes will sometimes originate in a trifle. A Margate steamer entailed a life of suffering upon me. My fortune vanished, my wife deceived me—laughed at by my friends, and ridiculed by my enemies — from all these complicated misfortunes, I have learned but one simple fact—Alas! '*That I should never do for Galway!*'"

---

## CHAPTER XXXVIII.

Morning alarm—Death of the otter-killer—General grief—Night excursion—Herring-fishery—Our reception—Beal fires—The wake—The funeral—Anecdote of a dog—A deserted house.

I SLEPT soundly: my servant found me still a-bed, when he came at his customary hour; as he unclosed the curtains I heard a hum of voices, and appearances of domestic hurry were visible; next moment the well-known *Currakeen*, whose celebrity as a courier is truly remarkable, passed the window at a " killing pace." I found upon inquiry, that the otter-killer was dying, and that " the runner" I had just observed, had been dispatched for Father Andrew.

T

The ancient retainer of an Irish family generally establishes a bond upon the affections of the wild household, that causes his loss to make a greater sensation, than so humble an event might be supposed to occasion. Antony for half a century had been attached to this family. Three generations have passed since he first settled beneath the roof-tree ; and he has been associated with every earlier recollection of the present master. No wonder I found my kinsman in considerable distress. The old man was dying—and youthful scenes, and youthful days, when the stormier passions had not broken "the sunshine of the breast," were now vividly recalled by the approaching dissolution of his ancient and devoted follower.

The summons to the priest was instantly attended,— Father Andrew returned with the messenger, and was immediately closeted with the penitent. Poor Antony's simple life had few dark recollections to harrow his parting hour. His shrift was short and satisfactory ; and at his own request, when the rites of the Roman Catholic church had been duly celebrated, my cousin and myself were summoned to his bedside.

The old man was supported by Hennessey, as a difficulty in breathing obliged him to be raised up ; and the scene was at once simple and imposing. The early monitor of his youthful fishing-days—the being who had in mountain pastimes been so frequently his companion, possibly recalled softer recollections, and a deep shade of sorrow overspread the countenance of the "stern homicide." The black-eyed girl, who held a teaspoon to his lips, vainly endeavouring to introduce some nourishment, wept over him like a lamenting child. His faithful terrier sat at the bed-foot, and the fixed and melancholy look that the poor animal turned on her dying master, would have half persuaded me that Venom knew she was about to lose him. Dim as his eye was, it lighted as my kinsman's tall figure darkened the entrance of the chamber ; and feebly putting forth his hand, he clasped that of his beloved master with affection, and while weakness and imperfect breathing sadly interrupted his "last farewell," we could with some difficulty thus collect his words.

" I'm going, Master Julius, and may the blessing of the Almighty attend ye ! Sure I should be thankful, with all

about me to make me easy to the last. I saw your grand
father stretched—I sat beside your father when he departed,
may the Lord be merciful to both! and I die with yourself
and the clargy to comfort my last hour, praises be to Mary,
Master Julius, will you listen to a dying man; he that
carried ye in his arms, and loved ye better than all the
world besides ?—ye'll take my advice. *Marry*, Julius
avourneen—the ould name that since the days of Shamul
a Croaghah held land and honour—surely you won't let it
pass? Mind the old man's last words—and now Heaven
bless ye!" And in feeble tones he continued muttering
benedictions upon all around him. My cousin was really
affected, and the Priest perceiving the increasing feebleness
of the otter-killer, requested us to retire. We were obey-
ing, when Antony rallied suddenly and unexpectedly :—
" You will mind the dog, for my sake, Master Julius—and
ye'll let trap and fishing-rod hang up in the hall, to put ye
in mind of old Antony?" These were his last connected
words—his strength failed fast; his memory wandered to
other times; "he babbled of green fields," he murmured
the names of lakes and rivers—and while the affectionate
Priest prayed fervently beside his old and innocent companion,
the otter-killer rendered his last sigh in the arms of Hennessey
and the weeping Alice!

Talk of parade around the couch of fortune, and what a
heartless display is it! *I* saw a rich man die; I saw the
hollow mockery of hireling attendants and interested friends;
but here, that simple unsophisticated being had a sincerity of
grief bestowed upon his death-bed, that to wealth and grandeur
would be unattainable!

There was a loud and agonizing burst of sorrow when the
otter-killer's death was communicated to those in the hall
and kitchen, who, during the closing scene, had been with
difficulty prevented from crowding the apartment of the
sufferer. But this noisy demonstration of regard was speedily
checked by old John, who knew that his master would be
doubly displeased should any tumultuary wailings render me
uncomfortable.

In a short time, order was tolerably established; and with
one exception, a quiet and respectful silence supervened. A
stout, though aged crone, occasionally burst into wild lament,

accompanied by a beating on her breast, which, like the signal to a chorus, elicited a fresh ebullition from the subordinate mourners. John, however, interposed his authority effectually.—" *Badahust, hanamondioul, badahust,* I say ! ye may *keinagh* at the funeral, but ye mustn't disturb the master and the company." This jobation restored tranquillity, and in " decent grief" the otter-killer's corpse was duly laid out in its funeral habiliments.

The evening wore on heavily—my kinsman was sensibly affected ; his old monitor in the gentle art was gone ; and though full in years, and ripe for the tomb, his master felt, that " he could have better spared a better man." There was heart-sinking about our party which I had never marked before. The wine had lost its charm ; and while the Colonel and the Priest commenced a game of piquet, my cousin ordered the gig, and proposed that we should pull over to the herring-boats, which in the next estuary, and on the preceding night, had been unusually successful. Accordingly, having lighted our pipes and procured our boat-cloaks, we left the pier-head in the four-oared galley.

The night was unusually dark and warm ; not a breath of wind was on the water ; the noise of the oars, springing in the coppered rullocks, was heard for a mile off, and the whistle of sandpipers and jack curlews, as they took wing from the beach we skirted, appeared unusually shrill. Other noises gradually broke the stillness of the night—the varied hum of numerous voices chanting the melancholy songs which are the especial favourites of the Irish, began to be heard distinctly—and we soon bore down upon the midnight fishers, directed by sound, not sight.

To approach the fleet was a task of some difficulty. The nets, extended in interminable lines, were so frequent, that much skill was necessary to penetrate this hempen labyrinth. without fouling the back ropes. Warning cries directed our course, and with some delay we threaded the crowded surface, and, guided by buoys and *puckawns,* found ourselves in the very centre of the flottilla.

It was an interesting scene. Momently the boats glided along the back ropes, which were supported at short intervals by corks, and at a greater by inflated dog-skins, and, raising the curtain of network which these suspended, the herrings were removed from the meshes, and deposited in the boats. Some of the nets were particularly fortunate, obliging their proprietors to frequently relieve them of the fish ; while others, though apparently stretched within a few yards, and consequently in the immediate run of the herrings, were favoured but with a few stragglers ; and the indolent fisherman had to occupy himself with a sorrowful ditty, or in moody silence watched the dark sea " like some dull ghost waiting on Styx for waftage."

Our visit appeared highly satisfactory, for the *ceade feal-teagh*, with a lament for " ould Antony," was universal, while every boat tossed herrings on board, until we were obliged to refuse further largess, and these many " trifles of fish" accumulated so rapidly, that we eventually declined receiving further compliments, or we might have loaded the gig gunnel deep.

The darkness of the night increased the scaly brilliancy which the phosphoric properties of these beautiful fish produce. The bottom of the boat, now covered with some thousand herrings, glowed with a living light, which the imagination could not create, and the pencil never imitate. The shades of gold and silvery gems were rich beyond description ; and much as I had heard of phosphoric splendour before, every idea I had formed fell infinitely short of its reality.

The same care with which we entered disembarrassed us of the midnight fishing : every boat we passed pressed hard to throw in a " cast of *skuddawns** for the strange gentleman," meaning me ; and such was the kindness of these hospitable creatures, that had I been a very Behemoth I should have this night feasted to satiety on their bounty.

The wind, which had been asleep, began now to sigh over the surface, and before we had cleared the outer back-ropes, the sea-breeze came curling " the midnight wave." The tide was flowing fast, and having stepped the mast, we spread our large lug, and the light galley slipped speedily ashore. A fire which I had noticed above the Lodge kindling gradually, fanned by the rising night-breeze, sprang at once into a glorious flame ; and through the darkness its intense light

* *Anglice*, Herrings.

must have been for many leagues discernible.  I broke my
cousin's musing, to ask what it was.

" That, my friend, is one of our ancient customs ; that is
our *beal-fire*.  It is lighted to notify that a death has occurred, and ere long you will see it answered by some of our
friends and kindred.  Poor old man ! none deserved it better,
for he would have attended religiously to such observances,
had any of my family preceded him to the grave.  He lighted
my father's beal-fire, and possibly kindled that of my grand-
sire; old John has probably performed the ceremony for him:
thus the kindlier offices are continued, and ' thus runs the
word away.'—Who,"—and he stopped, evidently embarrassed
at some passing thought—" Who shall say that the ceremonial bestowed upon the wandering otter-killer may not be
refused to the last descendant of a line of centuries !"

I would have interrupted these melancholy forebodings, but
just then, from the lofty brow of an inland hill which I had
frequently observed before, a light appeared, first faintly
struggling, but presently reddening to the sight ; and two
fires in Achil, in a time of incredible briefness, flung their
deep glow across the waters, and, as I afterwards remarked,
were repeated for miles along the coast and high grounds.

The rapidity with which the beal-fire was replied to,
evidently pleased my kinsman's family vanity ; and with
higher spirits, we watched the lights tremble in the windows
of the Lodge, until these *stellæ minores* directed our voyage
to its termination.

The Colonel and his companion were waiting for us on the
the pier ; they insisted on adding to our supper some of the
fish which we had brought home—and while this was being
done, my cousin and myself entered the wake, to pay our last
duties to the departed otter-killer.

To give additional *éclat* to his funeral rites, the corpse had
been removed to the barn, which, from its unusual size, was
well-fitted to admit the numerous mourners who would attend
the ceremony.  Upon a rude bier the old man rested, and the
trap and fishing-rod were, by a fancy of Hennessey, placed
above his head.  The barn was filled, but immediate room
was made for *the master* and his company.  I have seen the
corpse when carefully arranged ; when the collapsing features
were artificially moulded, to imitate a tranquillity that had

been foreign to the last event. But here was a study for a painter. The old man's face was puckered into the same conscious smile with which I have heard him terminate his happiest otter-hunt, or some mountain exploit of my kinsman, which appeared to him equally dear; his long hair, released from the band with which he usually confined it, wantoned in silvery ringlets across his neck and shoulders : all else was in wonted form ; only that the number of candles round the bier might have been called extravagant, and the plate of snuff upon the bosom of the corpse was heaped with a munificence that would stamp the obsequies as splendid.

Everybody has heard an Irish wake described, and there is no dissimilarity among a hundred, only that, according to the opulence of the family, and the quantity of funeral refreshments, the mirth and jollity of the *mourners* is invariably proportionate. That the master's ancient retainers should be nobly waked was fully expected by the country, and certainly they were not disappointed. Whisky in quantities passing all understanding, tobacco in all its preparations, were fearfully consumed on this important ceremony ; and during the two days and nights which the otter-killer was above ground, the barn, spacious as it was, proved unequal to accommodate the hundreds who flocked from a distance of even twenty miles to have "a last look at ould Antony."

When the evening fell on which the corpse was to be carried to its resting-place, a scene of great novelty and great interest ensued. From the insulated situation of the Lodge, in connexion with the burying-ground, it was necessary that the body should be carried across the estuary by water. At the appointed hour, from every creek and harbour, the peasantry were seen afloat : and when the funeral left the house, more than a hundred boats accompanied that in which the corpse was deposited. My kinsman followed next to the body with all his visitors and servants ; and when the opposite strand was reached, he and his foster-brother placed their shoulders under the coffin, and supported it for a short distance along the beach.

This was, I was afterwards informed, the highest honour that could be conferred upon the departed by his master ; and even the magnificence of the otter-killer's wake was held inferior to this proud and public testimony of his patron's affections.

One circumstance was remarked which was powerfully indicative of animal affection. The dead man's terrier had remained night and day beside his bier, since the morning of his death. Unnoticed, she crept on board the boat that conveyed the coffin to the churchyard ; and when the grave was filled, she was with difficulty carried home by an attendant, but escaping during the night, crossed the estuary by swimming, and again lay down upon the turf, beneath which her beloved master was sleeping. Every care and kindness was bestowed upon her in the Lodge. No one addressed her but as "*poor Venney.*" Notwithstanding, she drooped visibly, and in three weeks after her interment, in death the otter-killer's favourite " bore him company."

When we reached the Lodge, we made a discovery which, possibly with some people, might lead to an opposite conclusion, and either prove the security or insecurity of the country.

Not a living being had remained within the walls, and consequently, for several hours, the house and household goods were abandoned to the mercy of chance and chance travellers. The guardian saint, however, acquitted herself like a gentlewoman. We found every thing in pious order ; and had the Lodge been under the especial care of the glorious Santa Barbara herself, watch and ward could not have been more faithfully maintained.

## CHAPTER XXXIX.

Weather changes—Symptoms of winter—Animal appearances—Night passage of Barnacles—Grey plover—Hints for shooting plover—Wild geese—Swans—Ducks—Burke transported—Evening at the lodge—Feminine employments.

A MONTH had passed : winter comes on with giant strides, and the last lingering recollections of autumn are over. The weather becomes more rainy and tempestuous ; and bogs, which we once crossed easily, owing to the continued wet, are now quite impassable. The swell, which during the summer months came in in long and measured undulations, breaks in masses across the bar, and sends a broken and tumbling sea inside the estuary, so as to render it unsafe to expose any boat of heavy tonnage to its influence. Pattigo seldom ventures from his anchorage, and when last he ventured to pass a night at the pier, he ground away a hawser against the stones, notwithstading every pains were bestowed in renewing its *service*. The springs are usually high ; and two nights since, the Lodge and paddocks were completely insulated, and our communications with the mainland carried on by ferriage. The river rises fearfully, and the huge masses of turf left along the strand, prove how violent the mountain torrents must be at this advanced season. The sweet and crystal stream is nowhere seen ; and Scott's beautiful lines happily describe the turbid river that has replaced it :—

> " Late, gazing down the steepy linn
> That hems our little garden in,
> Low in its dark and narrow glen,
> You scarce the rivulet might ken,
> So thick the tangled greenwood grew,
> So feebly trill'd the streamlet through ;
> Now, murmuring hoarse, and frequent seen,
> Through bush and briar no longer green,
> An angry brook it sweeps the glade,
> Brawls over rock and wild cascade."

But other, and no less certain, tokens harbinger the wild season that has arrived. Yesterday a six-months' puppy, who crept after me across, the adjoining paddocks, stopped in a rushy field. Suspecting that he had a hare before him, I passed on to. push her from the *form :* I was mistaken— a *wisp* * of snipes, possibly thirty in number, sprang, and scattering in all directions, pitched loosely over the ad-joining bogs. To-day I saw a flock of barnacles ;† and the

* *Wisp*, in sporting parlance, means a flock of snipes.

† The *barnacle* weighs about five pounds, and measures more than two feet in length, and nearly four and a half in breadth. The bill, from the tip to the corners of the mouth, is scarcely an inch and a half long, black, and crossed with a pale reddish streak on each side ; a narrow black line passes from the bill to the eyes, the irides of which are brown ; the head is small, and as far as the crown, together with the cheeks and throat, white ; the rest of the head and neck, to the breast and shoulders, is black. The upper part of the plumage is prettily marbled or barred with blue, gray, black, and white ; the feathers of the back are black, edged with white, and those of the wing coverts and scapulars blue **grey**

herdsman on the sand-banks apprises us of the first appearance of a *Crowour Keough.** This is the earliest woodcock
announced, but my kinsman has no doubt but *the flight* †
has fallen in Achil : and we shall cross in a few days, if the
weather answers, and try Slieve More, he says, with excellent
success.

I had been some hours in bed, when I was awakened by a
quarrelling among the dogs, which I overheard the keeper
settling with the whip.    I remained, and it is rather an unusual thing with me, a long time awake.    An hour passed,
all was again in deep repose, and I too was sinking into
sleep, when a strange and unaccountable noise roused me.
It seemed to be at first faint and distant, but momently increasing, grew louder and more distinct, until it passed to all
appearance directly above my head.    The sounds were wild
and musical—varied in tone beyond any thing I could describe, and continuing, until they gradually became remote
and indistinct, and at length totally died away.    I was
amazingly puzzled, but was obliged to reserve my curiosity to
be satisfied in the morning.

My cousin smiled at my inquiry :—" And you heard these
strange noises as well as I?    This, if you remained here,
would be little marvel, as nightly *the Barnacle* cross the Lodge
in passing from one estuary to the other.    There they sit
on yonder point ;"—and, taking me to the window, I saw a
considerable extent of sand literally black with this migratory
tribe : they come here in immense multitudes, but from their

bordered with black near the margins, and edged with white ; the quills
black, edged a little way from the tips with blue grey ; the under parts
and tail coverts, white ; the thighs are marked with dusky lines or spots,
and are black near the knees ; the tail is black, and five inches and a half
long ; the legs and feet are dusky, very thick and short, and have a stumpy
appearance.

* Why this title, literally meaning " the blind cock," should be conferred by the peasantry of Ballycroy on a bird so remarkable for the
extraordinary quickness of his vision, is a paradox.    Such is the known
acuteness of the woodcock's vision, that the cover-shooter chooses a
masked position, or the *Crowour Keough* would seldom come within range
of the gun.

† *Flight* is the term used to describe a flock of woodcocks, as they
arrive in this country, in their annual migration from the north of
Europe.

coarse and fishy flavour, afford little occupation to the water-shooter.

The land barnacles are less numerous, although they are found in tolerable abundance. During the day I saw two flocks, of one or two hundred pairs, upon the bogs. They are, when sufficiently rested from their journey, sought for with great avidity by the few gunners in this district, and are very delicious when kept a sufficient time after being shot, before the cook transfers them to the spit.

Gray plover must also migrate in thousands hither. Nothing else could account for the immense flocks, that have been seen, and will continue, as I am informed, to arrive. The shores and moors are everywhere crowded with them; and within a hundred yards of the lodge, Hennessey, with two barrels, killed seven couple and a half last evening. The bent-banks are their favourite fixture : and I have never crossed them of late without finding at least one *stand*. These vary in numbers ; but I am certain I have seen three hundred of these birds thus congregated.

There is, in shoting plover, a common remark made by sportsmen, that the *second* is always the more productive barrel. The rapidity with which they vary their position when on the ground, seldom admits of a grand combination for a sitting, or rather a running shot. But when on the wing, their mode of flight is most favourable for permitting the shot to tell; and it is by no means unusual to bring down a number. When disturbed, they frequently wheel back directly above the fowler, and offer a tempting mark if he should have a barrel in reserve ; and even when too high for the shot to take effect, I have often thrown away a random fire ; for the plover, on hearing the report, directly make a sweep downwards on the wing, and I have by this means brought them within range of the second barrel.

When the season advances, the number of geese* that

* The time that wild geese feed in this country is by night, and par-ticularly during moonlight. I have never known them either *netted or decoyed ;* and all the shooter has to rely upon is patience and a long barrel. Of all the prizes that a wildfowl-shooter could wish to meet with, a flock of teal is the very first. Independently of their being by far the best birds of the whole Anas tribe, they are so much easier of access, and require such a slight blow, that no matter whether you are prepared for wildfowl, partridges, or snipes, you may, at most times, with very little

visit this wild peninsula is astonishing. For miles I have traced their night feedings along a river bank, where the marshy surface afforded them their favourite sustenance. They are far more wary than the barnacle, and are extremely difficult of access in moderate weather; but chance and storm occasionally favour the sportsman, and in spite of the

caution of these birds, the flock will be surprised, and the patient gunner reap in a lucky moment the reward of many a weary vigil and bootless attempt.

The last and greatest of the wild visiters, are the swan tribe. Their being scarce or plentiful depends much upon the season—and in winters of extreme severity thousands of these birds will be found upon the estuaries and inland lakes. The noise they make is wild and musical, and with *a little*

trouble, contrive to get near them; and this being once done, you have only to shoot straight to be pretty sure of killing.

I have seen teal "duck the flash," though never but once, and then I had rather a slow-shooting-gun.

*fancy,* my kinsman says, the ear will trace modulations almost extending to infinity. These birds, during severe frosts and snow-storms, are easily surprised and shot; and the skins, when carefully stripped off, will well repay the shooter for his trouble.

To enumerate the varieties of the duck tribe that an inclement winter brings to these shores, would be difficult. I have already noticed the *Pintail,* and the *Golden-eye* upon the estuary. Widgeons come here in immense flocks; and that beautiful bird the teal, the smallest and most delicate of the whole species, is found for the remainder of the season on loughs and rivers in abundance. The Grebe and Tringa tribes furnish numerous and interesting varieties; and an ornithologist, as well as a sportsman, would have here an ample field, could he but set the season at defiance, and pass his winter on this exposed and stormy coast.

But the note of dissolution of our happy party has sounded. The Colonel, having divers premonitory twinges, has named an early day for his departure. To be caught by the gout here, would be a hazardous experiment; and the portmanteau, whose captivity was likely to occasion such desperate results, is again packed and confided to *Andy Bawn.* But the commander's baggage is not to be exposed to a second interruption. The attempt was fatal to Mr. Burke; for, emboldened by the feud which his unadvised aggression created between my kinsman and this modern Cacus, the *Sweenies** seized the opportunity, and the outlaw was arrested in a whisky-house, tried, and escaped by a miracle from being hanged,—but was, alas! consigned to Australasia for the course of his natural life

To do Mr. Burke justice, he left his native soil with regret. Finding all chance of commuted punishment over, he endeavoured to obtain his liberty by an ingenious plan to strangle the turnkeys, and emancipate all and every victim of judicial tyranny who pleased to accept his freedom. He did, poor man, make an excellent offer to choke a jailer—but fortune frowned upon the attempt; the half-throttled janitor was

---

* This numerous clan derive their origin from a northman. They are, I know not with what justice, reckoned a treacherous and vindictive tribe, and a feud with them is consequently held to be a dangerous affair.

saved—and the hero of the bridge of Ballyveeny will cross the equator at the public expense.

To-morrow, wind and weather permitting, the commander takes his departure, and to-night will consequently be a high and solemn festival. Would it were over! I cannot, dare not, offer an excuse for cavilling at bumpers, even were they "fathoms deep;" and all the consolation that an aching head will claim to-morrow, will be a saw from old John about "the dog that bit me," and the merciless badinage of that black-eyed coquette who embodies all that Moore idealized in sketching his *Nora Crina*.

How soft the evening twilight falls on the waters of the estuary! the tide kisses the very verge of the greensward, and looks so treacherously calm, as if its storms were for ever ended. Boat after boat hurries down the inlet to shoot their herring-nets for the night; and many an ancient ditty, or ruder tale, will while away the time till morning. Occasionally a struggle between two rival barks ensues—and I remark, the contest invariably takes place before the windows of the Lodge. One very singular one amused me much. A boat rowed by four women challenged, and actually out-pulled another, though propelled by a similar number of the coarser sex.

Indeed, the occupations of the ladies of Ballycroy are not essentially feminine: the roughest and most dangerous employments they share in common with the men. A Mahratta woman, they told me in India, regularly shampoos her husband's horse. Were I of the fair sex, I would rather operate on a quadruped than row a fishing-boat by the day, and cut sea-weed up to the waist in water, with the expectation of being swept from my precarious footing by the first mountainous surge.

## CHAPTER XL.

Colonel leaves us—Last visit to Achil—Snipes and woodcocks—Their
migration—Solitary snipe—Cock-shooting in Achil—Mountain covers
—Cock-shooting: its accidents—Anecdotes—An unlucky companion.

THE Colonel has left us, and we lose in him the best and
safest of friends—a true buon camarado.  With spirits of
youthful buoyancy, a temper unsoured by time, and indifferent to worldly annoyances, years have only mellowed his com-
panionable qualities, while they added deeply to his anecdote
and information.  Few men of *a certain age* succeed in retaining their places as first favourites with others some quarter of
a century their juniors; but the Colonel is an exception: we
shall feel a blank in our society; and in this gay and careless
spirit lose a dear companion, who seemed to put time at defiance, and forbade gout itself to interrupt his comfort, or
" mar his tranquillity."

The last two days have been dry, the wind is favourable, a
white frost has been visible this morning, and we are about to
pay our parting visit to Achil.  We have again sent to our
ancient entertainers, the Water Guards, to beg a shelter for
the night; for the days so sensibly shortened, that we
shall have enough to do to reach Dugurth at nightfall.

" Merrily, merrily bounds the bark," and an hour landed
us at the Ridge Point.  Our establishment is on a minor scale
to what we sported on our first descent; we have only some
two or three *hangers-on*, and have brought but two brace of
orderly and antiquated setters.

I have seen much of snipe-shooting* in many parts of

---

* The common residence of the snipe is in small bogs, or wet grounds,
where it is almost constantly digging and nibbling in the soft mud, in
search of his food, which consists chiefly of a very small kind of red
transparent worm, about an half inch long; it is said also to eat slugs,
and the insects and grubs, of various kinds, which breed in great abundance in those slimy stagnant places.  In these retreats, when undisturbed,
the snipe walks leisurely with its head erect, and at short intervals keeps
moving the tail.  But in this state of tranquillity it is very rarely to be
seen, as it is extremely watchful, and perceives the sportsman or his dog
at a great distance, and instantly conceals itself among the variegated
withered herbage so similar in appearance to its own plumage, that it is
almost impossible to discover it while squatted motionless in its seat: it
seldom, however, waits the near approach of any person, particularly in

Ireland, but I could not have imagined that the number of these exquisite birds could be found within the same space,

that one particular marsh which bounds the rabbit-banks produced. Independently of a quantity of detached birds, several

open weather, but commonly springs and takes flight at a distance beyond the reach of the gun. When first disturbed, it utters a kind of feeble whistle, and gently flies against the wind, turning nimbly in a zigzag direction for two or three hundred paces, and sometimes soaring almost out of sight; its note is then something like the bleating of a goat, but is changed to a singular humming or drumming noise, uttered in its descent.

From its vigilance and manner of flying, it is one of the most difficult birds to shoot. Some sportsmen can imitate their cries, and by that means draw them within reach of their shot; others of a less honourable description, prefer the more certain and less laborious method of catching them in the night by a springe, like that which is used for the woodcock.

The snipe is migratory, and is met with in all countries; like the woodcock, it shuns the extremes of heat and cold by keeping upon the bleak moors in summer, and seeking the shelter of the valleys in winter. In severe frosts and storms of snow, driven by extremity of the weather, snipes seek the unfrozen boggy places, runners from springs, or any open streamlet of water, and they are sure to be found, often in considerable numbers in these places, where they sometimes sit till nearly trodden upon before they will take their flight.

Although it is well known that numbers of snipes leave Great Britain in the spring, and return in the autumn, yet it is equally well ascertained

*wisps* sprang wildly, as they always do; and I have no doubt that this fen had been their temporary resting-place after their autumnal migration from the north. We were the more inclined to this opinion, from finding many of the birds we killed extremely lean; while others, that sprang *singly*, were in admirable condition. Achil is a natural resting-place for migratory birds: and hence I can well believe the accounts given by the islanders, of the immense numbers of woodcocks and snipes which are here found, in their transit from a high latitude to our more genial climate. The same remark is made touching the vernal visit of these strangers to this island. After woodcocks have for days vanished from the inland covers, they have been found in flocks on the Achil and Erris highlands, evidently congregating for their passage, and preparing for the attempt.

It may be easily conceived, that whether the winter stock of snipes and woodcocks be limited or abundant, will mainly depend upon the state of the winds and weather at the period of migration. Hence, when the latter end of October and the succeeding month have continued stormy, with south or south-easterly gales, a lamentable deficiency of game has been invariably observed. That multitudes perish on their passage, or are obliged to change their course, is certain—and the exhausted state in which the small portion of the survivors reach these shores, attests how difficult the task must be to effect a landing, when opposed by contrary winds and stormy weather.

We crossed the bent-banks, occasionally knocking a rabbit over as we went along, and wheeled to the westward to skirt the base of Slieve More. We had not proceeded far, before

---

that many constantly remain, and breeds in various parts of the country, for their nests and young ones have been so often found as to leave no doubt of this fact. The female makes her nest in the most retired and inaccessible part of the morass, generally upon the stump of an alder or willow; it is composed of withered grass and a few feathers; her eggs, four or five in number, are of an oblong shape, and of a greenish colour, with rusty spots; the young ones run off soon after they are freed from the shell, but they are attended by the parent birds until their bills have acquired a sufficient firmness to enable them to provide for themselves.

The snipe is a very fat bird, but its fat does not cloy, and very rarely disagrees even with the weakest stomach. It is much esteemed as a delicious and well-flavoured dish, and is cooked in the same manner as the woodcock.

U

an islander, who was herding cows, told us that there was a *crowour keough beg** in the next ravine. We accordingly put a setter in, and were gratified with a steady point in the place the herdsman had intimated. The bird sprang, and was knocked over by my companion, when the little woodcock proved to be a double snipe. These birds are extremely scarce here, and a few couple only are seen during a whole season by persons most conversant in traversing the bogs. There cannot be a doubt but this bird is a distinct species; but for its extreme rarity and solitary habits naturalists are puzzled to account.

We shot, before we began to ascend the hill, a couple of woodcocks lying out upon the moors. They were very shy, never allowing the dogs to come to a set. This is usually the case when these birds are outlying; and I have followed a cock for miles before I got him within fire, teased by his getting up before I could approach, and removing some hundred yards from the gun. Some favourable inequality of surface has at last enabled me to close with my wild quarry, and, notwithstanding the keenness of his eye, got the wary stranger eventually within range of shot.

There grows in the valleys and water-courses which are so frequent in the Achil and Ballycroy hills, that large and shrub-like heather that reaches nearly to the height of brushwood. Here, in the earlier season, the woodcocks repose after their passage, and at times the numbers found in these ravines are stated to be extraordinary. With the first frost or snow they move off to the interior, dropping as they go along in the different covers, until a part of the flight reaches the very centre of the kingdom. We met, during our day's fag, about fifteen couple, out of which eight and a half were brought to bag. To these we added three brace and a half of grouse, and a brace of hares. When with these were united snipes, plovers, and rabbits, it is not too much to say that our bags were most imposing, and produced above fifty head of game. From our kind friends, the Water Guards, we received a hospitable reception; and next morning were run across the bay in their galley, and landed safely upon our own shores.

The cock-shooting, to use my cousin's words, in the west

---

* A little woodcock.

of Ireland is acknowledged to be very superior ; and when *the flight* has been large, and the season is sufficiently severe to drive the birds well to cover, there is not, to a quick eye, more beautiful shooting in the world. Some of the covers are copses of natural wood, situated in the very centre of the mountains. Consequently, when the snow falls, every wood-cock for miles around deserts the heath and seeks the nearest shelter. Then will the sportsman be amply repaid for all his labour. From a copse of not more than thirty acres extent, I have seen fifty couple of woodcocks flushed ; and as several excellent covers lay in the immediate vicinity, it was no un-usual thing for two or three guns to bring home twenty, nay, thirty couple. I have known a party fire a number of shots that appeared incredible ; and I have more than once ex-pended my last charge of powder, and left, for want of am-munition, one or more copses untried.

The best cock-shooting cannot be had without a good deal of fag. Like fox-hunting, it is work for hardy spirits ; and *non sine pulvere palma*, will apply to both. To reach a mountain-cover, the sportsman must be on the alert two or three hours before daylight, for he has likely some ten Irish miles to ride or drive over, by a rough and dangerous road,

now rendered scarcely discernible from the adjacent bogs, and hardly passable from the snow-drifts. The short day is hardly sufficient for shooting the different woods; and then the same distance must be again traversed, for which the shooter will be a borrower from the night. Then he must reckon on divers delays and sundry accidents; horses will come down, dog-carts capsize, a trace break, or a spring fail; and what has annoyed me more than all together, probably a fog rise so suddenly and densely, as to render the road undistinguishable from the surrounding heaths. But when all this is achieved,—when a cover-party have fairly encircled the table, after the luxury of a complete toilet,—when the fire sparkles, the curtains are drawn, and the wine circulates,—why then, without let the storm blow till it bursts its cheeks—and within, Father Care may hang himself in his own garters.

There are others perils, also, to which the cover-shooter is obnoxious. The eye is sometimes endangered by pressing unguardedly through the copse wood; and I knew one case where the sight was totally lost from a twig springing from a person who was struggling through the underwood and striking the next who followed. The legs also are frequently and severely wounded by the sharp stumps which remain after a thicket has been thinned. But from random shots the chief danger arises; and to prevent accidents occurring, a party, and particularly if it be numerous, should be guarded in selecting their stands and altering their positions. I have been struck a dozen times, but never with any worse effect than receiving a shot or two in my cheek and ear; but many a time I have felt a shower rattle against my fustian jacket, which, however, endured it bravely, as a garment of proof should do.

Some men, from carelessness or stupidity, are really a nuisance to a cover-party; and to others, one would almost ascribe a fatality, and avoid them like an evil genius. In the former case, I have found, after remonstrance failed, and they continued throwing their shot liberally around, without apparently caring one farthing upon whose person it alighted, the best cure was instantly to turn a barrel as nearly in the direction of the report as possible. A well-distributed charge rattling through the brush wood, and falling upon the delinquent, gave, practically, a hint that made him more cautious for the future, and proved more effective than the most powerful jobation. Of the latter class—I mean unlucky companions I shall particularize one. Captain M—— shot with me an entire season. He was a pretty shot, and an excellent fellow; but I never entered a cover with him that I was not certain to be struck before we returned home. Every precaution to evade his shot was useless. If in a copse of a mile long there was a solitary opening to admit its passage, he was opposite it to a certainty; and my first intimation that such an alley did exist, would be a fall of withered leaves from the bushes above, and most likely a few grains lodging in my hat or jacket. If I moved to avoid a chance of accident, something induced him to make a corresponding change; and at last I became so nervous, that I obliged him momently to call out, that I might ascertain our relative positions, and guard, if possible, against injury.

We once, during a severe frost, shot the beautiful islands in the lake of Castlebar, which belong to the Marquis of Sligo. There were an immense number of cocks in cover, and we had been particularly successful; but the wonder was, I had that day escaped unwounded, and my prayer to " keep lead out of me" had been heard. On our return, my friend was pluming himself on this result. " It was foolish," he said, " to reckon him unlucky. To be sure, some shots of his had been unfortunate, but such would ever be the case." We had now left off shooting, and were within a few fields of the barracks, when a jack snipe sprang from a drain on the road-side, and flying to the top of the field, pitched in the upper ditch. I followed it merely to discharge my barrels— it sprang, and the report of my gun disturbed a hare in the bottom of the field; she moved, and my companion instantly discharged both barrels. From the hardness of the surface, the shot rose; a shower fell upon the protected parts of my person, while two struck me in the lip, and cut me deeply. I was more than one hundred yards from him, yet from the hard frost, the *ricochet* of the shot came as sharply upon me, as if I had been within point-blank distance. After that incident, need I add? much as I loved him, I never pulled a trigger in his company again.

## CHAPTER XLI.

### Dull evening—Memoir of Hennessey.

WE sat down to dinner *téte-à-tete,* and although both my-self and my kinsman made an exertion to banish unpleasant reminiscences, the evening was the most sombre that I had yet passed. The happy party who once tenanted our " merrie home," are never to meet again. The otter-killer " sleeps the sleep that knows no breaking"—the Colonel has retired to his winter quarters—the Priest's confessions call him from us for a season—and some secret intelligence which reached the Lodge over night, has caused Hennessey to disappear.

To gratify a strong expression of curiosity on my part respecting the latter, my cousin told me the following parti-culars of this singular personage :

" If ever man came into the world with the organ of destructiveness surcharged, it was my unhappy foster-brother. He was a lively and daring boy, and being a favourite with my late father, had opportunities of improvement afforded to him, which persons in his sphere seldom can obtain. But Hennessey showed little inclination for literary pursuits, the gun was more adapted to him than the pen—and at fifteen, when but a very indifferent scribe, he was admitted by the whole population to be the best shot of his years that ' ever laid stock to shoulder.' Encouraged by my father's par-tiality, from this period he led an idle careless life, and ram-bled over the country, breaking dogs, or amusing himself with the gun and fishing-rod.

" I was at the college when the first of his misfortunes occurred. He had imprudently ventured into a dancing-house, where a number of the *Sweenies* were assembled, with whom he had previously been at feud, and, as might have been anticipated, a quarrel quickly arose. Hennessey, too late, perceived his danger ; but with that daring determina-tion for which he has ever been remarkable, when the assault began, he made a sudden dash for the door, and overturning all that opposed him, succeeded in escaping. He was, how-ever, closely pursued. From his uncommon activity, he far outstripped all but one of his enemies. He had nearly reached the river—but his enemy was close behind. Intending to disable his pursuer, Hennessey picked up a stone, and unfortunately threw it with such fatal precision, that the skull of his opponent was beaten in, and he expired on the spot.

" Well, this was an unfortunate affair, but it was homicide in self-defence. My father accommodated matters with the Sweenies, and my foster-brother was discharged without a prosecution.

" A year passed, but the Sweenies had not forgotten or forgiven the death of their kinsman. Hennessey's rambling habits exposed him to frequent encounters with this clan : and one night, when returning late from the fair of Newport, with two or three companions, he came into unexpected collision with a party of his ancient enemies. A scuffle ensued— in the struggle he wrested a loaded whip from his antagonist, and struck the unhappy wretch so heavily with his own weapon, that after lingering nearly a month, he died from the contusion.

" This second mishap occasioned us a deal of trouble ; but Hennessey surrendered, was tried, and acquitted, and we all trusted that his misfortunes were at an end. He abjured the use of spirits, avoided late hours, and such meetings as might expose him to any collision with that clan who had been so unfortunate, and religiously determined to avoid every cause of quarrelling ; but fate determined that it should be otherwise.

" Having been invited to a *dragging home*, as the bridegroom was his near relative, Hennessey could not without giving offence decline attending on the happy occasion. He was then a remarkably handsome fellow—and you would vainly now seek in those gaunt and careworn features, the manly beauty which then caused many a rustic heart to beat. The bride's cousin accompanied her ; she was remarkably pretty, and was, besides, reported to be the largest heiress in the barony. With such advantages, no wonder ' of lovers she'd plenty,' as the ballad says :—my foster-brother met her, danced with her, drank with her—loved her, and was beloved in turn. Every rival was double-distanced ; but she was unfortunately betrothed by her father to a wealthy *Kearne* ;* and although I, in person, interposed, and used my power-

* *Anglice*, a rich vulgar clown.

ful influence, the old fellow her father was obstinate in refusing to break off the match.

" Hennessey was no man to see his handsome mistress consigned without her own consent to the arms of a rival. He made the usual arrangements, and I encouraged him to carry her off. The evening came—he left the Lodge in a boat, with six fine young peasants ; and crossing the bay, landed by moonlight at a little distance from the village where his inamorata dwelt.

" That very night a multitude of the Malleys had accompanied the accepted suitor to conclude all necessary preliminaries. The cabin of the heiress was crowded, and all within was noisy revelry. Hennessey, with one companion, stole to the back of the house.

" He knew the chamber of the bride elect, for he had more than once ' when all the world were dreaming,' visited his pretty mistress. He looked through the little casement, and, sight of horror ! there she was, seated on the side of the bed, and the Kearne's arm around her waist, with all the familiarity of a privileged lover ! There, too, was the priest of Inniskea, and divers elders of ' both the houses'—while the remainder of the company, for whose accommodation this grand chamber was insufficient, were indulging in the kitchen or dancing in the barn.

" Since the days of Lochinvar, there never was a more daring suitor than my foster-brother ; yet he did not consider it a prudent measure to enter the state apartment ' 'mong bridesmen, and kinsmen, and clansmen, and all,'—but waited patiently at the window, to see what some lucky chance might do. Nor did he wait in vain. Kathleein turned her pretty eyes on the moonlit casement, and thought, poor girl ! how often her young lover had stolen there in secret, and told his tale of passion. A tap, too light for any but the ear of love to detect, arrested her attention, and she saw the indistinct form of a human face outside ; and whose could it be but her favoured youth ? Seizing an early opportunity, she stole from the apartment ; she soon was in her lover's arms ; a few words, and a few kisses,—and all was settled :—and while the Kearne, the priest, and the father, were regulating the exact quantities of cattle and plenishing,* that were to dower the hand-

* *Plenishing*, means household furniture, beds, blankets, &c.

some bride, Kathleein was hurrying to the shore with her young and daring suitor.

" An attempt so boldly and so fortunately begun, was, however, doomed to end unhappily. One of the Malleys had discovered the interview, and witnessed the elopement. Having silently observed the route of the fugitives, he apprized the parties within, that their negotiations were likely to become nugatory, and a fierce and vindictive pursuit was instantly commenced. The distance, however, to the beach was short: the companion of the bold abductor had run forward; the bride was won—the boat was launched—the oars were dipping in the water—when, alas! the rush of rapid footsteps were heard, and oaths and threats announced that the fugitives were closely followed. Two or three of the Malleys had far outstripped the rest; but a minute more, and pursuit would have been hopeless. One man had passed the others far, and on the brink of the tide he caught the fair runaway in his arms, while the companions of the gallant were actually pulling her on board. The chase was hard at hand—twenty feet were heard rushing over the loose shingle—not a moment was to be lost, or the bride was gone for ever. Like lightning Hennessey caught up a stretcher from the bottom of the boat, discharged one murderous blow upon the man who held back his beloved mistress, a deep-drawn moan was heard, and the unhappy Kearne, for it was himself, sank upon the beach without life or motion! Off went the boat—off went the lady —and the athletic crew pulled through the sparkling water, little dreaming that their exulting leader was for *the third time* a homicide! Great God! I cannot tell you what I suffered next morning, when the tragical result of an attempt I had myself encouraged was told me. My first care was to look to the safety of my foster-brother and his bride; and until pursuit was over, I had them conveyed by Pattigo in the hooker to Innisboffin. There they remained in safe concealment, and for six months it was not deemed prudent to permit them to return, as the clan of the deceased were numerous and vindictive.

" Time flew. They came back, and for some time remained here unmolested. Kathleein was near her confinement, when one day we received information that the Malleys had procured a warrant with a civil force to execute it, and were determined at every hazard to arrest my foster-brother. I, a magistrate myself, could not openly protect him; and that evening he left the lodge at night-fall, to shelter himself in the island of Innisbiggle until the threatened danger passed. Kathleein unfortunately accompanied him; although we told her that there was but one poor family on the place, and its difficulty of approach, while favourable to the concealment of her husband, was unsuited to any female situated like her.

" On landing on the island, the solitary family, who generally resided in the single cabin it contained, were absent at the fair of Westport. Hennessey and his wife took possession of the hut, lighted a fire, and made themselves as comfortable as the wretched hovel would admit. Even then he urged her to return to the Lodge—but to leave him in perfect solitude on this desolate place was more than she could determine. Night came, and the weather, which had been squally all day, became worse momently, and at midnight blew a gale. The outlaw and his wife were now shut out from all the world, for a raging sea was roaring round the island, and all communication with the main was interrupted. Whether fear precipitated the dreaded event I know not; but in the middle of the night, while the elemental war was in its fury, symptoms of approaching travail were perceived by poor Kathleein, and the unhappy girl became more and more sensible of the terrible danger that was coming on. God of mercy! what was to be done? It wanted some hours of morning, and even were it light, until the tide fell no mortal could cross that stormy water.

" Poor wretch! with a withered heart, all that he could do to cheer his sinking companion was done; but every hour she became worse, and every moment her pain and danger were increasing. Driven to madness, at the first dawn of morning he rushed madly to the beach, and though the retiring tide rushed between the island and the main with furious violence, he plunged into the boiling eddies, and with great strength and desperate courage made good his passage to the opposite shore.

" To obtain help was of course attended with delay ; at last, however, it was accomplished, and the tide fell sufficiently to permit some females to cross the *farset*.* He, the unhappy

* The stand communicating at low water between an island and the main.

husband, far outstripped them : like a deer he bounded over the beach that interposed between the cabin and the sands— he reached it—a groan of exquisite agony was heard from within—next moment he was stooping over his exhausted wife a dead infant was pressed wildly to her bosom : she turned a dying look of love upon his face, and was a corpse within the arms of the ill-starred homicide!

" When the tidings of the melancholy fate of poor Kathleein were carried to the Lodge, I got the hooker under weigh and stood over to the island. My unhappy foster-brother appeared paralysed with sorrow, and incapable of any exertion. We brought him, with the bodies of the young mother and the dead babe, to the house ; and the latter were in due season interred with every mark of sympathy and respect.

" For a time I dreaded that the unfortunate homicide would have sunk into hopeless idiocy ; but he suddenly appeared to rouse his torpid faculties ; he became gloomy and morose— and, deaf to all my remonstrances, to the least of which formerly he would have paid the most marked regard, he wandered over the country and seemed to court an arrest, or rather an attempt at it ; for from his desperation, I am inclined to think he would have done some new deed of blood had his enemies ventured to assail him. All I could do to prevent mischief I did. I had the bullets drawn from his fire-arms when he slept ; I kept him under constant espionage, and retained him as much about my person as I could possibly contrive. Whether none would grapple with a desperate and well-armed man, or that some feeling for his sufferings softened the rancour of his enemies for a time, I know not, but he passed unmolested through the country ; and the most daring of the Sweenies and Malleys left the road when they accidentally met my unhappy foster-brother. Time has gradually softened his distress, and the asperity of his temper has subsided ; he has lost the fierce and savage look that lately no stranger could meet without being terror-stricken ; and I shall endeavour to get the death of his miserable rival, which decidedly was unpremeditated and accidental, accommodated. Some intelligence has made it advisable for Hennessey to leave the Lodge, although I hardly think any of his enemies would dare to seek him here ; but still we cannot be too cautious, and to be placed in the power of his former foeman at this moment, would be to involve his life in imminent peril.

" His misfortunes have given me more distress than any thing that has ever befallen myself personally. His attachment to me is so devoted, that I cannot but have brotherly feelings for this ill-starred fosterer. Although he would follow me to the corners of the earth, if I required, he would rather risk a trial than leave the country, which I have often and earnestly entreated him to do."

I offered here to take Hennessey under my protection to England, but my kinsman shook his head.

" It is a kind intention, Frank, but he would not leave me. I am the last link that binds him to the world, and while life lasts, we must run our wild career in the same couples. Poor Hennessey! there are worse men than he, although misfortune has made him *thrice* a homicide."

It was late: John brought oysters at the customary hour, and soon after we separated for the night.

---

## CHAPTER XLII.

My departure fixed—Coast suited to an ornithologist—Godsend—An ocean waif—My last day—Coursing—Size of hares—Fen-shooting— Kill a bittern—Castle of Doona—Fall of the tower—Netting rabbits— Reflections—Morning—Passage through the Sound—Hennessey—Departure from the kingdom of Connaught.

THE day of my departure from this wild retreat, where so many months have happily passed over, is determined: indeed, the season hardly admits a longer sojourn, and circumstances beyond my control require an immediate return to England. My kinsman has made arrangements for passing the genial season of Christmas, and the remainder of the winter, with his relations in the interior; and in the morning fox-hunt and evening dance, the dullest months of gloomy winter will merrily disappear.

For me, were I not encumbered with a fortune, and " all the ills that flesh is heir to" when one is afflicted with independence, this place would suit me admirably. Though these shores be wild, and weather savage, yet every day brings its novelty along with it. The winter fisheries on the coast are magnificent; and birds, known only to a naturalist elsewhere, are daily presented during the stormy season to the active and intelligent shooter. That wild being, Hennessey, has preserved an infinity of curious specimens; and many a rare production that the ornithologist would prize, is here shot, and disregarded by the peasant who is so fortunate as to possess a gun.

Among the natural advantages which this remote coast possesses, the ocean contributes largely to the stock, and even the tempest does not rage in vain. The prevailing westerly winds drive many a serviceable waif to the shore; and seldom a winter passes, but some valuable wreck or derelict property adds to my kinsman's limited resources. True, these " angel visits" are irregular, and come in questionable shape; but still, be they in form of butter or rum, train-oil or mahogany, they answer " for the nonce," and even a dead body has not been profitless to the finder.

I possibly have thus digressed from having witnessed the triumphant arrival of a huge beam of Dantzic oak and a ship's topmast, which certain retainers of my gentle cousin have towed in. It appears that these " spolia opima" were discovered early in the morning about the centre of the bay, and a boat from both shores approached them nearly at the same time. Both, like true vassals, claimed on behalf of their respective master; and it being impossible, on what an Irishman would very naturally term " debatable land," to settle the question of property, the respective crews fought the thing fairly out, and my kinsman's representatives being men of thews and sinews, after breaking two heads, and chucking one gentleman of " the Capulets" overboard, brought the godsends safely hither. Law there will be, of course. The rival claimant was formerly an attorney, who managed to spoliate an unhappy fool who was litigiously inclined, and of course became owner of the property. He who thus gets them will be most tenacious of ill-acquired rights; and this log and spar will most likely terminate in being made a droit of the Admiralty.

We started on our last chassé—and the *ultima dies* of our sporting wanderings has come. The shortened days and wet moors have made us desert grouse-shooting, and we crossed the estuary to shoot a fen some three miles off, which at this season is thickly tenanted with snipes and waterfowl.

The day was particularly favourable; dark and quiet,* with a gentle breeze. As we had to traverse a hill which bounds the tillage-grounds of several of the opposite villages, we brought the greyhounds with us, to get a run or two while passing this otherwise unprofitable beat. For my own part I had early given up coursing in disgust. The hares were not plenty—difficult to find—and when we did get them a-foot, they either made for the sea-shore, or ran into some morass, where dogs had no chance whatever, and one became weary of seeing them cut themselves on rocks, or flounder in a bog; and latterly I gave up the business as a bad concern. But on this occasion I was agreeably disappointed. The hill afforded a sound and level surface; from its contiguity to the corn-fields, the hares were tolerably numerous, and before we reached the shooting-ground, we had had six excellent courses, and killed four hares.

I never observed a more striking contrast in point of size than these hares exhibited. Two of them were of the smallest mountain class; dark-coloured meagre animals, who certainly made matchless running while they lasted. The others were of the fullest size, and in point of good condition, though neither so large nor so white as Byron's, would have done honour to any hare-park in Great Britain.

The fen we sought was situate in a valley between two gentle slopes, and formed by a deep and sluggish stream which passed through its centre, extended for about four miles, varying its breadth from a few yards to more than a quarter of a mile. The morass was interspersed with shrubs and underwood, and alders of inconsiderable size were occasionally clumped along the borders. Part of the surface was

---

* Snipes, when plenty, afford very excellent sport, it being allowed to be the pleasantest, on account of the quick succession of shots; this is also the best shooting for practice, seldom failing to make indifferent shots most excellent ones. There is no shooting that presents such a variety of shots, scarcely any two being alike. These birds usually fly against the wind, therefore every snipe-shooter should walk down it, as by that means the bird, if he rises before him, will fly back, and coming round him, describe a kind of circle, or at least his flight, for a certain distance, will not lengthen the shot, allowing him a certain time to cover the bird, and take good aim; for if he gets up before him, and should by chance go down the wind or from him, it is then the most difficult shot. It will be proper in this case to let the bird get a little distance from him, as then he will fly steadier, and the slightest grain will fetch him to the ground.

too unsound to admit its being traversed by the lightest foot, but generally it was broken into tammocks, which a bold and practised shooter might pass with little difficulty. We took opposite sides, and consequently few birds sprang without affording one or the other of the guns a fair shot. The number of snipes that flushed in this fen went far beyond my expectation, though considerably excited; and besides, we met at least fifteen couple of that sweet little duck the Teal. We followed the morass to its extremity, and then returned— and our beat homewards was pleasanter, and, so far as the game-bags went, more profitable than the first range.

Out of seventy head, we reckoned one woodcock and a brace of old *stagers* that we found among the heathy banks bordering the fen. We shot six couple of teal; and, with one exception, the remainder of the count were snipes, of which at least a fourth were jacks. In the most impassable section of the morass, old York pointed with more than customary steadiness ; and, " it might be fancy," actually looked round with peculiar expression, as if he would intimate that no common customer was before him ! I got within twenty yards and encouraged the old setter to go in ; but he turned his grizzled and intelligent eyes to mine, and wagged his tail as if he would have said, " Lord ! you don't know what I have here." A tuft of earth flung by one of the aides-de-camp, obliged the skulker to get up, and to our general surprise a fine bittern arose. I knocked him over, but though he came down with a broken wing and wounded leg, he kept the old dog at bay until my companion floundered through the swamp and secured him. On this exploit I plumed myself, for bitterns are here extremely scarce, and in Ballycroy they are seldom heard or found.

On our return home we passed the old castle of Doona, once supposed to have been honoured by the residence of Mrs. Grace O'Malley, who, if fame tells truth, was neither a rigid moralist nor over-particular in her ideas of " meum and tuum." Some wild traditions are handed down of her exploits ; and her celebrated visit to that English vixen Elizabeth, is fairly on record. The castle of Doona was, till a few years since, in excellent preservation, and its masonry was likely to have puzzled Father Time himself; but Irish ingenuity achieved in a few hours what as many centuries had hitherto failed in effecting.

A rich and hospitable farmer,* whose name will be long remembered in this remote spot, had erected a comfortable dwelling immediately adjoining the courtyard wall of the ancient fortress ; and against the tower itself was piled in wealthy profusion a huge supply of winter fuel. It was a night of high solemnity, for his first-born son was christened. No wonder then that all within the house were drunk as lords. Turf was wanted, and one of *the boys* was despatched for a cleaveful—but though Patt could clear a fair, and " bear as much beating as a bull," he was no man to venture into the old tower in the dark, " and it haunted." Accordingly to have fair play " if the ghost gripped him," he provided himself with a brand of burning bog-deal. No goblin assailed him, and he filled his basket and returned unharmed to the company, but unfortunately forgot the light behind him. The result may be anticipated. The turf caught fire, and from the intense heat of such a mass of fuel, the castle-walls were rent from top to bottom, and one side fell before morning with a crash like thunder. Nor was the calamity confined to fallen tower and lost fuel. Alas ! several kegs and ankers of contraband spirits were buried beneath the walls, and the huge masses of masonry that came down, burst the concealed casks of Cognac and Schiedam.

---

We found the warrener netting rabbits in the sand-banks. They were intended for sale in the interior, and many dozens were already taken. Formerly the skins were valuable, and a well-stocked burrow was a valuable appendage to a country gentleman ; but of late these furs have fallen so considerably in value, that the warren does not produce a tithe of what it did " when Boney, the Lord speed him ! was uppermost." Indeed, many a hearty lament is made in Ballycroy for poor Napoleon, and his name is ever associated with times of past prosperity.

I cannot describe the melancholy reflections which crowded over my mind, as I squibbed off my barrels on the beach, while the boat was crossing the channel to carry us over the estuary. It was for *the last time*, and with that thought, all the happy events I spent by " flood and fell" passed over my

* John Conway.

memory in ‘‘ shadowy review.’’ The jovial commander, the burly priest, my merry cousin, the stern homicide, the ancient butler, and the defunct otter-killer, all were before me. I trod in fancy the banks of Pullgarrow, or couched among the rocks of our highland ambuscade; I saw the startled pack spring from the purple heather, while the red deer,

> Like crested leader proud and high,
> Toss'd his beam'd frontlet to the sky;
> A moment gaz'd adown the dale,
> A moment snuff'd the tainted gale—

and vanished in the rocky pass of Meeltramoe. My imaginary wanderings continued till we landed at the pier, and with a deep sigh I hastened to my chamber, to make, for the last time, my toilet after a day of sylvan exercise.

---

Morning—the last morning has arrived, and all is bustle and packing up. Travers, though a cold-blooded Englishman who scarcely can tell a grouse from a game-cock, seems to feel regret at leaving this hospitable cabin—old John is sensibly affected—and Alice's black eyes are dim with weeping. For once she kissed me without coquetry, and as she received my farewell present, invoked the Lord to bless me with such unaffected ardour as proved that her fervent benison came warmly from the heart.

Over the parting with this rude but affectionate family I shall hurry. My cousin accompanied me to Westport, and we left the lodge after an early dinner, in full expectation of reaching that town for supper, though the distance is some ten or twelve leagues, and by an intricate passage with very difficult and perplexing tides. As if fortune wished to offer me a parting compliment, the wind blew from the north-west, and there was as much of it as we could well carry our full sails to. We entered the Bull's Mouth at three-quarter tide, and brought plenty of water over the sands, and in an hour cleared the Sound, and rushing through the boiling currents of Bearnaglee, found ourselves in Clew Bay. The wind blew fresh and steadily, and at nine o'clock we were moored along the quay of Westport.

One incident occurred: at a rocky point which ran from the

x

Achil side into the Sound, and there narrowed the channel considerably, we observed a human being couched on a stone among the sea-weed. The deep water passed within an oar's length of the spot, and as the boat flew like a falcon past the point, the man rose and hailed us. We hove the hooker to. It was Hennessey—and nothing could dissuade him, notwithstanding the risk was considerable, from coming on board to give me a parting escort.

Early next morning I found, myself in his majesty's mail, and with many a sincere adieu, bade farewell to my kind cousin and his wild but warm-hearted followers.

## CHAPTER XLIII.

Moral and physical condition of the west, past and present.

HERE I am, safely over the Shannon : a laudable improvement in the mode and rate of travelling of the Westport mail facilitates one's intercourse with the kingdom of Connaught ; and in course of time I have little doubt but Erris will be as approachable as Upper Canada, or any of the remoter provinces.

After my rambling observations upon men and manners, you must permit me, like the last lawyer in a cause, to condense the evidence, and make a general wind-up.

With regard to the moral condition of the West, I cannot conscientiously assert that any great improvement will be traced for the last half-century. The two great classes, the gentry and peasantry, have undergone a mighty revolution in conduct, manners, and modes of thinking ; and yet one will look in vain for commensurate advantages. It is admitted that the former body have changed their generic character altogether. We have the old school stigmatized now for its aristocratic tyranny and petty assumption ; and many a modern squire blesses God that he is not as others were who preceded him. And yet our fathers were, I verily believe, wiser in their generation, and better fitted for their own times, than we. True, these days were little better than barbarous. Denis Browne, and Dick Martin, and

Bowes Daly, and many a far-famed name of minor note, were then in all their glory, and they lived, it must be acknowledged in very curious times. In those days, the qualifications of a representative were determined by wager of battle, and a rival for senatorial fame was probably requested by the old member to provide his coffin, before he addressed the county. Doctors rode on horseback over the country in cauliflower wigs and cocked hats; and if they differed about a dose or decoction, referred the dispute to mortal arbitrement. In these happy times, a client would shoot his counsellor if he lost a cause—the suitor sought his mistress at pistol-point—and there was but one universal panacea for every known evil, one grand remedy for all injuries and insults.

It was then, indeed, a bustling world. Men fought often, drank deep, and played high ; ran in debt, as a matter of course ; scattered fairs and markets at their good pleasure ; put tenants in the stocks *ad libitum* ; and cared no more for the liberty of the subject than they did for the king's writ. Yet where they merry times. Under all these desperate oppressions, the tenants throve and the peasantry were comfortable. Every village could point out its rich man— every cabin had food sufficient for its occupants. When the rent was required it was ready ; and though a man was sometimes in the guard-house, his cow was rarely in the pound. *Tempora mutantur !* Who dare now infringe upon the liberty of the subject ? "Who put my man i' the stocks ?" would be hallooed from Dingle to Cape Clear. Doubtless, civil rights are now most scrupulously protected ; but I suspect that food is abridged in about the same proportion that freedom is extended.

There was one class of persons who, in these old-world times, were conspicuously troublesome, who have since then fortunately disappeared. These were a nominal description of gentry, the proprietors of little properties called *fodeeins*, who continued the names and barbarisms of their progenitors. Without industry, without education, they arrogated a certain place in society, and idly imitated the wealthier in their vices. Poverty and distress were natural results, and desperate means were used to keep up appearances. The wretched serfs, whom they called their tenants, were ground to powder, till, happily for society, the *fodeeins* passed into other hands, and the name and place ceased to be remembered. The ivied walls, and numerous and slender chimneys one sees in passing through this country, will, in nine out of ten cases, point a moral of this sort.

In times like those of forty years ago, this extinct tribe were from the peculiar temper and formation of society, occasionally a sad nuisance. The lord of a *fodeein*, like Captain Mac Turk, was "precisely that sort of person who is ready to fight with any one; whom no one can find an apology for declining to fight with; in fighting with whom considerable danger is incurred; and, lastly, through fighting with whom no *éclat* or credit could redound to the antagonist." Hence, generally, the larger proprietors saw this class sink by degrees, without an attempt to uphold them, and the *fodeein*, to the great joy of the unhappy devils who farmed it, was appended by general consent to the next estate.

Many examples of dangerous and illegal authority, as usurped and exercised by the aristocracy within the last half-century, are on record, that would appear mere romance to a stranger. One of the Fitzgerald family was probably more remarkable than any person of his times. He was the terror of the upper classes—and to such as arrogated the privileges of the aristocracy, without, as he opined, a prescriptive right, he was the very devil. If a man aspired to become a duellist, or even joined the hounds, without being the proper *caste*, George Robert would flog him from the field without ceremony. He actually for years maintained an armed banditti, imprisoned his own father, took off persons who were obnoxious—and when he was hanged—and fortunately for society this eventually occurred—it required a grand cavalry and artillery movement from Athlone to effect it.

Denis Browne was an autocrat of another description; a useful blundering bear, who did all as religiously in the king's name as ever Mussulman in that of the prophet. He did much good and some mischief—imprisoned and transported as he pleased; and the peasantry to this day will tell you, that he could hang any one whom he disliked. Yet both these men were favourites with their tenantry, and under them their dependents prospered and waxed wealthy.

Sometimes the memoir of an individual will give a more graphic picture of the age wherein he flourished than a more elaborate detail ; and in the strange eventful histories of these two singular men, the leading characters of their times will be best portrayed.

No persons were more dissimilar—none were bitterer enemies—none in every point, personal and physical, were more essentially opposite. In one point alone there was a parallel—both were tyrants in disposition, and both would possess power, and no matter at what price.

George Robert Fitzgerald was middle-sized, and slightly but actively formed; his features were regular, his address elegant, and his manners formed in the best style of the French school. In vain the physiognomist would seek in his handsome countenance for some trace of that fierce and turbulent disposition which marked his short and miserable career. No one when he pleased it, could delight society more ; and with the fair sex he was proverbially successful. It is said that gallantry, however, was not his forte, and that he seldom used his persuasive powers with women, but for objects ultimately pecuniary or ambitious.

Added to his external advantages, he was an educated man ; and that he possessed no mean literary talent, may be inferred from his celebrated " Apology," which is neatly and spiritedly written.

His courage was undoubted. In Paris and London he was noted as a duellist ; and in Mayo, his personal encounters are still remembered. His duel with Doctor Martin, his encounter with Cæsar French, the most notorious fire-eaters of the day, placed him foremost in that class. He was, moreover, a dead shot, and reported to be one of the ablest swordsmen in the kingdom. As a sportsman he was justly celebrated. He was an elegant horseman, and his desperate riding was the theme of fox-hunters for many a year. No park-wall or flooded river stopped him—and to this day, leaps that he surmounted, and points where he crossed the Turlough river, are pointed out by the peasantry.

The dark act which clouded his memory, and his unhappy fate, are generally known ; and considering the other traits of his strange and mingling character, the apology offered by his friends on the score of occasional insanity, is not improbable.   One circumstance would strengthen this conclusion.   He was interred by night, and with so much privacy, in the old churchyard of Turlough, that the place where his remains lay was for a time uncertain.   Accident in some degree revealed it.   In the confusion attendant upon his hurried sepulture, it is said that a ring was forgotten and left upon the finger.   Afterwards, in opening the ground, this relic was discovered ; and what more satisfactorily proved it was that the skull was distinctly fractured ; and it was a matter well known, that Fitzgerald had been dangerously wounded by a pistol-bullet in the head, in one of his numerous and sanguinary duels on the continent.

Denis Browne, when a young man, is said to have been extremely handsome : but early in life he became corpulent and engrossed in other pursuits, gradually careless and slovenly in his person, and neglected any means to restrain his constitutional obesity.   To strong natural abilities, he united decision of character and mental energy.   He started in dangerous times; several influential families disputed political power with him—he had a fierce and dangerous aristocracy to overcome—men cold to every argument " but the last and worst one," the pistol.   Hence in the very outset of his voyage, his vessel all but foundered.   It was his first contest for the county, and he was opposed by the late Lord Clanmorris.   The Bingham party was bold and powerful, and after a protracted contest, matters looked gloomily enough, and the Brownes were likely to be defeated.

" In this dilemma," to use his own words, " I have applied to Counsellor ——, my legal adviser.   I told him how badly things were, and inquired what was to be done?

" ' My dear Dennis,' said he, with a grave and serious movement of his full-bottomed wig, ' the thing admits but one remedy, and that lies in a nut-shell.   You are one-and-twenty years old, and you have never yet been on the sod—why that one fact would lose you your election —you must fight—my dear boy,'

" ' Fight ! to be sure I will, when I'm insulted.'

' Of course you would, and so would any body : but you must fight, and that too this very evening.'

" ' Impossible! how could it be managed ?'

" ' How! arrah whihst, Denis!—maybe ye think I have nothing but law in my head; you must knock down Bingham!'

" ' Knock down a man who never offended me—with whom I have no dispute?'

" ' And what does this matter? The blow will settle that difficulty. But as you are particular, can't ye say some friend of his affronted one of yours—some devil you never heard of will answer—and as John Bingham is a reasonable man, he'd not lose time in asking idle questions.'

" Accordingly, I followed this excellent advice, struck Bingham on the steps of the court-house, was called out in half an hour, fought in the barrack-yard, was there wounded, and won my election."

From that period Denis Browne rose rapidly into power. His able brother, the late Marquis of Sligo, supported him with all his influence and talent. Denis overcame every obstacle, distanced every competitor, and at last was absolute in authority, dictator for twenty years, and ruled the county during that period with a rod of iron.

No one was warmer in his friendship or more virulent in his antipathies. These feelings blinded his better judgment, and many of his greatest mistakes arose from an anxiety to aggrandize a favourite or annoy an enemy. He unfortunately outlived his power, and that circumstance embittered his latter years. He had not resolution to quit public life while he might have retired with *éclat*; he saw his influence expire, and his power partitioned insensibly among men with whom, but a few years before, his will was law.

In private life Denis Browne was cheerful and hospitable. Full of anecdote, an excellent story-teller, one who had mixed largely with the world and knew mankind intimately, he was an amusing and instructive companion. Young and lively society he delighted in; and though, from increased corpulency, and all " the ills that flesh is heir to," life was latterly a burden, the mind was vigorous to the last—and the death-bed of Denis Browne was marked with a firmness and philosophy that was in perfect keeping with the energy and determination of his life.

Another order of things has succeeded. Men talk now

with horror of acts of oppression and arbitrary power, which then every country justice committed ; but after all, the times have changed for the worse—and the outcry about invaded rights and an enslaved population, was, after all, mere verbiage, "signifying nothing."

The last fading gleam of western prosperity was during the power of Napoleon, and with his dynasty it vanished. The terrible change from war to peace ; the bursting of the banking bubbles, which supplied for that time an imaginary capital ; over-population and high rents, have ruined this wild district, and reduced its peasantry, with few exceptions, to abject wretchedness and want.

Is there for this any remedy ? Cannot modern landlords, acting on what they call enlightened principles, remove the causes of distress, and restore the peasantry to that scale of comfort they enjoyed under the rude and tyrannical *régime* of their fathers ? *They cannot.* They will talk *"scholarly"* of tithes and local taxation, and vainly attribute the insolvency of their tenants to these and such like causes ; this is *vox et præterea nihil*—an unreal and fanciful conceit. The true cause of the misery of the western population is over-population and excessive rents ; and before the peasantry could be tolerably comfortable, the lands must, on the average, be lowered at least *one third.* Even then, at present prices, the occupant will be hardly able to manage to pay the rent and live.

But can the landlords do this ? Can they afford to equalize their rental to the times, and throw a third portion from their nominal income overboard ? *They cannot.* The majority of the owners of western estates, from family burdens and national unthriftiness, are heavily and hopelessly encumbered ; and a reduction on such scale as would be necessary to ensure their tenants' comforts, would completely pauperize themselves. Hence, to keep off the evil day, every pretext but the true one will be assigned for local wretchedness —and every reason but the right one offered to the starving tenant, to persuade him that ruinous rents will never occasion want and poverty.

---

In personal appearance, the western peasantry are very inferior to those of the other divisions of the kingdom.

Generally, they are undersized and by no means so good-looking as their southern neighbours—and I would say, in other points they are equally deficient. To overcome their early lounging gait and slovenly habits, is found by military men a troublesome task; and while the Tipperary man speedily passes through the hands of the drill-sergeant, the Mayo peasant requires a long and patient ordeal, before a martial carriage can be acquired, and he be perfectly *set-up* as a soldier. These defects once conquered, none are better calculated for the profession. Hardy, active, patient in wet and cold, and accustomed to indifferent and irregular food, he is admirably adapted to endure the privations and fatigue incident to a soldier's life on active service—and in dash and daring, no regiments in the service hold a prouder place than those which appertain to the kingdom of Connaught.

It is said that the physical appearance of the Irish peasantry deteriorates as the northern and western sea-coasts are approached; and, certainly, on the latter the population are very inferior to that of the adjacent counties. Even the inhabitants of different baronies in the same county, as their locality advances inland, will be found to differ materially; and in an extensive cattle-fair, the islander will be as easily distinguished from the borderer, whether he be on the Galway or Roscommon frontier, as from the stock-master of Leinster, or the jobber *from the North*.

Indeed, fifty years back, the communication between the islands and the interior was so difficult and unfrequent, that the respective occupants looked on each other as very strangers. Naturally, slowly as civilization crept westward, the islands and remoter coasts, from local causes, were last visited, and many curious circumstances to this day would prove it. In this age of machinery, when the minutest matters are produced by its agencies, and the lowest occupations of human labour are transacted by powers unknown to our fathers, there are extensive tracts upon the western portions of the island, where even a mill has never been erected, and where the corn is prepared for distillation or food by the same rude methods used by barbarous nations one thousand years ago. Trituration between two stones, by the hand labour of an individual, is the means employed to reduce the corn into meal; and the use of that ancient hand-mill the *querne*, is still general throughout Ballicroy and the islands on the coast.

The inhabitants of this district are extremely hospitable to passing travellers, but by no means fond of encouraging strangers to sojourn permanently among them. This latter inherent prejudice may arise from *clannish* feelings, or ancient recollections of how much their ancestors were spoliated by former settlers, who by artifice and the strong hand managed to possess the better portions of the country. They are also absurdly curious, and will press their questions with American pertinacity, until, if possible, the name, rank, and occasion of his visit, is fully and faithfully detailed by the persecuted traveller.

The credulity of these wild people is amazing, and their avidity for news, if possible, exceeded by the profound reliance they place in the truth of the intelligence. Hence, the most absurd versions of passing events circulate over the district—and reports prevail, by turns, of a ridiculous or mischievous tendency, generally according to the mental temperament of the story-teller.

It formerly was not uncommon for people in the islands to live and die without ever having seen a town. Of course, they were a simple and unsophisticated race—and their natural mistakes, if they did by accident come in collision with other beings, were the source of many an inland jest. One very old story is told, in which an Achil man is the hero; and as to its truth, old Antony would as soon have doubted the existence of the holy trout in Kilgeever,* as have questioned its authenticity.

An islander was once obliged to go into the town of Castlebar upon business; and among other marvellous things which there met his sight, he was particularly struck with the appearance of an earthen jar in a shop-window. He inquired what this unknown article might be, and was informed that it was a mare's egg, which, if placed beside the fire during the winter, would infallibly produce a foal the ensuing spring. The price was moderate, and the Achil man determined to possess the treasure, and thus become master of a horse. Having effected the purchase,

---

* A sacred well in the west, tenanted by a trout of surpassing sanctity.

he set out on his way rejoicing—and before evening fell, came within view of his own home, and sat down upon a heathy bank to rest himself. He placed his recent acquisition beside him— but alas! from its spherical form, it rolled down the hill, and, striking against a rock at the bottom, was shivered by the blow. A hare which had couched beneath the stone, startled at the crash, sprang from her form, and went off at speed. The unhappy Achil man gazed, in an agony of despair, after what he believed the emancipated quadruped—and then exclaimed with a bitter groan, " *Mona mon diaoul*! What a horse he would have been!—Lord! if he was but two years old! *the Devil himself would not catch him.*"

Now, the most curious part of this story is, that although a standing joke upon Achil simplicity for a century, it is to be found *verbatim* in a German jest-book, with this only difference, that a *gourd* is there substituted for a *jar*.

In alluding to the strange employments of the female peasantry, I noticed those coarse and laborious exercises which elsewhere are confined to the lords of the creation. That the appearance of the fair inhabitants of the western highlands should harmonize with their rude avocations, might be expected; and hence the female peasantry, in personal advantages, are very inferior indeed to those of the interior. The constant exposure to sun and storm injures the complexion, and gives them an old and faded look ; and the habit of dispensing with shoes renders the feet large and misshapen. Among the *Coryphées* who frequented our mountain balls, there was but one girl who might be termed decidedly handsome. Her face was uncommonly intelligent—I never saw so dark an eye, and her teeth were white as ivory. But there was a natural ease in all she did—whether she brought a pitcher from the spring, or danced a merry strathspey, every movement was graceful. Even her simple toilet evinced instinctive taste, though no corset was required to regulate a form moulded by the hand of Nature, and her magnificent hair boasted no arrangement beyond the simple cincture of a ribbon—

> But seldom was a snood amid
> Such wild luxuriant ringlets hid,
> Whose glossy black to shame might bring
> The plumage of a raven's wing.

And yet I have seen that young beauty bending beneath a basket of potatoes which would have overloaded me—and, on one occasion, carry a strapping fellow across the river, who was coming on some state affair to the cabin, which, as he conceived, required him to appear in the presence with dry legs.

On the score of propriety of conduct, I would assign the female peasantry of this district a high place. When the habits of the country are considered, one would be inclined to suspect that excessive drinking, and the frequent scenes of noctural festivities which wakes and dances present, would naturally lead to much immorality. This, however, is not the case :—broken vows will no doubt occasionally require the interference of the magistrate or the priest; but generally the lover makes the only reparation in his power, and the deceived females and deserted children are seldom seen in Erris.

## CHAPTER XLIV.

Hunting—Men—Horses and hounds—Game—Conclusion.

If ever a district were designed by Nature for field sports, a person, from even a cursory glance upon the map, would point to Mayo. Its great extent of mountain surface, interspersed with bogs and morasses—its numerous and expansive waters—and its large tracts of downs and feeding-grounds, render it available for every purpose of the sportsman; and few species of game indigenous to Britain, in their peculiar seasons, will here be sought in vain.

As a hunting country, *the plains* have been justly chronicled—and the adjacent counties of Galway and Roscommon yield to none in the empire. The extensive sheep-farms afford superior galloping-ground—and the fences, though few and far between, from their size and character, require a powerful horse and dashing rider. Hence, in the annals of fox-hunting, the bipeds and quadrupeds of Connaught are held in due estimation; and it has been stated, without contradiction, that in their *own country* no men or horses can compete with them.

During the last century, the West of Ireland was celebrated for its breed of horses. They were of that class denominated "the old Irish hunter,"—a strong, well-boned, and enduring animal, that without any pretension to extraordinary speed, was sufficiently fast for fox-hounds, an excellent weight-carrier, and, better still, able to live with any dogs and in any country. As *fencers*, this breed was unequalled; and for a crack hunter to carry ten or eleven stone over *six feet six* of solid masonry, was no extraordinary event;—*seven* feet has been achieved repeatedly—and there are still, I have no doubt, many horses in the province capable of performing the latter feat. But, alas! this noted class of hunters is now comparatively rare—a higher-blooded, and, as all admit, an inferior caste has been substituted—the racing hunter fills the stables that formerly were occupied by the old Roscommon weight-carrier —and in a few years this celebrated and valuable animal will be seldom seen. The number of English thorough-bred horses introduced within the last thirty years into the Connaught racing studs, gradually introduced a slight and unserviceable hybrid—and, too late, gentlemen discovered the error of endeavouring to procure a cross, which should combine increased speed with those durable qualities that alone can enable a horse, under reasonable weight, to live with fast hounds in a country where they can go for miles without a check, and where the leaps are always severe, and occasionally tremendous.

Of the riders, it may be observed that, much as Connaught has been celebrated for desperate horsemanship, no charge of degeneracy will lie against the present race. To the curious in break-neck fencing, I would recommend a sojourn with a Connaught club—or if that should be inconvenient, a visit to the steeple-chases on *the plains* or at Knockcroghery would be sufficient—he will there see *six feet walls* especially built "for the nonce," under the inspection of conscious stewards, who would give nothing but honest measure, taken at racing speed, and that too in the middle of a bunch of gentlemen, who would ride over an adopted child;—or let him join a drag after a champaign lunch at Lord C.'s;—let him do this, and then form his estimate of Connaught horsemanship.

A mistake prevails in England, as to the supposed inferiority in value of the horses commonly employed by the Western sportsmen. I have seen a field out, when, of twelve horses, ten would probably average at one hundred guineas each; and the remaining two (brothers, Jerry and Lancet) were reported to have cost the noble owner five hundred guineas apiece. When the dangers of a stone-wall country and the desperate riding of the men are considered, these are indeed sporting prices. And yet accidents of a serious character are not frequent; every horse that has been ridden to hounds is generally blemished more or less; but it is astonishing in such a country and with such riders, how long some noble hunters have lasted.

The hounds, with few exceptions, are inferior. They are seldom properly kennelled, or regularly hunted. Masters of hounds in the West seem careless to all considerations beyond having a pack that can *go high* and keep tolerably well together. In sizing aud draughting dogs* they are by no means particular, and hence the *ensemble* of many a kennel is materially injured. In home management and field turn-out, they are infinitely behind their English brethren:—the packs are carelessly hunted—the kennel servants badly appointed—and I have met men upon the plains able to take a horse over any thing that hand and heart could carry him, who to a stranger would appear, from "the wildness of their attire," to be desperate apprentices levanting with their master's property.

And yet, after this eulogy upon the splendid horsemanship of the Western gentlemen, it may appear singular that I add, few of them ride well to hounds. An impatience in the field, and the anxiety to be foremost where all are forward, interferes constantly with the dogs, and causes a pressure upon the

---

* The same remark may be made respecting the setters and pointers in general use among the Connaught sportsmen. Many admirable dogs will be met occasionally; but there appears to be little pains taken in matching the females; and in the same kennel you will find an intermixture of different and discordant stocks. Not unfrequently I have seen a man shooting to setters, pointers, and droppers, on the same heath, and hunting all indiscriminately.

As to greyhounds, they are in little request excepting in the mountain districts—and those principally kept are of the rough and wiry species, or the small smooth breed, which from their lightness are best adapted for the soft bogs which form the coursing-grounds.

pack, very unfavourable to good hunting. Riding rather *a the field* than to the hounds, is the prevailing error. Fences are crossed which would be better evaded—horses unnecessarily distressed ; and I have seen a man actually go out of his way to take a regular *rasper*, when he had a *gap* within thirty yards.

Game in Mayo would be much more abundant than it is were it not sadly thinned by irregular shooters, and an infinity of vermin. To prevent the spoliations of the former would be a difficult task—as, from the quantity of wild fowl that every winter brings to the Western shores, a number of *guerilla* sportsmen are employed or countenanced by the resident gentry ; to whom it is too strong a temptation, when lying for ducks, or stealing upon plovers, to discover a pack or covey grouped upon the snow, and yet have sufficient philosophy to keep the finger from the trigger. The vermin, however, are the main cause of the scarcity of game, and no means are taken to destroy these marauders. From the eagle to the sparrow-hawk, every variety abounds in the woods and mountains, and every species of kite and crow that an ornithologist would admire, and a sportsman abominate, infests the Western counties.

Of fallow deer, there is a large stock in the parks throughout the province—and buck-hunting has of late seasons been getting into fashion on *the plains*. I have already, in speaking of the red-deer, lamented the prospect of their extinction. That event I look upon as fast approaching—and I am convinced that nothing can avert this national calamity but a vigorous determination of the mountain proprietors to extend protection to those limited herds which are still found, though in lessened numbers, upon the Alpine heights bordering on Burrishoole and Tyrawley.

Foxes are tolerably abundant in the hunting districts, and mischievously so in the mountains and islands. From the latter any quantity could be procured, and there is no place in Britain where covers could be so easily formed, and stocked with less trouble and expense. I have seen healthy foxes for days hawked over the country before a purchaser could be found, and at last disposed of for a few shillings. I once bought a fine dog-fox for half-a-crown, and, had I not become his owner, I verily believe the captor must have turned him out upon the street.

Hares are in most places tolerably plentiful; in point of numbers differing according to local situation and the relative protection afforded to them. In the moors, the mountain hares are scarce; but, from the quantity of winged and four-footed vermin, it is surprising that so many are occasionally seen.

Rabbits abound in the West of Ireland. On the coast, the immense sand-banks are for miles perforated with their burrows—and, notwithstanding that they are unmercifully abandoned to cur-dogs, cats, and vermin, their numbers continue unabated. In the woods and coppices bush rabbits are numerous, and cover-shooters, when beating for woodcocks, will have their amusement diversified by many a running shot.

Other wild animals, in every variety, may be met with in parts of Connaught. Badgers and wild cats, martins and weasels will be found in their customary haunts; while on the coast and estuaries, the lakes and inland waters, seals and otters are plentiful in the extreme.

Of winged game, pheasants and partridges excepted, I have already spoken. With regard to the first, they are scarce, and, it would appear, difficult to rear in this moist and stormy climate. I speak only of the places contiguous to the coast, where the experiment has been tried; for inland, where they have been duly attended to, and the English system adopted, they have thriven amazingly. As to partridges, they are generally scarce, and in Erris and Ballycroy almost unknown. In the wheat counties, and especially in certain parts of Galway, I believe they are tolerably abundant—but by comparison with the quantity a sportsman meets in an English beat, the best partridge-shooting procurable in Connaught will be very indifferent indeed.

---

My task is ended—I have chronicled " the short but simple annals" of a sporting summer, passed in a remote and unfrequented corner of the earth, and protracted until " winter and rough weather" forbade a longer stay. Into these solitudes I carried prejudices as unfair as they were unfavourable

—I came prepared to dislike a people who, unhappily for themselves, are little known and less regarded. I found my estimate of their character false, for kindnesses were returned tenfold, and the native outbreakings of Milesian hospitality met me at every step. What though the mountaineer had nothing but his potato-basket to offer—it was freely open to my hand. Did I wander from the road? his loy* was left in the furrow, and he ran miles to put me in the right path. If it rained and I sheltered in a cabin, the hearth was swept, the driest log placed upon the fire, and the bed-covering taken off to keep my saddle from the shower. If possible, my wishes were anticipated—and labour was unheeded when my pleasure or comfort could be attained.

One incident I must mention, for it marks the character of this simple and devoted peasantry. It was the hottest of the dog-days, and we had toiled over a barren moor, and missed some packs that we were aware were in that neighbourhood. A hill of most discouraging altitude was before us—and as its face was difficult beyond description, I hesitated to attempt it. But beyond it was a land of promise—a valley where wonders might be expected—and *malgré* fatigue, I *did* muster courage for the ascent. I gave my gun to a young peasant who acted as my henchman, and, as he was already loaded heavily, I observed him stagger more than once before we gained the summit. Throughout the day he never left my side—when the river was forded, he led the way—and yet I observed that he was unusually flushed, and at times sighed heavily. When we reached the cabin, he tottered to a seat, and the next moment became insensible. Then, and not till then, the truth was disclosed: he had been attacked with measles on the preceding night ; but rather than surrender his post to another, he actually, and under the fever of the disease, worked for twelve hours beneath a burning sun. Old Antony, by some simple means, brought the eruption plentifully to the skin, and in another week my gallant henchman was at my side, without any apparent trace of lassitude.

---

I have left these mountains, and never shall I enjoy the

* *Loy*, a narrow spade.

unalloyed excitement—the calm luxurious solitude, which I found among their wastes. What has refinement to offer me in exchange? Will the over-stocked preserve replace the moorland *chase*, with its glorious ridge of purple highlands —its silver lake, and sparkling river—my wild followers—my tried friends—and the dear cabin and its snowy tent, peeping from the dark expanse of heather, like a white sea-bird from the lap of ocean? Alas! nothing will compensate for these —or give me an equivalent for the joyous intercourse with kindred spirits, which I realized and left in *the wilds of Bally-croy.*

**THE END.**

LONDON:

Printed by Schulze and Co., 13, Poland Street.